The OXFORD

Primary School

THESAURUS

Compiled by
Alan Spooner

D1353111

OXFORD UNIVERSITY PRESS

Oxford University Press, Walton Street, Oxford OX2 6DP

Oxford New York
Athens Auckland Bangkok Bombay
Calcutta Cape Town Dar es Salaam Delhi
Florence Hong Kong Istanbul Karachi
Kuala Lumpur Madras Madrid Melbourne
Mexico City Nairobi Paris Singapore
Taipei Tokyo Toronto

and associated companies in
Berlin Ibadan

Oxford is a trade mark of Oxford University Press

© **Oxford University Press 1992**

First published 1992
3 5 7 9 10 8 6 4

ISBN 0 19 910284 8

A CIP catalogue record for this book is available from the British Library

Printed in Great Britain by
HarperCollins Manufacturing, Glasgow

Do you have a query about words, their origin, meaning, use, spelling,
pronunciation, or any other aspect of the English language? Then write to
OWLS at Oxford University Press, Walton Street, Oxford OX2 6DP.

All queries will be answered using the full resources of the
Oxford Dictionary Department.

Preface

I have designed this thesaurus to enable young people to make good use of the words they already know, and to help them to improve their knowledge and understanding of language generally. I hope that it is simple to use, but that at the same time it includes a wide enough vocabulary to make it interesting and thought-provoking.

Our language is an extremely complicated system. Clearly, a book of this kind cannot give all the information a young person needs in order to judge whether a word is likely to convey a particular shade of meaning, or to be appropriate to a particular spoken or written context. It will often be important, therefore, for young people to be helped in their use of the book, as in their general language development, by parents, teachers, and other experienced users of English. Indeed, I hope that teachers may find it a useful book not only for children to refer to, but also for them to work from in various kinds of language work in the classroom.

AJS

Headwords
The first word of each entry (the *headword*) is printed in bold type so that you can find it easily.

Cross-references
If we don't have space for all the information you might want under a particular headword, we suggest that you look up another entry. This is called *cross-referencing*.

gentleman SEE **man**.

Warnings
When you need to be particularly careful about how you use a word, a warning goes in brackets before the word or phrase concerned.

germ bacteria, (informal) bug, microbe, virus.! *Bacteria is a plural word.*

germinate *Our seeds have germinated.* to grow, to shoot, to spring up, to sprout, to start growing.

gesture 1 action, movement, sign. 2 WAYS TO MAKE GESTURES: to beckon, to nod, to point, to salute, to shake your head, to shrug, to wave, to wink.

Notes
Occasionally, we draw your attention to some interesting fact or problem about a word. This goes at the end of an entry after a big exclamation mark.

get 1 *What did you get for Christmas? What can I get for £10?* to acquire, to be given, to buy, to gain, to get hold of, to obtain, to procure, to purchase, to receive. 2 *Tell the dog to get the ball.* to bring, to fetch, to pick up, to retrieve. 3 *Did you get a prize?* to earn, to take, to win. 4 *I got a cold.* to catch, to contract, to develop, to suffer from. 5 *Get him to do the washing-up.* to cause, to persuade. 6 *Let's get tea now.* to make ready, to prepare. 7 *I don't get what he means.* to comprehend, to follow, to grasp, to understand. 8 *What time did you get to school?* to arrive at, to reach.

Related words
An explanation in small capitals tells you that the words we give are not synonyms but are related in some other way.

Synonyms
Most entries give you *synonyms*, words which are similar in meaning to the headword.

Numbers
When a word has more than one meaning, or can be used in more than one way, numbers separate the main meanings or uses of a word from each other.

Examples
Phrases or sentences printed in *italics* are examples of how the headword can be used.

What is a thesaurus for?

A thesaurus helps you find the words you need to make your language more interesting and more effective in saying what you want to say. It gives you words with similar meaning to the word you look up, so that you can choose the best word for your purpose. It also helps you find words which are related in other ways: names of various foods, words to describe the weather, terms to do with medical treatment, and so on.

What will you find in this thesaurus?

Headwords
The first word of each entry (the *headword*) is printed in bold type so that you can find it easily. All the headwords are arranged in alphabetical order.

Numbers
When a word has more than one meaning, or can be used in more than one way, numbers separate the main meanings or uses of a word from each other.

Examples
Phrases or sentences printed in *italics* are examples of how the headword can be used.

Synonyms
Most entries give you *synonyms*, words which are similar in meaning to the headword. Synonyms hardly ever mean exactly the same, so you should think carefully about how you use them. Which is the word which gives *most exactly* the meaning you have in mind? Which words are more informal, and which more formal? Which words are more old-fashioned, and which are more up-to-date?

Related words
Sometimes an explanation in small capitals tell you that the words we give are not synonyms but are related in some other way. *For example*: *to nod* and *to point* do not mean the same, but they are both ways to make gestures. So under **gesture** we say WAYS TO MAKE GESTURES: ... and *to nod* and *to point* are listed.

Cross-references
If we don't have space for all the information you might want under a particular headword, we suggest that you look up another entry. This is called *cross-referencing*. When you look up a cross-reference you will find synonyms or related words which may help you. *For example*: if you look up **gentleman**, it says: SEE *man*. Under *man* you will find *gentleman* listed with other words to do with men.

Warnings
When you need to be particularly careful about how you use a word, a warning goes in brackets before the word or phrase concerned. *For example*: (informal) means that the word or phrase which comes next is

usually *informal*, or more likely to be used in conversation than in writing. Similar warnings mark words which are *old-fashioned*, *insulting*, etc.

Notes

Occasionally, we draw your attention to some interesting fact or problem about a word. This goes at the end of an entry after a big exclamation mark.

Definitions

A thesaurus does not give definitions of words, although it helps you to understand words by putting them with other words of similar or related meaning. If you want a definition of a word, you must look it up in a dictionary.

A

abandon 1 *It rained so hard we had to abandon the game.* to cancel, to discard, to drop, to give up, to postpone, to scrap. 2 *Abandon ship!* to desert, to evacuate, to forsake, to leave, to quit. 3 *They abandoned Ben Gunn on Treasure Island.* to maroon, to strand.

abbey cathedral, church, monastery, priory.

abdicate *to abdicate the throne.* to give up, to renounce, to resign.

abdomen belly, stomach, (informal) tummy.

abduct SEE **kidnap**.

abhorrent *The idea of eating meat is abhorrent to vegetarians.* disgusting, hateful, horrifying, repulsive, revolting. SEE ALSO **unpleasant**.

abide 1 (old-fashioned) to remain, to stay. 2 *I can't abide people who smoke.* to bear, to endure, to put up with, to stand, to tolerate. 3 *Abide by our rules.* to conform to, to keep to, to obey.

ability *artistic ability.* aptitude, capability, capacity, competence, gift, intelligence, knack, know-how, knowledge, power, prowess, skill, talent, training.

able 1 *Are you able to play today?* allowed, fit, free, permitted. 2 *an able player.* capable, clever, competent, effective, experienced, gifted, intelligent, proficient, qualified, skilful, skilled, talented, trained.

abnormal *It's abnormal to have frost in June.* curious, eccentric, exceptional, freak, funny, irregular, odd, peculiar, queer, rare, singular, strange, uncommon, unconventional, unusual.

abolish *He wishes they would abolish income tax.* to eliminate, to end, to finish, to get rid of, to remove.

abominable *abominable cruelty.* appalling, awful, beastly, brutal, cruel, dreadful, hateful, horrible, nasty, odious, terrible.

about 1 *Is anyone about?* around, close, near. 2 *It costs about £1.* almost, approximately, around, close to, nearly, roughly. 3 *a book about sharks.* concerning, connected with, involving, regarding, relating to, telling of.

abridged *an abridged book.* abbreviated, condensed, cut, shortened.

abroad overseas.

abrupt 1 *an abrupt ending.* hasty, quick, sharp, sudden, unexpected. 2 *an abrupt manner.* blunt, curt, impolite, rude, short, unfriendly.

abscess boil, inflammation, sore.

abscond to elope, to escape, to flee, to run away.

absent *absent from school.* away, off.

absolute *Our rehearsal was absolute chaos!* complete, perfect, pure, sheer, total, unrestricted, utter.

absorb 1 to soak up. 2 *absorbed in your work.* immersed, interested, preoccupied. 3 *an absorbing hobby.* fascinating, interesting.

abstain *to abstain from voting.* to do without, to refrain from.

abstract *That maths was too abstract for me.* theoretical.

absurd *absurd clowning.* amusing, comic, crazy, farcical, foolish, funny, grotesque, illogical, irrational, laughable, ludicrous, mad, preposterous, ridiculous, senseless, silly, stupid, unreasonable, zany.

abundant *an abundant supply of fresh water.* ample, copious, generous, liberal, plentiful, profuse.

abuse SEE **insult**.

abysmal *Our team gave an abysmal performance.* appalling, awful, dreadful, worthless. SEE ALSO **bad**.

abyss chasm, crater, hole, pit.

academic SEE **brainy**.

accelerate to go faster, to quicken, to speed up.

accent *a London accent, an Irish accent.* brogue, dialect, language.

accept 1 *Please accept this small gift.* to receive, to take. 2 *Most people accept that it's wrong to steal.* to acknowledge, to admit, to agree, to believe, to think.

acceptable *Flowers make an acceptable present.* adequate, appropriate, passable, pleasing, satisfactory, suitable, tolerable.

access *There is no direct access to our school from the main road.* approach, entrance, entry, way in.

accident 1 *Was anyone injured in the accident?* calamity, catastrophe, crash, disaster, misadventure, misfortune, mishap. 2 *We met by accident.* chance, coincidence, fluke, luck.

accidental *accidental damage, an accidental meeting.* casual, chance, fortunate, haphazard, lucky, unfortunate, unintentional, unplanned.

accommodate *The refugees were accommodated in tents.* to board, to house, to lodge, to put up.

accommodating SEE **considerate**.

accommodation SEE **holiday**.

accompany *We accompanied our visitors to their car.* to escort, to go with.

accomplice *a burglar's accomplice.* ally, assistant, collaborator, confederate, partner.

accomplish *We accomplished our mission successfully.* to achieve, to carry out, to complete, to do, to finish, to fulfil, to perform.

accomplished *an accomplished pianist.* brilliant, clever, experienced, gifted, masterly, skilful, talented.

accomplishment *Have you got any special accomplishments?* gift, skill, talent.

accordingly consequently, so, therefore, thus.

account 1 *Can you account for your mistake?* to explain, to make excuses. 2 *The shopkeeper gave us the account.* bill, receipt. 3 *We wrote a detailed account of our museum trip.* commentary, description, diary, explanation, log, narration, narrative, record, report, story, tale.

accumulate *We accumulate a lot of rubbish in our garage.* to assemble, to bring together, to collect, to concentrate, to gather, to heap up, to hoard, to mass, to pile up, to store up.

accurate *accurate measurements.* correct, exact, meticulous, precise, right, true.

accuse *You should have evidence before you accuse someone of a crime.* to blame, to charge, to condemn, to incriminate, to prosecute.

accustomed *We went home by our accustomed route.* conventional, customary, habitual, normal, ordinary, regular, routine, traditional, usual.

ache 1 *an ache in a bad tooth.* discomfort, pain, pang, soreness, twinge. 2 *She ached all over after running in the half marathon.* to be sore, to hurt, to sting, to throb.

achieve 1 *See what you can achieve in an hour.* to accomplish, to carry out, to complete, to do, to finish, to fulfil, to manage, to perform. 2 *Did they achieve their aim?* to gain, to get to, to reach.

achievement *It's a great achievement to get into the county team.* accomplishment, attainment, feat, success.

acid *Lemons taste acid.* sharp, sour, tangy, tart.

acknowledge *He acknowledged that I was right.* to accept, to admit, to agree, to grant.

acquaintance SEE **friend**.

acquire *Where did she acquire that hat?* to buy, to gain, to get, to get hold of, to obtain, to procure, to purchase, to receive.

acquit *The prisoner was acquitted.* to discharge, to excuse, to free, to let off, to liberate.

acrid *an acrid smell of burning.* bitter, unpleasant.

act 1 *a brave act.* action, deed, exploit, feat, performance. 2 *He's putting on an act.* deception, hoax, pretence. 3 *He's acting like a fool.* to behave, to conduct yourself, to pretend to be. 4 *She loves to act in plays.* to appear, to perform, to play. 5 *Give the medicine time to act.* to function, to operate, to work.

action 1 *a helpful action.* act, deed, exploit, feat, performance. 2 *I prefer films with plenty of action.* activity, drama, excitement, liveliness, movement. 3 *Grandad saw action in the Second World War.* battle, combat, conflict, fighting.

activate *Press that button to activate the alarm.* to set off, to start.

active 1 *an active puppy.* agile, energetic, lively, vigorous. 2 *active in charity work.* busy, employed, engaged, involved, occupied.

activity 1 *School is full of activity near Christmas.* action, excitement, liveliness, movement. 2 *What is your favourite activity?* hobby, occupation, pastime, project, task.

actual *That old oak tree isn't the actual tree Robin Hood lived in.* authentic, genuine, real, true.

acute 1 *acute pain.* extreme, intense, keen, severe, sharp, sudden. 2 *an acute angle.* pointed, sharp.

adamant SEE **determined**.

adapt 1 *They adapted our minibus so that handicapped children can use it.* to adjust, to convert, to modify, to transform, to vary. 2 *We adapted a play by Shakespeare.* to alter, to change, to edit, to rewrite.

add 1 *Add these numbers together.* to combine, to join, to put together, to unite. 2 *What does it all add up to?* to amount to, to come to, to make, to total. 3 *Add up what we have collected so far.* to calculate, to count, to reckon, to work out.

addict *a snooker addict.* enthusiast, fan, fanatic.

addiction habit, need, obsession.

additional *We need additional information.* extra, further, more, supplementary.

address 1 *Write the address clearly.* directions. 2 *The vicar addressed the congregation.* to speak to, to talk to.

adequate *The food was just adequate.* acceptable, enough, passable, satisfactory, sufficient, tolerable.

adhere *Limpets adhere to rocks.* to attach yourself, to cling, to fasten, to stick.

adhesive 1 glue, gum, paste. 2 *adhesive tape.* gluey, gummed, sticky.

adjacent *the house adjacent to ours.* closest, nearest, neighbouring, next.

adjourn *to adjourn a meeting.* to break off, to defer, to postpone, to put off, to suspend.

adjudicate SEE **judge**.

adjust *I adjusted the saddle on my bike.* to alter, to amend, to change, to modify, to put right, to vary.

administer 1 *The head administers the school.* to administrate, to command, to control, to direct, to govern, to look after, to manage, to rule, to run, to supervise. 2 *to administer corporal punishment.* to deal out, to give, to hand out.

admirable *The actors gave an admirable performance.* creditable, excellent, (informal) fabulous, fine, marvellous, praiseworthy, wonderful. SEE ALSO **good**.

admire 1 *We admired the firemen's courage.* to approve of, to honour, to marvel at, to praise, to respect, to revere, to value, to wonder at. 2 *We admired the view.* to appreciate, to enjoy, to like, to love.

admit 1 *Persons under sixteen are not admitted.* to allow in, to let in. 2 *She admitted that she broke the window.* to accept, to acknowledge, to agree, to confess, to own up.

adolescence growing up, puberty, (informal) your teens.

adolescent 1 *adolescent behaviour.* juvenile, youthful. 2 *Most adolescents like pop music.* teenager, youngster, youth.

adore to dote on, to idolize, to love, to revere, to worship.

adorn *The table was adorned with flowers.* to decorate.

adornment decoration, ornament.

adrift *adrift in the middle of the lake.* afloat, drifting, floating.

adult 1 *That film is for adults only.* grown-up. 2 *adult ideas.* developed, grown-up, mature.

adultery infidelity, unfaithfulness.

advance 1 *We advanced towards our objective.* to approach, to come near, to go on, to make headway, to move forward, to proceed. 2 *Computers have advanced a lot in recent years.* to develop, to evolve, to improve, to move on, to progress.

advanced

advanced 1 *advanced technology.* modern, sophisticated, up-to-date. 2 *advanced mathematics.* complicated, difficult, hard.

advantage *It's an advantage to be tall when you play basketball.* asset, benefit, gain, help, profit.

advantageous beneficial, good, helpful, profitable, useful.

adventure *an exciting adventure.* escapade, excitement, exploit.

adventurous bold, brave, courageous, daring, enterprising, fearless, heroic, intrepid.

adversary enemy, foe, opponent, opposition, rival.

adverse *adverse weather conditions.* contrary, hostile, opposing, unfavourable.

adversity *It's good to have friends in times of adversity.* calamity, catastrophe, difficulty, disaster, distress, hardship, misfortune, trouble.

advertise *We advertised our jumble sale.* to make known, (informal) to plug, to promote, to publicize.

advertisement (informal) ad, (informal) advert, bill, commercial, notice, placard, (informal) plug, poster, publicity, sign.

advice *Dad gave me some advice.* help, suggestion, tip, warning.

advisable *It's advisable to wrap up warm.* proper, prudent, sensible, wise.

advise 1 *They will advise us when the TV is mended.* inform, notify, tell. 2 *What medicine did the doctor advise?* prescribe, recommend, suggest.

aerodrome airfield, airport, airstrip, landing-strip.

aeroplane SEE **aircraft**.

affair 1 *Don't interfere in my affairs.* business, concern, matter. 2 *The robbery at the police station was a strange affair.* event, happening, incident, occasion.

affect 1 *Alcohol affects your driving.* to alter, to change, to influence, to modify. 2 *We were affected by the music.* to impress, to move, to stir, to touch.

affectionate attached, fond, friendly, kind, loving, tender, warm.

afflict *afflicted by boils.* to distress, to hurt, to torment, to torture, to trouble.

affliction ailment, blight, disease, disorder, illness, sickness.

affluent SEE **rich**.

afford *Can you afford 50p?* to manage, to provide, to spare.

afloat adrift, floating.

afraid apprehensive, cowed, fearful, frightened, scared, terrified.

age 1 *the Victorian age.* era, period. SEE ALSO **time**. 2 *Wine must be allowed to age.* to develop, to grow older, to mature, to ripen.

aged ancient, elderly, old.

aggravate 1 *Scratching aggravates the soreness.* to make worse, to worsen. 2 (informal) *Don't aggravate mum by asking for money.* to annoy, to bother, to exasperate, to irritate. ! Some people think this is a wrong use of *aggravate*.

aggressive *aggressive animals.* attacking, belligerent, hostile, militant, pugnacious, warlike.

agile *Gymnasts need to be agile.* acrobatic, active, deft, graceful, lively, nimble, quick-moving, swift.

agitate *The thunder agitated the animals.* to disturb, to excite, to stir up.

agonizing *an agonizing wound.* excruciating, painful, unbearable.

agony anguish, pain, suffering, torment, torture.

agree 1 *I agreed to pay for the damage.* to consent, to undertake. 2 *Do you agree that I was right?* to accept, to acknowledge, to admit. 3 *We agreed to play indoors.* to choose, to decide, to establish, to fix, to settle. 4 *His story didn't agree with hers.* to coincide, to correspond, to match.

agreeable *an agreeable companion.* amiable, decent, friendly, nice. SEE ALSO **kind, pleasant**.

agreement 1 *We have quarrels, but they usually end in agreement.* accord, concord, consent, harmony. 2 *After much arguing, we reached an agreement.* alliance, arrangement, bargain, contract, deal, pact, pledge, settlement, treaty, understanding.

agriculture farming.

aground stranded.

ahead forwards, onwards.

aid 1 *to aid someone in trouble.* to assist, to back, to help, to relieve, to support. 2 *They need our aid.* assistance, backing, co-operation, help, support.

ailment SEE **illness**.

aim 1 *Aim the gun at the target.* to direct, to point. 2 *I aim to arrive for dinner.* to intend, to plan, to try. 3 *What's your aim in life?* ambition, cause, goal, intention, object, objective, plan, purpose, target.

air 1 *They fired into the air.* atmosphere, sky. 2 *to air a room.* to dry, to freshen, to ventilate. 3 *to air your opinions.* to display, to make known, to reveal, to show.

aircraft 1 KINDS OF AIRCRAFT: aeroplane, airliner, airship, balloon, biplane, bomber, fighter, glider, hang-glider, helicopter, jet, jumbo jet, jump-jet, microlight, plane, seaplane, supersonic aircraft. 2 PARTS OF AIRCRAFT: fin, fuselage, jet engine, joystick, propeller, rotor, rudder, tail, undercarriage, wing.

airport aerodrome, airfield, airstrip, landing-strip.

airy *an airy room.* breezy, draughty, fresh, ventilated.

akin alike, related, similar.

alarm 1 *The thunder alarmed the animals.* to dismay, to disturb, to frighten, to scare, to shock, to startle, to surprise, to terrify, to upset. 2 *Alarm spread when the siren sounded.* consternation, dismay, fear, fright, panic, surprise. 3 *Move quickly into the playground when you hear the alarm.* bell, fire-alarm, gong, signal, siren, warning.

album 1 SEE **book**. 2 SEE **record**.

alcohol (informal) booze, liquor, spirits. SEE ALSO **drink**.

alcoholic 1 *alcoholic drink.* intoxicating. 2 *an alcoholic.* addict, drunkard.

ale beer.

alert 1 *You must stay alert if you play in goal.* attentive, awake, careful, lively, observant, vigilant, watchful. 2 *When the floods came, they rang the church bell to alert the villagers.* to caution, to warn.

alien *alien beings from outer space.* foreign, strange, unfamiliar.

alike akin, identical, similar.

alive existing, live, living.

allegiance *allegiance to the king.* duty, faithfulness, loyalty.

alley SEE **road**.

alliance *an alliance between two sides.* agreement, association, combination, league, pact, treaty, union.

alligator crocodile.

allot *We allotted half our food to the visitors.* to allow, to deal out, to distribute, to divide, to give out, to ration, to share out.

allow 1 *They allowed us to use the first team's pitch.* to approve, to authorize, to enable, to let, to license, to permit. 2 *We allowed £5 for spending money.* to allot, to give, to grant, to provide, to set aside.

alloy SEE **metal**.

all right 1 *Are you all right again after your illness?* fit, healthy, well. 2 *Is my work all right?* acceptable, adequate, passable, satisfactory, tolerable.

allude *Did mum allude to the spilt paint?* to mention, to refer to.

alluring SEE **beautiful**.

ally collaborator, confederate, friend, partner.

almighty omnipotent.

almost about, approximately, around, nearly, not quite, practically.

alone 1 *to be alone.* friendless, isolated, lonely, solitary. 2 *to perform alone.* solo.

alongside *Our friends parked their car alongside ours.* adjacent to, beside, next to.

aloud *to read aloud.* audibly, clearly, distinctly.

also additionally, besides, furthermore, moreover, too.

alter *Don't alter your story: it's excellent as it is.* to adapt, to adjust, to affect, to amend, to change, to convert, to edit, to modify, to transform, to vary.

alteration change, difference, modification.

alternative *The alternatives are beef or chicken.* choice, option, possibility.

altitude height.

altogether *We were not altogether satisfied.* absolutely, completely, entirely, quite, totally, utterly, wholly.

always continually, continuously, eternally, evermore, for ever, repeatedly, unceasingly.

amalgamate *Because they had so few players, the two teams amalgamated.* to combine, to come together, to integrate, to join, to merge, to put together, to unite.

amateur *an amateur player.* unpaid. ! *Amateur* is the opposite of *professional*.

amaze **1** *His speed amazed us.* to astonish, to astound, to bewilder, to confuse, to shock, to stun, to surprise. **2** *amazed:* dazed, dumbfounded, nonplussed, thunderstruck. **3** *amazing:* exceptional, extraordinary, notable, phenomenal, remarkable, special, unusual.

ambassador consul, diplomat, representative.

ambiguous *When you ride your bike, don't give ambiguous signals.* confusing, uncertain, unclear, vague.

ambition **1** *You need ambition to succeed in business.* drive, enterprise, enthusiasm. **2** *My ambition is to play for the county team.* aim, desire, goal, intention, objective, wish.

amble SEE **walk.**

ambush *The outlaws ambushed the travellers in the mountains.* to attack, to ensnare, to intercept, to pounce on, to swoop on, to trap.

amend *I amended the wording of my letter.* to adapt, to adjust, to alter, to change, to improve, to modify.

amiable *an amiable smile.* agreeable, friendly, good-humoured, kind-hearted, nice, pleasant. SEE ALSO **kind.**

ammunition KINDS OF AMMUNITION: bullet, cannonball, cartridge, grenade, missile, round, shell, shrapnel. SEE ALSO **weapon.**

amnesia forgetfulness.

amnesty pardon.

amount **1** *What did the collection amount to?* to add up to, to come to, to make, to total. **2** *a cheque for the full amount.* quantity, sum, total.

amphibious AMPHIBIOUS ANIMALS: frog, newt, toad.

ample *The spring provided an ample supply of water.* abundant, copious, generous, liberal, plentiful.

amplify *Can you amplify your explanation?* to develop, to enlarge, to expand, to magnify.

amputate *to amputate a limb.* to cut off, to remove, to sever.

amuse **1** *A comedian's job is to amuse people.* to cheer up, to delight, to divert, to entertain. **2** *amusing:* SEE **funny.**

amusement *What's your favourite form of amusement?* diversion, enjoyment, fun, hobby, joke, laughter, merriment, pastime, play, pleasure, recreation.

analyse *Tomorrow we're going to analyse our traffic survey.* to examine, to study.

anarchy *There would be anarchy if we had no police.* chaos, confusion, disorder, lawlessness.

anatomy *A doctor has to know all about anatomy.* the body.

ancestor *Mum's hobby is tracing her ancestors.* forefather, predecessor.

anchor **1** *to anchor a ship.* to berth, to moor, to tie up. **2** *to anchor something firmly.* SEE **fasten.**

anchorage harbour, haven, marina.

ancient aged, antiquated, antique, early, old, old-fashioned, prehistoric, primitive, venerable.

anger **1** *filled with anger.* exasperation, fury, rage, temper, wrath. **2** *They angered me with their insults.* to aggravate, to annoy, to enrage, to exasperate, to incense, to inflame, to infuriate, to madden, to provoke, to vex.

angle bend, corner.

angler fisherman.

angling fishing.

angry 1 bad-tempered, cross, enraged, fiery, fuming, furious, incensed, indignant, infuriated, irate, livid, mad, raging, raving, vexed, wild, wrathful. 2 *to be angry*: to be in a temper, to boil, to fume, to rage, to rave, to seethe. 3 *to make someone angry*: to enrage, to incense, to infuriate, to vex.

anguish agony, distress, pain, suffering, torment, torture.

animal 1 beast, brute, creature. 2 KINDS OF ANIMAL: amphibian, bird, carnivore, fish, herbivore, insect, mammal, marsupial, mollusc, pet, predator, quadruped, reptile, rodent, scavenger. 3 SOME ANIMALS: antelope, ape, ass, baboon, badger, bat, bear, beaver, bison, boar, buffalo, bull, bullock, camel, cat, cattle, cheetah, chimpanzee, cow, deer, dinosaur, dog, dolphin, donkey, dormouse, dromedary, elephant, elk, ferret, fox, gerbil, giraffe, goat, gorilla, grizzly bear, guinea-pig, hamster, hare, hedgehog, hippopotamus, horse, hyena, jackal, jaguar, kangaroo, koala, leopard, lion, llama, mammoth, mastodon, mink, mole, mongoose, monkey, moose, mouse, mule, octopus, otter, ox, panda, panther, pig, platypus, polar bear, porcupine, porpoise, rabbit, rat, reindeer, rhinoceros, seal, sea-lion, sheep, shrew, skunk, squirrel, stoat, tiger, tortoise, turtle, vole, wallaby, walrus, weasel, whale, wolf, zebra. 4 SEE ALSO **amphibious, bird, fish, insect, reptile, snake.**

animated *an animated conversation.* boisterous, bright, brisk, cheerful, energetic, excited, exuberant, lively, quick, spirited, sprightly, vivacious.

annexe *They built an annexe for the extra class.* extension, wing.

annihilate *Nuclear weapons can annihilate whole cities.* to destroy, to eliminate, to eradicate, to exterminate, (informal) to finish off, to kill, to slaughter, to wipe out.

anniversary birthday, jubilee.

announce 1 *They announced their engagement.* to declare, to proclaim, to publish, to report, to state. 2 *The DJ announced the next record.* to introduce.

announcement *a special announcement.* bulletin, communication, communiqué, declaration, message, notice, proclamation, report, statement.

annoy *Don't annoy the bull.* (informal) to aggravate, to bait, to bother, to cross, to displease, to exasperate, to irritate, to molest, to offend, to pester, to tease, to torment, to trouble, to try, to upset, to vex, to worry.

annual 1 *Sports day is an annual event.* yearly. 2 *a football annual.* SEE **book.** 3 *I planted annuals in the garden.* SEE **plant.**

anonymous nameless, unidentified, unnamed.

answer 1 *the answer to a question.* reaction, reply, response, retort. 2 *the answer to a problem.* explanation, solution, sum, total.

antagonism *the antagonism between two fighters.* conflict, hostility, opposition.

anticipate *In chess, you have to anticipate your opponent's next move.* to expect, to forecast, to foresee, to predict, to prevent. ! Some people think this is a wrong use of *anticipate*.

antiquated *Do you remember that antiquated car of grandpa's?* aged, old, old-fashioned, out-of-date, quaint.

antique *antique furniture.* aged, ancient, old, old-fashioned.

antisocial *an antisocial person.* disagreeable, nasty, obnoxious, offensive, rude, unfriendly.

anxiety care, concern, dismay, doubt, dread, fear, misgivings, strain, stress, tension, worry.

anxious 1 *I was anxious about travelling by air.* apprehensive, concerned, fearful, jittery, nervous, uneasy, worried. 2 *He is always anxious to do his best.* eager, keen.

apart divided, separate.

apartment flat.

ape monkey.

apex *The steeplejack climbed to the apex of the spire.* crown, head, peak, tip, top.

apiary hive.

apologetic *apologetic about his mistakes.* penitent, regretful, remorseful, repentant, sorry.

apologize *I apologized for being rude.* to regret, to repent, to say sorry.

apostle disciple, follower.

appal 1 *The crowd's bad behaviour appalled us.* to alarm, to disgust, to dismay, to frighten, to horrify, to shock, to terrify. **2** *What an appalling piece of work!* SEE **bad.**

apparatus appliance, device, equipment, instrument, machinery, tool.

apparent *It was apparent that he was lying.* blatant, clear, evident, obvious, plain, self-explanatory.

apparition see **ghost.**

appeal 1 *to appeal for help.* to ask, to beg, to entreat, to plead, to request. **2** *The picture appealed to me.* to attract, to fascinate, to interest. **3** *appealing:* SEE **attractive.**

appear 1 *Our visitors appeared an hour late.* to arrive, to come, to turn up. **2** *A difficulty has appeared.* to arise, to emerge, to loom, to materialize, to show. **3** *This appears to be the coat I lost.* to look, to seem. **4.** *We all appeared in the nativity play.* to act, to perform.

appease *a sacrifice to appease the gods.* to calm, to pacify, to soothe.

appetite *an appetite for food, an appetite for adventure.* craving, desire, greed, hunger, longing, lust, passion, zest.

applaud *The audience applauded our performance.* to approve of, to cheer, to clap, to commend, to praise.

appliance apparatus, device, equipment, instrument, machinery.

applicant candidate, entrant, participant.

apply 1 *to apply for a job.* to ask. **2** *to apply ointment to a wound.* to administer, to spread. **3** *to apply your strength.* to employ, to use.

appoint *Who did they appoint as captain?* to choose, to elect, to name, to nominate, to select.

appointment *I've got an appointment with a friend after tea.* date, engagement, fixture, meeting, rendezvous.

appreciate 1 *Do you appreciate classical music?* to admire, to approve of, to enjoy, to like, to prize, to respect, to value. **2** *I appreciate that you must be tired.* to know, to realize, to see, to understand.

apprehensive *He was apprehensive about his exam.* afraid, anxious, concerned, fearful, frightened, nervous, uneasy, worried.

apprentice beginner, learner, novice.

approach 1 *The approach to the school is off Church Street.* access, entrance, entry, way in. **2** *The lion approached its prey.* to come near, to draw near, to move towards. **3** *approaching traffic.* advancing, oncoming.

appropriate *an appropriate punishment, appropriate clothes.* apt, becoming, deserved, due, fit, fitting, proper, right, suitable, timely.

approve 1 *I approve of what he did.* to admire, to applaud, to commend, to like, to love, to praise, to value. **2** *The council approved our application to build an extension.* to allow, to authorize, to permit, to tolerate.

approximately about, around, close to, nearly, roughly.

apt 1 *an apt pupil.* clever, quick, skilful. **2** *an apt reply.* appropriate, deserved, fitting, proper, right, suitable.

aptitude *She has some aptitude for music.* ability, gift, knack, skill, talent.

aqueduct SEE **bridge.**

arbitrary *an arbitrary decision.* unplanned, unreasonable.

arbitrate *When the captains quarrelled, the referee had to arbitrate.* to make peace, to negotiate.

arc curve.

arch *The cat arched its back.* to bend, to curve.

arctic 1 SEE **geography. 2** *arctic weather.* bitter, bleak, freezing, frozen, (informal) perishing. SEE ALSO **cold.**

arduous *The mountaineers faced an arduous climb.* difficult, gruelling, hard, laborious, strenuous, tough.

area 1 *I like the area where I live.* district, locality, neighbourhood, region, sector, territory, vicinity, zone. 2 *a large area of ice.* expanse, sheet, surface.

arena *a sports arena.* field, ground, pitch, stadium.

argue 1 *to argue about politics.* to debate, to discuss, to dispute, to quarrel. 2 *to argue about the price.* to bargain, to haggle. 3 *The lawyer argued that the man was guilty.* to contend, to reason.

argument 1 *an argument about what to watch on TV.* controversy, debate, disagreement, dispute, quarrel. 2 *We weighed up the arguments for and against.* evidence, grounds, justification, proof, reason.

arid 1 *arid desert.* barren, dry, lifeless, parched, sterile. 2 *an arid subject.* boring, dull, uninteresting.

arise *We'll deal with any problems as they arise.* to appear, to begin, to come up, to crop up, to emerge, to occur, to result, to spring up.

aristocrat lord, noble, peer.

arm 1 SEE **body**. 2 *an arm of a tree.* branch, limb. 3 *They armed themselves with sticks.* to provide, to supply.

armada *an armada of ships.* convoy, fleet, navy.

armed services GROUPS OF FIGHTING MEN: air force, army, battalion, brigade, cavalry, commandos, company, corps, fleet, foreign legion, garrison, infantry, marines, mercenaries, navy, paratroops, patrol, platoon, recruits, regiment, reinforcements, squad, squadron, task-force, troop. SEE ALSO **fighter**.

armistice *The armistice ended the fighting.* pact, peace, treaty, truce.

armour *Soldiers used to wear armour in battle.* mail, protection.

armoury arsenal, weapons.

army SEE **armed services**.

aroma fragrance, odour, perfume, scent, smell, whiff.

arouse 1 *The alarm clock aroused us.* to awaken, to call, to rouse, to wake up. 2 *The sound of music aroused our interest.* to excite, to incite, to inspire, to provoke, to stimulate, to stir.

arrange 1 *I arranged the books in the library.* to classify, to distribute, to group, to put in order, to set out, to sort. 2 *We arranged an outing.* to fix, to organize, to plan, to prepare, to settle.

arrangement *We have an arrangement to buy eggs from a local farmer.* agreement, bargain, contract, deal, pact, settlement, understanding.

arrest 1 *The police arrested the suspect.* to capture, to catch, to detain, (informal) to nab, to seize, to take prisoner. 2 *A landslide arrested our progress.* to bar, to block, to check, to halt, to hinder, to stop.

arrive 1 *We arrived at our destination.* to come to, to reach. 2 *When will granny arrive?* to appear, to come, to turn up.

arrogant *an arrogant manner.* boastful, bumptious, (informal) cocky, conceited, disdainful, haughty, insolent, pompous, presumptuous, proud, scornful, self-important, snobbish, (informal) stuck-up, vain.

arsenal armoury.

art 1 KINDS OF ART AND CRAFT: architecture, carpentry, cartoons, collage, crochet, drawing, embroidery, engraving, fashion design, graphics, illustrations, jewellery, knitting, metalwork, mobiles, modelling, mosaic, murals, needlework, origami, painting, patchwork, photography, portraits, pottery, prints, sculpture, sewing, sketching, spinning, stencils, weaving, wickerwork, woodwork. SEE ALSO **music, picture, theatre**. 2 VARIOUS ARTISTS AND CRAFTSMEN: architect, blacksmith, carpenter, engraver, goldsmith, painter, photographer, potter, printer, sculptor, weaver. FOR PERFORMING ARTISTS SEE **entertainment, music, theatre**. 3 *There's an art in lighting a bonfire.* craft, knack, skill, talent, technique, trick.

artful *People say that foxes are artful creatures.* astute, clever, crafty, cunning, ingenious, knowing, shrewd, skilful, sly, tricky, wily.

article 1 *articles for the jumble sale.* item, object, thing. 2 *an article in a magazine.* SEE **writing**.

artificial *an artificial beard.* bogus, faked, false, feigned, man-made, manufactured, (informal) phoney, pretended, synthetic, unnatural, unreal.

artist SEE **art**.

artistic attractive, beautiful, creative, imaginative.

ascend 1 *We ascended the hill.* to climb, to go up, to mount, to scale. 2 *The road ascends to the church.* to rise, to slope up.

ash *the ashes of a fire.* cinders, embers.

ashamed *ashamed of doing wrong.* distressed, embarrassed, upset.

ask 1 *to ask a question, to ask for help.* to beg, to demand, to enquire, to entreat, to implore, to inquire, to pose a question, to query, to question, to request. 2 *to ask someone to a party.* to invite.

asleep dormant, hibernating, inactive, resting, sleeping.

aspect *There's one aspect of this affair we don't understand.* circumstance, detail, feature.

assail *The defenders were assailed with missiles.* to assault, to attack, to bombard, to set on.

assassinate to murder. SEE ALSO **kill.**

assault SEE **attack.**

assemble 1 *A crowd assembled.* to accumulate, to collect, to come together, to congregate, to crowd together, to group, to herd, to meet, to muster, to swarm, to throng. 2 *We assembled our belongings.* to bring together, to gather, to get together, to pile up. 3 *These cars are assembled in Britain.* to build, to construct, to fit together, to make, to manufacture, to put together.

assembly *an assembly of Scouts.* conference, congress, council, gathering, meeting.

assert *He asserted that he was innocent.* to argue, to claim, to contend, to declare, to emphasize, to insist, to maintain, to proclaim, to state, to stress.

assess *The garage assessed the damage to the car.* to calculate, to estimate, to reckon, to value, to work out.

asset 1 *Good health is a great asset.* advantage, benefit, blessing. 2 *What assets have you got?* capital, funds, money, resources, savings, wealth.

assignment *an assignment to be done by Monday.* job, project, task, work.

assist *Can you assist us?* to aid, to back, to help, to second, to serve, to support.

assistant accomplice, collaborator, deputy, helper, partner, second.

association *an association of youth clubs.* alliance, body, club, combination, company, group, league, organization, party, society, union.

assorted *assorted colours.* different, diverse, miscellaneous, mixed, varied, various.

assortment *an assortment of colours.* collection, mixture, variety.

assume *I assume you like ice-cream?* to believe, to guess, to imagine, to presume, to suppose, to think.

assumed *an assumed name.* false, feigned, pretended.

assumption *My assumption is that you will be hungry.* guess, supposition, theory.

assurance *We had his assurance that all was well.* guarantee, oath, pledge, promise, vow.

assure *He assured me the work was finished.* to promise, to tell, to vow.

assured SEE **confident.**

astonish *The acrobats astonished the crowd.* to amaze, to astound, to dumbfound, to surprise.

astound *The unexpected news astounded us.* to amaze, to astonish, to dumbfound, to shock, to stagger, to surprise.

astronaut cosmonaut, space-traveller.

astronomy WORDS USED IN ASTRONOMY: asteroid, comet, constellation, cosmos, eclipse, galaxy, meteor, meteorite, moon, planet, satellite, shooting star, sun, universe, world.

astute *It was an astute move to bring on a substitute.* artful, clever, crafty, cunning, ingenious, observant, perceptive, shrewd.

asylum *The refugees hoped to find asylum in our country.* haven, refuge, retreat, safety, sanctuary, shelter.

asymmetrical lop-sided, unbalanced, uneven.

athletics EVENTS IN ATHLETICS: cross-country, decathlon, discus, high-jump, hurdles, javelin, long-jump, marathon, pentathlon, pole-vault, relay race, running, shot, sprinting, triple jump.

atmosphere 1 *a stuffy atmosphere.* air. 2 *There was a happy atmosphere at the party.* feeling, mood, tone.

atom 1 molecule, particle. 2 *an atom bomb.* SEE **weapon.**

atrocious *an atrocious terrorist attack.* barbaric, evil, hateful, wicked. SEE ALSO **cruel.**

atrocity crime, outrage.

attach 1 to anchor, to bind, to connect, to fasten, to fix, to join, to link, to secure, to tie, to unite. SEE ALSO **fasten.** 2 *The twins are very attached.* close, fond, friendly, loving.

attack 1 *They launched an attack at dawn.* ambush, assault, blitz, charge, counter-attack, invasion, onslaught, raid. 2 *An attack of coughing.* bout, fit, outbreak, turn. 3 *They attacked us for no reason.* to ambush, to assail, to assault, to bombard, to charge, to molest, to mug, to raid, to rape, to set on, to storm.

attainment achievement, success.

attempt *to attempt to break a record.* to endeavour, to exert yourself, to make an effort, to strive, to try.

attend 1 *Attend to your work.* to concentrate on, to observe, to think about, to watch. 2 *Who will attend to the goldfish while we are away?* to care for, to look after. 3 *Do you attend church?* to go to, to visit.

attention 1 *Give attention to your work.* care, concentration, diligence, heed, notice, regard. 2 *Thank you for your attention while I was ill.* consideration, kindness, politeness, thoughtfulness.

attentive *attentive listeners.* alert, observant, thoughtful, vigilant, watchful.

attic loft.

attire clothes, clothing, costume, dress, garments.

attitude 1 *I didn't like her attitude.* behaviour, disposition, manner. 2 *What's your attitude towards smoking?* belief, feeling, opinion, standpoint, thought.

attract 1 *Magnets attract iron.* to draw, to pull. 2 *The old steam engines attracted me.* to appeal to, to captivate, to entice, to fascinate, to lure.

attractive *an attractive person, an attractive dress.* alluring, appealing, artistic, bewitching, captivating, charming, (informal) cute, endearing, enticing, fascinating, fetching, glamorous, good-looking, handsome, inviting, lovable, pleasing, pretty, quaint, seductive, tempting. SEE ALSO **beautiful.**

auction SEE **sale.**

audible *an audible voice.* clear, distinct.

audience crowd, spectators.

audio equipment KINDS OF AUDIO EQUIPMENT: amplifier, cassette recorder, compact disc player, earphones, gramophone, headphones, hi-fi, high-fidelity equipment, juke-box, loudspeaker, microphone, music centre, personal stereo, pick-up, radio, record-player, stereo, stylus, tape-recorder, tuner, turntable.

au revoir farewell, goodbye.

austere 1 *an austere man.* forbidding, hard, harsh, severe, stern, strict. 2 *an austere dress.* plain, simple.

authentic *an authentic antique.* actual, genuine, real, true.

author composer, creator, dramatist, novelist, playwright, poet, scriptwriter, writer. SEE ALSO **writer.**

authority 1 *We've got the head's authority to have a party.* approval, consent, permission. 2 *The police have the authority to stop the traffic.* control, influence, power, right. 3 *an authority on steam trains.* expert, specialist.

authorize 1 *The head authorized the purchase of a new computer.* to agree to, to allow, to approve, to consent to, to permit. 2 *You aren't authorized to buy cigarettes for your dad.* to entitle, to license.

autograph signature.

automatic 1 *an automatic reaction.* impulsive, involuntary, spontaneous, unconscious, unintentional, unthinking. 2 *an automatic dishwasher.* mechanical, programmed. 3 *an automatic machine.* robot. 4 *an automatic weapon.* SEE **weapon.**

automobile car, motor car. SEE ALSO **vehicle.**

auxiliary *auxiliary engines.* additional, helping, supplementary, supporting.

available *There are plenty of books available in the library.* accessible, handy, obtainable, ready.

average *an average sort of day.* common, mediocre, medium, middling, normal, typical, usual. SEE ALSO **ordinary.**

aversion *an aversion to spiders.* contempt, disgust, dislike, hatred, loathing, revulsion.

avid *an avid reader.* eager, enthusiastic, fervent, greedy, keen.

avoid *I will do anything to avoid gardening!* to dodge, to elude, to escape, to evade, to fend off, to shirk.

awake *A sentry must stay awake.* alert, attentive, conscious, lively, vigilant, watchful.

awaken *The alarm awakened us.* to arouse, to call, to rouse, to wake.

award 1 *They awarded her first prize.* to give, to hand over, to present. 2 VARIOUS AWARDS: badge, cup, decoration, medal, prize, reward, scholarship, trophy.

aware *When cycling, be aware of the traffic.* conscious, observant.

away *away from school.* absent, off.

awe *They watched the erupting volcano with awe.* admiration, fear, respect, reverence, wonder.

awful *Murder is an awful crime.* abominable, appalling, beastly, dreadful, hateful, horrible, nasty, shocking, terrible. SEE ALSO **bad**.

awkward 1 *an awkward machine.* cumbersome, inconvenient, unwieldy. 2 *I'm awkward with tools.* blundering, clumsy, gawky, ungainly, unskilful. 3 *Are you trying to be awkward?* difficult, unco-operative.

axe chopper.

B

babble SEE **talk**.

baby child, infant, toddler.

babyish childish, immature, infantile.

back 1 *the back of the train.* end, rear, tail. 2 *the back of the envelope.* reverse. 3 *He backed away.* to move back, to retreat, to reverse, to withdraw. 4 *Will you back our plan?* to aid, to assist, to help, to promote, to second, to sponsor, to subsidize, to support.

backbone spine.

backer *a new backer for our team.* promoter, sponsor, supporter.

background *Tell me the background to this affair.* circumstances, setting.

backing *If we go ahead will you give us your backing?* aid, assistance, help, sponsorship, subsidy, support.

backside behind, bottom, buttocks, rear, rump.

backward handicapped, retarded, slow, underdeveloped, undeveloped. ! These words may sound insulting.

bacon gammon, ham, rashers.

bacteria (informal) bugs, germs, microbes, viruses.

bad 1 *a bad man, a bad deed.* abhorrent, base, beastly, corrupt, criminal, cruel, deplorable, detestable, evil, immoral, infamous, malevolent, malicious, malignant, mean, naughty, offensive, regrettable, reprehensible, rotten, shameful, sinful, unworthy, vicious, vile, villainous, wicked, wrong. 2 *a bad accident.* appalling, awful, calamitous, dire, dreadful, frightful, ghastly, hair-raising, hideous, horrible, nasty, serious, severe, shocking, terrible, unfortunate, unpleasant, violent. 3 *a bad performance, a bad piece of work.* abominable, abysmal, appalling, awful, cheap, defective, deficient, dreadful, faulty, feeble, hopeless, imperfect, inadequate, incompetent, incorrect, ineffective, inefficient, inferior, (informal) lousy, pitiful, poor, unsound, useless, weak, worthless. 4 *bad food.* decayed, decomposing, diseased, foul, mildewed, mouldy, polluted, putrid, rotten, smelly, spoiled, tainted. 5 *a bad smell.* loathsome, nauseating, objectionable, obnoxious, odious, offensive, repellent, repulsive, revolting, sickening, vile. 6 *Smoking is bad for you.* damaging, dangerous, destructive, harmful, injurious, unhealthy. 7 *I feel bad today.* diseased, feeble, ill, indisposed, (informal) poorly, queer, sick, unwell. ! *Bad* has many shades of meaning, and these are only some of the other words you could use.

badge *the school badge.* crest, emblem, medal, rosette, sign, symbol.

bad-tempered angry, cross, disgruntled, gruff, grumpy, irascible, irritable, moody, morose, peevish, petulant, rude, short-tempered, snappy, sulky, sullen, testy.

baffle 1 *The police were baffled by the strange crime.* to bewilder, to confuse, to frustrate, to perplex, to puzzle. 2 *baffling:* inexplicable, insoluble, mysterious.

bag basket, carrier bag, case, handbag.

baggage bags, cases, luggage, suitcases, trunks.

bait *The bully was baiting the younger children.* to annoy, to persecute, to pester, to tease, to torment, to worry.

bake 1 SEE **cook.** 2 to harden, to heat.

balance 1 *He lost his balance and fell off.* equilibrium, stability, steadiness. 2 *Balance the boat so that it doesn't lean to one side.* to equalize, to even up, to make steady, to make symmetrical. 3 *The chemist weighed the pills on the balance.* scales, weighing-machine.

bald bare, hairless.

balderdash (informal) *He talks a lot of balderdash!* (informal) bilge, drivel, gibberish, nonsense, rubbish, (informal) tripe, (informal) twaddle.

bale *a bale of straw.* bundle.

ball 1 *a glass ball.* globe, sphere. 2 *Cinderella went to a ball.* dance, disco, party, social. SEE ALSO **party.**

ballerina ballet-dancer, dancer.

ballet dance, dancing.

ballot *We held a ballot to choose the captain.* election, poll, vote.

ball-point pen.

balmy *a balmy evening.* gentle, mild, peaceful, pleasant, soothing.

ban *Some people would like to ban all smoking.* to bar, to forbid, to make illegal, to outlaw, to prevent, to prohibit, to veto.

band 1 *Our football shirts have a white band round the chest.* belt, hoop, line, loop, ribbon, ring, strip, stripe. 2 *a band of robbers.* company, crew, gang, group, horde, troop. 3 *a recorder band.* ensemble, group, orchestra.

bandage dressing, lint, plaster.

bandit brigand, buccaneer, highwayman, hijacker, outlaw, pirate, robber, thief.

bandy-legged SEE **leg.**

bang 1 *a bang on the head.* blow, knock. SEE ALSO **hit.** 2 *a loud bang.* blast, boom, crash, explosion, report. SEE ALSO **sound.**

banish *They used to banish criminals as a punishment.* to deport, to eject, to exile, to expel, to send away.

bank 1 *a grassy bank.* embankment, mound, ridge, shore, slope. 2 *The plane banked as it turned to land.* to heel, to incline, to lean, to list, to slant, to slope, to tilt.

banner *waving banners.* colours, ensign, flag, standard, streamer.

banquet dinner, feast, meal, spread.

banter teasing.

baptize to christen.

bar 1 *a wooden bar.* beam, girder, rail, rod. 2 *a refreshment bar.* café, counter, pub, saloon. 3 *He was barred from the club because he was too young.* to ban, to exclude, to keep out, to prohibit. 4 *A fallen tree barred their way.* to block, to deter, to hinder, to impede, to obstruct, to prevent, to stop.

barbarian heathen, pagan, savage. ! It is insulting to use these words to describe people of other nations.

barbaric *a barbaric attack.* atrocious, cruel, fierce, savage, violent. SEE ALSO **cruel.**

barbarous *a barbarous tribe.* savage, uncivilized.

barbecue SEE **party.**

barber hairdresser.

bard minstrel, poet, singer. SEE ALSO **writer.**

bare 1 *bare legs, a bare patch.* bald, naked, nude, unclothed, uncovered, undressed. 2 *a bare hillside.* barren, bleak, desolate, windswept. 3 *a bare room.* empty, plain, unfurnished. 4 *He is not the sort of person to bare his private thoughts.* to betray, to disclose, to expose, to reveal, to uncover.

barely hardly, scarcely.

bargain 1 *After some arguing, they made a bargain.* agreement, arrangement, contract, deal, understanding. 2 *In the market people bargain over the prices.* to argue, to discuss terms, to haggle, to negotiate.

barmaid, barman waiter, waitress.

barrage 1 gunfire. 2 *a barrage across the river.* barrier, dam.

barrel cask, tub. SEE ALSO **container**.

barren *barren desert.* arid, bare, lifeless, sterile.

barricade *a barricade across a road.* barrier, obstacle, obstruction.

barrier 1 *We built a barrier to keep the spectators off the pitch.* barricade, fence, hurdle, obstacle, railings, wall. 2 *They built a barrier across the river.* barrage, dam.

barrow cart, wheelbarrow.

base 1 *Dad made a concrete base for the new shed.* basis, bottom, foot, foundation, rest, stand, support. 2 *The climbers set up a base at the foot of the mountain.* depot, headquarters. 3 *He based his argument on what he read in the paper.* to establish, to found, to set up. 4 *Stealing from old people is a base crime.* contemptible, cowardly, depraved, evil, immoral, low, mean, wicked.

basement cellar, crypt, vault.

bash SEE **hit**.

bashful *There's no need to be bashful about getting first prize!* coy, demure, faint-hearted, modest, reserved, self-conscious, sheepish, shy, timid, timorous.

basic *the basic facts.* chief, elementary, essential, foremost, fundamental, important, main, primary, principal.

basin bowl, dish.

basis *What was the basis of your story?* base, foundation, starting-point.

basket bag, carrier.

bastard illegitimate. ! Nowadays *bastard* is often insulting while *illegitimate* is a polite word.

bat *You hit the ball with the bat.* club, racket.

batch *Is there anything good in the latest batch of records?* bunch, collection, consignment, group, set.

bath 1 *a bath of water.* SEE **container**. 2 *to have a bath.* sauna, shower, wash.

bathe 1 *to bathe in the sea.* to go swimming, to swim, to take a dip. 2 *to bathe a wound.* to clean, to rinse, to swill, to wash.

bathroom THINGS YOU FIND IN A BATHROOM: bath, bath mat, bath salts, comb, cosmetics, curlers, extractor fan, flannel, foam bath, medicine cabinet, mirror, nail-brush, nail-scissors, pumice-stone, razor, scales, shampoo, shaver, shower, soap, sponge, taps, tiles, toilet, toilet roll, toothbrush, towel, towel rail, tweezers, ventilator, wash-basin.

baton *a policeman's baton.* cane, club, rod, stick.

battalion SEE **armed services**.

batter *We battered on the door.* to bang, to bash, to beat, to hammer, to knock, to pound, to strike, to thump. SEE ALSO **hit**.

battle *Many died in the battle.* action, campaign, clash, combat, conflict, confrontation, encounter, engagement, struggle. SEE ALSO **fight**.

bawl SEE **shout**.

bay *The ship sailed into a quiet bay.* cove, estuary, fiord, gulf, inlet.

bazaar *We held a bazaar to raise money for our camping trip.* auction, fair, jumble sale, market.

be 1 *Will I still be here in 50 years?* to continue, to exist, to live, to remain, to survive. 2 *When will the next eclipse be?* to happen, to occur, to take place.

beach *a sandy beach.* coast, sands, shore. SEE ALSO **seaside**.

bead 1 *pretty beads.* SEE **jewellery**. 2 *beads of sweat on her face.* blob, drip, drop.

beaker *a beaker of water.* SEE **cup**.

beam 1 *That beam holds up the ceiling.* bar, girder, joist, rafter. 2 *a beam of light.* gleam, ray, shaft. 3 *He beamed at us happily.* to grin, to laugh, to smile.

bear 1 *Will that pillar bear the weight?* to carry, to hold up, to prop up, to support. 2 *The angels bore good tidings.* to bring, to convey. 3 *Our dog bore six puppies.* to give birth to, to produce. 4 *I can't bear the smell of onions.* to abide, to cope with, to endure, to put up with, to stand, to suffer, to tolerate, to undergo.

bearings *We lost our bearings in the fog.* course, direction, position, way.

beast *a wild beast.* animal, brute, creature, monster.

beastly 1 *beastly cruelty.* abominable, brutal, hateful, horrible. SEE ALSO **cruel.** 2 *beastly weather.* awful, nasty, terrible. see also **unpleasant.**

beat 1 *They beat him mercilessly.* to batter, to cane, (informal) to clout, to flog, to knock about, to lash, to manhandle, to pound, to scourge, to strike, to thrash, to thump, to wallop, to whack, to whip. SEE ALSO **hit.** 2 *The cook beat the mixture until it was creamy.* to agitate, to mix, to stir, to whisk. 3 *Our opponents beat us easily.* to conquer, to crush, to defeat, (informal) to lick, to master, to outdo, to overcome, to overpower, to overthrow, to overwhelm, to rout, to subdue, (informal) to thrash, to vanquish. 4 *Our car could beat yours any day!* to exceed, to excel, to outdo, to surpass, to top, to win against. 5 *This music has a good beat.* pulse, rhythm, throb.

beautiful *a beautiful bride, beautiful embroidery, beautiful weather.* admirable, alluring, appealing, artistic, attractive, bewitching, brilliant, captivating, charming, dainty, elegant, exquisite, (old-fashioned) fair, fascinating, fetching, fine, glamorous, glorious, good-looking, gorgeous, graceful, handsome, imaginative, irresistible, lovely, magnificent, neat, picturesque, pleasing, pretty, quaint, radiant, scenic, seductive, spectacular, splendid, superb, tempting. ! The word *beautiful* has many shades of meaning. The words given here are only some of the other words you could use.

become 1 *This little puppy will become a big dog!* to change into, to grow into, to turn into. 2 *That dress becomes you.* to be appropriate for, to fit, to suit.

becoming *a becoming dress.* appropriate, apt, attractive, decent, fitting, proper, suitable.

bed 1 bedstead, berth, bunk, divan, four-poster, hammock. 2 *a flower bed.* border, patch, plot. 3 *the bed of a river.* bottom, course.

bedclothes, bedding THINGS YOU USE TO MAKE A BED: bedspread, blanket, bolster, continental quilt, counterpane, coverlet, duvet, eiderdown, electric blanket, mattress, pillow, pillowcase, pillowslip, quilt, sheet, sleeping-bag.

bedlam *bedlam in the classroom.* chaos, hubbub, pandemonium, riot, rumpus, turmoil, uproar. SEE ALSO **commotion.**

bedraggled *We came in from the rain very bedraggled.* dishevelled, scruffy, untidy, wet.

bedridden *The sick woman was bedridden.* infirm. SEE ALSO **ill.**

bedroom SEE **room.**

beefy *The wrestler looked a beefy character.* big, brawny, burly, hefty, muscular, strong, tough.

beer ale.

befall *The travellers told us what had befallen them.* to come about, to happen, to occur, to take place.

before earlier, previously, sooner.

beg 1 *to beg for food.* to cadge, to scrounge. 2 *Granny begged us to visit her.* to ask, to entreat, to implore, to plead, to request.

beggar destitute person, homeless person, pauper, poor person, ragamuffin, tramp, vagrant.

begin 1 *When did the trouble begin?* to arise, to commence, to start. 2 *She wants to begin a new business.* to create, to embark on, to found, to initiate, to introduce, to open, to originate, to set up.

beginner apprentice, learner, novice.

beginning 1 *the beginning of life on earth.* birth, commencement, creation, origin, start. 2 *the beginning of a book.* introduction, opening, preface, prelude, prologue.

begrudge *I don't begrudge him his good luck.* to be bitter about, to envy, to resent.

behave *I hope you'll behave well.* to act, to conduct yourself.

behaviour *They said our behaviour was excellent.* attitude, conduct, manners.

behead to decapitate. SEE ALSO **execute, kill.**

behold (old-fashioned) *He beheld a vision of a golden city.* to discern, to look at, to make out, to see, to witness.

being creature.

belated *It was two weeks before we sent belated thanks.* delayed, late.

belch *The chimneys belched filthy smoke.* to discharge, to emit, to erupt, to fume, to send out, to smoke, to vomit.

belfry steeple, tower.

belief *religious beliefs.* attitude, conviction, creed, faith, opinion, religion, thought, trust, view.

believe 1 *You can't believe anything he says.* to accept, to have confidence in, to have faith in, to rely on, to trust. 2 *I believe he cheated.* to consider, to feel, to judge, to reckon, to think. 3 *I believe you finished off the chocolates?* to assume, to presume, to suppose.

bell 1 *Didn't you hear the bell?* alarm, signal. 2 VARIOUS WAYS BELLS SOUND: to chime, to clang, to jangle, to jingle, to peal, to ping, to ring, to tinkle, to toll.

belligerent *a belligerent fighter.* aggressive, hostile, martial, militant, pugnacious, warlike.

bellow SEE **shout.**

belly abdomen, stomach, (informal) tummy.

belong 1 *This book belongs to me.* to be owned by. 2 *Do you belong to the youth club?* to be a member of.

belongings *Remember to take your belongings when you get off the train.* possessions, property, things.

beloved darling, dearest, loved.

belt 1 *a belt around her waist.* (old-fashioned) girdle, loop, strap. 2 *a belt of trees.* band, line, strip.

bench 1 *a park bench.* form, seat. 2 *a carpenter's bench.* table, worktop.

bend 1 *The blacksmith bent an iron bar.* to arch, to buckle, to coil, to curl, to curve, to distort, to fold, to loop, to turn, to twist, to warp, to wind. 2 *We bent down to go under the low branch.* to bow, to crouch, to duck, to kneel, to stoop. 3 *a bend in the road.* angle, corner, curve, turn, twist.

benediction blessing.

benefactor *A benefactor paid for our new sports gear.* donor, sponsor.

beneficial *They say that garlic is beneficial to your health.* advantageous, constructive, good, healthy, helpful, profitable, useful.

benefit *Clean air is one of the benefits of living in the country.* advantage, asset, blessing, gain, help, privilege, profit.

benevolent *a benevolent old gentleman.* considerate, good, helpful, humane, kindly, merciful, sympathetic, warm-hearted. SEE ALSO **kind.**

bent *a bent nail.* angled, crooked, curved, distorted, twisted, warped.

bequest *a small bequest from grandmother's will.* inheritance, legacy.

bereavement *a bereavement in the family.* death, loss.

berserk *The dog went berserk when the wasp stung him.* crazy, demented, frantic, frenzied, mad, violent, wild.

berth 1 *There were four berths in each cabin.* bed, bunk. 2 *The ship tied up at its berth.* anchorage, dock, landing-stage, moorings, pier, quay, wharf.

besides additionally, also, furthermore, moreover, too.

besiege *The Greeks besieged Troy for 10 long years.* to blockade, to cut off, to encircle, to surround.

bet 1 *You don't often gain anything by betting.* to do the pools, to enter a lottery, to gamble. 2 *How much was your bet?* stake, wager.

betray 1 *to betray someone who trusts you.* to cheat, to double-cross, to let down. 2 *to betray a secret.* to disclose, to divulge, to expose, to reveal.

betrayal disloyalty, treachery, treason.

betrothed engaged.

better *Are you better after your flu?* cured, healed, improved, recovered, recovering, well.

beverage SEE **drink.**

bewilder 1 *The flashing lights bewildered me.* to baffle, to confuse, to distract, to muddle, to perplex, to puzzle. 2 *bewildered:* dazed, stunned.

bewitch 1 *The magical atmosphere bewitched us.* to captivate, to charm, to enchant, to fascinate. 2 *bewitched:* entranced, spellbound. 3 *bewitching:* SEE **attractive.**

biased *a biased referee*. influenced, one-sided, prejudiced, unfair, unjust.

bicycle 1 (informal) bike, penny-farthing. SEE ALSO **cycle**. 2 PARTS OF A BICYCLE: brake, frame, gear, handlebar, pedal, saddle, spoke, wheel.

bid *to bid in an auction*. to offer, to propose.

bifocals glasses, spectacles.

big 1 *a big amount, a big person, a big shop, etc*. ample, bulky, colossal, considerable, enormous, extensive, fat, giant, gigantic, grand, great, hefty, high, huge, hulking, husky, immeasurable, immense, incalculable, infinite, large, lofty, mammoth, massive, mighty, monstrous, roomy, sizeable, spacious, substantial, tall, (informal) terrific, towering, tremendous, vast. 2 *a big decision, a big moment, etc*. grave, important, major, momentous, notable, serious, significant, weighty.

bilious ill, queasy, sick.

bill 1 *a bird's bill*. beak. 2 *Keep the bill to prove you've paid*. account, receipt. 3 advertisement, notice, poster.

billow *billowing waves*. to bulge, to rise, to swell.

bin SEE **container**.

bind 1 *to bind things together*. to attach, to connect, to join, to secure, to tie. SEE ALSO **fasten**. 2 *to bind a wound*. to cover, to wrap.

binoculars field-glasses.

bird 1 chick, cock, fledgling, hen, nestling. 2 VARIOUS BIRDS: albatross, blackbird, budgerigar, bullfinch, buzzard, canary, chaffinch, chicken, coot, cormorant, crane, crow, cuckoo, curlew, dove, duck, eagle, emu, falcon, finch, flamingo, goldfinch, goose, grouse, gull, hawk, heron, jackdaw, jay, kingfisher, kiwi, lapwing, lark, magpie, nightingale, ostrich, owl, parrot, partridge, peacock, peewit, pelican, penguin, petrel, pheasant, pigeon, plover, puffin, quail, raven, robin, rook, seagull, skylark, sparrow, starling, stork, swallow, swan, swift, thrush, tit, turkey, vulture, wagtail, warbler, woodpecker, wren, yellowhammer. 3 VARIOUS PARTS OF A BIRD: beak, bill, claw, crest, down, feather, plumage, tail, talon, wing.

birth appearance, beginning, creation, origin, start. SEE ALSO **pregnant.**

biscuit cracker, wafer.

bit 1 *a bit of chocolate, a bit of stone, etc*. block, chip, chunk, crumb, dollop, fragment, grain, hunk, lump, morsel, particle, scrap, slab, speck. 2 *I don't need it all, just a bit of it*. division, fraction, helping, part, piece, portion, section, segment, share, slice.

bite 1 to chew, to gnaw, to munch, to nip, to snap, to sting. 2 *I'll just have a bite*. morsel, mouthful.

bitter 1 *a bitter smell*. acrid, harsh, sharp, unpleasant. 2 *a bitter experience*. distressing, painful, unhappy. 3 *bitter feelings*. cruel, embittered, envious, jealous, resentful, sour, spiteful. 4 *a bitter quarrel*. angry, vicious, violent. 5 *a bitter wind*. biting, cold, freezing, (informal) perishing, piercing, raw.

black *a black night*. dark, inky, pitch-black, sooty, starless, unlit. 2 *a black mood*. bad, depressing, evil, gloomy, sad, sinister, sombre.

blackberry bramble.

blacken to darken.

blackguard knave, rascal, rogue, scoundrel, villain.

blacksmith THINGS USED BY A BLACKSMITH: anvil, bellows, forge, hammer, tongs.

blade *a sharp blade*. edge, knife, razor, sword.

blame 1 *They blamed me, but I didn't do it!* to accuse, to charge, to condemn, to criticize, to denounce, to incriminate, to rebuke, to reprimand, to scold. 2 *He admitted that the blame was his*. fault, guilt, responsibility.

blameless guiltless, innocent.

blank 1 *blank paper, a blank tape*. clean, empty, unmarked, unused. 2 *a blank look*. expressionless, vacant.

blare *The trumpets blared*. to bray, to roar, to shriek.

blasphemous *It would be blasphemous to tear up a Bible*. irreverent, sacrilegious, sinful, wicked.

blast 1 *a blast of air*. gale, wind. 2 *a bomb blast*. bang, boom, explosion, noise, report.

blatant *a blatant mistake*. conspicuous, evident, obvious, open, unconcealed, undisguised, unmistakable.

blaze 1 *The fire blazed up*. to burn, to flame, to flare. 2 *The firemen couldn't control the blaze*. conflagration, fire, inferno.

bleach *The sun bleached our curtains.* to discolour, to fade, to whiten.

bleak *a bleak moor.* bare, barren, cold, desolate, dismal, windswept.

blemish *There wasn't a blemish in her work.* blot, defect, fault, flaw, imperfection, mark, spot, stain.

blend *He blended the ingredients for his cake.* to combine, to mingle, to mix.

blessed hallowed, holy, sacred.

blessing 1 *The vicar said the blessing.* benediction, grace, prayer. 2 *The fine weather this year is a great blessing to the farmers.* advantage, asset, benefit, comfort, help.

blight affliction, ailment, disease, illness, sickness.

blind 1 sightless, unseeing. 2 *Please close the blind.* curtain, screen, shade, shutters.

blink *blinking lights.* to flicker, to wink.

bliss *It's bliss to have a nice hot bath!* delight, ecstasy, happiness, joy, pleasure, rapture.

blitz attack, onslaught, raid.

blizzard SEE **storm**.

bloated distended, swollen.

blob *a blob of paint.* bead, drop, spot.

block 1 *a block of ice-cream.* brick, chunk, hunk, lump, slab. 2 *The drain was blocked with leaves.* to bung up, to clog, to fill, to jam, to stop up. 3 *An overturned lorry blocked our way.* to bar, to barricade, to deter, to hamper, to hinder, to hold back, to impede, to obstruct, to prevent, to prohibit.

blockade siege.

blockage *a blockage in a drain.* block, hindrance, impediment, obstacle, obstruction.

bloke (informal) fellow, guy, man.

blond, blonde *blond hair.* fair, light. ! A man is *blond*; a woman is *blonde*.

bloodshed carnage, killing, massacre, murder, slaughter.

bloodthirsty brutal, ferocious, fierce, inhuman, murderous, pitiless, ruthless, savage, vicious, violent. SEE ALSO **cruel**.

bloody blood-stained, gory.

bloom *Most flowers bloom in summer.* to blossom, to flourish, to flower.

blossom to bloom, to flower.

blot 1 *a blot of ink.* blotch, spot, stain. 2 *a blot on the landscape.* blemish, eyesore. 3 *You've made me blot the page!* to mar, to mark, to smudge, to spoil, to stain. 4 *The fog blotted out the view.* to conceal, to cover, to erase, to hide, to mask, to rub out, to wipe out.

blow 1 *The wind blew.* to puff, to whistle. 2 *The tyres need blowing up.* to inflate. 3 *The bomb blew up.* to burst, to detonate, to explode, to go off. 4 *a nasty blow on the head.* bang, bump, hit, knock. 5 *It was a terrible blow when she lost her purse.* bombshell, jolt, shock, surprise.

blubber *Stop blubbering and help me clear up!* to cry, to snivel, to sob, to wail, to weep.

blue 1 azure, indigo, lavender, navy blue, turquoise. 2 *I'm feeling blue today.* dejected, depressed, gloomy, melancholy, unhappy.

bluff *Don't believe him: he's bluffing.* to deceive, to fool, to hoax, to hoodwink, (informal) to kid, to lie, to mislead, to pretend, to take in, to trick.

blunder 1 *to blunder about.* to stagger, to stumble. 2 *to make a blunder.* (informal) clanger, error, (informal) howler, mistake, (informal) slip-up. 3 *blundering:* awkward, bungling, clumsy, gawky, lumbering, ungainly.

blunt 1 *a blunt knife.* dull, unsharpened, worn. 2 *a blunt reply.* abrupt, candid, curt, direct, frank, honest, impolite, outspoken, plain, rude, straight, straightforward.

blurred *a blurred photograph.* cloudy, confused, dim, faint, fuzzy, hazy, indistinct, misty, unclear.

blush to colour, to flush, to glow, to redden.

blustery *blustery weather.* gusty, squally, windy. SEE ALSO **weather**.

board 1 *wooden boards.* plank, timber. 2 *to board a ship.* to embark. 3 *He boards in a hotel.* to live, to lodge.

boarder guest, lodger, resident, tenant.

boast to brag, (informal) to crow, to gloat, to show off, (informal) to swank.

boastful arrogant, conceited, haughty, proud, (informal) stuck-up.

boat craft, ship. SEE ALSO **vessel.**

bobsleigh sledge.

body 1 *Doctors know about the body.* anatomy. 2 *the body of a dead animal.* carcass, corpse, remains. 3 *The boxer aimed blows at his opponent's body.* trunk. 4 PARTS OF YOUR BODY: abdomen, adenoids, ankle, appendix, arm, artery, backbone, belly, bladder, blood, bone, bowels, brain, breast, buttocks, calf, cheek, chest, chin, ear, elbow, eye, finger, foot, forehead, funny-bone, gland, gullet, gums, guts, hand, head, heart, heel, hip, intestines, jaw, kidney, knee, knee-cap, knuckle, leg, limb, lip, liver, lung, marrow, mouth, muscle, navel, neck, nerve, nipple, nose, nostril, pores, rib, saliva, scalp, shin, shoulder, shoulder-blade, skeleton, skin, skull, spine, stomach, thigh, throat, thumb, toe, tongue, tonsils, tooth, trunk, vein, vertebra, waist, windpipe, womb, wrist.

bodyguard *The President always has a bodyguard.* guard, protector.

bog *Don't get stuck in the bog.* fen, marsh, quagmire, quicksands, swamp.

bogus *a bogus £5 note.* counterfeit, faked, false, feigned, (informal) phoney, pretended.

boil 1 *It's uncomfortable to have a boil on your bottom.* abscess, inflammation, sore. 2 *Are the potatoes boiling yet?* to bubble, to seethe, to simmer, to stew. SEE ALSO **cook.**

boisterous *boisterous behaviour.* animated, disorderly, irrepressible, lively, noisy, obstreperous, rough, rowdy, unruly, wild.

bold 1 *a bold adventure.* adventurous, brave, courageous, daring, enterprising, fearless, heroic, intrepid, self-confident, valiant. 2 *a bold request.* brazen, cheeky, forward, impertinent, impudent, insolent, presumptuous, rude, shameless. 3 *bold writing.* big, clear, large.

bolster cushion, pillow.

bolt 1 *a bolt on the door.* bar, catch, latch, lock. 2 *We bolt the door when we go out.* to close, to fasten, to lock, to secure. 3 *The animals have bolted!* to escape, to flee, to run away. 4 *Don't bolt your food.* to gobble, to gulp.

bombard *They bombarded us with missiles.* to assail, to assault, to attack, to fire at, to pelt, to shell, to shoot at.

bombshell *The £100 prize came as a complete bombshell.* shock, surprise.

bond 1 *a prisoner's bonds.* chain, cord, fetters, handcuffs, rope, shackles. 2 *There's a strong bond between twins.* connection, link, relationship.

bondage slavery.

bonnet *a woolly bonnet.* cap, hat.

bonus *a Christmas bonus.* addition, extra, supplement.

boo to hoot, to jeer.

booby trap ambush, snare, trap.

book 1 publication, volume. 2 KINDS OF BOOK: album, annual, anthology, atlas, booklet, diary, dictionary, encyclopaedia, fiction, hardback, hymn-book, manual, manuscript, omnibus, paperback, reference book, scrap-book, scroll, textbook. SEE ALSO **magazine, writing.** 3 PARTS OF A BOOK: chapter, epilogue, index, introduction, preface, prologue, title. 4 *Have you booked tickets for the pantomime?* to order, to reserve.

booklet book, brochure, leaflet, pamphlet.

boom bang, blast, crash, explosion.

boost *Winning a race boosts your morale.* to encourage, to help, to improve, to increase, to raise.

boot, bootee SEE **shoe.**

booth *a voting booth.* compartment, cubicle, kiosk, stall, stand.

booty *The thieves dropped their booty.* contraband, loot, plunder, (informal) swag, takings, trophies.

border 1 *We showed our passports at the border.* boundary, frontier. 2 *We put a colourful border round the edge.* edging, frame, frieze, frill, fringe, hem, margin, verge. 3 *a flower border.* bed.

bore 1 *to bore a hole.* to drill, to penetrate, to perforate, to pierce. 2 *The long speech bored most of the audience.* to tire, to weary.

boring *a boring book.* arid, commonplace, dreary, dry, dull, flat, long-winded, monotonous, tedious, unexciting, uninteresting, wordy.

borrow *Can I borrow your pen?* to be lent, to use.

bosom breast, chest, heart.

boss *Who's the boss here?* chief, controller, director, employer, foreman, governor, head, leader, manager, master, proprietor, ruler, superintendent, supervisor.

bossy *You may be captain, but don't get bossy!* dictatorial, domineering, masterful, tyrannical.

bother 1 *There was some bother in the playground.* ado, disorder, disturbance, fuss, to-do. SEE ALSO **commotion**. 2 *Is the dog a bother to you?* inconvenience, nuisance, trouble, worry. 3 *Are the wasps bothering you?* to annoy, to disturb, to exasperate, to irritate, to molest, to pester, to plague, to trouble, to upset, to vex, to worry. 4 *Don't bother to wash up.* to care, to mind.

bottle SEE **container**.

bottom 1 *the bottom of a wall.* base, foot, foundation. 2 *The wasp stung me on the bottom.* backside, behind, buttocks, rear, rump. 3 *the bottom of the sea.* bed, depths.

bough *a bough of a tree.* branch, limb.

boulder rock, stone.

bounce *The ball bounced over the fence.* to bound, to jump, to rebound, to recoil, to ricochet, to spring.

bound 1 *Grandpa is bound to be here soon.* certain, compelled, obliged, required, sure. 2 *The rocket was bound for the moon.* aimed at, destined for, directed towards. 3 *He bounded over the fence.* to bounce, to hop, to jump, to leap, to skip, to spring, to vault.

boundary *A fence marked the boundary.* border, circumference, edge, frontier, limit, margin, perimeter.

boundless *boundless energy.* endless, everlasting, limitless, unlimited, unrestricted.

bounty charity, generosity.

bouquet *a bouquet of flowers.* arrangement, bunch, posy, spray, wreath.

bout 1 *a boxing bout.* combat, contest, fight, match, round. 2 *a bout of coughing.* attack, fit, turn.

boutique SEE **shop**.

bow 1 *Tie it in a bow.* SEE **knot**. 2 *the bow of a ship.* front. 3 *to bow before the queen.* to bend, to curtsy, to stoop.

bowl 1 *a bowl of soup.* basin. SEE ALSO **container**. 2 *He bowled a faster ball.* to fling, to hurl, to lob, to pitch, to throw, to toss.

box 1 carton, case, chest, crate. 2 *boxing:* SEE **fight**.

boy (insulting) brat, lad, (insulting) urchin, youngster, youth.

brace couple, pair.

brag *Even if you did win, don't brag about it.* to boast, (informal) to crow, to gloat, to show off, (informal) to swank.

braid band, ribbon.

brain *Use your brains!* intellect, intelligence, reason, sense, understanding, wisdom, wit.

brainwash *People can be brainwashed by advertising.* to indoctrinate.

brainwave SEE **idea**.

brainy *She is the brainy one in the family.* academic, bright, clever, intellectual, intelligent, studious.

branch 1 *the branch of a tree.* arm, bough, limb. 2 *a branch of the bank.* department, part, office, section. 3 *The road branches.* to divide, to fork.

brand 1 *a brand of margarine.* kind, make, trademark. 2 *to brand cattle with a hot iron.* to mark, to stamp.

brandish *He brandished his umbrella to catch our attention.* to flourish, to shake, to twirl, to wave.

brass KINDS OF BRASS INSTRUMENTS: bugle, cornet, horn, trombone, trumpet, tuba.

brave *She was brave to go back into the burning house.* adventurous, bold, courageous, daring, fearless, gallant, heroic, intrepid, noble, plucky, spirited, undaunted, valiant.

bravery *Everyone praised her bravery.* courage, daring, determination, fortitude, (informal) grit, (informal) guts, heroism, nerve, (informal) pluck, prowess, spirit, valour.

brawl *a brawl outside the football ground.* clash, confrontation, fight, quarrel, row, scrap, scuffle, squabble, struggle, tussle.

brawny *That weightlifter looks a brawny fellow.* beefy, burly, muscular, strong, tough.

brazen *It was brazen to march up to the prince and ask for a kiss!* bold, cheeky, forward, impertinent, impudent, insolent, rude, shameless.

breach *a breach in the sea wall.* break, crack, gap, hole, opening, space, split.

bread loaf, roll.

break 1 *to break an egg, to break a leg, to break down a wall.* to burst, to chip, to crack, to crumble, to crush, to damage, to demolish, to destroy, to fracture, to knock down, to ruin, to shatter, to smash, to splinter, to split, to squash, to wreck. 2 *The sandcastle broke up.* to collapse, to crumble, to decay, to deteriorate, to disintegrate, to fall apart, to tumble down. 3 *to break the law.* to disobey, to disregard, to infringe, to violate. 4 *a break in a pipe.* breach, chink, crack, cut, gap, gash, hole, leak, opening, rift, slit, split, tear. 5 *a break between lessons.* interlude, interval, lapse, lull, pause, respite, rest.

breaker *The breakers crashed on the shore.* surf, waves.

breakneck *breakneck speed.* dangerous, hasty, headlong, suicidal.

breast bosom.

breathless *She was breathless after her race.* exhausted, gasping, panting, tired out.

breathe *Don't breathe the fumes.* to inhale.

breeches SEE **trousers.**

breed 1 *Mice breed rapidly.* to increase, to multiply, to produce young, to reproduce. 2 *What breed of dog is that?* kind, species, variety.

breeze *a cool breeze.* air, draught, wind.

bribe *You mustn't try to bribe the judge.* to corrupt, to entice, to influence, to pervert, to tempt.

brick block.

bride, bridegroom, bridesmaid SEE **wedding.**

bridge KINDS OF BRIDGE: aqueduct, fly-over, suspension bridge, viaduct.

brief 1 *a brief visit to granny.* little, momentary, passing, short, temporary, transient. 2 *a brief summary of a story.* abbreviated, abridged, compact, concise, condensed, terse.

briefs knickers, panties, pants, shorts, trunks, underpants.

brigand bandit, buccaneer, desperado, gangster, highwayman, outlaw, pirate, robber, thief.

bright 1 *bright colours, bright lights.* brilliant, clear, flashy, gaudy, gleaming, radiant, resplendent, shining, shiny, showy, sparkling, sunny, vivid. 2 *a bright manner, a bright voice.* animated, cheerful, happy, lively. 3 *a bright idea, a bright pupil.* brainy, clever, ingenious, intelligent, quick, shrewd, (informal) smart.

brighten *We need to brighten this gloomy place up.* to cheer up, to illuminate, to lighten, to light up.

brilliant 1 *brilliant lights.* bright, dazzling, gleaming, glittering, resplendent, shining, sparkling. 2 *a brilliant scientist.* brainy, clever, gifted, intelligent, marvellous, outstanding, talented, wonderful. 3 (informal) *a brilliant game.* SEE **excellent.**

brim *full to the brim.* brink, edge, rim, top.

brimming full, overflowing.

bring 1 *to bring the shopping home.* to carry, to fetch, to take. 2 *A change in the wind will bring snow.* to cause, to create, to generate, to give rise to, to induce, to lead to, to provoke. 3 *We plan to bring out a new magazine.* to introduce, to issue, to produce, to publish, to release, to start. 4 *Parents bring up their children.* to care for, to educate, to look after, to raise, to rear, to train.

brink *He stood on the brink of the pool.* brim, edge, rim.

brisk *brisk exercise.* animated, energetic, fast, lively, quick, rapid, speedy, sprightly.

bristle hair.

brittle *Eggshell is extremely brittle.* breakable, crisp, fragile, frail.

broad 1 *a broad path.* wide. 2 *a broad plain.* expansive, extensive, large. 3 *a broad outline of a story.* general, imprecise, indefinite, vague.

broadcast *to broadcast a concert.* to relay, to send out, to transmit, to televise.

brochure *We got a brochure from the travel agent.* booklet, catalogue, leaflet, pamphlet, prospectus.

brogue 1 SEE **shoe.** 2 *an Irish brogue.* accent, dialect, language.

brooch clasp.

brood 1 *a brood of chicks.* family, litter. 2 *It's no use brooding about past mistakes.* to meditate, to mope, to ponder, to reflect, to sulk, to think.

brook burn, stream.

broom brush.

broth soup, stock.

brown beige, fawn, khaki, tan, tawny.

bruise to damage, to injure.

brush 1 broom. 2 *Brush out the garage when you have finished your woodwork.* to clean, to sweep.

brutal *a brutal murder.* atrocious, beastly, bloodthirsty, ferocious, inhuman, murderous, pitiless, ruthless, savage, vicious, violent. SEE ALSO **cruel.**

brute animal, beast, creature.

bubble 1 *soap bubbles.* foam, froth, lather, suds. 2 *The water was bubbling.* to boil, to fizz, to fizzle, to foam, to froth, to seethe.

bubbly *bubbly drinks.* effervescent, fizzy, foaming, sparkling.

buccaneer bandit, brigand, highwayman, marauder, outlaw, pirate, robber.

buck (informal) *Buck up!* see **hurry.**

bucket pail. SEE ALSO **container.**

buckle 1 *the buckle of a belt.* clasp, fastener, fastening. 2 *The framework buckled under the heavy weight.* to bend, to collapse, to crumple, to curve, to dent, to distort, to twist, to warp.

budge *The stubborn donkey wouldn't budge.* to move, to shift.

buffet *We went to the buffet for a snack.* bar, café, cafeteria, snack-bar.

bug (informal) 1 *bugs on the roses.* insects. 2 *a bug in a computer program.* error, fault, mistake.

build 1 *to build models.* to assemble, to construct, to erect, to make, to put together, to put up. 2 *to build up a business.* to develop, to enlarge, to expand, to increase, to strengthen.

building 1 construction, edifice, structure. 2 KINDS OF BUILDING: abbey, arcade, art gallery, barn, barracks, boat-house, bungalow, cabin, castle, cathedral, chapel, château, church, cinema, complex, cottage, crematorium, dovecote, factory, farmhouse, filling station, flats, garage, granary, gymnasium, hall, hotel, inn, library, lighthouse, mansion, mill, minaret, monastery, mosque, museum, observatory, orphanage, outhouse, pagoda, palace, pavilion, pier, pigsty, police station, post office, power-station, prison, pub, public house, restaurant, shed, silo, skyscraper, slaughterhouse, stable, studio, synagogue, temple, theatre, tower, villa, warehouse, waterworks, windmill, woodshed. SEE ALSO **house, shop.** 3 PARTS OF BUILDINGS: arch, balcony, banister, basement, battlements, bay window, belfry, bow window, brickwork, buttress, ceiling, cellar, chimney, cloisters, courtyard, crypt, dome, drawbridge, dungeon, eaves, floor, foundations, foyer, gable, gallery, gateway, gutter, joist, keep, lobby, masonry, parapet, porch, portcullis, quadrangle, rafter, rampart, roof, room, sill, spire, staircase, steeple, tower, turret, vault, veranda, wall, window, window-sill. 4 MATERIALS USED IN BUILDING: asbestos, asphalt, brick, cement, concrete, fibreglass, glass, hardboard, metal, mortar, plaster, plastic, plywood, slate, stone, tile, timber, wood.

bulb 1 *an electric bulb.* lamp, light. 2 FLOWERS THAT GROW FROM BULBS: bluebell, crocus, daffodil, hyacinth, lily, snowdrop, tulip.

bulge 1 bump, hump, knob, lump, swelling. 2 *The shopping bag was bulging with interesting shapes.* to billow, to protrude, to stick out, to swell.

bulk *The bulk of the airship amazed us.* largeness, magnitude, size, volume.

bulletin *a news bulletin.* announcement, communiqué, dispatch, notice, proclamation, report, statement.

bullfighter matador, toreador.

bull's-eye *to hit the bull's-eye.* centre, target.

bully *to bully younger children.* to frighten, to intimidate, to persecute, to terrorize, to threaten, to torment.

bump 1 *We had a bump in the car.* blow, collision, crash, hit, knock. 2 *How did you get that bump on the head?* bulge, hump, lump, swelling. 3 *He bumped us deliberately.* to bang, to collide with, to crash into, to jolt, to knock, to ram, to strike, to thump, to wallop. SEE ALSO **hit**.

bumptious *The man next door has got bumptious since he was promoted.* arrogant, boastful, (informal) cocky, conceited, officious, self-important.

bumpy *a bumpy road.* irregular, rough, uneven.

bun SEE **cake**.

bunch 1 *a bunch of carrots, a bunch of friends.* batch, bundle, clump, cluster, collection, crowd, gathering, group, pack, set. 2 *a bunch of flowers.* bouquet, posy, spray.

bundle *a bundle of waste paper.* bale, bunch, collection, package, parcel, sheaf.

bung *Who took the bung out of the barrel?* cork, plug, stopper.

bungalow SEE **house**.

bungle *to bungle a job.* to mess up, to spoil.

bunk bed, berth.

burden 1 *to carry a burden.* load, weight. 2 *It may help to share your burdens.* problem, trouble, worry.

bureau 1 desk. 2 *an information bureau.* office.

burglar intruder, robber, thief.

burial SEE **funeral**.

burly *a burly figure.* beefy, big, brawny, hefty, husky, muscular, strong, tough.

burn 1 VARIOUS WAYS THINGS BURN: to blaze, to flame, to flare, to smoulder. 2 WAYS TO BURN THINGS: to char, to cremate, to ignite, to kindle, to light, to scald, to scorch, to set fire to, to singe. 3 *a Scottish burn.* brook, stream.

burnished *burnished brass.* polished, shiny.

burrow 1 *a rabbit's burrow.* hole, tunnel, warren. 2 *The rabbits burrowed under the fence.* to dig, to excavate, to tunnel.

burst *The tyre burst. They burst into laughter.* to blow out, to break, to erupt, to explode, to force open.

bury to conceal, to cover, to hide.

bush SEE **shrub**.

business 1 *The new shop does a lot of business.* buying and selling, commerce, industry, trade. 2 *What sort of business do you want to go into?* calling, career, employment, job, occupation, profession, trade, work. 3 *He works for a sports equipment business.* company, concern, corporation, establishment, firm, organization. 4 *It's none of your business.* affair, concern, matter.

busy 1 *Mum is busy in the garden.* active, diligent, employed, engaged, industrious, involved, occupied. 2 *It's busy in town on Saturdays.* bustling, frantic, hectic, lively.

busybody *to be a busybody:* SEE **interfere**.

butt 1 *a water butt.* SEE **container**. 2 *The goat butted her.* to bump, to knock, to strike, to thump. SEE ALSO **hit**. 3 *Please don't butt in.* to interfere, to interrupt, to intervene, to intrude, to meddle.

buttocks backside, behind, bottom, rear, rump.

button *Button your coat!* SEE **fasten**.

buy to acquire, to gain, to get, to get on hire purchase, to obtain, to pay for, to procure, to purchase.

bystander *The police asked the bystanders to describe the accident.* eyewitness, observer, onlooker, passer-by, spectator, witness.

C

cab taxi.

cable 1 *an anchor cable.* chain, cord, hawser, line, rope. 2 *an electric cable.* flex, lead, wire. 3 *They sent a cable to say they'd arrive tomorrow.* telegram, wire.

cache *a cache of arms.* depot, dump, hoard, stores.

cadge *to cadge food.* to beg, to scrounge.

café bar, buffet, cafeteria, canteen, restaurant, snack-bar.

cage *an animal's cage.* coop, enclosure, hutch, pen.

cake KINDS OF CAKE: bun, doughnut, éclair, flan, fruit cake, gingerbread, meringue, scone, shortbread, sponge, tart.

caked *caked with mud.* dirty, muddy.

calamitous *a calamitous mistake.* dire, disastrous, dreadful, serious, terrible, tragic, unfortunate, unlucky.

calamity *The hotel fire was a terrible calamity.* accident, catastrophe, disaster, misadventure, misfortune, mishap, tragedy.

calculate *Calculate how many sandwiches we need for the party.* to add up, to assess, to compute, to estimate, to figure out, to reckon, to total, to work out.

call 1 *Did you hear someone call?* to cry out, to exclaim, to shout, to yell. 2 *The head called me to his office.* to summon. 3 *I couldn't call because the phone was out of order.* to dial, to phone, to ring, to telephone. 4 *When did granny call?* to drop in, to visit. 5 *On Saturdays mum calls us at nine o'clock.* to arouse, to awaken, to rouse, to wake up. 6 *What did they call the baby?* to baptize, to christen, to name. 7 *What will you call your story?* to entitle.

calling *What was grandpa's calling in life?* business, career, employment, job, occupation, profession, trade.

callous *a callous murder.* cold-blooded, hard-hearted, heartless, insensitive, merciless, pitiless, ruthless, unfeeling. SEE ALSO **cruel.**

calm 1 *calm water.* even, flat, motionless, placid, smooth, still. 2 *a calm mood.* peaceful, quiet, sedate, serene, tranquil, untroubled. 3 *Keep calm!* cool, level-headed, patient, sensible. 4 *He was upset and it took ages to calm him.* to appease, to lull, to pacify, to quieten, to soothe.

camel dromedary.

camouflage *We camouflaged our hide-out.* to conceal, to cover up, to disguise, to hide, to mask, to screen.

campaign *a campaign against litter.* action, battle, crusade, fight, operation, struggle, war.

campus *the school campus.* grounds, site.

can *a can of beans.* tin.

canal channel, waterway.

cancel 1 *We cancelled the game because of the snow.* to abandon, to give up, to postpone, to scrap. 2 *They cancelled our order.* to cross out, to delete, to erase, to wipe out.

candid *Give me a candid answer.* direct, frank, honest, open, outspoken, plain, straightforward.

candidate *a candidate for an exam.* applicant, competitor, entrant.

cane *We put up some canes for our runner beans.* rod, stick.

canister SEE **container.**

canteen *a snack in the canteen.* buffet, café, cafeteria, restaurant, snack-bar.

canyon *a deep canyon.* defile, gorge, pass, ravine, valley.

cap 1 SEE **hat.** 2 *the cap off the ketchup bottle.* cover, covering, lid, top.

capable *a capable organizer.* able, accomplished, clever, competent, efficient, gifted, handy, practical, proficient, skilful, skilled, talented.

capacity 1 *the capacity of a container.* size, volume. 2 *It isn't within my capacity to run 100 metres in ten seconds.* ability, capability, competence, skill, talent.

caper *The lambs capered about the field.* to dance, to frisk, to jump, to leap, to play, to prance, to romp, to skip.

capital *You need capital to start a business.* funds, money, property, riches, savings, wealth.

capitulate *The town capitulated after a long siege.* to give in, to submit, to surrender, to yield.

capsize *The boat capsized.* to overturn, to tip over, to turn over, to turn turtle.

capsule *The doctor gave her some capsules for her rheumatism.* pill, tablet.

captain *the captain of a ship.* commander, master, skipper.

caption *Write a caption under your picture.* heading, headline, title.

captivate 1 *The kittens captivated us.* to attract, to bewitch, to charm, to delight, to enchant, to entrance, to fascinate. 2 *captivating:* SEE **attractive**.

captive *They guarded their captives closely.* convict, hostage, prisoner.

capture *Did they capture the thief?* to arrest, to catch, to corner, (informal) to nab, to seize, to take.

car automobile, estate car, hatchback, motor car, saloon, sports car, taxi.

carcass *the carcass of an animal.* body, corpse, remains.

card 1 cardboard. 2 *a game of cards.* SEE **cards.**

cards 1 playing cards. 2 CARD GAMES: bridge, patience, pontoon, rummy, snap, whist. 3 SUITS: clubs, diamonds, hearts, spades. 4 VALUES: ace, jack, joker, king, knave, number 2 to 10, queen.

care 1 *We should care about the starving.* to bother, to concern yourself, to mind, to trouble, to worry. 2 *He cares for his dog.* to attend to, to cherish, to guard, to keep, to look after, to mind, to mother, to protect, to tend, to watch over. 3 *Work with care.* attention, carefulness, caution, concentration, diligence, exactness, heed, pains, thoroughness. 4 *He doesn't have a care in the world!* anxiety, concern, trouble, worry. 5 *She left the baby in my care.* charge, custody, keeping, protection, safe-keeping.

career 1 *She's training for a career in industry.* business, calling, employment, job, occupation, profession, trade, work. 2 *They careered along.* to dash, to hurtle, to race, to rush, to speed, to tear, (informal) to zoom.

carefree *Our dog lives a carefree life.* contented, easy, easygoing, happy, light-hearted, untroubled.

careful 1 *a careful driver.* alert, attentive, cautious, diligent, observant, prudent, vigilant, wary, watchful. 2 *careful work.* conscientious, deliberate, exhaustive, methodical, meticulous, neat, orderly, organized, painstaking, precise, scrupulous, systematic, thorough.

careless 1 *careless driving.* inattentive, inconsiderate, irresponsible, negligent, rash, reckless, uncaring. 2 *careless work.* confused, disorganized, hasty, jumbled, messy, scatterbrained, shoddy, slapdash, sloppy, slovenly, thoughtless, untidy.

caress *She caressed the baby's skin.* to fondle, to kiss, to pat, to pet, to stroke, to touch.

cargo *to transport cargo.* freight, goods, load, merchandise.

carnage *a terrible scene of carnage.* bloodshed, killing, slaughter.

carnival *We want good weather for our carnival.* celebration, fair, festival, fête, gala, jamboree, show.

carpenter joiner.

carpentry woodwork.

carry 1 *Can we carry this wardrobe up the stairs?* to bring, to lift, to manhandle, to move, to remove, to take, to transfer. 2 *Aircraft carry passengers and goods.* to convey, to ferry, to ship, to transport. 3 *The foundations carry the weight of the building.* to bear, to hold up, to support. 4 *Have you carried out my orders?* to accomplish, to achieve, to complete, to do, to enforce, to execute, to finish, to perform. 5 *Shall we carry on?* to continue, to go on, to keep on, to last, to persevere, to persist, to remain, to stay, to survive.

cart barrow.

cart-horse SEE **horse.**

case 1 box, carton, crate. SEE ALSO **container.** 2 *an obvious case of favouritism.* example, illustration, instance. 3 *The detective said he'd never known a case like this one.* inquiry, investigation.

cash change, coins, money, notes.

cask barrel, tub. SEE ALSO **container.**

cast 1 *We cast a coin into the well.* to bowl, (informal) to chuck, to fling, to hurl, to lob, to pitch, to sling, to throw, to toss. 2 *The sculptor cast his statue in bronze.* to form, to mould, to shape.

castle 1 château, citadel, fort, fortress, palace. 2 PARTS OF A CASTLE: battlements, buttress, courtyard, drawbridge, dungeon, gate, keep, magazine, moat, parapet, portcullis, rampart, tower, turret, wall.

casual 1 *a casual meeting.* accidental, chance, unexpected, unintentional, unplanned. 2 *casual clothes, a casual manner.* careless, easygoing, informal, relaxed.

casualty *Although it looked a bad accident, there were no casualties.* dead person, fatality, injured person, victim, wounded person.

cat kitten, (informal) pussy, tabby, tomcat.

catalogue *a shopping catalogue, a library catalogue.* brochure, directory, index, list, register.

cataract *There are many cataracts along the river.* rapids, torrent, waterfall.

catastrophe *The plane crash was a terrible catastrophe.* accident, calamity, disaster, misfortune, mishap, tragedy.

catch 1 *to catch a ball.* to clutch, to grab, to grasp, to hang on to, to hold, to seize, to snatch, to take. 2 *to catch a rabbit, to catch a fish.* to ensnare, to hook, to net, to trap. 3 *to catch a thief.* to arrest, to capture, to corner, (informal) to nab, to stop. 4 *to catch an illness.* to be infected by, to contract, to get. 5 *a catch on a door.* bolt, latch, lock.

catching *a catching disease.* contagious, infectious.

catchy *a catchy tune.* attractive, memorable, tuneful.

category *The cars were in categories depending on the size of the engine.* class, group, kind, set, sort.

cater *We catered for twelve people at Christmas.* to cook, to provide.

caterpillar grub, larva, maggot.

cathedral SEE **church.**

cattle bullocks, bulls, calves, cows, heifers, oxen, steers.

catty *catty remarks.* malevolent, malicious, nasty, sly, spiteful, vicious.

cauldron pot, saucepan.

cause 1 *What was the cause of the trouble?* grounds, occasion, origin, reason, source. 2 *It'll cause trouble if we don't share the sweets fairly.* to bring about, to give rise to, to induce, to lead to, to provoke, to result in.

caution 1 *Proceed with caution.* attentiveness, care, heed, vigilance, wariness. 2 *The police let him off with a caution.* reprimand, warning. 3 *They cautioned us about the danger of falling rocks.* to alert, to warn.

cautious *a cautious driver.* attentive, careful, deliberate, vigilant, wary, watchful.

cavalcade parade, procession.

cave cavern, cavity, grotto, hole, pothole.

cavity cave, hole, hollow.

cease *Cease work!* to break off, to cut off, to discontinue, to end, to finish, to stop, to terminate.

ceaseless *Their ceaseless chatter annoys me.* chronic, constant, continual, continuous, incessant, interminable, non-stop, permanent, persistent, relentless, unending.

celebrate 1 *Let's celebrate!* to be happy, to rejoice, to revel. 2 *How shall we celebrate granny's seventieth birthday?* to keep, to observe, to remember.

celebrated *a celebrated actor.*
distinguished, eminent, famous, noted,
popular, renowned, well-known.

celebration KINDS OF CELEBRATION:
anniversary, banquet, birthday,
carnival, feast, festival, festivity,
jamboree, jubilee, party, wedding.

celestial *celestial music.* blissful, divine,
heavenly.

cell 1 *a monk's cell, a prison cell.* den,
prison, room. 2 *an electric cell.* battery.

cellar basement, crypt, vault.

cemetery burial-ground, churchyard,
graveyard.

censor *They censored the violent film.* to
ban, to cut, to forbid, to prohibit.

censure 1 *He deserved the referee's
censure for that foul.* condemnation,
criticism, disapproval, rebuke,
reprimand. 2 *The referee censured him.*
to reproach, to scold, (informal) to tick
off.

centre *the centre of the earth, the centre
of town.* core, focus, heart, hub, inside,
middle, nucleus.

cereal 1 corn, grain. 2 CEREALS GROWN
BY FARMERS: barley, maize, oats, rice,
rye, sweetcorn, wheat. 3 *breakfast
cereal.* cornflakes, porridge.

ceremony 1 *They held a ceremony to
open the sports centre.* event, function,
occasion. 2 *The wedding was conducted
with great ceremony.* formality,
grandeur, pageantry, pomp, ritual,
spectacle.

certain 1 *When the brakes failed,
disaster seemed certain.* destined, fated,
inescapable, inevitable, sure,
unavoidable. 2 *The shop is certain to
refund your money.* bound, compelled,
obliged, required, sure. 3 *Are you
certain it will rain?* assured, confident,
definite, positive, sure.

certificate *a certificate for swimming.*
award, degree, diploma, document.

chain 1 *The prisoners were in chains.*
bonds, fetters. 2 *Form a chain.* column,
cordon, line, row, sequence, series.
3 *The slaves were chained together.* to
link, to tie. SEE ALSO **fasten.**

chair armchair, deck-chair, pew,
rocking-chair, seat, settee, sofa.

chalet SEE **house.**

challenge 1 *The sentry challenged the
intruder.* to confront. 2 *He challenged his
rival to fight a duel.* to dare, to defy.

chamber room.

champion hero, victor, winner.

championship *a snooker
championship.* competition, contest,
tournament.

chance 1 *It happened by chance.*
accident, coincidence, destiny, fate,
fluke, fortune, luck, misfortune.
2 *There's a chance of rain.* danger,
possibility, risk. 3 *Now it's your chance
to try.* opportunity, turn. 4 *a chance
meeting.* accidental, casual, lucky,
unexpected, unintentional, unplanned.

chancy *It's chancy driving on icy roads.*
dangerous, hazardous, risky.

change 1 *to change your mind, to
change the rules, etc.* to adapt, to adjust,
to affect, to alter, to amend, to convert,
to influence, to modify, to process, to
reform, to transform, to vary. 2 *to
change clothes, to change places, etc.* to
exchange, to replace, to substitute, to
switch, to swop. 3 *The pumpkin changed
into a coach.* to become, to turn into.
4 *Have you any change?* cash, coins,
money, notes.

changeable *The weather in Britain is
very changeable.* erratic, fickle,
inconsistent, temperamental,
unpredictable, unreliable, variable.

channel 1 *a channel to take away water.*
canal, dike, ditch, gully, gutter,
waterway. 2 *Which channel is your
programme on?* (informal) side, station,
wavelength.

chaos *It was chaos when he let off the
fire-extinguisher.* anarchy, bedlam,
confusion, lawlessness, shambles.

chaotic *a chaotic mess.* confused,
disorderly, haphazard, higgledy-
piggledy, incoherent, jumbled, mixed
up, muddled, topsy-turvy.

chapel SEE **church.**

char *charred remains.* to blacken, to
burn, to scorch, to singe.

character 1 *an interesting character.*
human being, individual, person. 2 *a
character in a pantomime.* part, role.
3 *This brand of tea has a character of its
own.* characteristic, flavour, quality,
taste. 4 *He has a nice character.* attitude,
disposition, manner, nature,
personality, temperament. 5 *the
characters of the alphabet.* letter, sign,
symbol.

characteristic *A red breast is the characteristic feature of the robin.* distinctive, essential, individual, particular, recognizable, special, unique.

charge 1 *Their charges are reasonable.* cost, fare, fee, payment, price, rate, terms, toll, value. 2 *They left the dog in my charge.* care, command, control, custody, keeping, protection, safe-keeping. 3 *Did the police charge him?* to accuse, to blame, to prosecute. 4 *The cavalry charged.* to assault, to attack, to storm.

charity 1 *The animals' hospital depends on your charity.* generosity, kindness, love. 2 *We collected for a charity.* good cause.

charm 1 *People used to believe in the power of charms.* enchantment, magic, sorcery, spell, witchcraft, wizardry. 2 *He charmed us with his music.* to attract, to bewitch, to captivate, to enchant, to entrance, to fascinate, to spellbind. 3 *charming*: SEE **attractive**.

chart 1 map, plan. 2 diagram, graph.

charter *We chartered a bus for our trip to the zoo.* to hire, to rent.

chase *Our dog chased that rabbit for miles.* to follow, to hound, to hunt, to pursue, to track, to trail.

chasm *We nearly fell into the chasm.* abyss, crater, hole, pit.

chaste *Holy people are expected to be chaste.* decent, good, innocent, modest, pure, virgin, virtuous.

château castle, mansion, stately home.

chatter to chat, to gossip, to prattle. SEE ALSO **talk.**

chauffeur driver.

cheap 1 *You can find cheap clothes in the sales.* cut-price, economical, inexpensive, reasonable. 2 *It was cheap stuff which didn't last.* inferior, poor, shoddy, tawdry, tinny.

cheat 1 to deceive, to defraud, to dupe, to fool, to hoax, to hoodwink, to outwit, to swindle, to take in. SEE ALSO **trick.** 2 *to cheat in an examination.* to crib.

check 1 *Check your answers.* to compare, to examine, to test. 2 *A fallen tree checked our progress.* to arrest, to bar, to block, to curb, to delay, to foil, to halt, to hamper, to hinder, to impede, to stop. 3 *We took the car to the garage for a check.* examination, investigation, test.

cheek 1 face. 2 (informal) *She's got a cheek!* nerve.

cheeky *cheeky remarks.* arrogant, bold, brazen, discourteous, disrespectful, forward, impertinent, impolite, impudent, insolent, insulting, presumptuous, rude, saucy, shameless.

cheer 1 *The audience cheered.* to applaud, to clap, to shout. 2 *The clowns cheered us up.* to amuse, to brighten, to divert, to entertain.

cheerful *a cheerful mood.* animated, bright, delighted, elated, festive, gay, glad, gleeful, good-humoured, happy, jolly, jovial, joyful, laughing, light-hearted, lively, merry, optimistic, pleased, rapturous, spirited, warm-hearted.

chef cook.

chemical VARIOUS CHEMICALS: acid, alcohol, alkali, ammonia, arsenic, carbon, chlorine, fluoride, litmus, sulphur.

cherish *I shall cherish the lovely present you gave me.* to care for, to look after, to love, to prize, to protect, to treasure, to value.

chess 1 PIECES USED IN CHESS: bishop, castle or rook, king, knight, pawn, queen. 2 TERMS USED IN CHESS: checkmate, mate, stalemate.

chest *a chest full of treasure.* box, case, crate, trunk.

chew to bite, to crunch, to eat, to gnaw, to munch, to nibble.

chicken cockerel, fowl, hen, rooster.

chief 1 *What was the chief lesson you learned?* basic, dominant, essential, fundamental, greatest, important, leading, main, major, outstanding, primary, prime, principal, supreme. 2 *the chief cook.* head, leading, senior. 3 *Who's the chief around here?* boss, captain, chieftain, commander, director, employer, governor, head, leader, manager, master, president, principal, ruler.

chiefly generally, mainly, mostly, predominantly, primarily, usually.

child baby, boy, (insulting) brat, girl, infant, (informal) kid, (informal) nipper, offspring, toddler, (insulting) urchin, youngster, youth.

childish *childish behaviour.* babyish, immature, infantile, juvenile.

chill *to chill food.* to freeze, to refrigerate.

chilly *a chilly evening.* cold, cool, frosty, icy, (informal) nippy, raw, wintry.

chime SEE **bell.**

china earthenware, porcelain, pottery. SEE ALSO **crockery.**

chink *a chink in the curtains.* crack, gap, opening, slit, split.

chip **1** *I knocked a chip off the plate.* bit, flake, fragment, piece, scrap, slice, splinter. **2** *Who chipped this cup?* to break, to crack, to damage, to splinter.

chivalrous *a chivalrous knight.* courteous, gallant, gentlemanly, heroic, noble, polite.

choice *Can we have a choice?* alternative, option, pick, selection.

choir choral society, chorus.

choke **1** *The smoke choked us. This collar is choking me.* to smother, to stifle, to strangle, to suffocate, to throttle. **2** *The firemen choked in the smoke.* to gasp, to suffocate.

choose *We chose a captain.* to appoint, to decide on, to draw lots, to elect, to name, to nominate, to opt for, to pick, to prefer, to select, to settle on, to vote for.

chop *to chop wood.* to hack, to hew, to slash, to split. SEE ALSO **cut.**

chopper axe.

chores *We help with chores around the house.* drudgery, errands, jobs, tasks, work.

chorus **1** *She sings in the chorus.* choir. **2** *We joined in the chorus.* refrain.

christen *He was christened Antony.* to baptize, to name.

Christmas yule, yuletide.

chronic *a chronic illness.* ceaseless, constant, continual, continuous, everlasting, incessant, lifelong, permanent, persistent, unending.

chubby *a chubby figure.* dumpy, fat, plump, podgy, portly.

chuck (informal) *Stop chucking things into the water.* to fling, to hurl, to lob, to sling, to throw, to toss.

chuckle to giggle, to laugh, to titter.

chum companion, friend, mate.

chunk *a chunk of cheese, a chunk of wood.* bar, block, brick, dollop, hunk, lump, mass, piece, slab.

church **1** CHURCH BUILDINGS: abbey, cathedral, chapel, convent, monastery, parish church, priory. **2** PARTS OF A CHURCH: aisle, altar, belfry, buttress, chancel, chapel, cloisters, crypt, dome, gargoyle, porch, precinct, spire, steeple, tower, vestry. **3** THINGS YOU FIND IN CHURCH: Bible, candle, crucifix, font, hymn-book, lectern, memorial tablet, pews, prayer book, pulpit. **4** WORDS TO DO WITH CHURCH: Advent, angel, Ascension Day, Ash Wednesday, baptism, benediction, christening, Christmas, communion, confirmation, Easter, Good Friday, gospel, hymn, incense, Lent, martyr, mass, Nativity, New Testament, Old Testament, Palm Sunday, patron saint, Pentecost, prayer, preaching, psalm, requiem, Resurrection, sabbath, sacrament, saint, scripture, sermon, service, Shrove Tuesday, Whitsun, worship. **5** PEOPLE CONNECTED WITH CHURCH: archbishop, bishop, cardinal, chaplain, choir, clergyman, congregation, curate, deacon, deaconess, dean, evangelist, friar, minister, missionary, monk, nun, parson, pastor, Pope, preacher, priest, rector, verger, vicar.

churchyard burial-ground, cemetery, graveyard.

cinders *the cinders of a fire.* ashes, embers.

cinema (informal) the movies, the pictures.

circle **1** disc, hoop, ring. **2** *The plane circled before landing.* to go round, to turn, to wheel. **3** *The police circled the hide-out.* to encircle, to enclose, to ring.

circuit **1** *a racing circuit.* race-course, track. **2** *I completed one circuit.* circle, lap, orbit, revolution.

circulate *to circulate information.* to distribute, to issue, to send round.

circumference *It's a mile round the circumference of our playing-field.* boundary, edge, limit, perimeter.

circumstances *Don't jump to conclusions before you know the circumstances.* background, conditions, details, facts, position, situation.

circus WORDS TO DO WITH A CIRCUS: acrobat, clown, contortionist, juggler, lion-tamer, ring, tightrope, trapeze.

cistern *a water cistern.* tank.

citadel castle, fort, fortress, garrison.

citizen *the citizens of a town.* inhabitant, native, resident.

citrus fruit CITRUS FRUITS: grapefruit, lemon, lime, orange, tangerine.

city *London is a huge city.* conurbation, town.

civil *I know you're angry, but try to be civil.* considerate, courteous, polite, respectful, well-mannered.

civilized *a civilized nation.* cultured, orderly, organized.

claim 1 *I didn't claim my pocket-money last week.* to ask for, to demand, to request, to require. 2 *He claims that he's older than I am.* to assert, to declare, to insist, to maintain, to pretend, to state.

clamber *We clambered up the rocks.* to climb, to crawl, to scramble.

clammy *His hands were clammy.* damp, dank, humid, moist.

clamour *The starlings always make a clamour.* commotion, din, hubbub, noise, racket, row, screeching, shouting, uproar.

clamp SEE **fasten.**

clan family, group, tribe.

clap *The audience clapped.* to applaud, to cheer, to praise.

clarify *to clarify a confused situation.* to define, to explain, to make clear.

clash *the clash of cymbals.* SEE **sound.** 2 *a clash between two gangs.* battle, collision, combat, conflict, confrontation, contest, fight, struggle.

clasp 1 *a gold clasp.* brooch, buckle, fastener, fastening. 2 *She clasped the child in her arms.* to cling to, to embrace, to grasp, to grip, to hold, to hug, to squeeze. 3 *He clasped his hands.* to hold together, to wring.

class 1 *Whose class are you in?* form, group, set. 2 *In gymnastics she's in a class of her own.* category, classification, grade, group, kind, set, sort, species, type.

classic *This book is a classic!* masterpiece.

classical *classical music.* highbrow.

classify *to classify books in the library.* to arrange, to group, to put into sets, to sort.

claw 1 *a bird's claws.* nail, talon. 2 *The cat clawed me.* to scratch, to tear.

clean 1 *a clean floor.* hygienic, spotless, washed. 2 *clean water.* clear, fresh, pure. 3 *clean paper.* blank, unmarked, untouched, unused. 4 *to clean the house, to clean yourself, etc.* to bathe, to brush, to dust, to hoover, to mop up, to rinse, to sponge down, to sweep out, to swill, to wash, to wipe.

clear 1 *clear water.* clean, colourless, pure, transparent. 2 *a clear case of cheating.* apparent, blatant, evident, obvious, plain. 3 *clear handwriting.* bold, definite, legible, plain, simple. 4 *a clear sound.* audible, distinct. 5 *a clear picture.* focused, visible, well-defined. 6 *a clear explanation.* coherent, comprehensible, intelligible, lucid, unambiguous, understandable. 7 *a clear sky.* bright, cloudless, starlit, sunny, unclouded. 8 *a clear road.* free, open, passable, uncluttered, vacant. 9 *The fog cleared.* to disappear, to evaporate, to fade, to melt away, to vanish. 10 *Wait for the water to clear.* to become transparent, to clarify. 11 *When the alarm went, we cleared the building.* to empty, to evacuate. 12 *The horse cleared the fence.* to bound over, to jump, to leap over, to spring over, to vault. 13 *to clear up a mystery.* to clarify, to explain, to make clear.

clearing *a clearing in the forest.* gap, space.

clench *to clench your teeth.* to clamp up, to close, to grit.

clergyman SEE **preacher.**

clerk office worker, secretary, typist.

clever *a clever child, a clever idea, etc.* able, academic, accomplished, apt, artful, artistic, astute, brainy, bright, brilliant, crafty, cunning, cute, deft, expert, gifted, handy, imaginative, ingenious, intellectual, intelligent, quick, quick-witted, sharp, shrewd, skilful, skilled, slick, smart, talented, wily, wise.

client *a client of the bank.* customer.

climate SEE **weather.**

climax *The music built up to a climax.* crisis, highlight, peak.

climb *to climb a ladder.* to ascend, to clamber up, to go up, to mount, to scale.

climber CLIMBING PLANTS: honeysuckle, hops, ivy, vine.

cling 1 *Ivy clings to the wall.* to adhere, to stick. 2 *The baby clung to its mother.* to clasp, to clutch, to grasp, to hug.

clinic health centre, infirmary.

clip 1 *a paper-clip.* fastener. 2 *a clip from a film.* excerpt, extract. 3 *to clip a hedge.* to crop, to shear, to snip, to trim. SEE ALSO **cut.**

clock KINDS OF CLOCK: alarm clock, digital clock, grandfather clock, hourglass, pendulum clock, stopwatch, sundial, watch.

clog 1 SEE **shoe.** 2 *Don't clog the drain with all that paper.* to block, to bung up, to jam, to obstruct, to stop up.

close 1 *Close the door.* to bolt, to fasten, to lock, to seal, to secure, to shut. 2 *They closed the road.* to bar, to barricade, to block, to stop up. 3 *We closed the concert with a song.* to conclude, to end, to finish, to stop, to terminate. 4 *Our house is close to the park.* adjacent, near, neighbouring. 5 *The twins are close to each other.* affectionate, attached, familiar, fond, friendly, intimate, loving. 6 *It's close in here: open a window.* airless, humid, muggy, oppressive, stifling, stuffy, sultry, warm. 7 *He's close with his money.* mean, mingy, miserly, stingy.

clot *a clot of blood.* lump.

cloth 1 *cloth to make curtains.* fabric, material, stuff, textile. 2 KINDS OF CLOTH: canvas, corduroy, cotton, denim, elastic, felt, flannel, gauze, lace, linen, muslin, nylon, patchwork, polyester, rayon, sacking, satin, silk, taffeta, tapestry, tartan, tweed, velvet, wool, worsted.

clothes 1 attire, costume, dress, garments, outfit. 2 VARIOUS GARMENTS: anorak, apron, bib, bikini, blazer, blouse, bra, braces, breeches, briefs, cagoule, cape, cardigan, cassock, cloak, coat, corset, drawers, dress, dressing-gown, duffle coat, dungarees, frock, garter, gauntlet, girdle, glove, gown, jacket, jeans, jersey, jodhpurs, jumper, kilt, knickers, leg-warmers, leotard, lingerie, livery, mackintosh, miniskirt, mitten, muffler, nightdress, oilskins, overalls, overcoat, panties, pants, panty-hose, parka, petticoat, pinafore, poncho, pullover, pyjamas, raincoat, rompers, sari, scarf, shawl, shirt, shorts, singlet, skirt, slacks, slip, smock, sock, sou'wester, stockings, suit, surplice, sweater, tie, tights, trunks, T-shirt, tunic, underpants, uniform, vest, waistcoat, wet-suit, wind-cheater, yashmak. SEE ALSO **hat, shoe.** 3 PARTS OF A GARMENT: bodice, button, button-hole, collar, cuff, hem, lapel, pocket, sleeve.

cloudless *a cloudless sky.* bright, clear, starlit, sunny, unclouded.

cloudy 1 *a cloudy sky.* dull, gloomy, grey, overcast. 2 *The windows are cloudy.* blurred, dim, milky, misty, murky, opaque, steamy, unclear.

clout (informal) *She clouted her brother with the newspaper.* to bang, (informal) to bash, to drive, to hammer, to knock, to punch, to slam, to slog, to smash, to strike, to swipe, to thump, to wallop, to whack. SEE ALSO **hit.**

clown fool, jester.

club 1 *to hit someone with a club.* baton, cudgel, stick. 2 *to hit a ball with a club.* bat. 3 *a football club, a book club.* association, league, organization, party, society, union.

clue *Give me a clue what I'm getting for Christmas.* hint, indication, inkling, key, sign, suggestion.

clump *a clump of daffodils.* bunch, cluster, collection, group, tuft.

clumsy 1 awkward, blundering, fumbling, gawky, hulking, lumbering, ungainly, unskilful. 2 *to be clumsy*: to be a butterfingers.

cluster *a cluster of trees.* bunch, clump, collection, crowd, gathering, group.

clutch *He clutched the rope.* to clasp, to cling on to, to grab, to grasp, to grip, to hold on to, to seize, to snatch.

clutter *Please get rid of the clutter in your bedroom.* confusion, jumble, junk, litter, mess, muddle.

coach 1 *We travelled by coach.* SEE **vehicle**. 2 *to coach a football team.* to instruct, to teach, to train.

coarse 1 *coarse cloth.* hairy, harsh, rough, scratchy. 2 *coarse language.* blasphemous, common, crude, foul, impolite, improper, indecent, offensive, rude, uncouth, vulgar.

coast 1 *In summer we sometimes go to the coast.* beach, sea-shore, seaside, shore. 2 *I coasted down the hill on my bike.* to drift, to free-wheel, to glide.

coat 1 SEE **clothes**. 2 *a coat of paint.* coating, cover, covering, film.

coax *We coaxed the animal back into its cage.* to entice, to induce, to persuade, to tempt.

cobble pebble, stone.

cobbler shoemaker.

cocky (informal) *Don't get cocky just because she said your work was the best.* arrogant, boastful, bumptious, cheeky, conceited, impudent, insolent, rude, self-satisfied.

code 1 *The Highway Code.* laws, regulations, rules. 2 *a message in code.* language, signals, signs.

coherent *a coherent argument, a coherent story.* clear, convincing, logical, reasonable, sound.

coil *to coil a rope.* to bend, to curl, to entwine, to loop, to turn, to twist, to wind.

coin cash, change, money.

coincide *Fortunately, our opinions about holidays coincide.* to agree, to correspond, to match.

coincidence *We met by coincidence.* accident, chance, luck.

cold 1 *cold weather, cold hands, etc.* Arctic, biting, bitter, bleak, chill, chilly, cool, freezing, frosty, frozen, icy, (informal) nippy, (informal) perishing, raw, shivery, wintry. 2 *cold feelings, a cold heart.* callous, cold-blooded, cool, cruel, half-hearted, hard, hard-hearted, heartless, indifferent, insensitive, uncaring, unconcerned, unfeeling, unfriendly, unkind. 3 *to have a cold*: to cough, to sneeze.

cold-blooded *a cold-blooded killing.* callous, cruel, hard-hearted, heartless, insensitive, merciless, pitiless, ruthless, unfeeling.

collaborate *We were allowed to collaborate on the project.* to co-operate, to work together.

collaborator accomplice, ally, assistant, partner.

collapse 1 *Several people collapsed in the heat.* to drop, to faint, to fall down. 2 *The building collapsed in the earthquake.* to buckle, to fall in, to fold up, to tumble down. 3 *The earthquake caused the collapse of many old buildings.* destruction, downfall, end, fall, ruin.

collapsible *a collapsible chair.* folding.

collect 1 *Squirrels collect nuts. A crowd collected.* to accumulate, to assemble, to bring together, to cluster, to come together, to crowd, to gather, to group, to hoard, to muster, to pile up, to store. 2 *Please collect the bread from the baker's.* to bring, to fetch, to get, to obtain.

collection *a collection of stamps.* accumulation, assortment, batch, crowd, gathering, hoard, mass, pile, set, stack. SEE ALSO **group**.

college polytechnic, university.

collide *The car collided with the gatepost.* to bump into, to crash into, to knock, to run into, to slam into, to smash into, to strike. SEE ALSO **hit**.

collision *There was a collision at the end of the road.* accident, bump, crash, impact, knock, smash.

colony 1 settlement. 2 *a colony of ants.* SEE **group**.

colossal *a colossal statue.* big, enormous, giant, gigantic, huge, immense, mammoth, massive, mighty, monstrous, towering, vast.

colour 1 dye, hue, shade, tinge, tint, tone. VARIOUS COLOURS: amber, azure, beige, black, blue, bronze, brown, cream, crimson, fawn, gilt, gold, golden, green, grey, indigo, ivory, jet-black, khaki, lavender, maroon, mauve, navy blue, orange, pink, purple, red, rosy, sandy, scarlet, tan, tawny, turquoise, vermilion, violet, white, yellow. 3 *I'm colouring a picture.* to dye, to paint, to stain, to tinge, to tint. 4 *My fair skin colours easily.* to blush, to flush, to redden, to tan. 5 *The regiment was carrying its colours.* banner, ensign, flag, standard.

colourful *colourful flowers.* bright, brilliant, flashy, gaudy, showy, vivid.

colourless *a colourless scene.* dingy, dismal, dowdy, drab, dreary, dull, grey, shabby.

column 1 pile, pillar, pole, post, prop, shaft, support. 2 *a column of soldiers.* file, line, procession, queue, rank, row.

coma unconsciousness.

comb *I've combed the house and still can't find my pen.* to ransack, to rummage through, to scour, to search.

combat *a fierce combat.* action, battle, bout, conflict, contest, duel, fight, struggle.

combination alliance, blend, compound, mixture, union.

combine 1 *We'll have enough players if we combine the first and second teams.* to add together, to amalgamate, to couple, to join, to merge, to put together, to unite. 2 *Combine the ingredients in a bowl.* to blend, to integrate, to mingle, to mix.

come 1 *Our visitors have come.* to appear, to arrive. 2 *Tell me when we come to my station.* to arrive at, to get to, to reach. 3 *There are dark clouds coming.* to advance, to approach, to draw near. 4 FOR OTHER WORDS YOU CAN USE SEE **move.**

comedian SEE **comic.**

comfort 1 *to live in comfort.* ease, luxury, relaxation. 2 *His friends gave him some comfort.* consolation, relief, sympathy. 3 *He was upset, so we tried to comfort him.* to calm, to console, to ease, to relieve, to soothe, to sympathize with.

comfortable *a comfortable chair.* cosy, easy, luxurious, relaxing, restful, snug, soft.

comic 1 absurd, amusing, comical, facetious, farcical, funny, humorous, hysterical, laughable, ludicrous, (informal) priceless, ridiculous, silly, uproarious, witty. 2 *A comic sang some songs and made us laugh.* comedian, fool, jester, wit. 3 *a comic to read on the train.* SEE **magazine.**

command 1 *The general issued a command that fighting should stop.* decree, instruction, order. 2 *He commanded that fighting should stop.* to decree, to demand, to direct, to instruct, to order, to require, to rule. 3 *A captain commands his ship.* to administer, to be in charge of, to control, to direct, to govern, to head, to lead, to manage, to rule, to supervise.

commander captain, head, leader. SEE ALSO **chief.**

commando SEE **soldier.**

commence *We're ready to commence.* to begin, to embark on, to initiate, to open, to start, to take the initiative.

commend *The head commended our efforts.* to applaud, to approve of, to praise, to recommend.

comment 1 *Did mum make any comment about your dirty clothes?* mention, observation, opinion, reference, remark, statement. 2 *He commented that the weather had been bad.* to explain, to mention, to observe, to remark, to say.

commentary *a commentary on the big match.* account, description, report.

commerce *A country depends on commerce to keep going.* business, buying and selling, trade, traffic.

commercial 1 *commercial affairs.* business, economic, financial. 2 *a TV commercial.* advertisement, (informal) plug.

commit *to commit a crime.* to carry out, to do, to perform.

committee *a school committee.* council.

common 1 *Friends often have common interests.* communal, general, joint, mutual, shared. 2 *a common happening.* commonplace, conventional, customary, everyday, familiar, frequent, habitual, normal, ordinary, prevalent, regular, typical, usual, well-known, widespread. 3 *common language.* coarse, crude, rude, vulgar. 4 *We play football on the common.* heath, park.

commonplace *a commonplace event.*
boring, common, everyday, indifferent,
mediocre, normal, ordinary, unexciting,
usual.

commotion *a commotion in the crowd.*
ado, bedlam, bother, chaos, clamour,
confusion, din, disorder, disturbance,
fuss, hubbub, hullabaloo, noise,
pandemonium, racket, row, rumpus,
to-do, tumult, turbulence, turmoil,
unrest, upheaval, uproar.

communal *communal washing
facilities.* common, joint, mutual,
shared.

communicate 1 *to communicate with
other people.* to contact, to correspond
with, to get in touch with, to speak to, to
talk to. 2 *to communicate our thoughts.*
to convey, to express, to indicate, to say,
to show, to speak, to write.

communication 1 *to send a
communication.* announcement,
information, message, report,
statement. 2 KINDS OF COMMUNICATION:
advertising, broadcasting, cable, cable
television, CB, correspondence,
intercom, letter, the media, newspaper,
note, the press, radar, radio,
telecommunications, telegram,
telephone, television, walkie-talkie,
wire, wireless.

communicative *a communicative
person.* chatty, talkative.

communiqué announcement,
bulletin, dispatch, message, report,
statement.

community nation, public, society.

compact 1 *a compact set of instructions.*
brief, compressed, concise, condensed,
short. 2 *a compact typewriter.* neat,
portable, small.

companion chum, comrade, escort,
friend, mate, partner.

company 1 *We enjoy other people's
company.* companionship, fellowship,
friendship, society. 2 *a company of
rebels.* band, crew, gang, troop. 3 *a
theatrical company.* association, club,
group, society. 4 *a shipping company.*
business, concern, firm, organization,
union.

compare 1 *Compare your answers with
your neighbour's.* to check against, to
contrast with, to set against. 2 *Their team
cannot compare with ours.* to compete
with, to match, to rival.

comparison *a comparison between
your work and mine.* contrast,
difference, similarity.

compartment 1 *a box with various
compartments.* division, section. 2 *At the
baths there are compartments where you
can change.* booth, cubicle.

compassion *The muggers showed no
compassion for their victim.* feeling,
mercy, pity, sympathy.

compel 1 *You can't compel me to play
for your side.* to drive, to force, to
oblige, to order, to press, to require, to
urge. 2 *compelled: They'll be compelled
to use the motorway if they want to get
here for tea.* bound, certain, obliged,
sure.

compensate *Will the insurance
compensate us for what we lost in the fire?*
to make up, to recompense, to repay.

compete 1 *We competed against a good
side in the final.* to conflict, to contend, to
contest, to oppose, to rival, to struggle.
2 *How many runners are competing in
this race?* to enter, to participate, to
take part.

competent *a competent worker.* able,
capable, effective, efficient, experienced,
handy, practical, proficient, qualified,
skilful, skilled, trained.

competition 1 *a darts competition.*
championship, contest, event, game,
match, tournament. 2 *intense
competition between the teams.*
competitiveness, rivalry.

competitor *competitors in a quiz.*
candidate, contestant, entrant,
opponent, participant, rival.

compile *We compiled a magazine.* to
arrange, to compose, to edit, to put
together.

complacent *We knew we mustn't be
complacent after winning the first round.*
self-righteous, self-satisfied, smug.

complain *We complained about the
awful food.* to grouse, to grumble, to
moan, to object, to protest.

complaint 1 *a complaint about the
food.* grievance, objection, protest. 2
Flu is a common complaint in winter.
affliction, ailment, disease, disorder,
illness, infection, malady, sickness.

complete 1 *When will you complete the work?* to accomplish, to achieve, to carry out, to conclude, to do, to end, to finish, to fulfil, to perform, to round off. 2 *We've got the complete story on video.* entire, full, intact, total, unabridged, whole. 3 *His story was complete rubbish.* absolute, perfect, pure, sheer, total, utter.

complex *A computer is a complex machine.* complicated, elaborate, intricate, involved, sophisticated.

complexion 1 *a person's complexion.* colour, skin, texture. 2 WORDS TO DESCRIBE PEOPLE'S COMPLEXIONS: black, brown, dark, fair, freckled, pasty, ruddy, swarthy, tanned, white.

complicated *complicated instructions.* complex, difficult, elaborate, hard, intricate, involved, sophisticated.

complication *We thought we had no problems, but then we discovered a complication.* difficulty, problem, set-back, snag.

compliment *It's nice to get compliments.* appreciation, congratulations, flattery, praise, tribute.

complimentary *complimentary remarks.* admiring, appreciative, approving, flattering.

component *components for the car.* bit, element, part, unit.

compose 1 *The team is composed of good players.* to compile, to constitute, to make up, to put together. 2 *to compose music.* to create, to write.

composition SEE music.

compound 1 *The chemist made up a nasty-looking compound.* blend, combination, mixture. 2 *a compound for animals.* enclosure, pen, run.

comprehend *I can't comprehend his attitude.* to appreciate, to follow, to grasp, to know, to realize, to see, to understand.

compress 1 *to compress something into a small space.* to crush, to press, to squash, to squeeze. 2 *compressed:* compact, concise, condensed.

comprise *This album comprises the best hits of the year.* to consist of, to contain, to include.

compulsion *Taking drugs can become a compulsion.* addiction, habit.

compulsory *At our school it's compulsory to have a shower after games.* necessary, required, unavoidable.

compute *to compute figures.* to add up, to calculate, to count, to reckon, to total, to work out.

computer WORDS TO DO WITH COMPUTING: chip, cursor, data, disc, disc drive, floppy disc, hardware, interface, joystick, keyboard, micro, microchip, microcomputer, micro-processor, monitor, printer, print-out, program, software, terminal, VDU, word-processor.

comrade chum, companion, friend, mate, partner.

conceal *to conceal the truth.* to blot out, to bury, to camouflage, to cover up, to disguise, to envelop, to hide, to hush up, to keep quiet, to mask.

conceited *He was so conceited when his poem went in the magazine!* arrogant, boastful, bumptious, (informal) cocky, proud, self-important, (informal) stuck-up.

conceive *to conceive an idea.* to create, to imagine, to invent, to plan, to think up.

concentrate 1 *Concentrate on your work.* to attend to, to think about. 2 *A crowd concentrated around the speaker.* to accumulate, to collect, to gather, to mass. 3 *to concentrate a liquid.* to condense, to reduce, to thicken.

concept *scientific concepts.* belief, idea, notion, thought.

concern 1 *concern for the starving.* care, interest, responsibility. 2 *It's no concern of theirs.* affair, business, matter. 3 *a business concern.* company, firm, organization. 4 *Paying her gas bill is a great concern to granny.* anxiety, cause of distress, fear, worry. 5 *Road safety concerns us all.* to affect, to be important to, to interest, to involve, to matter to. 6 *concerned:* anxious, bothered, caring, distressed, fearful, troubled, worried. 7 *concerning:* about, involving, regarding, relating to.

concert SEE entertainment.

concise *a concise dictionary.* brief, compact, condensed, short, small, terse.

conclude 1 *We concluded the concert with a song.* to close, to complete, to end, to finish, to round off, to stop, to terminate. 2 *When you didn't arrive, we concluded that the car had broken down.* to decide, to gather, to judge.

conclusion 1 *the conclusion of a journey.* close, end, finish. 2 *You have heard the evidence, so what is your conclusion?* decision, judgement, opinion.

concoct *to concoct excuses.* to counterfeit, to devise, to feign, to invent, to make up, to put together, to think up.

concord *It'd be nice if everyone lived in concord.* agreement, harmony, peace.

condemn 1 *The head condemned the vandals who broke the windows.* to blame, to denounce, to disapprove of, to rebuke. 2 *The judge condemned the muggers to a spell in prison.* to convict, to punish, to sentence.

condense 1 *to condense a book.* to abbreviate, to abridge, to compress, to shorten. 2 *to condense a liquid.* to concentrate, to reduce, to thicken.

condition 1 *The lavatories were in a bad condition.* order, situation, state. 2 *An athlete has to keep in condition.* fitness, health.

conduct 1 *good conduct.* attitude, behaviour, manners. 2 *to conduct visitors round a museum.* to escort, to guide, to lead, to pilot. 3 *to conduct a choir.* to be in charge of, to direct, to lead. 4 *to conduct yourself well.* to act, to behave.

conference *a teachers' conference.* assembly, committee, congress, debate, gathering, meeting.

confess *He confessed that he was guilty.* to acknowledge, to admit, to own up.

confide *to confide in:* to tell secrets to, to trust.

confidence *We have confidence in our goalie.* belief, faith, hope, trust.

confident 1 *I'm confident that you'll succeed.* certain, hopeful, optimistic, positive, sure. 2 *a confident person.* assertive, assured, definite.

confidential *confidential papers.* intimate, personal, private, secret.

confine *Battery hens are confined in a very small space.* to cramp, to curb, to detain, to enclose, to gaol, to imprison, to intern, to limit, to restrict, to shut in.

confirm *Our experiments confirmed our theory.* to demonstrate, to establish, to prove, to show, to verify.

confiscate *She confiscated my catapult.* to seize, to take away.

conflagration *Three fire-engines came to the conflagration.* blaze, fire, inferno.

conflict 1 *angry conflict.* antagonism, confrontation, discord, hostility, opposition, strife. 2 *Many men died in the conflict.* action, battle, clash, combat, encounter, fight, struggle, war, warfare. 3 *The twins' views seldom conflict.* to clash, to compete, to contend, to oppose each other.

conform *Conform to the rules.* to abide by, to keep to, to fit in with, to obey.

confront 1 *I won't confront the headmaster.* to argue with, to attack, to challenge, to defy, to face up to, to resist, to stand up to. 2 *We confronted a 'no entry' sign.* to encounter, to face, to meet.

confuse 1 *The complicated rules confused us.* to baffle, to bewilder, to distract, to mislead, to perplex, to puzzle. 2 *Don't confuse those two packs of cards.* to jumble, to mix up, to muddle. 3 *confused:* chaotic, disjointed, disorganized, flustered, fuddled, garbled, higgledy-piggledy, incoherent, jumbled, mixed up, muddled, rambling, topsy-turvy, unclear.

confusion *terrible confusion when the lights went out.* ado, anarchy, bedlam, bother, chaos, clutter, commotion, din, disorder, disturbance, fuss, hubbub, hullabaloo, jumble, mess, muddle, pandemonium, racket, riot, rumpus, shambles, tumult, turbulence, turmoil, uproar.

congested *The roads are congested at rush hour.* blocked, full, jammed, overcrowded.

congratulate *We congratulated her when she won.* to applaud, to commend, to praise.

congregate *On summer evenings, we congregate in the park.* to assemble, to cluster, to collect, to come together, to crowd, to gather, to get together, to group, to mass, to meet, to muster, to swarm, to throng.

congress assembly, conference, gathering, meeting.

conjuring SEE **magic**.

conjuror SEE **magician**.

connect *Connect these two bits of rope.* to attach, to fasten, to fix, to join, to link, to relate, to tie.

connection bond, link, relationship.

conquer to beat, to crush, to defeat, (informal) to lick, to master, to overcome, to overpower, to overthrow, to overwhelm, to rout, to subdue, to succeed against, to suppress, (informal) to thrash, to vanquish.

conquest capture, occupation, victory, win.

conscientious *a conscientious worker.* careful, diligent, dutiful, hard-working, honest, scrupulous, serious, thorough.

conscious 1 *In spite of the knock, he remained conscious.* alert, awake, aware. 2 *a conscious foul.* deliberate, intended, intentional, premeditated.

consecrated *The churchyard is consecrated ground.* blessed, hallowed, holy, religious, sacred.

consent *to consent to a request.* to agree to, to allow, to approve of, to authorize, to permit.

consequence *The floods were a consequence of all that snow.* effect, end, issue, outcome, result, sequel.

conservation *the conservation of the countryside.* preservation.

conservatory glasshouse.

consider 1 *to consider a problem.* to contemplate, to discuss, to meditate on, to ponder, to reflect on, to study, to think about. 2 *Do you consider he was telling the truth?* to believe, to judge, to reckon.

considerable *a considerable amount of rain.* big, biggish, noticeable, significant, sizeable, substantial, worthwhile.

considerate *It was considerate of you to lend granny your umbrella.* accommodating, attentive, friendly, helpful, kind, kind-hearted, obliging, polite, sympathetic, thoughtful, unselfish.

consignment *a fresh consignment of strawberries.* batch, delivery.

consist *What does this fruit salad consist of?* to be composed of, to contain, to include.

consistent 1 *a consistent player.* dependable, faithful, regular, reliable, steady. 2 *That is not consistent with what you said yesterday.* compatible with, in accordance with.

console *to console someone who is unhappy.* to comfort, to ease, to soothe, to sympathize with.

conspicuous *a conspicuous landmark, a conspicuous case of cheating.* blatant, impressive, notable, noticeable, obvious, prominent, pronounced, showy, striking, unconcealed, unmistakable, visible.

conspiracy *a conspiracy against the government.* intrigue, plot, scheme.

constable SEE **police**.

constant 1 *a constant cough, a constant rhythm.* ceaseless, chronic, continual, everlasting, incessant, invariable, non-stop, permanent, persistent, repeated, unending. 2 *a constant friend.* dedicated, dependable, devoted, faithful, firm, loyal, reliable, steady, trustworthy, unchanging.

constitute *In soccer, eleven players constitute a team.* to compose, to form, to make up.

construct *We constructed a den out of old planks.* to assemble, to build, to erect, to fit together, to make, to put together.

consul ambassador, diplomat, representative.

consult *I consulted the doctor about my cough.* to discuss with, to refer to.

consume *We consumed all the food.* to devour, to digest, to eat, to exhaust, to gobble up, to swallow, to use up.

contact 1 *She contacted the police about her lost brooch.* to communicate with, to correspond with, to get in touch with, to speak to, to talk to. 2 *When the wires contact each other the current flows.* to connect with, to touch.

contagious *a contagious disease.* catching, infectious.

contain 1 *What does this cake contain?* to be composed of, to consist of, to incorporate. 2 *What does this box contain?* to hold, to include.

container 1 receptacle. 2 VARIOUS CONTAINERS: bag, barrel, basin, basket, bath, beaker, billycan, bin, bottle, box, bucket, butt, can, canister, carton, cartridge, case, cask, casket, casserole, cauldron, chest, churn, cistern, coffin, cup, dish, drum, dustbin, envelope, flask, glass, goblet, hamper, handbag, haversack, hold-all, holster, jar, jug, keg, kettle, knapsack, money-box, mould, mug, pail, pan, pannier, pitcher, pot, pouch, purse, rucksack, sack, satchel, saucepan, suitcase, tank, tankard, teapot, test tube, Thermos, tin, trough, trunk, tub, tumbler, urn, vacuum-flask, vase, vat, wallet, watering-can, wineglass.

contaminate *The water was contaminated by chemicals.* to defile, to infect, to poison, to pollute, to soil.

contemplate 1 *We contemplated the lovely view.* to eye, to gaze at, to look at, to observe, to regard, to stare at, to view, to watch. 2 *We contemplated what to do next.* to consider, to meditate, to plan, to ponder, to reflect on, to study, to think about.

contemporary 1 *contemporary events.* current, simultaneous, topical. 2 *contemporary music.* fashionable, modern, newest, (informal) trendy, up-to-date.

contempt disgust, dislike, disrespect, loathing, scorn.

contemptible *The judge said that the muggers were contemptible.* despicable, detestable, hateful, pitiful, worthless.

contemptuous *Don't be contemptuous: we did our best.* disdainful, scornful, sneering.

contend 1 *We contended against strong opposition.* to compete, to contest, to dispute, to fight, to oppose, to rival, to struggle. 2 *He contended that he was right.* to argue, to assert, to claim, to declare, to maintain.

content *The cat looks content after his dinner.* carefree, comfortable, happy, relaxed, satisfied.

contest 1 *to contest a title.* to compete for, to contend for, to fight for, to struggle for. 2 *to contest a decision.* to argue against, to challenge, to oppose, to resist. 3 *a sporting contest.* bout, championship, combat, competition, conflict, duel, fight, game, match, struggle.

contestant competitor, participant.

continual *Stop your continual chattering!* ceaseless, chronic, constant, continuous, endless, eternal, everlasting, frequent, incessant, interminable, lasting, limitless, non-stop, permanent, perpetual, persistent, recurrent, relentless, repeated, unending, uninterrupted.

continue 1 *How long will the fine weather continue?* to carry on, to endure, to go on, to keep on, to last, to linger, to live on, to persist, to remain, to stay, to survive. 2 *Please continue with your work.* to carry on, to persevere, to proceed, to resume.

continuous SEE **continual**.

contraband *The smugglers hid their contraband.* booty, loot.

contract 1 *a legal contract.* agreement, bargain, deal, pact, settlement, treaty. 2 *Most substances contract as they get colder.* to decrease, to diminish, to dwindle, to lessen, to reduce, to shrink.

contradict *Are you contradicting me?* to oppose, to speak against.

contradictory *contradictory reports.* conflicting, incompatible, inconsistent, opposite.

contraption SEE **gadget**.

contrary 1 *I spoke for the proposal, and you put the contrary view.* opposite, reverse. 2 *contrary winds.* adverse, hostile, opposing, unfavourable. 3 *a contrary child.* defiant, disobedient, obstinate, perverse, rebellious, stubborn.

contrast 1 *The teacher contrasted my work with yours.* to compare, to set against. 2 *The colours of the two dresses contrasted.* to differ. 3 *an obvious contrast.* comparison, difference, distinction.

contribute *Everyone contributed something to eat.* to donate, to give, to provide, to supply.

contribution *Please make a contribution to the school fund.* fee, gift, offering, payment, subscription.

contrivance SEE **gadget.**

control 1 *Can't you control that dog?* to administer, to command, to cope with, to deal with, to direct, to dominate, to govern, to handle, to look after, to manage, to manipulate, to master, to regulate, to rule, to supervise. 2 *The dam controls the floods.* to check, to curb, to hold back, to restrain. 3 *Who is in control here?* charge, command, management, rule. 4 *She has good control over the class.* authority, discipline, influence, power.

controversy *a controversy about whether they should build a bypass.* argument, debate, disagreement, dispute, issue, quarrel.

conundrum riddle.

conurbation SEE **city.**

convalescent *Granny is convalescent in hospital after her operation.* getting better, improving, recovering, recuperating.

convenient *There's a convenient shop round the corner.* accessible, available, handy, suitable, useful.

convention *It's a convention to give presents at Christmas.* custom, formality, rule, tradition.

conventional *'How are you?' is a conventional greeting.* accustomed, common, commonplace, customary, everyday, habitual, normal, ordinary, orthodox, regular, traditional, usual.

converge *The motorways converge in a mile.* to come together, to intersect, to join, to meet, to merge.

conversation chat, chatter, dialogue, discussion, talk.

convert *We converted the attic into a games room.* to adapt, to alter, to amend, to change, to modify, to process, to transform, to turn.

convey 1 *Please convey our best wishes to your father.* to bear, to carry, to deliver, to send, to take. 2 *Lorries convey goods all over the country.* to carry, to take, to transfer, to transport. 3 *What does 'SOS' convey to you?* to communicate, to indicate, to mean.

convict 1 *The convicts were forced to work hard all day.* captive, criminal, prisoner. 2 *He was convicted for murder.* to condemn, to sentence.

conviction *religious conviction.* belief, creed, faith, opinion, view.

convince *He convinced the jury that he was innocent.* to persuade, to win over.

convoy *a convoy of ships.* armada, fleet.

convulsion fit, seizure, spasm.

cook 1 WAYS TO COOK: to bake, to barbecue, to boil, to brew, to fry, to grill, to pickle, to poach, to roast, to simmer, to steam, to stew, to toast. 2 OTHER THINGS YOU DO IN COOKING: to blend, to chop, to freeze, to grate, to knead, to mix, to peel, to sieve, to sift, to stir, to whisk. 3 CONTAINERS USED TO COOK IN: basin, billycan, casserole, cauldron, dish, frying-pan, kettle, pan, percolator, pot, saucepan. 4 *Would you like to be a cook?* chef.

cool 1 *cool weather.* chilly, cold. 2 *Keep cool!* calm, level-headed, sensible, unflustered. 3 *a cool response.* distant, half-hearted, indifferent, reserved, unconcerned, unenthusiastic, unfriendly. 4 *to cool food.* to chill, to freeze, to refrigerate.

coop *a chicken coop.* cage, enclosure, pen.

co-operate *He wouldn't co-operate with us.* to aid, to assist, to collaborate with, to help, to support, to work together with.

co-operative *The dealer was co-operative when the TV went wrong.* accommodating, constructive, helpful, willing.

cop SEE **police.**

cope *Can you cope with the housework?* to control, to deal with, to endure, to handle, to look after, to manage, to suffer, to tolerate, to withstand.

copious *copious supplies of food.* abundant, ample, generous, lavish, liberal, plentiful, profuse.

coppice, copse *a coppice of birch trees.* grove, thicket, wood.

copulate *Animals copulate when the time is right to have young ones.* to couple, to have sexual intercourse, to mate.

copy 1 *a copy of a painting.* double, duplicate, fake, forgery, imitation, likeness, model, photocopy, print, replica, reproduction, twin. 2 *to copy someone's work.* to counterfeit, to crib, to duplicate, to forge, to imitate, to photocopy, to print, to reproduce. 3 *to copy someone's voice.* to imitate, to impersonate, to mimic.

cord *a length of cord.* cable, lace, line, rope, string, twine.

cordial *a cordial welcome.* friendly, genial, kind, warm, warm-hearted.

cordon *a cordon of policemen.* chain, line, row.

core *the core of an apple, the core of the earth, etc.* centre, heart, inside, middle, nucleus.

cork *Put the cork back in the bottle.* bung, plug, stopper.

corn SEE **cereal.**

corner 1 *the corner of the room.* angle, nook. 2 *the corner of the road.* bend, crossroads, intersection, junction, turn. 3 *After a chase, they cornered him.* to capture, to catch, to trap.

coronation crowning.

coronet crown, diadem.

corporation 1 *the town corporation.* council. 2 *a business corporation.* organization.

corpse body, carcass, remains.

correct 1 *Can the garage correct the fault in the car?* to cure, to put right, to rectify, to remedy, to repair. 2 *The teacher corrected our maths.* to assess, to mark. 3 *Is that the correct time?* accurate, exact, faultless, precise, right, true.

correspond 1 *I correspond with a girl in Paris.* to communicate with, to send letters to, to write to. 2 *My answer doesn't correspond with yours.* to agree with, to coincide with, to match.

correspondent *a newspaper correspondent.* journalist, reporter.

corridor hall, passage.

corrode *Chemicals corroded the metal.* to eat away, to erode, to rot, to rust.

corrupt 1 *You don't expect a judge to be corrupt.* criminal, crooked, depraved, dishonest, evil, immoral, low, untrustworthy, wicked. 2 *You'd get into serious trouble if you tried to corrupt a judge.* to bribe, to influence, to pervert, to tempt.

cosmetics 1 make-up. 2 VARIOUS COSMETICS: cream, deodorant, eye-shadow, lipstick, lotion, nail varnish, perfume, scent, talcum powder.

cosmonaut astronaut, space-traveller.

cosmos universe.

cost *What's the cost of a return ticket?* charge, expense, fare, payment, price, value.

costly *costly jewels.* dear, exorbitant, expensive, precious, priceless, (informal) pricey, valuable.

costume *The actors wore weird costumes.* attire, clothing, dress, garments, outfit. SEE ALSO **clothes.**

cosy *a cosy room, a cosy atmosphere, etc.* comfortable, relaxing, restful, secure, snug, soft, warm.

cot cradle.

cottage SEE **house.**

cotton *If you find some cotton, I'll sew your button on.* thread.

council 1 *We held a council to decide what to do.* assembly, committee, conference. 2 *the town council.* corporation.

count 1 *The bank clerk counts the money.* to add up, to calculate, to compute, to figure out, to number, to reckon, to total, to work out. 2 *You can count on my support.* to bank on, to depend on, to rely on, to trust.

countenance *His countenance shows that he's had bad news.* appearance, expression, face, features, look.

counter 1 *You play ludo with counters.* disc, token. 2 *You can buy a drink at the counter.* bar, table.

counterfeit 1 *They were put in prison for counterfeiting £5 notes.* to copy, to fake, to forge, to imitate. 2 *They weren't really ill, only counterfeiting.* to pretend, to sham.

countless *There are countless stars in the sky.* frequent, innumerable, many, numberless, numerous, untold.

country 1 *the countries of the world.* land, nation, state. 2 KINDS OF COUNTRY: democracy, dictatorship, kingdom, monarchy, realm, republic. 3 *There's some lovely country near here.* countryside, landscape, rural surroundings, scenery.

couple 1 *a couple of rabbits.* brace, pair. 2 *to couple wagons to a locomotive.* to combine, to join, to link, to unite.

coupon *If you save ten coupons you get a free mug.* ticket, token, voucher.

courage *We admired the firemen's courage.* bravery, daring, determination, fortitude, (informal) grit, (informal) guts, heroism, nerve, (informal) pluck, prowess, spirit, valour.

courageous bold, brave, daring, determined, fearless, heroic, intrepid, plucky, valiant.

course 1 *The pilot checked the air-liner's course.* bearings, direction, route, way. 2 *a course of driving lessons.* series. 3 *a race-course.* circuit, track.

court 1 *The court decided that he was guilty.* court martial, lawcourt. 2 *to court someone.* to go out with, to make love to, to woo.

courteous *a courteous young man.* chivalrous, civil, considerate, gallant, gracious, polite, respectful, well-mannered.

courtesy good manners, politeness.

courtyard enclosure, quadrangle, yard.

cove *a sandy cove.* bay, inlet.

cover 1 *Fog covered the town.* to blot out, to bury, to camouflage, to clothe, to conceal, to enclose, to envelop, to hide, to mask, to obscure, to plaster, to protect, to shroud. 2 *An encyclopaedia covers many subjects.* to deal with, to include, to incorporate. 3 *a jam-pot cover, a cover to keep the rain off, etc.* cap, coat, covering, envelope, folder, lid, protection, roof, top, wrapper. 4 *The animals searched for cover in the bad weather.* hiding-place, protection, refuge, shelter.

covering *a light covering of snow.* cap, coating, layer, skin.

cowardly *a cowardly person, a cowardly action.* base, faint-hearted, fearful, spineless, timid, unheroic, (informal) yellow.

cowed *He seemed cowed in front of our famous visitor.* afraid, fearful, frightened, scared, terrified.

coy *Don't be coy: come and be introduced.* bashful, modest, self-conscious, sheepish, shy, timid.

crack 1 *a crack in the wall.* break, chink, cranny, crevice, flaw, fracture, gap, opening, rift, split. 2 *He cracked a bone in his leg.* to break, to chip, to fracture, to snap, to splinter, to split.

cracker 1 SEE **firework.** 2 biscuit.

cradle cot.

craft 1 *Few people know the craft of thatching.* handicraft, skill, technique, trade. 2 *There were many craft in the harbour.* boat, ship. SEE ALSO **vessel.**

crafty *They say the fox is a crafty creature.* artful, astute, clever, cunning, deceitful, ingenious, knowing, skilful, sly, sneaky, tricky, wily.

crag *The climb up the crag was dangerous.* cliff, precipice, rock.

cram 1 *The room was crammed with people.* to crowd, to fill, to jam, to pack. 2 *Don't cram any more in your mouth!* to squeeze, to stuff.

cramp *I'm sorry you are so cramped in this little room.* to confine, to enclose, to restrict.

crane derrick.

cranky (informal) *It seems a bit cranky to have jam with scrambled egg.* eccentric, odd, unconventional, weird, zany.

cranny *a cranny in a rock.* crack, gap, split.

crash 1 *The car crashed into the wall.* to bump, to collide, to knock, to smash. SEE ALSO **hit.** 2 *Did you see the crash?* accident, bump, collision, derailment, impact, knock, smash.

crate box, carton, case. SEE ALSO **container.**

crater *The explosion left a deep crater.* abyss, chasm, hole, pit.

crawl *He crawled along a narrow ledge.* to clamber, to creep, to edge, to worm.

craze *the latest craze.* diversion, enthusiasm, fashion, mania, pastime.

crazy 1 *The dog went crazy when it was stung by a wasp.* berserk, delirious, demented, deranged, frantic, frenzied, hysterical, insane, lunatic, mad, (informal) potty, unhinged, wild. 2 *a crazy comedy.* absurd, farcical, illogical, irrational, ludicrous, preposterous, ridiculous, silly, stupid, unreasonable, zany.

crease *to crease a piece of paper.* to crinkle, to crumple, to fold, to furrow, to pleat, to wrinkle.

create. *to create something beautiful, to create trouble, etc.* to begin, to breed, to bring about, to compose, to conceive, to construct, to establish, to form, to found, to generate, to initiate, to invent, to make, to originate, to produce, to think up.

creation *the creation of the world.* beginning, birth, construction, invention, origin.

creative *Artists are creative people.* artistic, imaginative, inventive, original, resourceful.

creator author, discoverer, inventor, maker, painter.

creature being. SEE ALSO **animal, bird, fish, insect, reptile, snake.**

crèche nursery.

credible *No one thought the story about Martians was credible.* believable, plausible, reasonable.

credit *Our win brought credit to the school.* honour, merit, reputation.

creditable *a creditable performance.* admirable, commendable, honourable, praiseworthy, respectable, worthy.

creed *a religious creed.* belief, conviction, faith.

creek inlet.

creep *to creep along the ground.* to crawl, to edge, to slink, to slither, to worm.

creepy *I don't like creepy noises in the dark.* eerie, frightening, ghostly, scary, spooky, uncanny, weird.

crescent *a crescent moon.* curved.

crest *the school crest.* badge, emblem, seal, sign, symbol.

crestfallen *He was crestfallen when he didn't win.* dejected, disappointed, discouraged, downcast, downhearted, forlorn, glum, miserable, wretched. SEE ALSO **sad.**

crevice *a crevice in the rock.* crack, cranny, gap, split.

crew *a ship's crew.* company, team.

crib *to crib in a test.* to cheat, to copy.

cricket WORDS TO DO WITH CRICKET: batsman, boundary, bowler, fielder, innings, lbw, maiden over, over, pads, slips, stumps, test match, wicket, wicket-keeper.

crime 1 dishonesty, misdeed, offence, racket, sin, wrongdoing. 2 VARIOUS CRIMES: abduction, arson, assassination, assault, blackmail, burglary, hijacking, hold-up, kidnapping, manslaughter, mugging, murder, pilfering, poaching, rape, robbery, shoplifting, smuggling, stealing, theft.

criminal 1 convict, (informal) crook, culprit, delinquent, hooligan, malefactor, offender, outlaw, thug, wrongdoer. 2 VARIOUS KINDS OF CRIMINAL: assassin, bandit, blackmailer, brigand, buccaneer, burglar, desperado, gangster, gunman, highwayman, hijacker, kidnapper, mugger, murderer, outlaw, pickpocket, pirate, poacher, robber, shoplifter, smuggler, terrorist, thief, vandal.

crimson SEE **red.**

cringe *The frightened dog cringed in his kennel.* to cower, to crouch, to flinch, to grovel, to quail, to wince.

crippled 1 *a crippled person.* disabled, handicapped, hurt, injured, lame, maimed, mutilated. 2 *a crippled vehicle.* damaged, immobilized.

crisis *We had a crisis when we found a gas leak.* danger, emergency.

crisp *a crisp biscuit.* brittle, crackly, fragile, hard and dry.

criticism *No one likes criticism.* censure, disapproval, reprimand, reproach.

criticize *She criticized us for being noisy.* to find fault with, to judge, to rebuke, to scold.

crockery 1 china, earthenware, porcelain, pottery. 2 VARIOUS ITEMS OF CROCKERY: basin, bowl, cup, dish, jug, plate, pot, saucer, teapot.

crocodile alligator.

croft farm.

crook SEE **criminal.**

crooked 1 *a crooked road.* angled, bent, twisted, zigzag. 2 *a crooked salesman.* corrupt, criminal, dishonest, untrustworthy.

crop 1 *to crop the grass.* to clip, to cut, to shear, to trim. 2 *A difficulty cropped up.* to arise, to come up, to emerge, to occur, to spring up, to turn up. 3 *a heavy crop of apples.* harvest, produce, yield. 4 *He hit the horse with his crop.* lash, whip.

cross 1 *The road crosses the river.* to go across, to intersect with, to pass over, to span. 2 *The trains crossed at high speed.* to pass. 3 *They crossed out my name.* to cancel, to delete, to erase, to wipe out. 4 *She was cross when I trod on her plants.* angry, annoyed, bad-tempered, grumpy, indignant, irate, irritated, short-tempered, upset, vexed.

cross-examine *to cross-examine a witness.* to examine, to question.

cross-eyed squinting.

crossroads interchange, intersection, junction.

crouch *They crouched in the low tunnel.* to bend, to bow, to cower, to duck, to kneel, to stoop.

crow SEE **boast.**

crowd 1 *a crowd of people.* bunch, cluster, collection, crush, gathering, horde, host, mob, multitude, pack, rabble, swarm, throng. SEE ALSO **group.** 2 *The crowd cheered.* audience, spectators. 3 *We crowded round to listen.* to assemble, to congregate, to flock, to gather, to herd, to swarm, to throng. 4 *They crowded us into a small room.* to cram, to crush, to huddle, to overcrowd, to pack, to press, to push, to shove, to squeeze.

crown 1 coronet, diadem. 2 *the crown of a hill.* apex, head, top.

crucify SEE **execute.**

crude 1 *crude oil.* natural, raw, unprocessed, unrefined. 2 *We made a crude table out of planks.* clumsy, primitive, rough, unskilful. 3 *crude language.* coarse, common, improper, indecent, rude, vulgar.

cruel *a cruel action, a cruel person.* atrocious, barbaric, beastly, bloodthirsty, bloody, brutal, callous, cold-blooded, ferocious, fierce, hard, hard-hearted, harsh, heartless, inhuman, merciless, murderous, pitiless, relentless, ruthless, sadistic, savage, severe, stern, tyrannical, unfeeling, unjust, unkind, vicious, violent.

cruise *to go on a cruise.* holiday, journey, sail, voyage. SEE ALSO **travel.**

crumb *a crumb of bread.* bit, fragment, particle, scrap, speck.

crumble *The road surface is crumbling.* to break up, to disintegrate.

crumple *Don't crumple the clothes I've just ironed!* to crease, to crush, to dent, to fold, to wrinkle.

crunch *to crunch a biscuit.* to break, to chew, to crush, to munch, to smash, to squash.

crusade *a crusade against drinking and driving.* campaign, struggle, war.

crush 1 *He crushed his finger in the door.* to break, to crumple, to crunch, to grind, to jam, to mangle, to mash, to pound, to press, to pulp, to smash, to squash, to squeeze. 2 *We crushed their best team.* to conquer, to defeat, to overcome, to overpower, to overthrow, to overwhelm, to rout, to subdue, (informal) to thrash.

crust *the crust of a loaf, the crust of the earth.* outside, rind, skin.

crutch *The lame man needed a crutch.* prop, support.

cry 1 *Baby cries when she's tired.* to blubber, to grizzle, to shed tears, to snivel, to sob, to wail, to weep. 2 *Who cried out?* to bawl, to call, to exclaim, to scream, to shout, to yell.

crypt *the church crypt.* basement, cellar, vault.

crystal *a crystal ball.* glass.

cubicle *changing cubicles at the baths.* booth, compartment, kiosk.

cuddle *Baby loves to cuddle her mother.* to caress, to embrace, to fondle, to huddle against, to hug, to kiss, to nestle against, to snuggle against.

cudgel *The bandits were armed with cudgels.* baton, cane, club, stick.

cue *In our play, I missed the cue for me to come on.* reminder, sign, signal.

cuff (informal) to clout, to hit, to knock, to slap, to smack, to swipe.

culprit *Have they caught the culprit yet?* offender, trouble-maker, wrongdoer.

cultivate *to cultivate the land, to cultivate crops.* to farm, to grow, to produce, to raise.

cultivated *a cultivated person.* courteous, cultured, educated, well-bred. SEE ALSO **polite.**

cultivation agriculture, farming, gardening.

cultural *cultural pursuits.* civilizing, educational, high-brow, improving, intellectual.

culture *a nation's culture.* art, background, education, learning.

cultured *a cultured person.* civilized, cultivated, educated, well-bred.

cumbersome *a cumbersome machine.* awkward, heavy, unwieldy.

cunning *a cunning trick.* artful, astute, clever, crafty, ingenious, knowing, skilful, sly, tricky, wily.

cup *I won a cup on sports day.* award, prize, trophy.

cur dog, mongrel.

curb *Curb your enthusiasm.* to check, to control, to hamper, to hinder, to hold back, to limit, to restrain.

curdle *curdled milk.* to clot, to go sour.

cure 1 *Can they cure arthritis?* to heal, to remedy. 2 *I cured the nasty noise in the car.* to correct, to put right, to rectify. 3 *a cure for the common cold.* medicine, remedy, therapy, treatment.

curious 1 *Our cat was curious about the puppy.* inquisitive, interested, nosey, prying. 2 *There's a curious smell in here.* abnormal, odd, peculiar, queer, strange, unusual.

curl to bend, to coil, to loop, to turn, to twist, to wind.

current 1 *Beware of currents in the water.* flow, stream, tide, undertow. 2 *What do you think of current fashion?* contemporary, fashionable, modern, present, prevailing, up-to-date.

curse 1 *He let out a curse.* exclamation, oath, swear-word. 2 *His dad cursed us for waking him.* to damn, to swear at.

cursory *The mechanic only gave the car a cursory inspection.* hasty, hurried, quick.

curt *His curt answer showed he was in a bad mood.* abrupt, rude, short.

curtail *They had to curtail their holiday.* to break off, to cut, to shorten.

curtain *Close the curtains.* blind, drape, screen.

curtsy *She curtsied to acknowledge the applause.* to bend, to bow.

curve 1 arc, arch, bend, curl, loop, turn, twist. 2 *curved:* arched, bowed, crescent, curled, looped, twisted.

cushion bolster, pillow.

custodian *the custodian of the museum.* guardian, keeper, warder.

custom *It's our custom to take flowers when we visit friends.* convention, habit, institution, practice, routine, tradition.

customary *It's customary to have mint sauce with lamb.* accustomed, common, conventional, habitual, normal, ordinary, regular, traditional.

customer buyer, client.

customs *customs duty.* duty, tax.

cut 1 VARIOUS WAYS TO CUT THINGS: to amputate, to carve, to chisel, to chop, to clip, to crop, to gash, to grate, to guillotine, to hack, to hew, to lop, to mince, to mow, to nick, to prune, to saw, to scalp, to sever, to shave, to shear, to shred, to slash, to slice, to slit, to snip, to split, to stab, to trim. 2 *We cut the story as it was too long.* to abbreviate, to abridge, to censor, to shorten. 3 *I was talking on the phone, but we were cut off.* to interrupt, to stop, to terminate. 4 *a cut on the finger.* gash, injury, nick, notch, slash, slit, tear, wound.

cute SEE **attractive, clever.**

cutlery ITEMS OF CUTLERY: bread-knife, carving knife, dessertspoon, fork, knife, ladle, spoon, tablespoon, teaspoon.

cut-price cheap, inexpensive.

cycle 1 KINDS OF CYCLE: bicycle, (informal) bike, moped, (informal) motor bike, motor cycle, pennyfarthing, scooter, tandem, tricycle. 2 *a cycle of events.* sequence, series.

cyclone hurricane, storm, tempest, tornado, typhoon.

D

dab SEE **touch.**

dainty *dainty embroidery.* delicate, exquisite, fine, neat, pretty.

dale *Yorkshire Dales.* glen, valley.

dally *Don't dally: we must move on.* to dawdle, to hang about, to linger, to loaf, to loiter.

dam *They built a dam across the stream.* bank, barrage, barrier, dike, embankment, wall, weir.

damage 1 *Did it cause any damage?* destruction, devastation, havoc, injury, sabotage. 2 *Did the accident damage the car?* to break, to chip, to cripple, to dent, to destroy, to harm, to hurt, to immobilize, to injure, to mar, to scratch, to spoil, to stain, to wound.

damn to condemn, to curse.

damp *The spare room feels damp.* clammy, dank, humid, moist.

dampen to moisten.

dance 1 *We danced for joy.* to caper, to jig about, to jump about, to leap, to prance, to skip. 2 KINDS OF DANCING: ballet, ballroom dancing, barn dancing, country dance, disco dancing, hornpipe, jig, limbo dancing, minuet, reel, square dance, tap-dancing, waltz. 3 *We went to a dance.* ball, disco, party, social.

danger 1 *There's a danger of catching cold in this weather.* chance, possibility, risk, threat. 2 *Astronauts are always facing danger.* crisis, distress, hazard, peril, pitfall, trouble.

dangerous 1 *a dangerous journey.* chancy, hazardous, perilous, precarious, risky, unsafe. 2 *a dangerous lion.* destructive, harmful, treacherous. 3 *a dangerous criminal.* desperate, violent.

dangle *The rope dangled just above his head.* to be suspended, to droop, to hang, to sway, to swing.

dank clammy, damp, moist.

dare 1 *Would you dare to jump off that rock?* to risk, to venture. 2 *I dared him to eat four ice-creams.* to challenge, to defy.

daring *a daring explorer, a daring feat, etc.* adventurous, bold, brave, fearless, intrepid.

dark 1 *a dark place, a dark sky, etc.* black, dim, gloomy, murky, shadowy, shady, sombre, starless, sunless, unlit. 2 *dark hair.* black, brown, brunette. 3 *a dark complexion.* swarthy, tanned.

darken *The sky darkened.* to blacken.

darling beloved, dear, love, sweetheart.

darn *to darn a hole in your jumper.* to mend, to patch, to repair, to sew, to stitch.

dart *to dart about.* SEE **move.**

dash 1 *He dashed his foot against a rock.* to beat, to smash, to strike. SEE ALSO **hit.** 2 *We dashed home.* to hasten, to hurry, to run, to rush, to speed, (informal) to zoom. SEE ALSO **move.**

data *Feed the data into the computer.* evidence, facts, information, statistics.

date *a date with a friend.* appointment, engagement, fixture, meeting, rendezvous.

daunt *The steepness of the climb daunted us.* to discourage, to dishearten, to dismay, to frighten, to intimidate, to put off.

dawdle *Don't dawdle: we haven't got all day.* to be slow, to dally, to hang about, to lag behind, to linger, to straggle.

dawn day-break, sunrise.

day-dream dream, fantasy, illusion, reverie.

dazed *The blow dazed him.* amazed, bewildered, confused, shocked, stunned.

dazzle SEE **light.**

dead 1 *the dead king.* deceased, late. 2 *Is that fish dead?* killed, lifeless. 3 *It's so cold my fingers are dead.* deadened, numb, paralysed.

deaden *The silencer deadens the noise of the engine.* to muffle, to quieten, to soften, to stifle, to suppress.

deadly *a deadly illness.* fatal, lethal, mortal, terminal.

deaf SEE **handicap.**

deafening *a deafening roar.* loud, noisy.

deal 1 *to deal cards.* to allot, to distribute, to divide, to give out, to share out. 2 *to deal with a problem.* to attend to, to control, to cope with, to grapple with, to handle, to look after, to manage, to sort out, to tackle. 3 *a book that deals with insects.* to be concerned with, to cover. 4 *Dad made a deal with the garage about his new car.* agreement, bargain, contract, pact, settlement, understanding. 5 *They went to a great deal of trouble.* amount, quantity, volume.

dealer *If you have a complaint, take the goods back to your dealer.* merchant, retailer, shopkeeper, stockist, supplier, trader.

dear 1 *dear friends.* beloved, darling, loved. 2 *dear goods.* costly, expensive, (informal) pricey.

death decease, end, passing.

debate 1 *We debated whether to go out to the pictures.* to argue, to discuss, to dispute. 2 *We had a debate about cruelty to animals.* argument, conference, controversy, discussion, dispute.

debris *The debris of the aircraft was scattered over a wide area.* fragments, remains, rubble, ruins, wreckage.

decapitate to behead. SEE ALSO **kill.**

decay *Meat decays quickly in warm weather.* to decompose, to deteriorate, to disintegrate, to go bad, to perish, to rot, to spoil.

deceased *the deceased king.* dead, late.

deceit *We saw through his deceit.* deception, dishonesty, fraud, hoax, pretence, ruse, trickery, untruthfulness.

deceitful *a deceitful person.* dishonest, false, furtive, lying, secretive, shifty, sneaky, treacherous, unfaithful, untrustworthy.

deceive *He tried to deceive us, but we discovered the truth.* to be an impostor, to bluff, to cheat, to defraud, to delude, to dupe, to fool, to hoax, to hoodwink, to kid, to lie, to mislead, to outwit, to pretend, to swindle, to take in, to trick.

decent 1 *decent behaviour.* becoming, chaste, good, honourable, law-abiding, modest, proper, respectable. 2 *a decent meal.* agreeable, nice, pleasant, satisfactory.

deception *We soon discovered the deception.* deceit, dishonesty, fraud, hoax, pretence, ruse, trickery.

deceptive *When you look into the pool, you get a deceptive impression of the depth.* deceiving, false, misleading, unreliable.

decide 1 *Have you decided what to say?* to conclude, to fix on, to resolve, to settle. 2 *We decided on fish and chips.* to choose, to elect, to opt for, to pick, to select.

decided *decided in his opinions.* adamant, determined, firm, resolute.

decimal *decimal scales.* metric.

decipher *I can't decipher his writing.* to decode, to interpret, to make out, to read, to understand.

decision *After all that talking, what was your decision?* conclusion, judgement, outcome, result.

deck *the deck of a ship.* floor, level.

declare *He declared that he would never play again.* to announce, to assert, to contend, to emphasize, to insist, to maintain, to proclaim, to pronounce, to report, to reveal, to state, to testify.

decline 1 *She declined the invitation to my party.* to refuse, to reject, to turn down. 2 *Their enthusiasm declined after a while.* to decrease, to degenerate, to deteriorate, to die, to diminish, to fail, to flag, to lessen, to sink, to weaken, to wilt, to worsen.

decode *We tried to decode their signal.* to decipher, to explain, to interpret, to understand.

decompose *The dead bird had begun to decompose.* to decay, to disintegrate, to go bad, to perish, to rot.

decorate 1 *to decorate a church with flowers.* to adorn, to make beautiful. 2 *to decorate a room.* to paint, to paper. 3 *The soldier was decorated for bravery.* to honour, to reward.

decoration 1 *Christmas decorations.* adornment, ornament. 2 *a decoration for bravery.* award, badge, medal.

decorator painter.

decoy *We had to decoy him away from the sweet stall.* to bait, to entice, to lure, to tempt.

decrease 1 *They ought to decrease the bus fares for a change.* to cut, to lessen, to lower, to reduce. 2 *The numbers of children in our school decreased this term.* to contract, to decline, to diminish, to dwindle, to fall, to lessen, to shrink, to wane.

decree 1 *an official decree.* command, declaration, order, proclamation. 2 *The government decreed that income tax would go up.* to command, to declare, to direct, to order, to proclaim.

decrepit *a decrepit old building.* broken down, derelict, dilapidated, old, ramshackle, worn out.

dedicated 1 *a dedicated fan.* devoted, faithful, loyal. 2 *This part of the church is dedicated to private prayer.* devoted to, set aside for.

deduct *He deducted £1 from my pocket-money.* to subtract, to take away.

deed 1 *a heroic deed.* act, action, adventure, exploit, feat. 2 *the deeds of a house.* documents, papers, records.

deep 1 *deep feelings.* earnest, intense, profound, serious, sincere. 2 *a deep conversation.* intellectual, learned, thoughtful. 3 *a deep colour.* dark, strong. 4 *a deep note.* base, low. 5 *deep snow.* thick.

deface *Vandals defaced the statue.* to disfigure, to mar, to spoil.

defeat *to defeat an enemy.* to beat, to conquer, to crush, to destroy, (informal) to flatten, (informal) to lick, to master, to outdo, to overcome, to overpower, to overthrow, to overwhelm, to rout, to subdue, to suppress, to thrash, to triumph over, to vanquish.

defect 1 *a defect in a piece of work.* blemish, failing, fault, flaw, imperfection, mark, shortcoming, spot, stain, weakness. 2 *The traitor defected to the enemy's side.* to desert, to go over.

defective *Our TV set was defective.* faulty, imperfect, out of order.

defence 1 *When you accused him, what was his defence?* excuse, explanation, justification. 2 *We built a defence against the cold wind.* guard, protection, shelter, shield.

defend 1 *They did what they could to defend their homes.* to fortify, to guard, to keep safe, to protect, to safeguard, to shelter, to shield. 2 *He defended himself before the judge.* to speak up for, to stand up for, to support.

defer *We deferred the match until the weather got better.* to adjourn, to delay, to postpone, to put off.

defiant *He was defiant when I told him to clear up.* disobedient, mutinous, obstinate, rebellious, unyielding.

deficient *Their diet is deficient in vitamins.* lacking, scarce, short.

defile *We thought the sewage works might defile our water supply.* to contaminate, to corrupt, to infect, to poison, to pollute, to soil.

define *A thesaurus simply lists words, whereas a dictionary defines them.* to clarify, to explain.

definite 1 *definite opinions.* assured, certain, confident, fixed, positive, settled, sure. 2 *a definite improvement in granny's health.* clear, distinct, noticeable, obvious, plain, pronounced.

deformed *a deformed tree.* disfigured, distorted, grotesque, mis-shapen, twisted, ugly, warped.

defraud *He tried to defraud the bank.* to cheat, to dupe, to swindle, to trick.

defrost to de-ice, to unfreeze.

deft *deft movements.* agile, clever, nimble, quick, skilful.

defy 1 *It isn't wise to defy the head.* to confront, to disobey, to face up to, to resist, to stand up to. 2 *I defy you to come any further.* to challenge, to dare.

degenerate *The sick man's condition degenerated.* to decline, to deteriorate, to sink, to weaken, to worsen.

dehydrated *dehydrated food.* dried, dry.

de-ice *to de-ice the fridge.* to defrost, to unfreeze.

deity *Ancient tribes worshipped many deities.* divinity, god, goddess.

dejected *He was dejected when he didn't get into the team.* crestfallen, depressed, discouraged, downcast, down-hearted, gloomy, melancholy, unhappy. SEE ALSO **sad.**

delay 1 *The snow delayed the traffic.* to detain, to hinder, to hold up, to keep, to obstruct, to slow down. 2 *We delayed the start of our journey.* to defer, to postpone, to put off. 3 *Don't delay if you want to catch that bus.* to hang back, to hesitate, to pause, to stall, to wait.

delete *They deleted my name from the list.* to cancel, to cross out, to erase, to remove, to wipe out.

deliberate 1 *a deliberate insult.* calculated, conscious, intentional, planned, premeditated, wilful. 2 *deliberate planning.* careful, cautious, methodical, painstaking, slow.

deliberately *He hit me deliberately.* intentionally, purposely.

delicate 1 *delicate material.* dainty, exquisite, fine, flimsy, fragile, frail, soft, tender. 2 *delicate health.* feeble, sickly, unhealthy, weak. 3 *delicate machinery.* intricate, sensitive. 4 *a delicate flavour.* faint, gentle, mild, subtle.

delicious appetizing, luscious, tasty.

delight 1 *The play delighted the children.* to amuse, to captivate, to charm, to enchant, to entertain, to please, to fascinate, to please, to thrill. 2 *Mum's greatest delight is a nice hot bath.* bliss, ecstasy, enjoyment, joy, pleasure, rapture.

delinquent *a juvenile delinquent.* criminal, culprit, hooligan, offender, wrongdoer.

delirious *delirious with joy.* crazy, demented, excited, frantic, frenzied, hysterical, mad, wild.

deliver *to deliver letters.* to convey, to distribute, to give out, to hand over, to present, to take round.

delivery *a fresh delivery of vegetables.* batch, consignment.

delude SEE **deceive.**

deluge *We got soaked in the deluge.* downpour, flood, rainstorm.

delusion hallucination, illusion.

demand *He demanded to have his money back.* to ask, to beg, to claim, to command, to order, to request, to require.

demented *The dog was demented when the wasp stung him.* berserk, crazy, delirious, deranged, frantic, frenzied, insane, lunatic, mad, wild.

demolish *They demolished a block of old flats.* to destroy, to dismantle, to knock down, to raze.

demon devil, imp, spirit.

demonstrate 1 *The local garage demonstrated a new car.* to display, to exhibit, to show. 2 *She demonstrated how to make a cake.* to describe, to explain, to illustrate, to show. 3 *They demonstrated that smoking does affect your health.* to establish, to prove. 4 *We demonstrated against experiments on live animals.* to march, to protest.

demonstration 1 *a cookery demonstration.* display, exhibition, presentation, show. 2 *a political demonstration.* demo, march, protest, rally.

demure *a demure expression.* bashful, coy, modest, quiet, retiring, shy.

den *We made a den in the garden.* hide-out, hiding-place, lair.

denounce *At the end of the play, the detective denounced the murderer.* to accuse, to blame, to complain about, to condemn, to inform against, to report, to reveal, to tell of.

dense 1 *dense fog.* heavy, impenetrable, thick. 2 *a dense crowd.* packed, solid. 3 *a dense pupil.* dim, dull, foolish, obtuse, slow, stupid, (informal) thick, unintelligent.

dent *Dad dented the wing of the car.* to bend, to buckle, to crumple, to knock in.

deny *Do you deny the accusation?* to contradict, to disclaim, to dispute, to reject. 2 *Within reason, grandad doesn't deny us anything.* to deprive of, to refuse.

depart *Are you ready to depart?* to embark, to emigrate, to go away, to leave, to quit, to set off, to set out.

department branch, part, section.

depend *We depend on your support.* to bank on, to count on, to need, to rely on, to trust.

dependable *a dependable friend.* consistent, faithful, regular, reliable, safe, sound, steady, true, trustworthy.

depict *We depicted a snowy scene.* to describe, to draw, to illustrate, to paint, to picture, to portray, to represent, to show.

deplorable *deplorable behaviour.* regrettable, reprehensible, unfortunate. SEE ALSO **bad.**

deport *to deport a criminal.* to banish, to exile, to expel, to send away.

depose *to depose a monarch.* to get rid of, to remove.

deposit 1 *Deposit your dirty plates by the hatch.* to leave, to place, to put down, to set down. 2 *I deposited some money in the bank.* to pay in, to save. 3 *a dirty deposit in the bottom of a cup.* dregs, sediment.

depot *The climbers established a depot at the foot of the mountain.* base, cache, dump, headquarters, hoard, store.

depraved *a depraved person.* base, corrupt, evil, immoral, vicious, wicked. SEE ALSO **bad.**

depress 1 *His dog's death depressed him.* to dishearten, to grieve, to sadden. 2 *depressed:* dejected, desolate, despondent, disconsolate, gloomy, heart-broken, low, melancholy, miserable, mournful, unhappy, wretched. SEE ALSO **sad.** 3 *depressing:* black, discouraging, disheartening, dismal, gloomy, sombre, tragic.

depression 1 *a mood of depression.* despair, gloom, hopelessness, melancholy, sadness. 2 *a depression in the ground.* dent, dip, hollow.

deprive *Would a vegetarian deprive a dog of his bone?* to deny, to refuse, to rob, to take away.

deputy *The mayor was ill, so he sent a deputy.* assistant, replacement, representative, reserve, stand-in, substitute.

derailment accident, crash.

deranged crazy, demented, insane, (informal) loony, lunatic, mad.

derelict *a derelict farmhouse.* abandoned, broken down, decrepit, deserted, dilapidated, forsaken, ruined, tumbledown.

derive *He derives a lot of pleasure from his garden.* to acquire, to get, to obtain, to procure, to receive.

descend to come down, to climb down, to drop, to fall, to move down, to sink.

descendants heirs, offspring, posterity.

describe *An eyewitness described what happened.* to depict, to explain, to express, to narrate, to portray, to recount, to relate, to represent, to tell.

description account, commentary, depiction, narration, portrait, representation, sketch, story.

desert *waterless desert.* wasteland, wilderness. 2 *a desert island.* barren, uninhabited, wild. 3 *Don't desert your friends.* to abandon, to forsake, to leave. 4 *They deserted him on an island.* to maroon, to strand. 5 *The soldiers deserted.* to defect, to run away.

deserter fugitive, outlaw, renegade, traitor.

deserve *Does he deserve a prize?* to earn, to merit.

design 1 *a design for a dress.* drawing, pattern, plan, sketch. 2 *Our car is an old design.* model, type, version. 3 *An architect designs buildings.* to draw, to plan, to plot, to scheme, to sketch.

desire 1 *What do you desire most?* to fancy, to hanker after, to long for, to want, to wish for, to yearn for. 2 *He stole because of his desire for money.* ambition, appetite, craving, hunger, itch, longing, love, lust, passion, thirst, urge, wish.

desolate 1 *a desolate place.* barren, bleak, deserted, dreary, empty, isolated, lonely, remote, windswept. 2 *He was desolate after his dog died.* depressed, forlorn, forsaken, neglected, unhappy, wretched. SEE ALSO **sad.**

despair *a state of despair.* depression, desperation, hopelessness.

desperate 1 *The shipwrecked sailors were desperate.* despairing, hopeless. 2 *a desperate situation.* bad, serious. 3 *a desperate criminal.* dangerous, reckless, violent.

despicable *a despicable crime.* base, contemptible, detestable, hateful.

despise *We sometimes despise people who can't do what we can.* to be contemptuous of, to detest, to disdain, to dislike, to hate, to look down on, to scorn, to sneer at.

despondent *He was despondent when he didn't get into the team.* depressed, desolate, gloomy, melancholy, unhappy. SEE ALSO **sad.**

dessert (informal) afters, pudding, sweet.

destination *This train's destination is London.* terminus.

destined *The plan was destined to fail.* doomed, fated, intended.

destiny chance, doom, fate, fortune, luck, providence.

destitute 1 *destitute beggars.* deprived, homeless, impoverished, needy, penniless, poor, poverty-stricken. 2 *the destitute:* beggars, paupers, tramps, vagrants.

destroy to abolish, to annihilate, to crush, to demolish, to devastate, to dismantle, to eliminate, to end, to eradicate, to exterminate, to finish off, to flatten, to get rid of, to knock down, to raze, to ruin, to stamp out, to uproot, to wipe out, to wreck. SEE ALSO **defeat, kill.**

destruction *a scene of destruction.* damage, devastation, havoc.

destructive *destructive animals.* dangerous, harmful, violent.

detach to disconnect, to divide, to part, to remove, to separate, to undo, to unfasten.

detached 1 *a detached house.* separate. 2 *a detached attitude.* disinterested, impartial, neutral, unbiased, unemotional, uninvolved, unprejudiced.

detail *The policeman noticed every detail.* circumstance, fact, feature, particular.

detain 1 *What detained you?* to delay, to hold up, to keep. 2 *The police detained the suspect.* to arrest, to capture, to confine, to gaol, to hold, to imprison.

detect *Did you detect anything wrong?* to diagnose, to discern, to discover, to find, to identify, to notice, to observe, to sense.

deter *We put up a scarecrow to deter the birds.* to daunt, to discourage, to dismay, to hinder, to impede, to obstruct, to prevent.

deteriorate *His health deteriorated in winter.* to decay, to decline, to degenerate, to disintegrate, to get worse, to weaken, to worsen.

determination *Marathon runners show great determination.* courage, (informal) grit, (informal) guts, spirit, will.

determined *He was determined that he would succeed.* adamant, decided, firm, resolute, resolved, strenuous.

detest *Our dog detests snow.* to despise, to dislike, to hate, to loathe.

detestable *a detestable crime.* contemptible, despicable, hateful, horrible, loathsome, odious.

detonate *to detonate a bomb.* to blow up, to discharge, to explode, to fire, to let off, to set off.

detour diversion.

devastate *The hurricane devastated the town.* to demolish, to destroy, to flatten, to ravage, to wreck.

develop 1 *Her piano-playing is developing well.* to advance, to evolve, to improve, to move on, to progress. 2 *The shop plans to develop next year.* to build up, to expand, to grow, to increase. 3 *Leave the apples on the tree to develop.* to age, to mature, to ripen. 4 *Your story starts well: you ought to develop it.* to amplify, to enlarge, to strengthen.

device *That tin-opener is a clever device.* appliance, contraption, contrivance, gadget, implement, instrument, invention, machine, tool, utensil.

devil demon, fiend, imp, spirit.

devious 1 *a devious route.* indirect, roundabout. 2 *a devious liar.* deceitful, dishonest, sly, sneaky, wily.

devise *I'm devising a scheme to make lots of money!* to concoct, to design, to invent, to make up, to plan, to think up.

devoted *a devoted companion.* constant, dedicated, devout, enthusiastic, faithful, loving, loyal, reliable.

devour *The lions devoured the meat greedily.* to consume, to gobble, to gulp. SEE ALSO **eat.**

devout *a devout worshipper.* committed, dedicated, devoted, genuine, religious, sincere.

diabolical *diabolical behaviour.* devilish, fiendish, hellish.

diadem coronet, crown.

diagnose *The doctor diagnosed mumps.* to detect, to find, to identify.

diagram chart, graph, figure, plan, outline, sketch.

dial *Did you dial the right number?* to call, to phone, to ring, to telephone.

dialect *a London dialect, a northern dialect.* accent, brogue, language.

dialogue conversation, discussion, talk.

diary *She writes a diary every day.* journal, log, record.

dictatorial *a dictatorial ruler.* bossy, domineering, tyrannical.

die 1 *All creatures must die.* to expire, to pass away, to perish. 2 *Our enthusiasm began to die.* to decline, to decrease, to fail, to lessen, to stop, to weaken.

diet *You need a good diet to keep healthy.* food, nourishment.

differ 1 *I wonder how our school differs from the one granny went to?* to contrast with. 2 *We often differ about what to watch on TV.* to argue, to disagree, to quarrel.

difference 1 *What's the difference between the cheap jeans and the expensive ones?* comparison, contrast, distinction. 2 *We told him to stop, but it didn't make any difference.* alteration, change, modification. 3 *There was a difference between us about who should pay.* argument, disagreement, quarrel.

different 1 *Have the chocolates got different centres?* assorted, contrasting, dissimilar, miscellaneous, mixed, unlike, varied, various. 2 *Everyone's handwriting is different.* distinct, particular, personal, separate, special, specific, unique. 3 *We have different views about music.* conflicting, contradictory, incompatible, opposite.

difficult 1 *a difficult problem.* advanced, complicated, hard, thorny, ticklish, tricky. 2 *a difficult climb.* arduous, laborious, strenuous, tough.

difficulty *Have you got a difficulty?* adversity, complication, dilemma, fix, hardship, hindrance, jam, obstacle, plight, predicament, problem, snag, trouble.

dig *to dig a hole.* to burrow, to excavate, to gouge out, to hollow out, to mine, to scoop, to tunnel.

digest SEE **eat**.

digit figure, integer, number, numeral.

dignified *a dignified ceremony.* calm, elegant, formal, grave, noble, proper, sedate, serious, sober, solemn, stately, tasteful.

dike 1 *They dug a dike across the marsh.* channel, ditch. 2 *They built a dike as a defence against flooding.* dam, embankment.

dilapidated *a dilapidated old building.* broken down, decrepit, derelict, ramshackle, rickety, ruined, tumbledown.

dilemma *a tricky dilemma.* difficulty, fix, jam, plight, predicament, problem.

diligent *a diligent worker.* careful, conscientious, earnest, hardworking, persevering, scrupulous, thorough.

dilute *You dilute squash with water.* to thin, to water down, to weaken.

dim 1 *a dim outline in the mist.* blurred, cloudy, dark, faint, gloomy, hazy, indistinct, misty, murky, obscure, shadowy, unclear. 2 (informal) *You are dim if you can't understand that!* dense, dull, foolish, obtuse, slow, stupid, (informal) thick.

dimensions *the dimensions of a room.* magnitude, measurements, proportions, size, volume.

diminish *Our supply of sweets diminished rather quickly.* to contract, to decline, to reduce, to shrink, to subside.

diminutive *We saw a diminutive figure in the distance.* little, miniature, minute, short, small, (informal) teeny, tiny, undersized, wee.

din SEE **noise**.

dingy *a dingy room.* depressing, dirty, dismal, drab, dull, gloomy, grimy.

dinner banquet, feast. SEE ALSO **meal**.

dip 1 *to dip in water.* to dive, to drop, to immerse, to lower, to plunge, to submerge. 2 *a dip in the sea.* plunge, swim. 3 *a dip in the ground.* dent, depression, hollow.

diploma award, certificate. SEE ALSO **qualification**.

diplomat ambassador, consul, representative.

diplomatic *a diplomatic reminder.* discreet, polite, tactful.

dire *a dire calamity.* appalling, awful, calamitous, dreadful, serious, terrible. SEE ALSO **bad**.

direct 1 *a direct line.* straight, unswerving. 2 *a direct answer.* blunt, candid, frank, honest, outspoken, plain, straight, straightforward, uncomplicated. 3 *Can you direct me to the station?* to guide, to indicate, to show. 4 *Their guns were directed at us.* to aim, to point, to turn. 5 *The head directed us to come in.* to command, to instruct, to order, to tell. 6 *The fireman directed the rescue.* to administer, to command, to control, to govern, to manage, to regulate, to supervise.

director *the director of a business.* administrator, boss, captain, controller, executive, governor, head, manager, overseer, ruler, supervisor.

directory *a telephone directory.* catalogue, index, list, register.

dirt dust, filth, grime, (informal) muck, mud, pollution.

dirty 1 *a dirty room, dirty shoes, etc.* dingy, dusty, filthy, foul, grimy, grubby, messy, (informal) mucky, muddy, soiled, sooty, sordid, squalid, unclean. 2 *dirty language.* coarse, crude, improper, indecent, obscene, offensive, rude, smutty, vulgar.

disable 1 to damage, to weaken. 2 *disabled:* crippled, handicapped, lame, maimed.

disadvantage *It's a disadvantage to be short if you play basketball.* drawback, handicap, hindrance, inconvenience.

disagree *He disagrees with everything we say.* to argue, to differ, to quarrel.

disagreeable *a disagreeable remark, a disagreeable smell, etc.* distasteful, nasty, offensive, rude, unfriendly. SEE ALSO **unpleasant.**

disagreement argument, controversy, debate, dispute, opposition, quarrel.

disappear *The fog disappeared quickly.* to clear, to dwindle, to evaporate, to fade, to melt away, to pass, to vanish.

disappointed *We were disappointed when our team lost.* crestfallen, dejected, discontented, dissatisfied, downcast, down-hearted, let down, unhappy. SEE ALSO **sad.**

disapproval *She showed her disapproval of our behaviour.* censure, condemnation, criticism, dissatisfaction, reprimand, reproach.

disaster 1 accident, calamity, catastrophe, fiasco, mishap. 2 VARIOUS DISASTERS: air crash, avalanche, derailment, earthquake, flood, landslide, road accident, shipwreck, tidal wave, volcanic eruption.

disbelieving *Dad was disbelieving when I said I didn't want any pocket-money.* incredulous, sceptical.

disc 1 circle, counter, token. 2 *Do you buy discs or cassettes?* album, LP, single. SEE ALSO **record.**

discard *It's time we discarded these old comics.* to dispose of, to dump, to eliminate, to get rid of, to reject, to scrap, to shed, to throw away.

discern *We discerned a change in the weather.* to detect, to distinguish, to mark, to notice, to observe, to perceive, to recognize, to see, to spy, to understand.

discharge 1 *The judge discharged him.* to acquit, to excuse, to free, to let off, to liberate. 2 *His boss discharged him because he was lazy.* to dismiss, to fire, to sack. 3 *to discharge a gun.* to detonate, to fire, to shoot. 4 *The chimney discharged black smoke.* to belch, to eject, to emit, to expel, to give out, to release, to send out.

disciple admirer, apostle, follower.

discipline *Usually the discipline in our class is good.* control, management, obedience, order, system.

disclaim *Everyone disclaimed responsibility for the broken window.* to deny, to disown, to renounce.

disclose *to disclose a secret.* to bare, to betray, to divulge, to expose, to make known, to reveal, to uncover.

discolour *The spilt acid discoloured the table.* to bleach, to stain, to tarnish, to tinge.

discomfort *I hate the discomfort of wearing new shoes.* ache, distress, pain, soreness, uncomfortableness, uneasiness.

disconsolate SEE **sad.**

discontented *How can we cheer up this discontented crowd?* disappointed, disgruntled, displeased, dissatisfied, miserable, unhappy. SEE ALSO **sad.**

discontinue *They discontinued the Sunday bus service.* to cease, to end, to finish, to stop, to terminate.

discord *Was there any discord, or did you all agree?* argument, conflict, disagreement, dispute, quarrelling.

discount *Did you pay full price, or did you get a discount?* concession, reduction.

discourage *We were discouraged by the bad weather.* to daunt, to deter, to dishearten, to dismay, to dissuade, to frighten, to intimidate, to put off, to scare.

discourteous SEE **rude.**

discover *I discovered some interesting facts.* to come across, to detect, to explore, to find out, to identify, to learn, to locate, to notice, to observe, to perceive, to reveal, to search out, to track down, to uncover, to unearth.

discoverer creator, explorer, inventor.

discreet *discreet questions.* careful, diplomatic, polite, prudent, tactful.

discretion *You showed great discretion in choosing those nice colours.* good sense, judgement.

discriminate 1 *Can you discriminate between instant coffee and ground coffee?* to distinguish, to tell apart. 2 *It is wrong to discriminate against people because of their religion or colour or sex.* to be biased, to be intolerant, to be prejudiced, to show favouritism.

discrimination *racial discrimination.* bias, favouritism, intolerance, prejudice, racialism, racism.

discuss *Let's discuss the problem.* to argue about, to consider, to debate, to examine, to talk about.

discussion argument, conversation, debate, dialogue, talk.

disdain *That cat's too fussy: he disdains everything we give him.* to despise, to dislike, to look down on, to scorn, to snub.

disdainful *a disdainful smile.* arrogant, contemptuous, haughty, proud, scornful, snobbish, stuck-up.

disease affliction, ailment, blight, (informal) bug, complaint, disorder, infection, infirmity, malady, sickness. SEE ALSO **illness.**

disembark *to disembark from a ship.* to go ashore, to land.

disentangle *to disentangle a piece of string.* to untie, to untwist.

disfigured *He was disfigured in the fire.* defaced, deformed, scarred.

disgrace 1 *the disgrace of being punished.* dishonour, embarrassment, humiliation, shame. 2 *The way he treats his dog is a disgrace!* outrage, scandal.

disgraceful *disgraceful behaviour.* dishonourable, embarrassing, humiliating, shameful.

disgruntled SEE **bad-tempered.**

disguise 1 *The bird-watchers disguised their hide-out.* to camouflage, to conceal, to cover up, to hide, to mask. 2 *to disguise yourself as:* to counterfeit, to dress up as, to pretend to be.

disgust 1 *He couldn't hide his disgust for the rotten food.* aversion, contempt, dislike, hatred, loathing, revulsion. 2 *The rotten food disgusted him.* to appal, to horrify, to nauseate, to offend, to repel, to revolt, to shock, to sicken. 3 *disgusting:* SEE **unpleasant.**

dish basin, bowl, plate.

dishearten *They were disheartened by losing four games in a row.* to depress, to deter, to discourage, to dismay, to put off, to sadden.

dishevelled *dishevelled hair.* bedraggled, messy, scruffy, tangled, uncombed, unkempt, untidy.

dishonest cheating, corrupt, criminal, crooked, deceitful, deceptive, false, fraudulent, insincere, lying, misleading, underhand, unscrupulous, untrustworthy.

dishonour disgrace, shame.

disinclined hesitant, reluctant, unwilling.

disinfect to purify, to sterilize.

disintegrate *The wrecked ship disintegrated.* to break up, to crumble, to decay, to degenerate, to deteriorate, to fall apart, to shatter, to smash up.

disinterested *A referee is supposed to be disinterested.* detached, impartial, neutral, unbiased, uninvolved, unprejudiced.

disjointed *a disjointed account of what happened.* broken up, confused, incoherent, jumbled, mixed up, muddled.

dislike 1 *I dislike shopping.* to despise, to detest, to hate, to loathe, to scorn. 2 *He couldn't hide his dislike.* aversion, contempt, disgust, distaste, hatred, loathing, revulsion.

disloyal *a disloyal friend.* treacherous, unfaithful.

disloyalty *We found it hard to forgive his disloyalty.* betrayal, infidelity, treachery, treason, unfaithfulness.

dismal *Our garden looks dismal in the winter.* bleak, cheerless, depressing, dingy, dreary, gloomy, sombre. SEE ALSO **sad.**

dismantle *They dismantled the old chimney.* to demolish, to take down.

dismay 1 *He realized with dismay that the brakes were not working.* alarm, anxiety, consternation, dread, fear, horror. 2 *They were dismayed to see the damage.* to alarm, to appal, to daunt, to discourage, to disgust, to dishearten, to distress, to frighten, to horrify, to scare, to shock, to terrify.

dismiss 1 *The head dismissed the class.* to let go, to release, to send away. 2 *The boss dismissed him because he was lazy.* to discharge, to fire, to sack. 3 *We dismissed the idea of going abroad.* to discard, to disregard, to get rid of, to reject, to set aside.

disobedient *disobedient children.* contrary, defiant, insubordinate, mutinous, obstinate, perverse, rebellious, stubborn, troublesome, unmanageable, unruly.

disobey 1 *to disobey an order.* to defy, to disregard, to ignore. 2 *to disobey a rule.* to break, to infringe, to violate. 2 *to disobey your leader.* to mutiny, to rebel, to revolt.

disorder 1 *The police wanted to prevent disorder.* anarchy, chaos, commotion, confusion, disturbance, lawlessness, rioting, rumpus, turmoil, unrest. 2 *The burglars left the house in disorder.* mess, muddle, shambles.

disorderly *a disorderly class.* badly-behaved, boisterous, lawless, noisy, obstreperous, riotous, rough, rowdy, turbulent, undisciplined, unruly, wild.

disorganized *Your work is very disorganized.* careless, chaotic, confused, disorderly, haphazard, jumbled, messy, muddled, scatterbrained, slapdash, sloppy, slovenly, unsystematic, untidy.

disown *He disowned his dog when it misbehaved.* to renounce.

disparaging *disparaging remarks.* insulting, mocking, rude, uncomplimentary.

dispatch 1 *to dispatch a parcel.* to convey, to post, to send, to transmit. 2 *to dispatch a wounded animal.* (informal) to finish off, to put an end to. SEE ALSO **kill**. 3 *A messenger arrived with important dispatches.* bulletin, communiqué, letter, message, report.

dispense 1 *The chemist is qualified to dispense medicine.* to distribute, to give out, to provide. 2 *It's time we dispensed with that old bike in the garage.* to do without, to get rid of, to remove.

disperse *The crowd dispersed when it rained.* to scatter, to spread out.

display 1 *a gymnastics display.* demonstration, exhibition, presentation, show. 2 *to display your knowledge.* to air, to demonstrate, to exhibit, to present, to produce, to reveal, to show.

displease to annoy, to exasperate, to irritate, to offend, to trouble, to upset, to vex, to worry.

dispose 1 *to dispose of rubbish.* to discard, to dump, to get rid of, to give away, to sell, to throw away. 2 *to be disposed to:* to be inclined to, to be liable to, to be likely to, to be ready to, to be willing to.

disposition *a friendly disposition.* attitude, character, manner, mood, nature, personality, temperament.

dispute 1 *a dispute between two sides.* argument, debate, quarrel. 2 *No one disputed the referee's decision.* to argue against, to contradict, to deny, to oppose, to question.

disregard 1 *to disregard someone's advice.* to dismiss, to disobey, to forget, to ignore, to neglect, to overlook, to reject. 2 *I disregarded the hard sums.* to leave out, to miss out, to omit, to skip.

disreputable *a disreputable-looking character.* dubious, shady, suspicious, untrustworthy.

disrespectful cheeky, discourteous, impertinent, impolite, impudent, insolent, rude.

disrupt *The arrival of visitors disrupted our work.* to break up, to interrupt, to upset.

dissatisfied *a dissatisfied customer.* disappointed, discontented, displeased.

dissimilar *The teams need to wear dissimilar colours.* contrasting, different, distinct, unalike.

dissolve *Sugar dissolves in tea.* to disappear, to melt.

dissuade *She dissuaded me from buying the record she hated.* to advise against, to discourage.

distance *the distance between us and the moon.* gap, interval, length, measurement, space, stretch.

distant 1 *distant places.* far, far-away, outlying, remote. 2 *a distant manner.* cool, reserved, unenthusiastic, unfriendly.

distasteful *The job of clearing up when the cat was sick was distasteful.* disagreeable, horrid, nasty, objectionable, repellent, revolting. SEE ALSO **unpleasant**.

distended bloated, bulging, swollen.

distinct 1 *distinct footprints in the mud.* clear, definite, obvious, plain. 2 *My style is distinct from hers.* contrasting, different, dissimilar, separate. 3 *a distinct kind of handwriting.* SEE **distinctive**.

distinction 1 *Is there any distinction between different brands of soap powder?* contrast, difference. 2 *She has the distinction of being in the county team.* excellence, fame, honour, importance, renown.

distinctive *distinctive handwriting.* characteristic, different, distinct, individual, personal, special, typical, unique.

distinguish 1 *Can you distinguish butter from margarine?* to discriminate, to tell apart. 2 *In the dark I couldn't distinguish who he was.* to discern, to make out, to perceive, to recognize, to see. 3 *distinguished: a distinguished actor.* celebrated, eminent, famous, foremost, great, important, leading, notable, noted, outstanding, prominent, renowned, well-known.

distort *to distort the truth.* to bend, to deform, to twist, to warp.

distract *The flashing lights distracted us.* to bewilder, to confuse, to divert, to trouble, to worry.

distress 1 *The trapped animal was in distress.* adversity, agony, anguish, danger, difficulty, discomfort, pain, suffering, torment, torture. 2 *The news of the disaster distressed us.* to afflict, to alarm, to dismay, to frighten, to grieve, to hurt, to perturb, to scare, to shake, to shock, to terrify, to torment, to torture, to trouble, to upset, to worry.

distribute *to distribute the papers.* to allot, to circulate, to deal out, to deliver, to dispense, to divide, to give out, to hand round, to issue, to share out.

district *There are plenty of shops in our district.* area, locality, neighbourhood, region, vicinity, zone.

distrust *I distrust dogs that bark.* to doubt, to mistrust, to suspect.

disturb 1 *Don't disturb granny.* to annoy, to bother, to interrupt, to worry. 2 *A fox disturbed the chickens.* to agitate, to alarm, to excite, to frighten, to perturb, to scare, to stir up, to upset.

disused *a disused railway line.* abandoned, obsolete.

ditch channel, dike, drain, gutter, trench.

divan SEE **bed.**

dive *to dive into the water.* to dip, to go under, to nosedive, to plunge, to sink, to submerge, to subside, to swoop.

diver frogman.

diverge *The motorways diverge.* to branch, to divide, to fork, to separate, to split.

diverse *a diverse collection of things.* assorted, different, miscellaneous, mixed, varied, various.

diversion 1 *a traffic diversion.* detour. 2 *diversions to keep people amused.* amusement, entertainment, game, hobby, pastime, recreation.

divert 1 *They diverted the plane to another airport.* to change direction. 2 *He diverted us with funny stories.* to amuse, to cheer up, to distract, to entertain.

divide 1 *The road divides: which way do we go?* to branch, to diverge, to fork, to separate. 2 *How shall we divide these sweets?* to allot, to deal out, to distribute, to give out, to halve, to share out. 3 *We'll divide the class into two.* to part, to separate, to split.

divine celestial, god-like, heavenly, holy, religious, sacred.

division 1 *The box has divisions for different tools.* compartment, part, section, segment. 2 *a division of a business.* branch, department.

divorce to separate, to split up.

divulge *to divulge a secret.* to betray, to disclose, to expose, to make known, to publish, to reveal, to tell.

dizzy confused, faint, giddy, reeling, unsteady.

do 1 *Have you done your work?* to accomplish, to achieve, to carry out, to commit, to complete, to execute, to finish, to perform. 2 *Will you do the potatoes?* to attend to, to cope with, to deal with, to handle, to look after, to manage. 3 *Will four big potatoes do?* to be enough, to be satisfactory, to be sufficient, to be suitable. ! *Do* can mean many things. The words given here are only some of the other words you can use.

docile *a docile animal.* gentle, meek, obedient, patient, tame.

dock *The ship came in to the dock.* berth, dockyard, harbour, haven, jetty, landing-stage, pier, port, quay, wharf.

document certificate, deed, form, licence, paper, passport, records, visa, warrant, will.

dodder SEE **walk.**

dodge 1 *I dodged out of the way.* to avoid, to duck, to elude, to evade, to swerve, to turn, to veer. 2 *a dodge for opening lemonade bottles.* knack, trick.

dog 1 bitch, cur, hound, mongrel, pedigree, puppy. 2 VARIOUS BREEDS: Alsatian, beagle, bloodhound, bulldog, collie, dachshund, Dalmatian, foxhound, greyhound, husky, Labrador, mastiff, Pekingese, poodle, pug, retriever, sheepdog, spaniel, terrier, whippet.

dogged *dogged persistence.* determined, firm, obstinate, persistent, resolute, stubborn, unwavering, wilful.

dole 1 social security, unemployment benefit. 2 *on the dole:* out of work, unemployed.

doleful SEE **sad.**

dollop *a dollop of ice-cream.* chunk, hunk, lump, mass.

domestic *domestic animals.* domesticated, house-trained, tame.

dominant 1 *The teacher is usually the dominant influence in a class.* chief, main, outstanding, prevailing, principal, ruling. 2 *The church is the dominant feature in the landscape.* biggest, highest, largest, tallest.

dominate *Their captain dominated the game.* to control, to govern, to influence, to manage, to rule.

domineering *a domineering personality.* bossy, dictatorial, tyrannical.

donate *to donate money to charity.* to contribute, to give, to grant, to provide, to supply.

donation *a donation to OXFAM.* contribution, gift, offering, present.

donor *a generous donor.* benefactor, contributor, giver, provider, sponsor.

doodle *I wasn't drawing properly, just doodling.* to jot, to scribble.

doom 1 *We shall never know the doom of the missing ship.* destiny, fate. 2 *The dying woman faced her doom bravely.* death, end.

door doorway, entrance, entry, exit, French windows, gate.

dormant *Many plants are dormant in winter.* asleep, hibernating, inactive, resting, sleeping.

dot mark, point, speck, spot.

dote *He dotes on his dog.* to adore, to idolize, to love, to worship.

double 1 dual, twice. 2 *I saw your double in town.* copy, duplicate, twin.

double-cross to betray, to cheat.

double-decker bus.

doubt 1 *Have you any doubt about whether we can trust him?* anxiety, hesitation, misgiving, qualm, suspicion, uncertainty, worry. 2 *Do you doubt my word?* to distrust, to mistrust, to question, to suspect.

doubtful *The weather made us doubtful about our picnic.* dubious, hesitant, uncertain, undecided, unsure.

dowdy *dowdy clothes.* colourless, drab, dull, shabby, sloppy, unattractive.

down *a pillow filled with down.* feathers.

downpour *I got soaked in the downpour.* deluge, rainstorm, shower.

downs fells, hills, moors.

downtrodden *downtrodden slaves.* exploited, oppressed.

downy *The jacket was made of downy material.* feathery, fleecy, furry, fuzzy, soft, woolly.

doze *I often doze in the evening.* to nod off, to sleep, to snooze, to take a nap.

drab *drab colours.* cheerless, colourless, dingy, dismal, dowdy, dreary, dull, grimy, shabby, sombre, unattractive.

drag 1 *The tractor dragged a load of logs.* to draw, to haul, to lug, to pull, to tow, to tug. 2 *Time drags when you are bored.* to crawl, to creep, to pass slowly.

drain 1 *They are repairing the drains.* ditch, drainage, gutter, pipe, sanitation, sewer. 2 *He drained the oil out of his engine.* to clear, to draw off, to empty, to take off. 3 *The long game drained our energy.* to consume, to exhaust, to sap, to spend, to use up. SEE ALSO **exhaust.**

drama 1 *Drama is one of our favourite lessons.* acting, improvisation, plays, the stage, theatre. 2 *We had a drama today when the fire-alarm went.* action, excitement, suspense.

drastic *It would be drastic to have all your teeth out.* extreme, severe.

draught breeze, wind.

draw 1 *to draw with crayons.* to depict, to portray, to represent, to sketch. 2 *The locomotive was drawing eleven coaches.* to drag, to haul, to lug, to pull, to tow, to tug. 3 *The dentist drew two of my teeth.* to extract, to remove, to take out. 4 *The show drew a big crowd.* to attract, to bring in, to entice, to lure. 5 *Even after extra time they still drew.* to be equal, to tie. 6 *She draws out her chewing-gum like a bit of string.* to elongate, to lengthen, to prolong, to stretch. 7 *The bus drew up.* to halt, to pull up, to stop. 8 *a prize draw.* competition, lottery, raffle.

drawback *Being tall can be a drawback when you are exploring caves.* disadvantage, handicap, hindrance, inconvenience.

drawing design, pattern, sketch. SEE ALSO **picture.**

drawing-room living-room, lounge, sitting-room.

dread 1 *There's no need to dread going to the dentist.* to be afraid of, to fear. 2 *a dread of spiders.* anxiety, fear, horror, terror.

dreadful *a dreadful accident.* alarming, appalling, awful, fearful, frightening, frightful, ghastly, grisly, horrifying, monstrous, shocking, terrible, tragic.

dream 1 *Extraordinary things happen in dreams.* day-dream, fantasy, hallucination, illusion, nightmare, reverie, vision. 2 *She dreamed that she was flying.* to fancy, to imagine.

dreary *dreary weather.* boring, cheerless, depressing, dismal, drab, dull, gloomy, joyless, melancholy, sombre, unhappy. SEE ALSO **sad.**

dregs *the dregs at the bottom of a bottle.* deposit, remains, sediment.

drench *The rainstorm drenched us.* to saturate, to soak, to wet.

dress 1 *a woman's dress.* frock, gown. 2 *Can a man's dress tell you the sort of person he is?* attire, clothes, clothing, costume, garments. 3 *You must dress when you come in from the beach.* to clothe yourself, to cover yourself, to wear clothes. 4 *A nurse dressed my wound.* to attend to, to bandage, to care for, to treat.

dribble *Blood dribbled down his face.* to drip, to flow, to leak, to ooze, to run, to seep, to trickle.

drift 1 *The boat drifted down the river.* to float. 2 *We had nowhere special to go, so we drifted about.* to ramble, to wander.

drill *to drill through something.* to bore, to penetrate, to pierce.

drink 1 to gulp, to guzzle, to lap, to sip, to swallow, (informal) to swig. 2 VARIOUS DRINKS: alcohol, ale, beer, brandy, champagne, cider, cocktail, cocoa, coffee, cordial, gin, juice, lager, lemonade, lime-juice, milk, mineral water, nectar, orangeade, pop, port, sherry, soda-water, squash, tea, vodka, water, whisky, wine. 3 CONTAINERS YOU DRINK FROM: beaker, cup, glass, goblet, mug, tankard, tumbler, wineglass.

drip 1 *The water dripped onto the floor.* to dribble, to leak, to sprinkle, to trickle. 2 *I felt a few drips of rain.* bead, drop.

drive 1 *The starving people were driven to stealing.* to compel, to force, to oblige, to press. 2 *The dog drove the sheep into a pen.* to propel, to push, to urge. 3 *Is it easy to drive a car?* to control, to operate, to pilot, to steer. 4 *He drove the ball over the boundary.* to hit, to strike. 5 *We went for a drive in the car.* excursion, journey, outing, trip. 6 *She does well because she's got lots of drive.* ambition, determination, energy, enthusiasm, keenness, zeal.

drivel SEE **nonsense.**

driver chauffeur.

drizzle mist, rain.

dromedary camel.

droop *The flag drooped in the windless air.* to be limp, to dangle, to flop, to hang, to sag, to wilt.

drop 1 *a drop of liquid.* bead, drip, tear. 2 *to drop to the ground.* to collapse, to descend, to dip, to dive, to fall, to lower, to plunge. 3 *They dropped me from the team.* to eliminate, to exclude, to leave out, to omit. 4 *It isn't nice when a friend drops you.* to abandon, to desert, to dump, to forsake, to leave. 5 *We dropped our plan when we knew what it would cost.* to give up, to scrap. 6 *Some trees drop their leaves in autumn.* to discard, to shed.

drown 1 SEE **kill.** 2 *The floods drowned everything for miles around.* to engulf, to flood, to immerse, to inundate, to overwhelm, to sink, to submerge, to swamp. 3 *The music drowned our voices.* to overpower, to overwhelm.

drowsy

drowsy *Go to bed: you look drowsy.* sleepy, tired, weary.

drudgery *Rich people used to have servants to do all their drudgery.* chores, labour, toil, work.

drug 1 ADDICTIVE DRUGS: (informal) dope, heroin, marijuana, narcotic, nicotine, opium. **2** *Doctors use drugs to cure illnesses.* cure, remedy, treatment. SEE ALSO **medicine**.

drum *an oil drum.* barrel.

drunk *He sounded drunk.* fuddled, intoxicated, (informal) tight.

drunkard alcoholic.

dry 1 *In the desert everything is dry.* arid, dehydrated, parched, thirsty. **2** *a dry book.* boring, dull, tedious, uninteresting. **3** *The flowers dried up.* to shrivel, to wither.

dual *a dual carriageway.* double.

dubious 1 *a dubious expression.* disbelieving, doubtful, incredulous, sceptical, uncertain, unconvinced. **2** *a dubious character.* shady, suspicious, unreliable, untrustworthy.

duck 1 drake, duckling. **2** *We ducked under the low branches.* to bend, to crouch, to dodge, to stoop, to swerve.

dud (informal) *a dud battery.* unusable, useless, worthless.

due 1 *Your club subscription is due.* outstanding, owed, owing, unpaid. **2** *I gave the matter due consideration.* appropriate, decent, fitting, proper, right, suitable. **3** *Is the bus due?* expected, scheduled.

duel *to fight a duel.* bout, combat, contest, fight.

dull 1 *a dull pupil.* dense, dim, obtuse, slow, stupid, (informal) thick, unintelligent. **2** *a dull film.* boring, dry, stodgy, tame, tedious, uninteresting. **3** *a dull sky.* cloudy, grey, overcast, sunless. **4** *dull colours.* dingy, dowdy, drab, gloomy, shabby, sombre. **5** *a dull sound.* deadened, indistinct, muffled.

dumb mute, silent, speechless, tongue-tied.

dumbfounded *When we heard we had won £1000 we were dumbfounded.* amazed, astonished, astounded, nonplussed, speechless, stunned, thunderstruck.

dummy 1 *a dummy revolver.* imitation, model. **2** *a ventriloquist's dummy.* doll, puppet.

dump 1 *a rubbish dump.* rubbish-heap, tip. **2** *an ammunition dump.* cache, depot, hoard, store. **3** *We dumped that old bike.* to discard, to dispose of, to get rid of, to reject, to scrap, to throw away. **4** *Just dump your things on the table.* to drop, to place, to throw down, to unload.

dumpy *a dumpy figure.* chubby, fat, plump, podgy, portly, short, squat, stocky.

dunce SEE **idiot**.

dung manure, muck.

dungeon gaol, prison.

dupe *He duped me into buying a dud radio.* to cheat, to deceive, to defraud, to fool, to hoax, to hoodwink, to swindle, to take in, to trick.

duplicate 1 *a duplicate of the original painting.* copy, double, imitation, likeness, replica, reproduction, twin. **2** *to duplicate a document.* to copy, to photocopy, to print, to reproduce.

durable *durable shoes.* hard-wearing, indestructible, lasting, strong, sturdy, tough, unbreakable, well-made.

dusk evening, gloom, sunset, twilight.

dust 1 *Wipe the dust off the shelf.* dirt, grit, powder, sawdust. **2** *I dusted the shelf.* to clean, to wipe.

dusty *The spare room is dusty.* dirty, filthy, grimy, gritty, grubby, (informal) mucky, sooty.

dutiful *a dutiful worker.* conscientious, diligent, faithful, hard-working, loyal, reliable, responsible, scrupulous, thorough, trustworthy.

duty 1 *a sense of duty towards your country.* allegiance, faithfulness, loyalty, obligation, responsibility. **2** *When we go camping, we each have special duties to perform.* assignment, function, job, task. **3** *customs duty:* customs, tax.

dwarf midget, pigmy. ! These words may be insulting.

dwell to inhabit, to live in, to occupy, to reside in.

dwelling abode, home, house, residence.

dwindle *Our stock of sweets seems to have dwindled.* to contract, to decrease, to diminish, to disappear, to fade, to lessen, to shrink, to shrivel, to subside, to wane.

dye to colour, to paint, to stain, to tint.

dynamic *a dynamic person.* active, energetic, forceful, powerful, vigorous.

E

eager *an eager pupil.* anxious, avid, earnest, enthusiastic, excited, fervent, impatient, intent, interested, keen, passionate, zealous.

early 1 *an early motor car.* ancient, antiquated, old, primitive. 2 *The baby was born early.* prematurely. 3 *earlier:* before, previously. 4 *earliest: the earliest motor car.* first, initial, original.

earn 1 *She earned her success with hard training.* to deserve, to merit. 2 *How much did you earn doing a paper round?* to clear, to gain, to get, to make, to receive, to take home.

earnest *an earnest worker.* conscientious, determined, diligent, grave, hard-working, industrious, serious, sincere, solemn, zealous.

earnings income, pay, salary, wages.

earth 1 *We live on the earth.* globe, world. 2 *Plants grow in the earth.* ground, land, loam, soil.

earthenware china, crockery, porcelain, pottery.

earthquake *The earthquake rocked the town.* shock, tremor.

ease 1 *Grandad hopes for a life of ease when he retires!* comfort, leisure, luxury, relaxation, repose, rest. 2 *Take an aspirin to ease the pain.* to calm, to comfort, to lessen, to quieten, to relieve, to soothe. 3 *Ease the tension in the guy ropes.* to relax, to slacken.

easy 1 *easy work.* effortless, elementary, light, painless. 2 *easy to use.* foolproof, simple, straightforward, uncomplicated. 3 *an easy life.* carefree, comfortable, contented, cosy, leisurely, peaceful, relaxed, relaxing, restful, soft, tranquil, untroubled.

easygoing *Our teacher last year was easygoing, but the new one is strict.* carefree, casual, genial, indulgent, informal, lenient, liberal, patient, relaxed, tolerant, unexcitable.

eat 1 WAYS TO EAT THINGS: to bite, to bolt, to chew, to consume, to devour, to digest, to dine, to feast, to feed on, to gnaw, to gobble, to graze, to gorge, to gulp, to guzzle, to live on, to munch, to nibble, to peck, to swallow, to taste, (informal) to tuck in. 2 *Acid can eat into metal.* to corrode, to rot, to rust. 3 *The river ate the bank away.* to erode, to wear away.

eatable *Is the food eatable?* edible.

eavesdrop *to eavesdrop on other people's conversations.* to listen, to overhear.

ebb *When the tide ebbed we walked out onto the beach.* to flow back, to go down, to recede, to retreat.

eccentric *eccentric behaviour.* cranky, odd, peculiar, strange, unconventional, weird, zany.

echo 1 *The sound echoed back across the valley.* to resound, to reverberate. 2 *The parrot echoed everything I said.* to imitate, to mimic.

economical 1 *It's more economical to walk than to go by bus.* careful with money, sparing, thrifty. 2 *Mum buys economical kinds of meat.* cheap, inexpensive, reasonable.

ecstasy bliss, delight, happiness, joy, pleasure, rapture.

ecstatic *They gave their heroes an ecstatic welcome.* delighted, elated, exultant, gleeful, joyful, overjoyed, rapturous.

eddy *an eddy in the water.* swirl, whirl, whirlpool.

edge 1 *the edge of a field.* border, boundary. 2 *the edge of the road.* side, verge. 3 *the edge of a crowd.* fringe. 4 *the edge of a picture.* frame, margin. 5 *the edge of a cup.* brim, brink, lip, rim. 6 *We edged cautiously away.* to creep, to slink.

edgy *The dog seems edgy: will he bite?* highly-strung, jittery, jumpy, irritable, nervous, tense, touchy, (informal) uptight.

edible *I don't think conkers are edible.* digestible, eatable.

edifice building, structure.

edit *We edited our articles for the magazine.* to adapt, to alter, to compile, to revise, to rewrite.

edition *When will the next edition of the magazine be ready?* issue, number, publication.

educate 1 to bring up, to coach, to indoctrinate, to inform, to instruct, to lecture, to teach, to train. 2 *educated: an educated person.* cultivated, cultured, knowledgeable, learned, literate, well-bred. 3 PLACES WHERE YOU CAN BE EDUCATED: academy, college, kindergarten, play-group, polytechnic, university. SEE ALSO **school.** 4 PEOPLE WHO EDUCATE US: coach, guru, instructor, lecturer, professor, trainer, tutor. SEE ALSO **teacher.**

eerie *The castle looked eerie in the moonlight.* creepy, frightening, ghostly, scary, spooky, uncanny, unearthly, weird.

effect *Did the head's warning have any effect?* consequence, impact, influence, outcome, result, sequel. 2 *The new wallpaper in the bathroom gives a nice effect.* impression.

effective *an effective goalkeeper, an effective cure for colds, etc.* capable, competent, efficient, powerful, productive, proficient, strong, successful.

effervescent *effervescent drinks.* bubbling, bubbly, fermenting, fizzy, foaming, sparkling.

efficient *an efficient worker.* capable, competent, effective, productive, proficient, useful.

effort 1 *You deserve a rest after all that effort.* exertion, labour, struggle, toil, trouble, work. 2 *We made a real effort to win.* attempt, endeavour, try.

effortless *She makes gymnastics look effortless.* easy, painless, simple.

egg (informal) *to egg someone on.* to encourage, to inspire, to prompt, to urge.

eject *He was ejected from the youth club because of his behaviour.* to banish, to discharge, to dismiss, to evict, to expel, (informal) to kick out, to send out, to throw out.

elaborate 1 *an elaborate plan.* complex, complicated, detailed, intricate, involved. 2 *elaborate embroidery.* decorated, fancy, intricate, showy.

elapse *A lot of time has elapsed since we met.* to go by, to pass.

elastic *an elastic band.* springy, stretching.

elated *We were elated by our win.* delighted, ecstatic, joyful, overjoyed. SEE ALSO **happy.**

elderly aged, old.

elect *The gymnastics team elected her as captain.* to appoint, to choose, to name, to nominate, to pick, to select, to vote for.

election *We had an election to choose a captain.* ballot, poll, vote.

electricity WORDS TO DO WITH ELECTRICITY: adaptor, battery, bell, bulb, cable, charger, circuit, dynamo, element, flex, fuse, generator, insulation, lead, meter, negative, plug, positive, power-point, power-station, pylon, socket, switch, terminal, torch, transformer, volt, watt, wire, wiring.

electrifying *an electrifying performance.* exciting, stimulating, thrilling.

elegant *an elegant palace, an elegant dance, etc.* dignified, graceful, handsome, noble, (informal) posh, refined, stately, tasteful. SEE ALSO **beautiful, splendid.**

element 1 *the main elements of a subject.* component, ingredient, part. 2 *The explorers battled against the elements.* weather.

elementary *an elementary problem.* basic, easy, fundamental, simple, uncomplicated.

elevate 1 *The gunners elevated the angle of the big guns.* to lift, to raise. 2 *elevated: an elevated position.* high, raised.

eligible *eligible to enter a race.* acceptable, allowed, authorized, qualified, suitable.

eliminate 1 *How can I eliminate the ants from my garden?* to abolish, to annihilate, to destroy, to end, to eradicate, to exterminate, to finish off, to get rid of, to remove, to stamp out. 2 *Our team was eliminated in the first round.* to knock out. 3 *I was eliminated because I wasn't fit.* to drop, to leave out, to omit, to reject.

elongated drawn out, extended, lengthened, stretched.

eloquent *an eloquent speaker.* fluent, persuasive.

elude *The thieves eluded the police.* to avoid, to dodge, to escape, to evade.

emaciated *The refugees were terribly emaciated.* bony, gaunt, scraggy, skinny, thin, wasted away.

emancipate *to emancipate slaves.* to free, to liberate.

embankment bank, dam.

embark 1 *The sailors embarked at high tide.* to board, to depart, to go, to leave, to set out. 2 *I embarked on my homework.* to begin, to commence, to start, to undertake.

embarrass 1 *He was embarrassed when mum bought him pink underwear.* to disgrace, to distress, to humiliate. 2 *embarrassing:* humiliating, shameful. 3 *embarrassed:* ashamed, distressed, flustered, humiliated, self-conscious, shy, upset.

embedded *My wellingtons were embedded in the mud.* fixed, set.

embers ashes, cinders.

embittered *embittered by failure.* bitter, envious, resentful, sour.

emblem badge, crest, seal, sign, symbol.

embrace *They embraced each other lovingly.* to clasp, to fondle, to grasp, to hold, to hug, to kiss.

embroidery needlework, sewing.

embryo foetus.

emerge *It's nice to see the flowers emerge in the spring.* to appear, to come out, to evolve, to issue, to materialize, to show, to surface.

emergency *We knew there was an emergency when we heard the fire-engine.* crisis, danger, predicament.

emigrate *Many people emigrated from Europe to America.* to depart, to leave, to quit.

eminent *an eminent TV personality.* celebrated, distinguished, famous, great, important, notable, outstanding, prominent, renowned, well-known.

emit *The exhaust of your car emits a lot of smoke.* to belch, to discharge, to expel, to give out, to radiate, to send out, to transmit.

emotion feeling, passion, sentiment.

emotional *Saying goodbye was an emotional moment.* moving, passionate, romantic, sentimental, touching.

emphasize *She emphasized that we must not wander off.* to assert, to insist, to stress, to underline.

employ 1 *The school employs a special teacher to teach music.* to give work to, to pay. 2 *Our doctor employs the most modern methods.* to apply, to use, to utilize. 3 *to be employed in something:* to be active, to be busy, to be engaged, to be involved, to be occupied.

employer boss, chief, head, manager, owner.

employment business, job, occupation, profession, trade, work.

empty 1 *an empty space.* hollow, unfilled, void. 2 *an empty room.* bare, unfurnished. 3 *an empty house.* deserted, desolate, forsaken, uninhabited, unoccupied, vacant. 4 *an empty page.* blank, clean, unused. 5 *Empty the cup. Empty the room.* to clear, to drain, to evacuate.

enable 1 *A little more money will enable us to have a really good time.* to aid, to assist, to help. 2 *A passport enables you to travel to certain countries.* to allow, to authorize, to entitle, to permit.

enchant 1 *The ballet enchanted us.* to allure, to bewitch, to captivate, to charm, to delight, to entrance, to fascinate. 2 *enchanted:* spellbound.

enchantment *The witch's enchantment held them in its power.* charm, magic, spell, witchcraft, wizardry.

encircle *We encircled the area where the tortoise was last seen.* to besiege, to circle, to enclose, to ring, to surround.

enclose *The lions were enclosed behind a high fence.* to confine, to encircle, to envelop, to fence in, to hedge in, to hem in, to imprison, to pen, to restrict, to ring, to shut in, to surround, to wall in.

enclosure *an enclosure for animals.* cage, compound, corral, courtyard, farmyard, fold, pen, run.

encounter 1 *a violent encounter.* battle, clash, confrontation, fight, meeting, struggle. 2 *The plan encountered fierce opposition.* to clash with, to confront, to face, to meet, to run into.

encourage 1 *The supporters encouraged their team.* to cheer up, (informal) to egg on, to inspire, to reassure, to support. 2 *Advertising encourages sales.* to boost, to help, to promote. 3 *Encourage people to pay their subscriptions.* to invite, to prompt, to urge. 4 *encouraging*: favourable, hopeful, promising, reassuring.

encouragement *The team needs encouragement.* boost, incentive, reassurance, support.

end 1 *the end of a film.* close, conclusion, ending, finale, finish. 2 *the end of an ambition.* collapse, death, destruction, downfall, fall, passing, ruin. 3 *the end of a train.* back, rear, tail. 4 *the end of a pin.* point, tip. 5 *What was the end of all your efforts?* consequence, effect, outcome, result. 6 *What end did you have in mind when you started?* aim, intention, objective, purpose. 7 *When does your club membership end?* to cease, to close, to expire, to finish, to stop. 8 *Do you want to end your club membership?* to discontinue, to terminate. 9 *Please end your work now.* to break off, to cut off, to halt, to round off. 10 *We have the power to end all life on earth.* to abolish, to destroy, to eliminate, to get rid of, to kill.

endanger *to endanger someone's life.* to threaten.

endearing *an endearing puppy.* appealing, attractive, charming, lovable.

endeavour *We endeavoured to behave.* to attempt, to exert yourself, to make an effort, to strain, to strive, to try.

endless 1 *an endless journey into space.* boundless, eternal, immeasurable, infinite, limitless, unlimited. 2 *endless chattering.* ceaseless, constant, continual, everlasting, incessant, interminable, non-stop, persistent, unending.

endure 1 *to endure pain.* to abide, to bear, to cope with, to experience, to put up with, to stand, (informal) to stick, to suffer, to tolerate, to undergo, to withstand. 2 *We hope that life on earth will endure for a long time yet.* to carry on, to continue, to exist, to last, to live on, to remain, to stay, to survive.

enemy adversary, antagonist, attacker, foe, opponent, opposition, rival.

energetic *an energetic player.* active, animated, brisk, dynamic, enthusiastic, forceful, hard-working, lively, powerful, spirited, sprightly, vigorous.

energy *The winning team played with tremendous energy.* force, liveliness, might, power, strength, vigour, vitality, zeal, zest.

enforce *The referee enforces the rules.* to carry out, to impose, to inflict, to insist on.

engaged 1 *an engaged couple.* betrothed. 2 *What are you engaged in?* busy, employed, involved, occupied.

engagement 1 *I have another engagement.* appointment. 2 *a fierce engagement between two armies.* battle, clash, encounter, fight, struggle.

engine 1 KINDS OF ENGINE: diesel engine, electric motor, internal combustion engine, jet engine, outboard motor, steam engine, turbine. 2 *a railway engine.* locomotive.

engulf *A tidal wave engulfed the town.* to flood, to inundate, to overwhelm, to submerge, to swallow up, to swamp.

enjoy *Do you enjoy snooker?* to admire, to appreciate, to be pleased by, to delight in, to like, to love, to relish, to revel in.

enjoyable agreeable, amusing, delightful, diverting, entertaining, likeable, pleasant, satisfying.

enjoyment *They ate the food with great enjoyment.* appreciation, delight, pleasure, satisfaction, zest.

enlarge to amplify, to build up, to develop, to expand, to extend, to fill out, to increase, to inflate, to lengthen, to magnify, to swell, to widen.

enlist *to enlist in the army.* to enrol, to join up, to register, to sign on, to volunteer.

enormous *an enormous elephant.* gigantic, gross, huge, immense, mammoth, massive, mighty, monstrous, towering, tremendous, vast. SEE ALSO **big.**

enough *Was there enough food?* adequate, sufficient.

enquire WAYS TO ENQUIRE: to ask, to beg, to demand, to entreat, to implore, to inquire, to query, to question, to request.

enrage to anger, to exasperate, to incense, to inflame, to infuriate, to madden, to provoke, to vex.

enrol 1 *to enrol in the army.* to enlist, to join up, to register, to sign on, to volunteer. 2 *How many people have we enrolled?* to accept, to recruit, to sign up, to take on.

ensemble *a recorder ensemble.* band, group, orchestra.

ensign *a ship's ensign.* banner, colours, flag, standard.

ensnare *to ensnare animals.* to ambush, to capture, to catch, to entangle, to trap.

ensure *Will you ensure that the goldfish gets fed?* to guarantee, to make certain, to secure.

enter *to enter a race.* to come in, to go in, to penetrate.

enterprising *Several enterprising children organized a sponsored walk.* adventurous, ambitious, bold, courageous, daring, energetic, enthusiastic, hard-working, industrious, intrepid, keen, resourceful.

entertain 1 *The comedian entertained the audience.* to amuse, to delight, to divert, to please. 2 *We usually entertain some friends at Christmas.* to cater for, to give hospitality to, to greet, to receive, to welcome.

entertainment 1 amusement, diversion, enjoyment, fun, recreation. 2 KINDS OF ENTERTAINMENT: acrobatics, ballet, cabaret, casino, cinema, circus, comedy, concert, dance, disco, drama, fair, gymkhana, musical, night-club, night-life, opera, pageant, pantomime, play, recital, recitation, radio, rodeo, show, tap-dancing, tattoo, television, variety show, waxworks, zoo. 3 VARIOUS ENTERTAINERS: acrobat, actor, actress, ballerina, broadcaster, clown, comedian, comic, compère, conjuror, contortionist, dancer, DJ, jester, juggler, lion-tamer, magician, matador, minstrel, musician, question-master, singer, star, stunt man, superstar, toreador, trapeze artist, ventriloquist.

enthusiasm 1 *You need plenty of enthusiasm to succeed in sport.* ambition, drive, eagerness, excitement, fervour, keenness, zeal. 2 *His enthusiasms include water-skiing.* craze, diversion, pastime.

enthusiast *a pop music enthusiast.* addict, fan, fanatic, supporter.

enthusiastic *an enthusiastic new manager.* avid, eager, energetic, fervent, keen, lively, passionate, spirited.

entice *I enticed the rabbit into the hutch with a carrot.* to attract, to bribe, to coax, to lure, to tempt.

entire *Did you read the entire book?* complete, full, intact, total, unbroken, whole.

entitle 1 *Grandad's bus pass entitles him to travel free of charge.* to allow, to authorize, to enable, to permit. 2 *What did you entitle your story?* to call, to name.

entrance 1 *You pay at the entrance.* access, door, entry, gate, opening, turnstile, way in. 2 *The ballet entranced everyone.* to bewitch, to captivate, to charm, to delight, to enchant, to fascinate, to spellbind.

entrant *How many entrants are there for the swimming gala?* applicant, candidate, competitor, contestant, participant, rival.

entreat *The captain entreated the passengers to remain calm.* to appeal to, to ask, to beg, to implore, to plead, to request.

entry access, door, entrance, gate, opening, turnstile, way in.

entwine *The wires became entwined.* to coil, to entangle, to tangle, to twist, to wind.

envelop *Fog enveloped the town.* to conceal, to cover, to encircle, to enclose, to surround, to wrap up.

envelope cover, wrapper.

envious bitter, grudging, jealous, resentful.

environment *What kind of environment do you live in?* surroundings.

envy to begrudge, to resent.

epidemic *an epidemic of measles.* outbreak, plague.

episode *What happened in the last episode?* instalment, passage, scene, section.

epistle letter.

epitaph *an epitaph on a tombstone.* inscription.

equal *equal amounts.* equivalent, even, identical, level, matching, the same.

equalize *to equalize the scores.* to balance, to even up.

equilibrium *to keep your equlibrium.* balance, poise, stability, steadiness.

equip *They equipped the hall with new lighting.* to furnish, to provide, to supply.

equipment apparatus, furnishings, gear, hardware, instruments, kit, machinery, outfit, paraphernalia, supplies, tackle.

equivalent *They'll refund the money or give you something of equivalent value.* equal, matching, the same.

era *the Roman era.* age, period, time.

eradicate to abolish, to annihilate, to destroy, to eliminate, to end, to exterminate, to get rid of, to remove, to uproot.

erase *It's easy to erase mistakes when you're using a word-processor.* to blot out, to cancel, to delete, to remove, to rub out, to wipe out.

erect 1 *to erect a tent.* to build, to construct, to pitch, to put up, to raise, to set up. 2 *Human beings stand erect.* upright, vertical.

erode *The river is eroding the bank.* to corrode, to eat away, to grind down, to wear away.

err *It is better to err by arriving early than by arriving late.* to do wrong, to go wrong, to misbehave, to miscalculate.

errand *an errand to the shops.* job, mission, task.

erratic *The team's performance has been erratic lately.* changeable, fickle, inconsistent, irregular, unpredictable, variable.

error *to correct errors in your work.* blunder, fallacy, fault, (informal) howler, inaccuracy, miscalculation, misconception, mistake, misunderstanding, oversight, (informal) slip-up.

erupt *A flow of lava erupted from the volcano.* to be discharged, to be emitted, to belch, to burst out, to gush, to issue, to pour out.

eruption *a volcanic eruption.* explosion, outburst.

escalate *The trouble escalated as more people joined in.* to become worse, to increase, to multiply, to step up.

escalator lift, staircase, stairs.

escapade *Don't get involved in any escapades!* adventure, mischief, prank, scrape.

escape 1 *The prisoner escaped.* to abscond, to bolt, to elope, to flee, to run away, to slip away. 2 *She always escapes the washing-up.* to avoid, to dodge, to elude, to evade, to get away from, to shirk. 3 *His escape wasn't noticed until the morning.* getaway, flight, retreat, running away.

escort 1 *The security man has an escort if he's carrying a lot of money.* companion, guard, guide, protector. 2 *Dad escorted the little ones home after the party.* to accompany, to conduct, to see.

espionage intelligence, spying.

essential 1 *the essential facts.* basic, chief, fundamental, important, indispensable, main, primary, principal. 2 *It's essential that you come.* imperative, necessary, vital.

establish 1 *to establish a new business.* to base, to begin, to construct, to create, to found, to initiate, to install, to introduce, to originate, to set up. 2 *We must establish what to do first.* to agree, to decide, to fix, to settle. 3 *Can you establish where you were last night?* to confirm, to demonstrate, to prove, to show, to verify.

establishment *What sort of establishment does uncle run?* business, company, concern, factory, firm, institution, office, organization, shop.

estate 1 *a housing estate.* area, development. 2 *a family estate.* fortune, inheritance, possessions, property, wealth.

estimate *We estimated the size of the crowd.* to assess, to calculate, to guess, to reckon, to work out.

eternal SEE **everlasting**.

ethnic *ethnic music*. national, racial.

evacuate 1 *The police evacuated everyone from the area*. to clear, to move out, to remove. 2 *The family had to evacuate the blazing house*. to abandon, to desert, to forsake, to leave, to quit.

evade *to evade the washing-up*. to avoid, to dodge, to elude, to escape from, to shirk.

evaporate *The dew evaporated during the morning*. to disappear, to dry up, to vaporize.

even 1 *even ground*. flat, level, smooth. 2 *an even temper*. calm, placid, serene, steady. 3 *the even ticking of the clock*. consistent, regular. 4 *to even up the teams*. to balance, to equalize. 5 *We evened out the wrinkled carpet*. to flatten, to level.

evening dusk, sunset, twilight.

event 1 *a special event*. affair, ceremony, entertainment, experience, function, happening, incident, occasion, occurrence, proceedings. 2 *a sporting event*. championship, competition, contest, match, meeting, tournament.

eventually finally, ultimately.

everlasting 1 *everlasting life*. endless, eternal, immortal, infinite, limitless, timeless, unending. 2 *We get tired of their everlasting quarrelling*. ceaseless, constant, continual, frequent, incessant, interminable, non-stop, perennial, permanent, perpetual, persistent, recurrent, relentless, repeated.

evermore always, eternally, for ever, unceasingly.

everyday *an everyday happening*. accustomed, common, commonplace, conventional, customary, familiar, habitual, normal, ordinary, orthodox, regular, routine, standard, typical, usual.

evict *The landlord evicted them for not paying the rent*. to eject, to expel, (informal) to kick out, to remove, to throw out, to turn out.

evidence *The judge examined the evidence*. data, facts, grounds, information, proof, sign, statistics, testimony.

evident *It is evident that he doesn't like work*. apparent, clear, obvious, plain, self-explanatory, unmistakable.

evil *an evil deed, an evil person*. atrocious, base, foul, hateful, immoral, infamous, malevolent, sinful, sinister, vicious, villainous, wicked, wrong. SEE ALSO **bad**.

evolve *Animals have evolved over millions of years*. to develop, to emerge, to grow, to improve, to progress.

ewe lamb, sheep.

exact *the exact time*. accurate, correct, precise, right, specific, true.

exaggerate to overdo it.

examination 1 *a school examination*. exam, test. 2 *a medical examination*. check-up, inspection, investigation, scrutiny.

examine 1 *We examined the evidence*. to analyse, to check, to inquire into, to inspect, to investigate, to probe, to study, to test. 2 *The police examined the witness*. to cross-examine, to interrogate, to question.

example 1 *Give an example of what you mean*. case, illustration, instance, sample, specimen. 2 *Can we have an example to copy?* model, pattern, prototype.

exasperate SEE **anger**.

excavate *to excavate a hole*. to burrow, to dig, to mine, to scoop, to tunnel, to uncover, to unearth.

exceed *to exceed a target*. to beat, to excel, to go over, to outdo, to outnumber, to surpass, to top.

exceedingly *exceedingly good*. exceptionally, extremely, outstandingly, specially, unusually, very.

excel *Our team excelled theirs in nearly every event*. to beat, to exceed, to outdo, to surpass, to top.

excellent *excellent advice, excellent food, etc*. admirable, brilliant, esteemed, exceptional, (informal) fabulous, (informal) fantastic, fine, first-class, gorgeous, great, impressive, magnificent, marvellous, outstanding, (informal) super, superb, (informal) terrific, tremendous, wonderful.

except besides, excluding.

exceptional 1 *exceptional weather*. abnormal, extraordinary, peculiar, rare, remarkable, special, uncommon, unusual. 2 *an exceptional performance*. SEE **excellent**.

excerpt *an excerpt from 'Treasure Island'*. clip, extract, quotation.

excessive 1 *excessive prices.* exorbitant, extreme, high, uncalled-for, unreasonable. 2 *an excessive amount of food.* extravagant, superfluous, unnecessary.

exchange *He exchanged his old bike for some roller-skates.* to change, to replace, to substitute, to switch, to swop, to trade, to trade in.

excite 1 to agitate, to arouse, to disturb, to electrify, to move, to provoke, to rouse, to stimulate, to stir, to thrill. 2 *excited:* animated, boisterous, delirious, exuberant, frenzied, hysterical, lively, spirited, vivacious, wild.

excitement action, activity, adventure, drama, (informal) kicks, stimulation, suspense, thrill.

exclaim to call, to cry out, to shout, to yell. SEE ALSO **talk.**

exclude to ban, to bar, to keep out, to omit, to prohibit, to shut out.

excruciating *excruciating pain.* agonizing, painful, unbearable.

excursion *an excursion to the seaside.* expedition, jaunt, outing, tour, trip.

excuse 1 *Have you any excuse for what you did?* explanation, defence, justification, pretext, reason. 2 *After hearing the facts, the judge excused him.* to forgive, to free, to let off, to overlook, to pardon.

execute 1 *The pilot executed a difficult manoeuvre.* to accomplish, to carry out, to complete, to do, to perform. 2 *to execute a criminal.* to put to death. 3 WAYS TO EXECUTE PEOPLE: to behead, to crucify, to decapitate, to electrocute, to gas, to guillotine, to hang, to lynch, to shoot, to stone.

executive *an executive in big business.* administrator, director, manager.

exercise 1 *Exercise helps to keep you fit.* activity, aerobics, games, gymnastics, PE, sport. 2 *army exercises.* drill, manoeuvres, training. 3 *to exercise in a gym.* to jog, to keep fit, to practise, to train. 4 *to exercise self-control.* to display, to employ, to show, to use, to wield.

exercise-book jotter, notebook, pad.

exert *to exert yourself:* to attempt, to endeavour, to strain, to strive, to try.

exertion *The exertion made us sweat.* effort, energy, labour, toil, work.

exhaust 1 *The car gives out a lot of exhaust.* fumes, gases, smoke. 2 *We exhausted our money.* to consume, to spend, to use up. 3 *Don't exhaust yourselves.* to drain, to sap, to strain, to tire, to weaken, to wear out, to weary. 4 *exhausted:* breathless, (informal) done in, drained, gasping, panting, tired out, weary, worn out. 5 *exhausting:* arduous, gruelling, hard, laborious, strenuous, tiring.

exhaustive *an exhaustive search.* careful, complete, meticulous, thorough.

exhibit *We exhibited our art work.* to demonstrate, to display, to present, to produce, to show.

exhibition *an exhibition of paintings.* demonstration, display, presentation, show.

exile 1 *to exile someone from his country.* to banish, to deport, to eject, to expel, to send away. 2 *An exile longs to be back in her own country.* outcast, refugee, wanderer.

exist 1 *Do dragons exist?* to be, to occur. 2 *We can't exist without water.* to endure, to keep going, to live, to remain, to survive.

exit door, outlet, way out.

exorbitant *exorbitant prices.* excessive, high, unreasonable.

expand *He hopes his business will expand.* to amplify, to build up, to enlarge, to fill out, to grow, to increase, to lengthen, to swell, to widen.

expanse *an expanse of water.* area, sheet, surface.

expect 1 *We are expecting snow.* to anticipate, to forecast, to foresee, to hope for, to wait for. 2 *expecting a baby:* expectant, pregnant.

expedition *a hunting expedition.* excursion, exploration, journey, mission, outing, safari, tour, trek, trip, voyage.

expel *to expel someone from school.* to banish, to deport, to discharge, to dismiss, to eject, to evict, to exile, (informal) to kick out, to send away, to throw out.

expense cost, expenditure, payment, price.

expensive *expensive jewellery.* costly, dear, exorbitant, extravagant, lavish, luxurious, precious, priceless, (informal) pricey, valuable.

experience 1 *He has a lot of experience.* knowledge, wisdom. 2 *Flying in a helicopter is an exciting experience.* event, happening, incident, occurrence. 3 *to experience pain.* to endure, to feel, to go through, to know, to live through, to see, to suffer, to undergo.

experienced *an experienced craftsman.* accomplished, competent, expert, knowledgeable, proficient, qualified, skilled, trained.

experiment *a scientific experiment.* test, trial.

expert 1 *an expert mechanic.* clever, experienced, knowledgeable, professional, proficient, qualified, skilful, skilled, talented, trained. 2 *Ask an expert.* authority, professional, specialist.

expire 1 *My club membership expires this month.* to cease, to end, to finish, to run out, to stop, to terminate. 2 *The wounded animal expired.* to die, to pass away, to perish.

explain *Can you explain how a computer works?* to account for, to analyse, to clarify, to define, to demonstrate, to describe, to illustrate, to interpret, to justify, to make clear, to show.

explanation *Do you believe his explanation?* account, answer, definition, description, excuse, justification, reason, theory.

explode to blow up, to burst, to detonate, to go off, to set off.

exploit 1 *the exploits of King Arthur.* act, adventure, deed, feat. 2 *The owners exploited the slaves.* to take advantage of, to use, to utilize. 3 *exploited:* downtrodden, oppressed.

explore 1 *We explored the woods.* to discover, to look around, to travel about. 2 *We explored the problem.* to examine, to inquire into, to investigate, to probe.

explorer discoverer, pioneer, prospector.

explosion bang, blast, eruption, outburst, report.

explosive KINDS OF EXPLOSIVE: dynamite, gelignite, gunpowder, TNT.

expose *to expose a secret.* to bare, to disclose, to display, to divulge, to make known, to reveal, to show, to uncover.

express *We expressed our thanks.* to communicate, to describe, to make known, to put into words, to say, to speak, to talk, to utter.

expression 1 *Her expression shows she's had bad news.* countenance, face, look. 2 EXPRESSIONS ON PEOPLE'S FACES: beam, frown, glare, glower, grimace, grin, laugh, leer, pout, scowl, smile, smirk, sneer, wince, yawn. 3 *We learned a few French expressions.* phrase, remark, saying, statement, word.

expressionless *an expressionless face.* blank, vacant.

exquisite *an exquisite piece of jewellery.* beautiful, dainty, delicate, elegant, fine, lovely, perfect.

extend 1 *The pier extends into the sea.* to project, to reach out, to stick out, to stretch out. 2 *You can extend this ladder.* to draw out, to elongate, to enlarge, to lengthen, to prolong, to stretch. 3 *We extend a warm welcome to all.* to give, to offer.

extension *an extension to a house.* addition, annexe, enlargement, wing.

extensive 1 *an extensive forest.* broad, large, vast, wide. 2 *extensive damage.* general, wholesale, widespread.

extent *the extent of a piece of land.* amount, area, breadth, degree, dimensions, distance, length, limit, magnitude, measure, measurement, range, reach, scope, size.

exterior *the exterior of a house.* outside, shell, skin, surface.

exterminate *Dad exterminated an ants' nest.* to annihilate, to destroy, to eliminate, to eradicate, (informal) to finish off, to kill, to slaughter, to wipe out.

external *The external appearance of the house was attractive.* exterior, outer, outside, outward.

extinct *Dinosaurs are extinct.* dead, died out.

extinguish *to extinguish a candle.* to put out, to quench, to snuff.

extra *We need extra milk for the weekend.* additional, further, more, spare, supplementary.

extract 1 *The dentist extracted the bad tooth.* to draw out, to pull out, to remove, to take out. 2 *an extract from 'Oliver Twist'.* clip, excerpt, passage, quotation.

extraordinary *We hardly believed his extraordinary story.* abnormal, amazing, curious, exceptional, fantastic, funny, incredible, miraculous, notable, odd, peculiar, phenomenal, queer, rare, remarkable, singular, special, strange, stupendous, unbelievable, uncommon, unusual.

extravagant *It was extravagant to buy the biggest ice-creams.* excessive, expensive, lavish, prodigal, wasteful.

extreme 1 *the extreme end of the runway.* farthest, furthest, furthermost, ultimate. 2 *extreme difficulties.* acute, drastic, excessive, great, intense, severe. 3 *from one extreme to the other.* end, limit, maximum, opposite.

exuberant *The winning team was in an exuberant mood.* animated, boisterous, cheerful, energetic, excited, lively, spirited, sprightly.

exultant *She was exultant when she won the cup.* delighted, ecstatic, elated, gleeful, joyful, overjoyed, rapturous.

eyesore *The quarry is an eyesore.* blemish, blot.

eyewitness *The police asked the eyewitness to describe the accident.* bystander, observer, onlooker, spectator, witness.

F

fabric cloth, material, textile.

fabulous 1 *fabulous monsters.* fictional, imaginary, legendary, mythical, non-existent. 2 (informal) *a fabulous record.* SEE **excellent**.

face 1 *He made a funny face.* countenance, expression, features, look. 2 *A cube has six faces.* front, side, surface. 3 *Our house faces the pie factory.* to look at, to overlook. 4 *The explorers faced many dangers.* to confront, to encounter, to meet.

facetious *facetious remarks.* amusing, comic, funny, humorous, joking, witty.

fact *I want the full facts.* circumstances, data, details, evidence, information, reality, statistics, truth.

factory *places where things are made:* forge, foundry, manufacturing plant, mill, refinery, workshop.

fade 1 *The sun faded the curtains.* to bleach, to discolour, to whiten. 2 *The light faded.* to decline, to diminish, to disappear, to dwindle, to fail, to melt away, to vanish, to wane, to weaken.

fail 1 *His attempt to beat the record failed.* to be unsuccessful, to fall through. 2 *The old man's health was failing.* to decline, to diminish, to disappear, to dwindle, to fade, to melt away, to vanish, to wane, to weaken. 3 *Don't fail to phone us!* to neglect, to omit.

failing *Her main failing is that she is untidy.* defect, fault, imperfection, shortcoming, vice, weakness.

failure *Our attempt to cook a cake was a failure.* disaster, fiasco.

faint 1 *a faint picture.* blurred, dim, faded, hazy, indistinct, misty, pale, shadowy, unclear, weak. 2 *a faint smell.* delicate, slight. 3 *a faint sound.* low, soft. 4 *I felt faint.* dizzy, exhausted, giddy, unsteady, weak. 5 *I fainted in the heat.* to become unconscious, to collapse.

faint-hearted *He made a faint-hearted attempt to stop the thieves.* cowardly, fearful, shy, spineless, timid, timorous, unheroic.

fair 1 carnival, fun-fair. 2 *a Christmas fair*. bazaar, exhibition, festival, fête, market, sale. 3 *fair hair*. blond, light. 4 *a fair referee, a fair decision*. honest, impartial, just, proper, right, unbiased, unprejudiced. 5 *a fair performance*. indifferent, mediocre, middling, moderate, ordinary, reasonable, satisfactory. 6 *fair weather*. bright, cloudless, fine, pleasant, sunny. 7 (old-fashioned) *a fair maiden*. attractive, beautiful, pretty.

fairly moderately, (informal) pretty, rather.

faith 1 *Your dog has faith in you*. belief, confidence, trust. 2 *a religious faith*. conviction, creed, religion.

faithful *The dog is his faithful companion*. consistent, constant, dependable, devoted, dutiful, loyal, reliable, true, trustworthy.

fake 1 *He faked her signature*. to copy, to counterfeit, to feign, to forge, to imitate, to pretend, to reproduce. 2 *faked*: artificial, bogus, false, (informal) phoney, synthetic, unreal. 3 *The £5 note was a fake*. copy, counterfeit, duplicate, forgery, fraud, hoax, imitation, replica, reproduction.

fall 1 *He fell into the river*. to collapse, to drop, to overbalance, to plunge, to tumble. 2 *The temperature falls at night*. to decline, to decrease, to diminish, to lessen. 3 *Millions fell in the war*. to be killed, to die, to perish.

fallacy *a fallacy in your reasoning*. error, inaccuracy, misconception, mistake, misunderstanding.

false 1 *a false idea*. deceptive, inaccurate, incorrect, misleading, mistaken, untrue, wrong. 2 *a false friend*. deceitful, dishonest, disloyal, lying, treacherous, unfaithful. 3 *a false £5 note*. artificial, bogus, counterfeit, fake, imitation, (informal) phoney, synthetic. 4 *a false name, a false story*. assumed, fictitious, made up, unreal.

falsehood (informal) fib, lie, untruth.

falter *He faltered when he saw the danger*. to flinch, to hesitate, to quail, to stagger, to stumble, to totter.

fame *A superstar's fame spreads everywhere*. distinction, glory, importance, prestige, renown, reputation.

familiar 1 *a familiar sight*. common, everyday, normal, regular, usual, well-known. SEE ALSO **ordinary**. 2 *a familiar companion*. close, friendly, intimate. 3 *to be familiar with*: to be acquainted with, to know about.

family 1 brood, clan, generation, kin, kinsmen, litter, relations, relatives, tribe. 2 MEMBERS OF A FAMILY: adopted child, ancestor, aunt, brother, cousin, daughter, descendant, divorcee, father, fiancé, fiancée, forefather, foster-child, foster-parent, godchild, godparent, grandchild, grandparent, guardian, husband, mother, nephew, niece, orphan, parent, quadruplet, quintuplet, sextuplet, sister, son, stepchild, step-parent, triplet, twin, uncle, ward, widow, widower, wife.

famine hunger, malnutrition, starvation.

famished *We were famished after our long walk*. hungry, (informal) peckish, ravenous, starving.

famous *a famous person*. celebrated, distinguished, eminent, great, historic, important, legendary, notable, noted, outstanding, prominent, renowned, well-known.

fan *a football fan*. addict, enthusiast, fanatic, follower, supporter.

fanciful *fanciful ideas*. fantastic, imaginary, make-believe, pretended, unreal.

fancy 1 *fancy patterns on a birthday cake*. decorated, elaborate, ornamental. 2 *I fancied I saw a pink elephant*. to dream, to imagine. 3 *What do you fancy to eat?* to desire, to hanker after, to like, to long for, to prefer, to wish for.

fang *an animal's fang*. tooth.

fantastic 1 *a fantastic story about dragons and wizards*. amazing, extraordinary, fabulous, grotesque, incredible, odd, remarkable, strange, unbelievable, unreal, weird. 2 (informal) *We had a fantastic time*. SEE **excellent**.

fantasy *Alice's adventures in Wonderland were a fantasy*. day-dream, dream, illusion, make-believe, reverie.

far far-away, distant, remote.

fare *How much is the fare to London?* charge, cost, payment, price.

farewell au revoir, goodbye.

far-fetched *a far-fetched story.* improbable, incredible, unbelievable, unconvincing, unlikely.

farm 1 croft, ranch. 2 CROPS GROWN ON FARMS: barley, cereals, corn, fodder, fruit, maize, oats, rye, sugar beet, sweetcorn, vegetables, wheat.
3 ANIMALS KEPT ON FARMS: bantam, bull, bullock, calf, cattle, chicken, cow, duck, goat, goose, hen, horse, lamb, livestock, pig, poultry, pullet, sheep, turkey. 4 FARM BUILDINGS: barn, cow-shed, farmhouse, farmyard, granary, haystack, outhouse, pigsty, rick, shed, silo, stable, sty. 5 FARM EQUIPMENT: baler, combine harvester, cultivator, harrow, harvester, mower, pitchfork, planter, plough, scythe, tractor, trailer.

fascinate 1 *Snakes fascinate some people.* to attract, to bewitch, to captivate, to charm, to enchant, to entice, to entrance, to interest, to spellbind. 2 *fascinating*: alluring, attractive, glamorous.

fashion 1 *the latest fashion.* craze, style, taste, trend, vogue. 2 *He acts in a business-like fashion.* manner, method, mode, style, way.

fashionable *fashionable clothes.* contemporary, modern, smart, sophisticated, stylish, tasteful, (informal) trendy, up-to-date.

fast 1 *a fast pace.* brisk, (informal) nippy, quick, rapid, smart, speedy, swift. 2 *fast colours.* fixed, indelible, permanent.
3 *The ship was fast on the rocks.* firm, immobile, immovable, secure. 4 *In some religions you fast on certain days.* to go without food, to starve.

fasten 1 WAYS OF FASTENING THINGS: to adhere, to attach, to bind, to cling, to close, to connect, to fix, to hitch, to join, to knot, to lash, to link, to lock, to moor, to seal, to secure, to stick, to tether, to tie, to unite, to weld. 2 THINGS USED TO FASTEN: anchor, bolt, buckle, button, cement, chain, clamp, clasp, clip, glue, hook, knot, lock, nail, padlock, paste, peg, pin, rivet, rope, safety-pin, screw, sellotape, solder, staple, strap, string, tack, tape, wedge, zip.

fastidious *fastidious about food.* (informal) choosey, finicky, fussy, particular, squeamish.

fat 1 KINDS OF FAT: butter, dripping, grease, lard, margarine, oil, suet. 2 *a fat person.* chubby, dumpy, flabby, gross, heavy, overweight, plump, podgy, portly, squat, stocky, stout, tubby. 3 *a fat book.* thick. 4 *a fat meat.* fatty, greasy, oily.

fatal *a fatal illness.* deadly, lethal, mortal, terminal.

fatality *There were no fatalities in the accident.* casualty, death.

fate *Fate was kind to him.* chance, destiny, doom, fortune, luck, providence.

fated *He believes he was fated to miss that train.* destined, doomed, intended.

father dad, daddy.

fatigue exhaustion, tiredness, weakness, weariness.

fault 1 *It was my fault.* blame, guilt, responsibility. 2 *Look for any faults in your work.* blemish, defect, error, failing, fallacy, flaw, imperfection, inaccuracy, mistake, shortcoming, slip, vice, weakness.

faulty *Take the faulty goods back.* defective, imperfect, out of order.

favour *Will you do me a favour?* good deed, kindness, service.

favourable 1 *a favourable wind.* beneficial, helpful. 2 *a favourable comment.* approving, encouraging, friendly, generous, kind, sympathetic.

favourite 1 *a favourite toy.* best, chosen, popular, preferred, well-liked. 2 *She's her mother's favourite.* darling, pet.

fear alarm, anxiety, awe, dread, fright, horror, panic, terror.

fearful 1 *fearful of spiders.* afraid, anxious, apprehensive, cowardly, cowed, frightened, scared, terrified.
2 *The volcano was a fearful sight.* alarming, appalling, awful, fearsome, frightening, frightful, horrifying, shocking, terrible, terrific, tremendous.

fearless *fearless rescuers.* bold, brave, courageous, daring, heroic, intrepid, valiant.

feasible *a feasible plan.* possible, practicable, realistic, viable, workable.

feast banquet, dinner, meal.

feat *a daring feat.* achievement, act, action, deed, exploit, performance.

feathers down, plumage, plumes.

feathery downy, fluffy, light.

feature 1 *One feature of the crime puzzled us.* aspect, characteristic, circumstance, detail. 2 *a person's features.* countenance, expression, face.

fee *a fee of £1.* charge, cost, fare, payment, price, subscription, toll.

feeble 1 *I felt feeble after my illness.* delicate, frail, helpless, ill, listless, (informal) poorly, sickly, (informal) weedy. 2 *a feeble defence.* puny, spineless, weak. 3 *feeble excuses.* flimsy, lame, poor, tame, weak.

feed to nourish, to strengthen.

feel 1 *Feel this lovely velvet.* to finger, to handle, to manipulate, to stroke, to touch. 2 *Can you feel your way in the dark?* to grope. 3 *It feels colder today.* to seem. 4 *Do you feel the cold?* to detect, to experience, to know, to notice, to perceive, to sense, to suffer. 5 *I feel it's time to go home.* to believe, to consider, to think.

feeling 1 *What were your feelings when you won?* emotion, passion, sensation, sentiment. 2 *Our feeling was that they didn't want to come.* attitude, belief, impression, opinion, thought. 3 *There was a happy feeling at the party.* atmosphere, mood, tone. 4 *I have a feeling I'm going to be lucky.* guess, hunch, instinct, intuition.

feign SEE **pretend.**

fell 1 down, hill. 2 *A lumberjack fells trees.* to cut down, to knock down.

fellow SEE **man.**

fellowship *Most people enjoy the fellowship of others.* companionship, company, friendship, society.

female FEMALE CREATURES: bitch, cow, doe, ewe, hen, lioness, mare, nanny-goat, sow, tigress, vixen.

feminine *feminine clothes.* female, girlish, ladylike, womanly.

fen bog, marsh, swamp.

fence 1 *a garden fence.* barrier, hedge, hurdle, obstacle, paling, palisade, railing, stockade, wall. 2 *We fenced in the animals.* to encircle, to enclose, to hedge in, to pen, to surround, to wall in.

fend *The boxer fended off his opponent's blows.* to keep off, to parry, to push away, to repel, to repulse, to ward off.

ferment to bubble, to effervesce, to fizz, to foam.

ferocious *a ferocious attack.* barbaric, barbarous, bloodthirsty, bloody, brutal, cruel, fierce, inhuman, merciless, murderous, pitiless, ruthless, sadistic, savage, vicious, violent.

ferry *The ship ferried us to the island.* to carry, to convey, to take, to transfer, to transport.

fertile *a fertile garden.* flourishing, fruitful, lush, productive.

fertilizer compost, manure.

fervent *I am a fervent follower of the local team.* avid, eager, enthusiastic, keen, passionate, zealous.

festering *a festering wound.* infected, inflamed, poisoned, putrid.

festival carnival, celebration, fair, feast, festivity, fête, gala, jamboree, jubilee.

festive *Christmas is a festive occasion.* cheerful, gay, gleeful, happy, joyful, joyous, light-hearted, merry.

fetch *Our dog fetches the newspaper.* to bring, to carry, to collect, to get, to obtain, to retrieve.

fetching *a fetching dress.* appealing, attractive, charming, lovely, pretty. SEE ALSO **beautiful.**

fête carnival, fair, festival, gala, jamboree.

fetters *The prisoner was in fetters.* bonds, chains, handcuffs, irons, shackles.

feud *a bitter feud between two families.* dispute, quarrel, strife, vendetta.

fiasco *Our play was a fiasco.* disaster, failure, (informal) flop, (informal) mess-up.

fib SEE **lie.**

fibre strand, thread.

fickle *Our weather is so fickle that you never know what clothes to wear.* changeable, erratic, inconsistent, unpredictable, unreliable, variable.

fictional, fictitious *His story was fictitious.* fabulous, false, fanciful, imaginary, invented, legendary, made-up, mythical, unreal.

fiddle 1 violin. 2 *Please don't fiddle with the knobs on the TV.* to fidget, to twiddle.

fidelity faithfulness, honesty, integrity.

fidget *It irritates me when you fidget!* to be restless, to fiddle, to jerk, to twiddle, to twitch.

fidgety *The horses became fidgety as the storm approached.* impatient, jittery, jumpy, nervous, restless.

field 1 *Cows grazed in the field.* enclosure, meadow, paddock, pasture. 2 *a games field:* arena, ground, pitch, stadium.

field-glasses binoculars.

fiend demon, devil, imp, spirit.

fierce *a fierce attack, a fierce animal, etc.* angry, barbaric, bloodthirsty, brutal, cruel, ferocious, merciless, murderous, savage, vicious, violent.

fiery 1 *a fiery furnace.* blazing, burning, flaming, hot, red, red-hot. 2 *a fiery temper.* angry, furious, livid, mad, raging.

fight KINDS OF FIGHT: action, attack, battle, bout, boxing-match, brawl, clash, combat, competition, conflict, confrontation, contest, counter-attack, duel, encounter, engagement, feud, hostilities, joust, quarrel, raid, rivalry, row, scramble, scrap, scuffle, squabble, strife, struggle, tussle, vendetta, war, wrestling.

fighter VARIOUS FIGHTERS: archer, boxer, gladiator, guerrilla, gunman, knight, marine, mercenary, paratrooper, partisan, troops, warrior, wrestler. SEE ALSO **soldier.**

figure 1 *the figures 1 to 10.* digit, integer, number, numeral. 2 *good at figures.* mathematics, sums, statistics. 3 *a plump figure.* form, outline, shape. 4 *a bronze figure.* carving, image, statue. 5 *Figure out how much we owe.* to add up, to calculate, to compute, to reckon, to total, to work out.

file 1 *single file.* column, line, queue, rank, row. 2 *Keep your papers in a file.* folder.

fill 1 *Fill the box with sweets.* to cram, to crowd, to load up, to pack, to occupy. 2 *The drain was filled with muck.* to block up, to jam, to obstruct, to plug, to stop up. 3 *Don't pick the peas until the pods fill out.* to enlarge, to expand, to swell.

film 1 VARIOUS CINEMA OR TV FILMS: cartoon, documentary, feature, movie, western. 2 *a film of oil.* coating, covering, layer, sheet, skin.

filter *You filter the liquid to remove the solid bits.* to sieve, to strain.

filth dirt, grime, (informal) muck, mud, pollution.

filthy 1 *filthy shoes, a filthy room, etc.* caked, dirty, dusty, foul, grimy, grubby, messy, (informal) mucky, muddy, soiled, sooty, sordid, squalid. 2 *filthy language.* coarse, crude, improper, indecent, offensive, rude, smutty, vulgar.

final *the final moments of the game.* closing, concluding, last, ultimate.

finally eventually, ultimately.

find 1 *Where do you find fossils?* to come across, to discover, to dig up, to locate, to uncover, to unearth. 2 *Did mum find her handbag?* to get back, to recover, to retrieve, to trace. 3 *Did you find your friends?* to encounter, to meet. 4 *Did the garage find the fault in the car?* to detect, to diagnose, to identify, to notice, to observe.

fine 1 *a parking fine.* charge, penalty. 2 *fine weather.* bright, cloudless, fair, pleasant, sunny. 3 *a fine thread.* narrow, slender, slim, thin. 4 *fine sand.* minute, powdered, powdery. 5 *fine embroidery.* beautiful, dainty, delicate, exquisite. 6 *a fine performance.* admirable, excellent, first-class. SEE ALSO **good.**

finger *Please don't finger the food.* to feel, to handle, to stroke, to touch.

finicky *finicky about food.* (informal) choosey, fastidious, fussy, particular.

finish 1 *Finish your work.* to accomplish, to complete, to conclude, to end, to round off, to stop, to terminate. 2 *Did we finish the sweets?* to consume, to exhaust, (informal) to polish off, to use up. 3 *When did they finish dinner?* to break off, to cease, to discontinue, to halt. 4 (informal) *to finish off:* to destroy, to dispatch, to exterminate. SEE ALSO **kill.**

fiord inlet.

fire 1 blaze, bonfire, conflagration, inferno. 2 *Modern houses don't always have a fire in the lounge.* fireplace, grate, hearth. 3 KINDS OF HEATING APPARATUS: boiler, central heating, convector, electric fire, forge, furnace, gas fire, heater, immersion heater, incinerator, kiln, oven, stove. 4 *The vandals fired a barn.* to burn, to ignite, to kindle, to light, to set fire to. 5 *to fire a gun.* to detonate, to discharge, to explode, to let off. 6 *The gunners fired at the ship.* to bombard, to shell. 7 *His boss fired him.* to dismiss, to sack.

firearms 1 guns. 2 VARIOUS FIREARMS: machine-gun, pistol, revolver, rifle, shotgun, sub-machine-gun. SEE ALSO **weapon**.

fireplace fire, grate, hearth.

firework VARIOUS FIREWORKS: banger, Catherine wheel, cracker, rocket, sparkler, squib.

firm 1 *Is the ice firm?* hard, rigid, solid, stable, stiff, unyielding. 2 *Is the nail firm?* fast, fixed, immovable, secure, steady, tight. 3 *a firm refusal.* adamant, decided, determined, dogged, obstinate, persistent, resolute, unwavering. 4 *a firm agreement.* agreed, settled, unchangeable. 5 *a firm friend.* constant, dependable, devoted, faithful, loyal, reliable. 6 *He wants to be boss of his own firm.* business, company, concern, corporation, establishment, organization.

first 1 *Who was first to arrive?* earliest, soonest. 2 *Who made the first aeroplane?* initial, original. 3 *Who is your first choice?* foremost, leading, prime.

first-class SEE **excellent**.

fish 1 VARIOUS FISH: carp, chub, cod, eel, goldfish, haddock, herring, jellyfish, mackerel, minnow, octopus, perch, pike, pilchard, plaice, salmon, sardine, shark, sole, squid, starfish, stickleback, tiddler, trout. 2 PARTS OF A FISH: dorsal fin, fin, gills, roe, scales, tail. 3 FISHING: angling, trawling.

fist hand, knuckles.

fit 1 *Is that old house fit to live in?* appropriate, fitting, proper, right, suitable. 2 *Will you be fit for the game?* able, capable, healthy, prepared, ready, strong, well. 3 *Do casual clothes fit the occasion?* to become, to suit. 4 *Can you fit the pieces together?* to assemble, to build, to construct, to put together. 5 *a fit of coughing.* attack, bout, convulsion, outbreak, seizure, spasm.

fitting appropriate, apt, due, proper, right, suitable, timely.

fix 1 *to fix something into place, to fix things together.* to attach, to bind, to join, to link, to make firm, to secure. SEE ALSO **fasten**. 2 *to fix a price for something.* to agree, to arrange, to decide, to establish, to settle. 3 *to fix a broken window.* to mend, to put right, to repair. 4 *to get into a fix.* difficulty, dilemma, jam, plight, predicament, problem.

fixture *a sporting fixture.* appointment, engagement, meeting.

fizz to bubble, to effervesce, to fizzle, to foam, to froth.

fizzy *fizzy drinks.* bubbly, effervescent, foaming, sparkling.

flabby *a flabby tummy.* fat, feeble, overweight, out of condition, weak.

flag 1 *decorated with flags.* banner, colours, ensign, streamer. 2 *Our interest flagged.* to decline, to flop, to sink, to weaken, to wilt, to worsen.

flake *flakes of old paint, flakes of flint.* bit, chip, scale, slice, splinter.

flame to blaze, to flare. SEE ALSO **burn**.

flap *The flag flapped in the wind.* to flutter, to swing, to wave.

flare to blaze, to flame. SEE ALSO **burn**.

flash SEE **light**.

flashy *flashy clothes.* bright, elaborate, fancy, gaudy, showy.

flask bottle.

flat 1 *a flat surface.* even, horizontal, level, smooth. 2 *a flat sea.* calm. 3 *to lie in a flat position.* prone, spread out. 4 *a flat voice.* boring, dull, monotonous, unexciting, uninteresting.

flatten 1 *We must flatten the lawn if we want to play cricket on it.* to even out, to iron out, to level, to press, to roll, to smooth. 2 *The hurricane flattened the town.* to crush, to demolish, to destroy, to devastate, to knock down. 3 *Vandals flattened the flowerbeds.* to run over, to trample. 4 *We flattened the opposition.* SEE **defeat**.

flatter 1 to humour. 2 *flattering*: *a flattering remark.* complimentary.

flavour character, characteristic, quality, taste.

flaw *a flaw in a piece of work.* blemish, crack, defect, error, fault, imperfection, inaccuracy, mistake, shortcoming, weakness.

flee *We fled when the lion roared.* to abscond, to escape, to run away.

fleet *a fleet of ships.* armada, convoy, navy, squadron.

flesh meat, muscle.

flex *The flex for our iron needs replacing.* cable, lead, wire.

flexible bendable, (informal) bendy, floppy, pliable, soft, springy, supple.

flick to flip. SEE ALSO **hit.**

flicker *The candles flickered.* to blink, to flutter, to glimmer, to quiver, to tremble, to twinkle, to waver.

flight escape, getaway, retreat, running away.

flimsy *A butterfly's wings seem so flimsy.* brittle, delicate, feeble, frail, fragile, rickety, shaky, slight, thin, weak.

flinch *He bore the pain without flinching.* to cringe, to falter, to jerk away, to quail, to recoil, to shrink back, to wince.

fling SEE **throw.**

flip to flick.

flit *Bats flitted about.* to dart, to fly, to skim.

float 1 *to float on water.* to drift, to sail, to swim. 2 *to float in the air.* to drift, to hang, to hover. 3 *We're ready to float our raft.* to launch.

floe ice, iceberg.

flog to beat, to cane, to lash, to scourge, to thrash, to wallop, to whip. SEE ALSO **hit.**

flood 1 *When the dam burst a flood of water swept through the valley.* deluge, inundation, spate, torrent. 2 *The water flooded the whole town.* to drown, to engulf, to inundate, to overflow, to submerge, to swamp.

floodlights SEE **light.**

floor 1 VARIOUS FLOOR COVERINGS: carpet, lino, mat, matting, rug, tiles. 2 *The bedrooms are on the top floor.* deck, level, storey.

flop *The seedlings began to flop.* to collapse, to dangle, to droop, to drop, to fall, to flag, to sag, to wilt.

floppy *The cabbage seedlings have gone floppy.* bendable, (informal) bendy, flexible, limp, pliable.

flounder *We floundered about in the mud.* to struggle, to wallow.

flourish 1 *My plants are flourishing now that we've had some rain.* to be fruitful, to be successful, to bloom, to blossom, to flower, to grow, to prosper, to strengthen, to succeed, to thrive. 2 *He flourished his umbrella to attract our attention.* to brandish, to shake, to twirl, to wave.

flow WAYS IN WHICH LIQUIDS FLOW: to dribble, to drip, to ebb, to gush, to leak, to move in a current, to ooze, to pour, to run, to seep, to stream, to trickle.

flower 1 *There are flowers in the garden.* bloom, blossom, petal. 2 *a bunch of flowers*: arrangement, bouquet, garland, posy, spray, wreath. 3 VARIOUS FLOWERS: bluebell, buttercup, carnation, catkin, chrysanthemum, cornflower, cowslip, crocus, daffodil, daisy, dandelion, forget-me-not, foxglove, geranium, hollyhock, hyacinth, iris, lilac, lupin, marigold, orchid, pansy, peony, pink, poppy, primrose, rhododendron, rose, snowdrop, sunflower, tulip, violet, wallflower, water-lily.

fluent *a fluent speaker of French.* eloquent, flowing, unhesitating.

fluffy *fluffy toys.* downy, feathery, fleecy, furry, fuzzy, woolly.

fluid *a fluid substance.* flowing, liquid, runny, sloppy, watery.

fluke *It was only a fluke that you scored.* accident, chance, luck.

flush 1 *to flush the lavatory.* to rinse out, to wash out. 2 *He flushed with embarrassment.* to blush, to colour, to glow, to redden.

flustered *Keep calm: don't get flustered.* confused, distressed, embarrassed, nervous.

flutter *The leaves fluttered in the wind.* to flap, to flicker, to quiver, to tremble.

fly 1 *Most birds fly.* to flit, to glide, to hover, to rise, to soar, to swoop. **2** *A flag was flying.* to flap, to flutter, to wave.

foam 1 froth, lather, scum, suds. **2** *What makes the water foam?* to bubble, to effervesce, to fizz, to froth, to lather.

focus 1 *Let's focus on the main problem.* to concentrate on, to look at, to think about. **2** *The market square is the main focus of the town.* centre, core, heart, hub.

fodder hay, silage.

foe adversary, antagonist, attacker, enemy, opponent, opposition, rival.

foetus embryo.

fog cloud, haze, mist.

foil 1 *The security officer foiled the thieves.* to block, to frustrate, to halt, to hamper, to hinder, to obstruct, to prevent, to stop. **2** *to fight with foils.* sword.

fold 1 *Fold the paper.* to bend, to crease, to double over. **2** *My umbrella folds up.* to collapse. **3** *The curtains hung in folds.* crease, pleat, wrinkle. **4** *The dog drove the sheep into the fold.* compound, enclosure, pen.

folder *a folder to keep papers in.* cover, file.

foliage *We want some foliage to put with the flowers.* greenery, leaves.

folk human beings, humanity, people.

follow 1 *Follow the car in front!* to chase, to hound, to hunt, to pursue, to shadow, to stalk, to tag on to, to tail, to track. **2** *Another bus follows this one in a few minutes.* to come after, to replace, to succeed. **3** *Follow the instructions.* to heed, to keep to, to obey, to observe, to take notice of. **4** *Did you follow what he said?* to comprehend, to grasp, to understand. **5** *Do you follow football?* to be interested in, to know about, to support.

follower admirer, apostle, disciple, fan, supporter.

fond *a fond kiss.* affectionate, attached, loving, partial, tender.

fondle *He fondled the dog's ears.* to caress, to kiss, to pat, to pet, to stroke, to touch.

food 1 delicacy, diet, fodder, (informal) grub, nourishment, protein, provisions, recipe, refreshments, swill, vitamins. **2** KINDS OF FOOD: batter, beans, blancmange, bran, bread, broth, caviare, cheese, chips, chop suey, cornflakes, cornflour, cream, crisps, curry, custard, dumplings, egg, flour, fritter, glucose, goulash, greens, haggis, hash, health foods, honey, hot-pot, ice-cream, icing, jam, jelly, junket, kipper, kosher food, lasagne, macaroni, malt, marmalade, milk, mincemeat, mince pie, mousse, noodles, oatmeal, omelette, pancake, pasta, pastry, pasty, pâté, pie, pizza, porridge, pudding, quiche, rice, risotto, rissole, rusk, sandwich, sausage, sausage roll, scampi, seafood, semolina, soufflé, soup, soya beans, spaghetti, stew, stock, stuffing, syrup, tart, toast, treacle, trifle, vegetarian food, wholemeal flour, yeast, yoghurt. SEE ALSO **biscuit, cake, cereal, fat, fish, fruit, meat, nut, salad, vegetable. 3** THINGS YOU ADD TO FOOD: chutney, colouring, dressing, garlic, gravy, herbs, ketchup, mayonnaise, mustard, pepper, pickle, preservative, salt, sauce, seasoning, spice, sugar, vanilla, vinegar.

fool 1 ass, blockhead, booby, dope, dunce, half-wit, idiot, ignoramus, imbecile, moron, nit, nitwit, twerp. !These words are mostly used informally and are often insulting. **2** *the king's fool.* clown, entertainer, jester. **3** *He fooled us by saying he'd won a prize.* to bluff, to cheat, to deceive, to dupe, to hoax, to hoodwink, to kid, to mislead, to swindle, to take in, to trick.

foolish *It's foolish to play with fire.* absurd, crazy, frivolous, idiotic, irrational, ludicrous, misguided, ridiculous, silly, stupid, unwise.

foot 1 hoof, paw. **2** PARTS OF A FOOT: ankle, heel, instep, sole, toe.

football 1 soccer. **2** WORDS USED IN FOOTBALL: ball, corner, cup tie, defender, draw, forward, foul, goal, goalkeeper, linesman, match, offside, penalty, pitch, referee, striker, touch-line.

forbid *They forbid smoking in the house.* to ban, to bar, to deter, to outlaw, to prohibit, to veto.

forbidding *forbidding storm-clouds.* gloomy, grim, menacing, ominous, stern, threatening, unfriendly.

force 1 *We used all our force to open the door.* energy, might, power, pressure, strength, vigour. 2 *You can't force me to play with you.* to compel, to drive, to make, to oblige, to order. 3 *We had to force the door.* to break open, to burst open, to wrench.

forceful *a forceful leader.* dynamic, energetic, enthusiastic, masterful, powerful, strong, vigorous.

foreboding *I had a foreboding that something nasty would happen.* omen, premonition, warning.

forefather ancestor, predecessor.

foreign 1 *a foreign country.* alien, strange, unfamiliar. 2 *foreign goods.* imported.

foreigner *Many foreigners pass through the airport.* alien, immigrant, outsider, visitor.

foreman boss, controller, head, superintendent, supervisor.

foresee *Do they foresee any improvement in the weather?* to anticipate, to expect, to forecast, to foretell, to predict, to prophesy.

forethought planning.

forfeit *to pay a forfeit.* fine, penalty.

forge 1 *a blacksmith's forge.* furnace. 2 *to forge £5 notes.* to copy, to counterfeit, to fake, to imitate.

forgery copy, fake, fraud, imitation, replica, reproduction.

forget 1 *We almost forgot Mother's Day last year.* to disregard, to ignore, to leave out, to miss out, to neglect, to overlook, to skip. 2 *I forgot my money.* to leave behind.

forgetful absent-minded, careless, inattentive, negligent, scatterbrained, thoughtless.

forgive to excuse, to pardon, to spare.

forked *a forked stick.* branched, divided, V-shaped.

forlorn SEE **sad.**

form 1 *a human form.* figure, outline, shape. 2 *What form of exercise do you like best?* kind, sort, type, variety. 3 *We're in the same form at school.* class, group, set. 4 *We sat on a form.* bench, seat. 5 *If you want a bus pass, you fill in a form.* document, paper. 6 *I formed the clay into a ball.* to cast, to mould, to shape. 7 *They form an excellent team.* to compose, to constitute, to create, to make up, to produce. 8 *Icicles formed under the bridge.* to appear, to develop, to grow, to take shape.

formal *The prize-giving was a formal occasion.* ceremonial, dignified, official, (informal) posh, proper, solemn, stately.

forsake *The dog never forsook his master.* to abandon, to desert, to evacuate, to give up, to leave, to quit, to renounce.

fort castle, citadel, fortress, garrison, stronghold.

forthwith directly, immediately, instantly, promptly.

fortify to defend, to protect, to reinforce, to strengthen.

fortitude *She endured the pain with fortitude.* bravery, courage, heroism, patience, (informal) pluck, valour.

fortress castle, citadel, fort, garrison, stronghold.

fortunate *a fortunate accident.* favourable, happy, lucky.

fortune 1 *good fortune, bad fortune.* chance, destiny, fate, luck, providence. 2 *The duke lost his fortune by gambling.* estate, inheritance, possessions, property, wealth.

fortune-teller prophet.

forward SEE **cheeky.**

forwards ahead, onwards.

foul 1 *a foul mess.* dirty, disgusting, filthy, nasty, nauseating, obnoxious, repulsive, revolting. SEE ALSO **unpleasant.** 2 *foul weather.* rainy, rough, stormy, violent, windy. 3 *foul language.* blasphemous, coarse, common, crude, improper, indecent, offensive, rude, uncouth, vulgar. 4 *a foul crime.* atrocious, cruel, evil, monstrous, vicious, vile, villainous, wicked. 5 *foul air.* contaminated, impure, infected, polluted, smelly, unclean. 6 *a foul stroke.* illegal, prohibited.

found 1 *Grandad founded a business in the High Street.* to begin, to create, to establish, to set up. 2 *They founded the castle on solid rock.* to base, to build, to construct, to erect.

foundation *the foundations of a building.* base, basis, bottom, foot.

fountain *a fountain of water.* jet, spray.

fowl bird, chicken, hen.

foyer entrance, hall, lobby.

fraction 1 *Only a fraction of the crowd could hear what was going on.* part, portion, section. 2 *to divide something into fractions.* shares.

fracture *to fracture a leg.* to break, to crack.

fragile *Eggshell is fragile.* breakable, brittle, delicate, frail, thin.

fragments 1 *The teapot smashed into fragments.* atoms, bits, particles, smithereens. 2 *Sweep up the fragments.* chips, crumbs, debris, pieces, remnants, scraps, snippets, specks.

frail 1 *As you get old, you get more frail.* delicate, feeble, infirm, unsteady, weak, (insulting) weedy. 2 *The first aircraft were frail machines.* brittle, flimsy, fragile, rickety.

frame 1 *a frame for a tent.* framework, skeleton. 2 *a frame for a picture.* border, edge, edging. 3 *He framed his picture in a coloured border.* to enclose, to mount, to surround.

framework frame, outline, plan, skeleton, structure.

frank *a frank reply.* candid, direct, honest, open, outspoken, plain, sincere, straightforward.

frantic *Dad went frantic when he lost his wallet.* berserk, crazy, demented, deranged, frenzied, hectic, hysterical, mad, wild.

fraud *The so-called magic was a fraud.* cheat, counterfeit, deceit, deception, dishonesty, fake, hoax, ruse, sham, trick.

fraudulent cheating, crooked, deceitful, dishonest, false, lying, underhand, unscrupulous.

frayed *a frayed collar.* ragged, tattered, (informal) tatty, worn.

freak *a freak storm.* abnormal, exceptional, peculiar, queer, unusual.

free 1 *Are you free to come?* able, allowed, permitted. 2 *The slaves wanted to be free.* emancipated, liberated, released. 3 *Our uncle is free with his money.* bounteous, generous, lavish, liberal. 4 *Is the lavatory free?* available, open, unoccupied, vacant. 5 *The judge freed him.* to acquit, to discharge, to let off, to let go, to pardon, to spare. 6 *Robin Hood freed his friends from the castle.* to liberate, to release, to rescue, to save, to set free.

freedom *The slaves wanted their freedom.* independence, liberty.

free-wheel *We free-wheeled downhill.* to coast, to drift, to glide.

freeze *to freeze food.* to chill, to ice, to refrigerate.

freight *Some aircraft carry passengers and some carry freight.* cargo, goods, load, merchandise.

frenzied *The frenzied fans screamed.* berserk, crazy, delirious, demented, frantic, hysterical, mad, wild.

frenzy *a frenzy of excitement.* hysteria, insanity, madness, mania.

frequent 1 *frequent bouts of illness, frequent trains.* constant, continual, countless, many, numerous, persistent, recurrent. 2 *The cuckoo is a frequent visitor to Britain.* common, habitual, regular.

fresh 1 *The detectives looked for fresh clues.* different, new, recent, up-to-date. 2 *We put fresh sheets on the bed.* airy, clean, unused, untouched. 3 *You feel fresh after a shower.* energetic, healthy, invigorated, lively, perky, rested. 4 *fresh water.* pure, unpolluted.

fret *The dog fretted while his master was away.* to grieve, to worry.

friend acquaintance, ally, chum, companion, comrade, (informal) mate, (informal) pal, partner, penfriend.

friendly affectionate, agreeable, amiable, attached, close, familiar, good-natured, favourable, gracious, helpful, hospitable, intimate, kind, kind-hearted, loving, sociable, sympathetic, tender, warm, welcoming.

frieze *a decorative frieze.* border, edging.

fright alarm, dread, fear, horror, panic, terror.

frighten 1 to alarm, to appal, to bully, to daunt, to dismay, to horrify, to intimidate, to make afraid, to menace, to persecute, to petrify, to scare, to shake, to shock, to startle, to terrify, to terrorize, to threaten. 2 *frightened*: afraid, apprehensive, fearful.
3 *frightening*: creepy, eerie, ghostly, hair-raising, scary, sinister, spooky, uncanny, weird.

frightful *a frightful accident.* appalling, awful, dreadful, fearful, fearsome, ghastly, grisly, hideous, horrible, horrid, horrifying, shocking, terrible.

frill border, edging, fringe.

fringe 1 *a fringe round the bottom of a curtain.* border, edging, frill. 2 *The fringe of a town.* edge, outskirts.

frisk *Lambs were frisking in the field.* to caper, to dance, to jump about, to leap, to prance, to romp, to skip.

frisky jaunty, lively, perky, playful, spirited, sprightly.

fritter *to fritter away your money.* to misuse, to squander, to waste.

frivolous *I hate frivolous questions.* foolish, ridiculous, silly, stupid, trivial, unimportant, worthless.

frock dress, gown.

frogman diver.

front *the front of an aircraft, the front of a house.* face, head, nose.

frontier *the frontier between two countries.* border, boundary.

frosty SEE **cold**.

froth bubbles, foam, lather, scum, suds.

frown to glower, to scowl.

fruit VARIOUS FRUITS: apple, apricot, banana, berry, blackberry, cherry, citrus fruit, coconut, crab-apple, currant, damson, date, fig, gooseberry, grape, grapefruit, greengage, hip, lemon, lime, melon, olive, orange, peach, pear, pineapple, plum, prune, raisin, raspberry, rhubarb, strawberry, sultana, tangerine, tomato.

fruitful 1 *a fruitful search.* profitable, successful. 2 *a fruitful garden.* fertile, flourishing, lush, productive.

fruitless *a fruitless search.* futile, pointless, unsuccessful, useless.

frustrate *The police frustrated an attempted robbery.* to foil, to halt, to hinder, to prevent, to stop.

fuddled 1 *I'm always fuddled when I wake up.* confused, flustered, mixed up, muddled. 2 *fuddled with alcohol.* drunk, intoxicated.

fuel KINDS OF FUEL: anthracite, butane, charcoal, coal, coke, electricity, gas, gasoline, logs, methylated spirit, nuclear fuel, oil, paraffin, peat, petrol, propane.

fugitive deserter, refugee, renegade.

fulfil 1 *I wonder if she will fulfil her ambition?* to accomplish, to achieve, to carry out, to complete, to perform.
2 *Did the shop fulfil your requirements?* to meet, to satisfy.

full 1 *The shops are full at Christmas.* bursting, congested, crammed, crowded, filled, jammed, packed, stuffed. 2 *My cup is full.* brimming, overflowing. 3 *Tell us the full story.* complete, entire, total, whole. 4 *She ran at full speed.* greatest, highest, maximum.

fumble *He fumbled the ball.* to grope at, to mishandle.

fume 1 *fuming chimneys.* to smoke. 2 *He was fuming because his money had been stolen.* SEE **angry**.

fumes exhaust, gases, smoke, vapour.

fun amusement, jokes, laughter, merriment, pastimes, play, pleasure, recreation. SEE ALSO **entertainment, game**.

function 1 *The function of the police is to keep order.* aim, duty, job, purpose, task, use. 2 *Our uncle's wedding was a happy function.* ceremony, event, gathering, occasion, party, reception.
3 *This computer isn't functioning properly.* to act, to behave, to operate, to perform, to work.

fundamental basic, elementary, essential, important, main, primary, principal.

funds *You need funds to start a business.* capital, money, resources, savings, wealth.

funeral 1 burial, cremation. 2 WORDS TO DO WITH FUNERALS: cemetery, coffin, crematorium, grave, graveyard, hearse, memorial, mortuary, mourner, tomb, undertaker, wreath.

fun-fair ENTERTAINMENTS AT A FUN-FAIR: dodgems, merry-go-round, roundabout, side-show.

fungus mushroom, toadstool.

funny 1 *a funny joke.* absurd, amusing, comic, crazy, facetious, farcical, hilarious, humorous, hysterical, laughable, ludicrous, (informal) priceless, ridiculous, uproarious, witty, zany. 2 *a funny pain in the stomach.* abnormal, curious, odd, peculiar, queer, strange, unusual.

funny-bone elbow.

fur 1 *animals covered in fur.* bristles, down, fleece, hair. 2 *people dressed in furs.* hide, skin.

furious *a furious bull.* angry, cross, enraged, fuming, incensed, indignant, infuriated, irate, livid, mad, raging.

furnace SEE **fire**.

furnish *a workshop furnished with the latest gadgets,* to equip, to fit up, to provide, to supply.

furniture KINDS OF FURNITURE: antique, armchair, bed, bench, bookcase, bunk, bureau, cabinet, chair, chest of drawers, cot, couch, cradle, cupboard, cushion, deck-chair, desk, divan, drawer, dresser, easel, fender, fireplace, mantelpiece, pew, pouffe, rocking-chair, settee, sideboard, sofa, stool, suite, table, trestle table, wardrobe, workbench.

furrow crease, groove, rut, wrinkle.

furry *furry animals.* bristly, downy, feather, fleecy, fuzzy, hairy, woolly.

further *further information.* additional, extra, more, supplementary.

furthermore additionally, also, besides, moreover, too.

furtive *We didn't like the furtive way he was looking round the shop.* crafty, deceitful, mysterious, secretive, shifty, sly, sneaky, stealthy, tricky, untrustworthy, wily.

fury *We were frightened by the fury of the storm.* anger, rage, violence, wrath.

fuss ado, bother, commotion, excitement, to-do, trouble, turmoil, uproar.

fussy *fussy about food.* (informal) choosey, fastidious, finicky, particular.

futile *It's futile to complain if you've lost the receipt.* fruitless, ineffective, pointless, unsuccessful, useless, vain, worthless.

future *future events.* approaching, coming.

fuzzy 1 *a fuzzy beard.* downy, feathery, fleecy, woolly. 2 *a fuzzy picture.* blurred, cloudy, dim, faint, hazy, indistinct, misty, unclear.

G

gabble *I can't understand what you say if you gabble.* to babble, to jabber, to mutter. SEE ALSO **talk**.

gadget contraption, contrivance, device, implement, instrument, invention, machine, tool, utensil.

gag 1 *The comedian told some old gags.* jest, joke. 2 *The gang tied him up and gagged him.* to silence.

gain 1 *What did they gain by fighting a war?* to acquire, to earn, to get, to obtain, to procure, to receive, to win.

2 *The explorers gained their objective.* to achieve, to get to, to reach. 3 *At the end of the day we added up our gains.* advantage, asset, benefit, profit.

gala carnival, fair, festival, fête.

gale blast, wind.

gallant *a gallant knight.* brave, chivalrous, courageous, fearless, gentlemanly, heroic, noble, polite, valiant.

gallop to race, to run, to rush.

gallows *hanged on a gallows.* scaffold.

gamble 1 WAYS OF GAMBLING: betting, bingo, cards, dice, drawing lots, lottery, pools, raffle, wager. 2 *She gambled her life to save the drowning man.* to risk, to venture.

game 1 *fun and games.* amusement, entertainment, fun, joke, pastime, playing, sport. 2 *a game of tennis.* competition, contest, match, tournament. 3 VARIOUS GAMES: billiards, bingo, charades, chess, crossword puzzle, darts, dice, dominoes, draughts, hide-and-seek, hopscotch, jigsaw puzzle, leap-frog, ludo, marbles, pool, skittles, snooker, table-tennis, tiddlywinks. SEE ALSO **cards.** 4 FOR MORE ACTIVE GAMES SEE **sport.**

gammon bacon, ham.

gang *a gang of workers.* band, company, crew, group, horde.

gangster brigand, criminal, crook, desperado, gunman, robber, ruffian.

gaol 1 dungeon, prison. 2 *He was gaoled for fraud.* to confine, to detain, to imprison, to intern, to shut up.

gap 1 *a gap in the fence.* break, hole, opening. 2 *a gap between lessons.* interval, lapse, lull, pause, respite, rest. 3 *Is the gap between the posts wide enough for the car?* distance, space.

gape to gaze, to stare. SEE ALSO **look.**

garbage *Put the garbage in the dustbin.* junk, litter, refuse, rubbish, trash, waste.

garbled *a garbled message.* confused, incoherent, jumbled, misleading, mixed up.

garden 1 allotment, patch, plot. 2 THINGS FOUND IN A GARDEN: bed, border, butt, compost heap, flagstones, hedge, lawn, orchard, path, patio, pond, rockery, rock garden, shrubbery, terrace, trellis, turf, window-box. SEE ALSO **flower, fruit, tree, vegetable.** 3 GARDEN TOOLS: broom, cultivator, fork, hoe, rake, riddle, secateurs, shears, shovel, sieve, spade, trowel, watering-can. 4 SUBSTANCES USED IN A GARDEN: compost, fertilizer, insecticide, manure, peat, pesticide, weed-killer.

garment attire, clothing, costume, dress. FOR VARIOUS GARMENTS SEE **clothes.**

garrison citadel, fort, fortress.

gas 1 *poisonous gas.* exhaust, fumes, vapour. 2 VARIOUS GASES: hydrogen, nitrogen, oxygen, tear gas.

gash cut, slash, slit, wound.

gasoline petrol.

gasp 1 *The smoke made them gasp.* to choke, to pant, to puff, to wheeze. 2 *gasping*: breathless, exhausted, puffed, tired out.

gate door, entrance, entry, exit, gateway, turnstile.

gather 1 *A crowd gathered. We gathered our belongings.* to accumulate, to assemble, to bring together, to cluster, to collect, to come together, to concentrate, to congregate, to crowd, to get together, to group, to herd, to hoard, to mass, to meet, to mobilize, to muster, to pile up, to round up, to store up, to swarm, to throng. 2 *We gathered strawberries.* to harvest, to pick, to pluck. 3 *I gather you've been ill.* to conclude, to learn, to understand.

gathering 1 *a gathering of people.* bunch, company, congregation, crowd, mass, swarm, throng. SEE ALSO **group.** 2 *a social gathering.* assembly, function, meeting, party, social.

gaudy *gaudy colours.* bright, colourful, flashy, lurid, showy, tawdry.

gauge *a narrow gauge railway.* measurement, size.

gaunt *The old man looked gaunt after his illness.* bony, emaciated, lean, skinny, starving, thin, wasted away.

gauntlet glove.

gawky awkward, blundering, clumsy, ungainly.

gay 1 *gay colours, gay laughter.* bright, cheerful, joyful, light-hearted, merry. SEE ALSO **happy.** 2 homosexual, (impolite) queer.

gaze SEE **look.**

gear *camping gear.* apparatus, equipment, instruments, kit, paraphernalia, rig, tackle.

gem jewel, precious stone.

general 1 *The bad weather is general this year.* common, communal, global, shared, universal, widespread. 2 *Smoking used to be more general than it is now.* customary, everyday, familiar, habitual, regular, usual. 3 *He only gave us a general idea of where we were going.* broad, indefinite, unclear, vague.

generally chiefly, mainly, mostly, predominantly, usually.

generate *to generate electricity, to generate business, etc.* to breed, to bring about, to create, to make, to produce.

generous 1 *a generous sponsor.* bounteous, charitable, free, kind, lavish, liberal, public-spirited, unselfish. 2 *generous portions of food.* abundant, ample, copious, large, liberal, plentiful, sizeable.

genial *Our friends gave us a genial welcome.* cheerful, cordial, easy-going, friendly, pleasant, relaxed, warm-hearted. SEE ALSO **kind.**

genius 1 *a mathematical genius.* expert, know-all, master-mind. 2 *He has a genius for maths.* gift, intellect, talent.

gentle 1 *a gentle person.* good-tempered, kindly, merciful, mild, pleasant, soft-hearted, tender. 2 *gentle music.* peaceful, quiet, relaxing, soft, soothing. 3 *a gentle dog.* docile, manageable, meek, obedient, tame. 4 *a gentle wind.* balmy, delicate, faint, light. 5 *a gentle hint.* indirect, subtle. 6 *a gentle hill.* gradual, moderate, steady.

gentleman SEE **man.**

genuine 1 *a genuine £5 note.* actual, authentic, real. 2 *genuine feelings.* devout, honest, sincere, true.

geography SOME GEOGRAPHICAL WORDS: Antarctic, archipelago, Arctic, bay, borough, canyon, cape, capital, city, climate, continent, contour, conurbation, country, county, creek, dale, delta, downs, east, equator, estate, estuary, fells, fen, fiord, geyser, glacier, glen, gulf, hamlet, heath, hemisphere, highlands, hill, industry, inlet, island, isthmus, lagoon, lake, land, latitude, longitude, mainland, nation, north, oasis, parish, pass, peninsula, plain, plateau, pole, prairie, province, reef, relief map, river, sea, south, strait, suburb, tide, town, tributary, tropics, valley, village, volcano, west, world.

germ bacteria, (informal) bug, microbe, virus.! *Bacteria* is a plural word.

germinate *Our seeds have germinated.* to grow, to shoot, to spring up, to sprout, to start growing.

gesture 1 action, movement, sign. 2 WAYS TO MAKE GESTURES: to beckon, to nod, to point, to salute, to shake your head, to shrug, to wave, to wink.

get 1 *What did you get for Christmas? What can I get for £10?* to acquire, to be given, to buy, to gain, to get hold of, to obtain, to procure, to purchase, to receive. 2 *Tell the dog to get the ball.* to bring, to fetch, to pick up, to retrieve. 3 *Did you get a prize?* to earn, to take, to win. 4 *I got a cold.* to catch, to contract, to develop, to suffer from. 5 *Get him to do the washing-up.* to cause, to persuade. 6 *Let's get tea now.* to make ready, to prepare. 7 *I don't get what he means.* to comprehend, to follow, to grasp, to understand. 8 *What time did you get to school?* to arrive at, to reach. 9 *How do you get to school?* to go to, to travel. 10 *It's getting cold.* to become, to grow, to turn.! *Get* can mean many things. The words given here are only some of the other words you could use.

getaway *They made their getaway in a fast car.* escape, flight, retreat.

ghastly *a ghastly disaster.* appalling, awful, dreadful, fearful, frightful, grim, grisly, horrible, horrifying, shocking, terrible.

ghost apparition, hallucination, illusion, phantom, poltergeist, spectre, spirit, (informal) spook, vision.

ghostly *a ghostly noise in the churchyard.* creepy, eerie, frightening, scary, spooky, uncanny, unearthly, weird.

giant 1 monster, ogre. 2 *a giant statue.* SEE **gigantic.**

gibberish (informal) balderdash, drivel, nonsense, rubbish, (informal) tripe, (informal) twaddle.

giddy *Heights make me feel giddy.* dizzy, faint, reeling, unsteady.

gift 1 *a birthday gift.* contribution, donation, offering, present. 2 *a gift for music.* ability, genius, knack, talent.

gifted

gifted *a gifted musician.* able, accomplished, brilliant, clever, masterly, skilful, skilled, talented, versatile.

gigantic *a gigantic monster.* colossal, enormous, giant, huge, immense, mammoth, massive, mighty, monstrous, vast. SEE ALSO **big.**

giggle to snigger, to titter. SEE ALSO **laugh.**

girder *a framework of girders.* bar, beam, joist, rafter.

girdle belt.

girl lass. OLD-FASHIONED WORDS: damsel, maid, maiden, virgin.

give 1 *to give someone a prize.* to award, to hand over, to offer, to pass, to present. 2 *How much did she give to you?* to allot, to allow, to contribute, to donate, to deal out, to distribute, to grant, to pay, to provide, to ration out, to supply. 3 *Give me the facts.* to display, to reveal, to show, to tell. 4 *Be careful: the roof might give.* to buckle, to collapse, to fall in, to fold up, to yield.

glad delighted, joyful, pleased. SEE ALSO **happy.**

glamorous 1 *a glamorous TV star.* alluring, attractive, beautiful, good-looking, gorgeous, lovely. 2 *a glamorous place for a holiday.* colourful, exciting, fascinating.

glance SEE **look.**

glaring *glaring lights.* bright, dazzling, harsh.

glass 1 pane, plate-glass. 2 *a glass ball.* crystal. 3 *a glass of water.* tumbler, wine-glass.

glasses bifocals, goggles, spectacles, sun-glasses.

glasshouse greenhouse.

glass-paper sandpaper.

gleam 1 *a gleam of light.* beam, flash, glimmer, glow, ray. SEE ALSO **light.** 2 *gleaming:* bright, brilliant, shining, shiny, sparkling.

gleeful delighted, ecstatic, exultant, joyful, merry, overjoyed, pleased. SEE ALSO **happy.**

glen dale, valley.

glide *to glide across the ice.* to coast, to drift, to fly, to skid, to slide, to slip.

glimmer *A distant light glimmered in the darkness.* to flicker, to gleam, to glow, to twinkle. SEE ALSO **light.**

glimpse *We glimpsed a deer in the woods.* to discern, to distinguish, to make out, to notice, to observe, to see, to sight, to spot.

glint *The light glinted on the bright metal.* to flash, to sparkle. SEE ALSO **light.**

glisten *The lights glistened on the wet road.* to gleam, to shine. SEE ALSO **light.**

glitter 1 *The diamond necklace glittered.* to flash, to sparkle, to twinkle. SEE ALSO **light.** 2 *glittering: The banquet was a glittering occasion.* brilliant, colourful, glamorous, resplendent, sparkling, splendid.

gloat to boast, to brag, to show off.

global *Do you think there's any danger of a global war?* general, universal, wholesale, widespread, worldwide.

globe 1 *the shape of a globe.* ball, sphere. 2 *the globe we live on.* earth, world.

gloom *We could hardly see in the gloom.* dimness, dusk, twilight.

gloomy 1 *a gloomy house, gloomy weather.* cheerless, cloudy, dark, depressing, dingy, dismal, dull, heavy, murky, overcast, shadowy, sombre. 2 *a gloomy person.* depressed, down-hearted, glum, grave, lugubrious, melancholy, miserable, morbid, unhappy. SEE ALSO **sad.**

glorious 1 *glorious scenery, glorious weather, etc.* beautiful, brilliant, excellent, gorgeous, grand, impressive, lovely, magnificent, majestic, marvellous, resplendent, spectacular, splendid, (informal) super, superb, wonderful. 2 *a glorious victory.* celebrated, distinguished, famous, heroic, noble.

gloss *We polished the table until we got a good gloss.* brightness, lustre, polish, sheen, shine.

glossy *glossy paint.* bright, gleaming, shiny, sleek.

glove gauntlet, mitten.

glow 1 *A fire glowed in the hearth.* to gleam, to glimmer, to radiate, to shine. SEE ALSO **light. 2** *the glow from a fire.* brightness, colour, redness, heat, warmth.

glower to frown, to scowl.

glue 1 *We need some glue to stick the pictures onto card.* adhesive, gum, paste. **2** *Can we glue the broken bits together?* to paste, to stick.

gluey adhesive, gummed, sticky, tacky.

glum *The defeated team looked glum.* depressed, down-hearted, gloomy, lugubrious, melancholy, miserable, unhappy. SEE ALSO **sad.**

gluttonous greedy.

gnarled *a gnarled old tree.* distorted, knobbly, lump, rough, twisted.

gnaw *The dog gnawed a bone.* to bite, to chew, to munch.

gnome dwarf, goblin.

go 1 *Let's go!* to advance, to begin, to be off, to commence, to depart, to disappear, to embark, to get away, to leave, to move, to proceed, to retire, to retreat, to set out, to start, to withdraw. **2** *I'd love to go to America.* to journey to, to travel to, to visit. **3** *This road goes to the rubbish dump.* to extend to, to lead to, to reach, to stretch to. **4** *The car won't go.* to act, to function, to operate, to perform, to run, to work. **5** *A holiday always goes quickly.* to elapse, to pass. **6** *Is he going mad?* to become, to grow, to turn. **7** *The bomb went off.* to blow up, to detonate, to explode. **8** *How long can you go on running?* to carry on, to continue, to keep on, to last, to persevere, to persist. **9** *She has gone through a serious illness.* to endure, to experience, to undergo. **10** *Who'll go with me to the shops?* to accompany, to escort. ! *Go* can be used in many ways. The words given here are just some of the other words you can use.

goal *a goal in life.* aim, ambition, objective, purpose, target.

goat billy-goat, kid, nanny-goat.

gobble *She gobbled her food greedily.* to bolt, to devour, to gulp, to guzzle. SEE ALSO **eat.**

goblet beaker, cup.

goblin brownie.

god deity, divinity.

goggles glasses, spectacles.

good 1 *a good deed, a good person.* admirable, appropriate, benevolent, caring, commendable, considerate, creditable, dutiful, esteemed, fair, great, helpful, holy, honest, honourable, humane, innocent, just, kind, kind-hearted, law-abiding, marvellous, moral, noble, obedient, outstanding, praiseworthy, proper, reliable, religious, right, righteous, saintly, thoughtful, upright, virtuous, well-behaved, wonderful, worthy. **2** *a good musician, a good worker.* able, accomplished, capable, clever, conscientious, creditable, efficient, (informal) fabulous, gifted, proficient, skilful, skilled, talented, thorough. **3** *a good holiday, good weather.* agreeable, delightful, enjoyable, excellent, fine, heavenly, lovely, nice, pleasant, pleasing, satisfactory, (informal) terrific, satisfactory, (informal) terrific.! *Good* can mean many different things. The words given here are only some of the other words you could use.

goodbye au revoir, farewell.

good-humoured amiable, cheerful, friendly, genial, kind, likeable, sympathetic, warm-hearted.

good-looking attractive, handsome, lovely, pretty. SEE ALSO **beautiful.**

good-natured friendly, helpful, kind-hearted, sympathetic. SEE ALSO **kind.**

goods *a train carrying goods.* cargo, freight, merchandise.

good-tempered gentle, mild, nice. SEE ALSO **kind.**

goose gander, gosling.

gorge 1 *He was sick after gorging himself on ice-cream.* to feast, to gobble, to guzzle. **2** *A river runs along the gorge.* canyon, defile, pass, ravine, valley.

gorgeous *a gorgeous dress, a gorgeous view.* colourful, glorious, lovely, magnificent. SEE ALSO **beautiful.**

gory *a gory battle.* blood-stained, bloody, grisly, gruesome.

gosling

gosling goose.

gossip 1 *Don't gossip while I'm reading to you!* to chatter, to prattle. SEE ALSO **talk.** 2 *Don't listen to unkind gossip.* rumour, scandal.

gouge *to gouge out a hole.* to dig, to scoop.

goulash stew.

govern *to govern a country.* to administer, to be in charge of, to command, to control, to direct, to guide, to head, to look after, to manage, to master, to regulate, to rule, to run, to supervise.

government WORDS CONNECTED WITH GOVERNMENT: administration, ambassador, cabinet, chancellor, civil service, commonwealth, constituency, constitution, consul, councillor, democracy, dictatorship, diplomat, embassy, empire, exchequer, kingdom, mayor, member of parliament, minister, ministry, monarchy, parliament, politician, politics, premier, president, prime minister, republic, statesman.

governor *Who is the governor here?* boss, chief, controller, director, head, manager, ruler, supervisor.

gown dress, frock.

grab *Grab the end of that rope!* to catch, to clutch, to grasp, to hold, to pluck, to seize, to snatch.

grace 1 *God's grace.* forgiveness, goodness, mercy. 2 *grace before dinner.* blessing, prayer.

graceful 1 *graceful movements.* agile, deft, flowing, nimble, supple. 2 *a graceful figure.* attractive, beautiful, dignified, elegant, slim, slender.

gracious *a gracious lady.* agreeable, courteous, friendly, good-natured, kind, polite.

grade *Our butcher sells top grade meat.* category, class, quality, standard.

gradient *a steep gradient.* ascent, hill, incline, slope.

gradual *a gradual improvement in the weather.* gentle, moderate, slow, steady.

grain 1 *Many farmers grow grain.* cereals, corn. 2 *a grain of sand.* bit, granule, particle, speck.

grand *a grand occasion.* big, great, important, imposing, impressive, lordly, magnificent, majestic, noble, (informal) posh, regal, royal, stately. SEE ALSO **splendid.**

grant 1 *a grant of money.* allowance, donation, expenses, loan, scholarship. 2 *The insurance company granted them the full value of the wrecked car.* to allot, to allow, to donate, to give, to pay, to provide. 3 *In the end he granted that I was right.* to acknowledge, to accept, to admit, to agree.

graph chart, diagram.

grapple 1 *to grapple with an intruder.* to struggle, to wrestle. 2 *to grapple with a problem.* to attend to, to cope with, to deal with, to handle, to manage.

grasp 1 *Grasp the bat firmly.* to catch, to clasp, to clutch, to grab, to grip, to hang on to, to hold, to seize. 2 *She quickly grasped the facts.* to comprehend, to follow, to learn, to master, to realize, to understand.

grasping *a grasping miser.* greedy, miserly, selfish, worldly.

grass *We sat on the grass.* green, lawn.

grate 1 *There's a fire in the grate.* fireplace, hearth. 2 *to grate cheese.* to shred.

grateful *He was grateful for the gift.* appreciative, thankful.

grave 1 *She looked grave when she heard the bad news.* dignified, earnest, gloomy, pensive, sedate, serious, sober, solemn, subdued, thoughtful. SEE ALSO **sad.** 2 *Stealing is a grave offence.* important, momentous, serious, weighty. 3 *graves in the churchyard.* burial-place, gravestone, memorial, tomb.

gravel grit, pebbles, shingle, stones.

graveyard cemetery, churchyard.

graze *grazing cattle.* to feed.

grease fat, oil.

greasy fatty, oily.

great 1 *a great mountain.* enormous, huge, immense, large, tremendous. SEE ALSO **big.** 2 *great pain.* acute, excessive, extreme, intense, severe. 3 *a great event.* SEE **grand.** 4 *a great piece of music.* brilliant, classic, excellent, (informal) fabulous, famous, (informal) fantastic, fine, outstanding, wonderful. 5 *a great composer.* celebrated, distinguished, eminent, gifted, notable, noted, prominent, renowned, talented, well-known. 6 *a great friend.* chief, close, main, valued.

greedy 1 *That greedy crowd ate everything!* avid, eager, famished, gluttonous, hungry, ravenous, starving. 2 *Don't be greedy: share things with the others.* grasping, miserly, selfish, worldly.

greenery foliage, leaves.

greenhouse glasshouse.

greet *We greeted our visitors at the door.* to receive, to welcome.

grief misery, regret, remorse, sadness, sorrow, unhappiness.

grievance *If you have a grievance, see the manager.* complaint.

grieve 1 *He grieved terribly when his dog died.* to fret, to lament, to mope, to mourn, to weep. 2 *It grieved us to see how cruelly the animal had been treated.* to depress, to distress, to hurt, to sadden.

grim *a grim expression, grim weather, etc.* bad-tempered, cruel, forbidding, frightful, ghastly, gloomy, grisly, gruesome, harsh, horrible, menacing, ominous, severe, stern, terrible, threatening, unfriendly.

grimace *to make a grimace.* face, look. SEE ALSO **expression**.

grimy *grimy windows.* dirty, dusty, filthy, grubby, sooty.

grin to beam, to smile. SEE ALSO **laugh**.

grind 1 *to grind corn.* to crush, to pound, to powder. 2 *to grind a knife.* to polish, to sharpen. 3 *to grind something away.* to eat away, to erode, to wear away.

grip *He gripped her hand.* to clasp, to clutch, to grab, to grasp, to hold, to seize.

grisly *a grisly accident.* appalling, dreadful, frightful, ghastly, gory, grim, gruesome, hideous, horrible, terrible. SEE ALSO **bad**.

gristly *gristly meat.* leathery, rubbery, tough.

grit 1 *I had some grit in my eye.* dust, gravel, sand. 2 (informal) *You need grit to climb that mountain.* bravery, courage, determination, (informal) guts, (informal) pluck, spirit. 3 *to grit your teeth.* to clench.

grizzle *The baby grizzled.* to cry, to weep, to whimper.

groan to moan, to wail.

groove cut, furrow, scratch, slot.

grope *We groped about in the dark.* to feel about, to fumble.

gross *He was gross: he never stopped eating.* enormous, fat, flabby, huge, monstrous, overweight, ugly.

grotesque *grotesque carvings.* absurd, deformed, distorted, fantastic, misshapen, ugly, weird.

grotto cave, cavern.

ground 1 *You sow seeds in the ground.* earth, loam, soil. 2 *We showed our visitors round the grounds.* campus, estate, gardens, playing-fields, surroundings. 3 *Whose ground are we playing on next week?* arena, field, pitch, stadium. 4 *Have you any grounds for accusing her?* argument, cause, evidence, proof, reason.

group 1 *We formed a group for railway enthusiasts.* alliance, association, body, club, combination, company, league, organization, party, society, union. 2 OTHER GROUPS: accumulation, assortment, band, batch, brood, bunch, bundle, category, clan, class, clump, cluster, clutch, collection, colony, company, congregation, convoy, crew, crowd, fleet, flock, galaxy, gang, gathering, herd, hoard, horde, host, litter, mass, mob, multitude, pack, party, picket, posse, pride, rabble, school, set, shoal, swarm, team, throng, troop. 3 *Group the specimens according to size.* to arrange, to assemble, to bring together, to classify, to collect, to set out, to sort.

grouse to complain, to grumble, to moan.

grove *a grove of small trees.* coppice, copse, forest, thicket, wood.

grovel *Stand up for yourself: don't grovel!* to cower, to cringe, to be too humble, to snivel.

grow 1 *The seeds have started to grow.* to emerge, to germinate, to spring up, to sprout. 2 *Many plants won't grow in cold weather.* to flourish, to live, to prosper, to survive, to thrive. 3 *Trees grow slowly.* to become longer, to become taller, to enlarge, to expand, to fill out, to increase in size, to lengthen, to swell. 4 *Her confidence grew when she started training seriously.* to build up, to develop, to improve, to increase. 5 *He grows lovely roses.* to cultivate, to produce, to raise.

grown-up adult, mature, well-developed.

grub *There's a grub in this apple!* caterpillar, larva, maggot.

grubby *a grubby shirt.* dirty, grimy, (informal) mucky, soiled.

grudging *He gave my plan his grudging approval.* envious, jealous, reluctant, resentful, ungracious, unkind.

gruelling *a gruelling climb.* arduous, exhausting, hard, laborious, stiff, strenuous, tiring, tough.

gruesome *a gruesome accident.* bloody, disgusting, grim, grisly, hideous, horrible, ghastly, gory, revolting, sickening.

gruff 1 *a gruff voice.* harsh, hoarse, husky, tough. 2 *a gruff answer.* bad-tempered, grumpy, surly, unfriendly.

grumble to complain, to grouse, to moan.

grumpy *He's grumpy because he's got toothache.* bad-tempered, cross, gruff, irascible, irritable, peevish, snappy, surly, testy.

guarantee 1 *He gave us his guarantee that it worked.* assurance, pledge, promise. 2 *He guarantees that it works.* to pledge, to promise, to swear, to vow. 3 *This ticket guarantees you a seat.* to ensure, to secure.

guard 1 *A mother always guards her young.* to care for, to defend, to keep safe, to look after, to preserve, to protect, to safeguard, to shelter, to shield, to tend. 2 *The sentry guarded the prisoners.* to prevent from escaping, to watch. 3 *A guard watched over the prisoner.* escort, look-out, patrol, sentinel, sentry, warder, watchman.

guardian *The guardian of the treasure was a fierce dragon.* custodian, keeper, protector, warder.

guess 1 *Make a guess.* assumption, estimate, guesswork, opinion, supposition, theory. 2 *I guess it will cost about £1.* to assume, to estimate, to suppose.

guest 1 *We had guests on Sunday.* caller, visitor. 2 *How many guests stay in this hotel?* boarder, customer, lodger, resident, tenant.

guide 1 *a guide to show us the way.* escort, pilot. 2 *Who can guide us out of the maze?* to conduct, to direct, to escort, to lead, to manoeuvre, to navigate, to pilot, to steer.

guilt *The evidence proved his guilt.* blame, fault, responsibility.

guilty 1 *The jury declared him guilty.* at fault, responsible. 2 *He looked guilty.* ashamed, regretful, remorseful, sheepish.

gullet throat.

gulp *We gulped our food as fast as we could.* to bolt, to devour, to gobble.

gum adhesive, glue, paste.

gummed *gummed paper.* adhesive, gluey, sticky.

gumption (informal) *Haven't you any gumption?* judgement, sense, wisdom.

gun 1 VARIOUS GUNS: airgun, artillery, automatic, blunderbuss, cannon, machine-gun, mortar, musket, pistol, revolver, rifle, shotgun, small arms, sub-machine-gun. 2 PARTS OF A GUN: barrel, breach, butt, magazine, muzzle, sight, trigger.

guru leader, teacher.

gush 1 *Oil gushed out of the pipe.* to flow, to pour, to run, to spout, to spurt, to squirt, to stream. 2 *to come in a gush.* flood, jet, rush, stream.

gusty *gusty weather.* blustery, squally, windy.

guts (informal) *They had guts to take the lifeboat out in that storm.* bravery, courage, determination, (informal) grit, nerve, (informal) pluck, spirit.

gutter *The water flows along the gutter.* channel, ditch, drain, sewer.

guzzle *It's not polite to guzzle your food.* to bolt, to gobble, to gulp.

gypsy nomad, traveller.

H

habit 1 *Don't let smoking become a habit!* addiction, compulsion. 2 *In our family, it's our habit to open presents on Christmas Eve.* custom, practice, routine.

habitual *We went home by our habitual route.* accustomed, conventional, common, customary, normal, ordinary, regular, routine, traditional, usual.

hack *We hacked down the undergrowth.* to chop, to hew, to slash. SEE ALSO **cut**.

haggle *If you haggle with the man in the market, he'll knock a pound off the price.* to argue, to bargain, to discuss terms, to negotiate.

hair 1 *Most animals have hairs on their skins.* bristles, fur. 2 *Does your mum do your hair?* curls, lock, tresses. 3 WAYS OF DOING HAIR: permanent wave, pigtail, plait, pony-tail. 4 WORDS TO DESCRIBE THE COLOUR OF HAIR: auburn, blond or blonde, brunette, dark, fair.

hairdresser barber.

hairless bald, bare.

hair-raising *The drive over the mountain road was hair-raising.* appalling, frightening, horrifying, scary, terrifying.

hairy *hairy skin.* bristly, downy, feathery, fleecy, fuzzy, shaggy, woolly.

half-hearted 1 *He made a half-hearted shot at goal.* feeble, ineffective, weak. 2 *She seems half-hearted about the party.* cool, indifferent, unenthusiastic.

half-wit SEE **idiot**.

hall 1 *Wipe your feet before you come into the hall.* corridor, foyer, lobby, passage. 2 *We do the nativity play in the hall.* assembly hall, concert hall, theatre.

hallowed *hallowed ground.* blessed, consecrated, holy, sacred.

hallucination apparition, delusion, dream, illusion, mirage, vision.

halt 1 *A red light halts the traffic.* to arrest, to block, to check, to stop. 2 *The traffic halts when the lights turn red.* to come to a standstill, to draw up, to pull up, to stop. 3 *All activity halted when the whistle went.* to break off, to cease, to end, to terminate.

halve 1 *The two explorers halved their rations.* to divide, to share. 2 *Dad threatened to halve my pocket-money.* to cut, to decrease, to lessen, to reduce.

hamlet settlement, village.

hammer *He hammered on the door.* to bash, to batter, to beat, to knock, to strike. SEE ALSO **hit**.

hamper *Work on the extension was hampered by bad weather.* to curb, to foil, to frustrate, to hinder, to hold back, to obstruct.

hand 1 *She hit me with her hand.* fist. 2 PARTS OF A HAND: finger, finger-nail, index finger, knuckle, palm, thumb, wrist. 3 *to hand in, to hand over*: to deliver, to give, to present, to submit. 4 *to hand round*: to circulate, to deal out, to distribute, to give out, to pass round, to share.

handbag bag, purse.

handicap 1 *It's a handicap to run a race in wellington boots!* disadvantage, drawback, hindrance, impediment, inconvenience, obstacle. 2 WAYS IN WHICH PEOPLE MAY BE HANDICAPPED: to be backward, blind, crippled, deaf, deformed, disabled, disfigured, dumb, lame, limbless, maimed, mute, paralysed, paraplegic, retarded, slow, spastic, to have a speech impediment.

handicraft art, craft, workmanship.

handkerchief tissue.

handle 1 *Hold it by the handle.* grip, hilt, knob. 2 *You must handle small animals carefully.* to feel, to finger, to stroke, to touch. 3 *The teacher handled the rowdy class firmly.* to control, to cope with, to deal with, to look after, to manage, to manipulate.

handsome 1 *a handsome man.* attractive, good-looking. 2 *a handsome piece of furniture.* beautiful, elegant, tasteful. 3 *a handsome present.* big, generous, sizeable, valuable.

handy 1 *Dad always has his tools handy.* accessible, available, close at hand, convenient, easy to reach, ready. 2 *Mum is handy at mending the car.* capable, clever, competent, helpful, practical, proficient, skilful.

hang 1 *Hang the washing on the line.* to dangle, to suspend. 2 *The smoke hung in the still air.* to drift, to float, to hover. 3 *Don't hang about.* to dally, to dawdle, to linger, to loiter. 4 *Come on, there's no need to hang back.* to hesitate, to pause, to wait. 5 *Hang on to the rope!* to catch, to grasp, to hold, to keep, to retain, to seize.

hangman executioner.

hanker *In winter we hanker after warm sunshine.* to desire, to fancy, to long for, to want, to wish for.

haphazard *The organization of the jumble sale was a bit haphazard.* accidental, chance, chaotic, confused, disorganized, random, unplanned, unsystematic.

happen *What happened next?* to befall, to come about, to occur, to take place.

happening event, incident, occasion, occurrence, phenomenon.

happy 1 *a happy bride, a happy event, etc.* blissful, cheerful, contented, delighted, ecstatic, elated, exultant, festive, gay, glad, gleeful, good-humoured, joyful, joyous, laughing, light-hearted, lively, merry, overjoyed, pleased, proud, radiant, rapturous. 2 *a happy accident.* favourable, fortunate, lucky.

harass *The dogs harassed the sheep.* to annoy, to bother, to disturb, to molest, to pester, to plague, to trouble, to worry.

harbour 1 *The ships tied up in the harbour.* anchorage, dock, haven, jetty, landing-stage, marina, moorings, pier, port, quay, wharf. 2 *I'd be in trouble if I harboured a criminal.* to give asylum to, to give refuge to, to protect, to shelter.

hard 1 *hard concrete.* firm, inflexible, rigid, solid, unyielding. 2 *a hard climb.* arduous, difficult, exhausting, gruelling, harsh, heavy, laborious, stiff, strenuous, tough. 3 *a hard problem.* baffling, complicated, confusing, difficult, involved, puzzling. 4 *a hard heart.* cruel, harsh, heartless, merciless, pitiless, ruthless, severe, stern, strict, unfeeling. 5 *a hard knock.* forceful, heavy, powerful, strong, violent. 6 *hard up:* SEE **poor.**

hardly barely, only just, scarcely, with difficulty.

hardship *They suffered great hardship when their father died.* adversity, difficulty, misery, suffering, trouble, unhappiness.

hardware equipment, instruments, machinery, tools.

hard-wearing *hard-wearing shoes.* durable, lasting, strong, sturdy, tough, well-made.

harm to damage, to hurt, to injure, to misuse, to spoil, to wound.

harmful *Eating stale food can be harmful.* bad, damaging, dangerous, destructive, injurious, unhealthy.

harmless *Don't you know that grass-snakes are harmless?* innocent, innocuous, inoffensive, mild, safe.

harmony *Wouldn't it be nice if we could all live in harmony?* agreement, concord, friendliness, peace.

harsh 1 *a harsh noise.* grating, jarring, raucous, shrill. 2 *harsh light, harsh colours.* bright, brilliant, dazzling, gaudy, glaring, lurid. 3 *a harsh smell.* acrid, bitter, unpleasant. 4 *harsh conditions.* arduous, austere, difficult, hard, severe, tough. 5 *a harsh texture.* bristly, coarse, hairy, rough, scratchy. 6 *a harsh judge.* cruel, stern, strict, unkind.

harvest 1 *The farmers hope for a good harvest.* crop, produce, yield. 2 *They harvest the corn in the summer.* to gather, to reap.

hash goulash, stew.

hear

hasty 1 *a hasty decision.* abrupt, hurried, impetuous, impulsive, quick, rash, reckless, speedy, sudden. 2 *hasty work.* brief, careless, cursory, hurried, slapdash.

hat KINDS OF HEAD-DRESS: beret, bonnet, bowler, cap, coronet, crash-helmet, crown, diadem, helmet, hood, sou'wester, turban, wig.

hatch 1 *to hatch eggs.* to brood, to incubate. 2 *to hatch a plot.* to concoct, to devise, to plan.

hate to despise, to detest, to dislike, to loathe, to scorn.

hatred aversion, contempt, dislike, loathing, revulsion.

haughty *a haughty manner.* arrogant, boastful, bumptious, (informal) cocky, conceited, disdainful, proud, self-important, (informal) stuck-up.

haul *The explorers had dogs to haul the sledge.* to drag, to draw, to lug, to pull, to tow, to tug.

haunt *We haunt the area near the sweet shop most evenings.* to hang around, to loiter about, to visit.

have 1 *She has her own TV.* to own, to possess. 2 *Our house has six rooms.* to consist of, to contain, to hold, to include, to incorporate, to involve. 3 *What did you have for Christmas?* to acquire, to be given, to gain, to get, to obtain, to receive. 4 *Who had the last biscuit?* to consume, to eat, to remove, to take. 5 *Did you have fun? Did you have any pain?* to endure, to enjoy. to experience, to feel, to go through, to know, to live through, to suffer, to undergo. ! *Have* has many meanings. These are only some of the other words you can use.

haven 1 *The ship reached the haven before the storm broke.* anchorage, harbour, port. 2 *The climbers found haven in a mountain hut.* asylum, refuge, retreat, safety, shelter.

haversack knapsack, rucksack.

havoc *The storm created havoc along the coast.* damage, destruction, devastation.

hawser cable, cord, line, rope.

hay fodder.

haystack rick.

hazard danger, peril, risk, threat, trouble.

hazardous *Crossing the sea in a rowing boat is hazardous.* chancy, dangerous, perilous, risky, unsafe.

haze fog, mist.

hazy *The view was hazy.* blurred, dim, faint, misty, unclear.

head 1 PARTS OF YOUR HEAD: brain, cheek, chin, ear, eye, forehead, gums, jaw, lip, mouth, nose, nostril, scalp, skull, teeth, tongue. 2 *the head of a mountain.* apex, crown, top. 3 *the head of an organization.* boss, director, employer, leader, manager, ruler. SEE ALSO **chief.** 4 *the head of a school.* headmaster, headmistress, headteacher, principal. 5 *Captain Scott headed an expedition to the South Pole.* to be in charge of, to command, to govern, to lead, to manage, to rule, to supervise. 6 *the head waiter.* chief, leading, most important, senior.

heading *Write the heading in big letters.* caption, headline, title.

headline *a newspaper headline.* caption, heading, title.

headlong *a headlong dash.* breakneck, hurried, impetuous, impulsive, reckless.

headquarters 1 *the headquarters of an expedition.* base, depot. 2 *the headquarters of a business.* head office, main office.

heal 1 *They claim that this ointment heals cuts.* to cure, to make better, to remedy. 2 *Wounds heal in time.* to get better, to mend, to recover.

health *We'd all like to have good health.* condition, fitness, strength, vigour.

healthy 1 *a healthy animal.* hearty, lively, perky, robust, sound, strong, vigorous, well. 2 *healthy surroundings.* hygienic, sanitary, wholesome.

heap 1 *a heap of rubbish.* mass, mound, pile, stack. 2 *We heaped up the rubbish.* to accumulate, to collect, to mass, to pile up, to stack up.

hear 1 *Have you heard this new single?* to listen to. 2 *Have you heard the news?* to discover, to find out, to gather, to learn.

heart *the heart of the forest, the heart of the problem.* centre, core, focus, hub, middle.

heart-broken SEE **sad.**

hearth fireplace, grate.

heartless SEE **cruel.**

hearty 1 *a hearty welcome.* enthusiastic, sincere, warm. 2 *a hearty appetite.* big, healthy, robust.

heat 1 *the heat of a fire.* glow, hotness, warmth. 2 WORDS FOR HEATING THINGS OR FOR BEING HOT: to bake, to blister, to boil, to burn, to cook, to fry, to grill, to melt, to roast, to scald, to scorch, to simmer, to sizzle, to smoulder, to steam, to stew, to swelter, to toast.

heath moor, moorland.

heathen atheist, barbarian, pagan, savage. ! These words are often insulting.

heave *They heaved the sacks onto the lorry.* to drag, to draw, to haul, to hoist, to lift, to lug, to pull, to raise, to throw, to tow, to tug.

heaven 1 paradise. 2 (informal) *Mum says it's heaven to have a hot bath.* bliss, ecstasy, happiness, rapture.

heavenly (informal) *What's that heavenly smell?* blissful, celestial, divine. SEE ALSO **pleasant.**

heavy 1 *a heavy load.* burdensome, massive, ponderous, weighty. 2 *heavy work.* arduous, difficult, hard, exhausting, laborious, strenuous, tough. 3 *heavy rain.* concentrated, considerable, severe, torrential. 4 *a heavy heart.* depressed, gloomy, miserable. SEE ALSO **sad.**

hectic *hectic activity.* active, bustling, busy, excited, frantic, lively, mad, wild.

hedge 1 fence, hedgerow. 2 *to hedge in*: to encircle, to enclose, to fence in, to hem in, to pen, to surround.

heed *If you're wise, you'll heed his warning.* to attend to, to follow, to keep to, to listen to, to mark, to mind, to note, to notice, to obey, to observe, to take notice of.

heel *The dinghy heeled over in the wind.* to lean, to list, to slope, to tilt.

hefty *a hefty man.* beefy, big, brawny, burly, mighty, muscular, strong, tough.

height *the height of a mountain.* altitude, tallness.

heir inheritor, successor.

hell underworld.

hellish diabolical, dreadful, ghastly. SEE ALSO **unpleasant.** ! *Hellish* is often used as slang.

help 1 *You can help each other if you want.* to aid, to assist, to back, to boost, to collaborate with, to co-operate with, to side with, to support. 2 *Give me a bit of help.* aid, assistance, backing, boost, co-operation, relief, support.

helpful 1 *a helpful person.* accommodating, benevolent, considerate, constructive, co-operative, neighbourly, obliging, thoughtful, willing. SEE ALSO **kind.** 2 *a helpful tool.* convenient, handy, useful. 3 *a helpful suggestion.* advantageous, informative, instructive, profitable, valuable.

helping *a helping of pudding.* portion, share.

helpless 1 *a helpless invalid.* feeble, impotent, incapable, weak, (informal) weedy. 2 *a helpless ship.* aground, disabled, drifting, stranded.

hem 1 *the hem of a skirt.* border, edge. 2 *to hem in*: to encircle, to enclose, to hedge in, to surround.

herald announcer, messenger, towncrier.

herb KINDS OF HERB: mint, parsley, sage.

herd 1 *a herd of cattle.* SEE **group.** 2 *to herd together.* to assemble, to congregate, to crowd, to flock, to gather, to swarm, to throng.

hereditary *a hereditary disease.* handed down, inherited, passed on.

hero, heroine champion, idol, star, superstar, victor, winner.

heroic *a heroic rescue.* bold, brave, chivalrous, courageous, daring, fearless, gallant, intrepid, noble, valiant.

hesitate *I hesitated before jumping into the cold water.* to delay, to falter, to hang back, to pause, to think twice, to wait, to waver.

hew *to hew down a tree.* to chop, to saw. SEE ALSO **cut.**

hibernating *a hibernating animal.* asleep, dormant, inactive.

hide 1 *They hid the money under the floorboards.* to bury, to conceal, to cover, to put away. 2 *The mist hid the view.* to blot out, to camouflage, to cloak, to mask, to obscure, to screen, to shroud. 3 *The runaway hid in an old warehouse.* to lie low, to lurk. 4 *an animal's hide.* fur, leather, skin.

hideous *a hideous wound.* frightful, ghastly, grisly, gruesome, repulsive, ugly, unsightly.

hide-out den, hiding-place, lair.

high 1 *a high building.* lofty, tall, towering. 2 *a high look-out.* elevated, raised. 3 *high prices.* excessive, exorbitant, unreasonable. 4 *a high rank in the army.* eminent, important, leading, powerful, prominent, top. 5 *a high wind.* great, intense, stormy, strong. 6 *a high reputation.* favourable, good, respected. 7 *a high sound.* piercing, sharp, shrill.

highbrow 1 *highbrow music.* classical. 2 *a highbrow book.* cultural, educational, improving, intellectual.

highlight *The highlight of our day out was a flight in a helicopter.* best moment, climax, peak.

highly-strung *Our dog yaps because he's highly-strung.* edgy, jittery, nervous, tense, touchy, (informal) uptight.

highwayman bandit, brigand, robber, thief.

hike *We hiked across the moors.* to ramble, to tramp, to trek. SEE ALSO **walk.**

hilarious *a hilarious joke.* amusing, comic, funny, humorous, hysterical, laughable, ridiculous, silly, uproarious, witty.

hill 1 *I climbed the hill.* mountain, peak, rise, summit. 2 *an area of hills*: downs, fells, highlands.

hinder *Deep snowdrifts hindered our progress.* to bar, to check, to curb, to delay, to deter, to hamper, to impede, to obstruct, to prevent, to stop.

hindrance *Our heavy rucksacks were a hindrance.* difficulty, disadvantage, handicap, impediment, inconvenience, obstacle.

hint 1 *I don't know the answer: give me a hint.* clue, implication, indication, inkling, suggestion, tip. 2 *Dad hinted that we might have a trip to London.* to imply, to indicate, to suggest.

hire 1 *We hired a bus.* to charter, to rent. 2 *to hire out*: to let.

historic *a historic battle.* celebrated, eminent, famous, important, notable, renowned, well-known.

hit 1 *The record was a hit.* success, triumph. 2 *I got a hit on the head.* blow, bump, knock. 3 VARIOUS WAYS TO HIT THINGS: to bang, to bash, to batter, to beat, to bump, to butt, to cane, to clout, to collide with, to cuff, to dash, to drive, to flick, to flip, to flog, to hammer, to head, to jab, to jar, to jog, to kick, to knock, to lash, to pat, to poke, to pound, to prod, to punch, to putt, to ram, to rap, to scourge, to slam, to slap, to slog, to smack, to smash, to spank, to strike, to stub, to swat, to swipe, to tap, to thrash, to thump, to wallop, to whack, to whip.

hive apiary.

hoard *Squirrels hoard nuts.* to accumulate, to collect, to gather, to keep, to mass, to pile up, to save, to store, to treasure.

hoarse *a hoarse voice.* croaking, grating, gruff, harsh, husky, rasping, raucous, rough.

hoax 1 *The firemen were angry when they heard that the emergency call was a hoax.* deception, fake, fraud, practical joke, trick. 2 *They realized that someone had hoaxed them.* to bluff, to deceive, to delude, to fool, to hoodwink, to mislead, to take in, to trick.

hobble to limp. SEE ALSO **walk.**

hobby interest, pastime, pursuit, relaxation.

hoist *The crane hoisted the boxes onto the deck.* to heave, to lift, to pull up, to raise.

hold 1 *Hold this rope!* to catch, to clutch, to grasp, to grip, to hang on to, to keep, to retain, to seize. 2 *He held the baby.* to bear, to carry, to clasp, to embrace, to hug, to support, to take. 3 *Our uncle held an important position in the bank.* to have, to occupy, to possess. 4 *The suitcases held all our things.* to contain, to enclose, to include. 5 *The lock gates hold back the water.* to block, to check, to control, to curb, to halt, to keep back, to retain, to stop. 6 *The police are holding a suspect.* to arrest, to confine, to detain, to keep. 7 *Hold that pose while I put a film in the camera!* to keep up, to maintain, to preserve, to retain. 8 *The church holds services every week.* to conduct, to have. 9 *I wonder how long this heat-wave will hold?* to carry on, to continue, to endure, to keep on, to last, to persist, to stay. 10 *to hold out: Hold out your hand.* to extend, to reach out, to stick out, to stretch out. 11 *to hold up: The traffic jam held up our journey.* to delay, to hinder, to obstruct, to slow down.

hold-up 1 *There was a hold-up at the bank.* SEE **crime.** 2 *My train was late because of a hold-up on the line.* delay, pause, postponement, wait.

hole 1 *a hole in the ground.* abyss, burrow, cave, chasm, crater, excavation, pit, pothole, tunnel. 2 *a hole in a fence, a hole in a tyre, etc.* breach, break, chink, crack, cut, gap, gash, leak, opening, puncture, slit, split, tear, vent.

holiday 1 *a holiday from school.* day off, leave, rest, time off, vacation. 2 VARIOUS KINDS OF HOLIDAY: camping, cruise, honeymoon, safari, seaside holiday, tour, trip, youth-hostelling. 3 KINDS OF HOLIDAY ACCOMMODATION: apartment, boarding-house, campsite, flat, guest-house, hostel, inn, motel, self-catering, villa, youth hostel.

hollow 1 *a hollow space.* empty, unfilled. 2 *a hollow in the ground.* dent, depression, dip, hole, valley. 3 *We hollowed out a pumpkin to make a lantern.* to dig, to gouge, to scoop.

holy *The temple is a holy place.* blessed, consecrated, divine, hallowed, heavenly, religious, sacred, saintly.

homage *to pay homage to:* to honour, to praise, to respect, to worship.

home abode, dwelling, residence. SEE ALSO **house.**

homeless *homeless people:* beggars, the destitute, tramps, vagrants.

homosexual gay, (impolite) queer.

honest 1 *an honest worker.* conscientious, honourable, law-abiding, moral, trustworthy, upright. 2 *an honest answer.* blunt, candid, direct, frank, genuine, open, sincere, straightforward, truthful. 3 *an honest judgement.* fair, impartial, just, unbiased, unprejudiced.

honour 1 *I had the honour of presenting a bouquet to our visitor.* distinction, fame, importance, renown, respect. 2 *If he had any honour, he would own up.* decency, honesty, integrity, loyalty, nobility, principle, sincerity, virtue. 3 *On Remembrance Day we honour those who died in war.* to admire, to pay homage to, to pay tribute to, to praise, to respect, to show respect to.

honourable *It was the honourable thing to hand over the money you found.* admirable, decent, good, honest, law-abiding, loyal, noble, respectable, upright, virtuous, worthy.

hoodwink SEE **deceive.**

hoof foot.

hook *to hook a fish.* to capture, to catch, to take.

hooligan delinquent, mugger, ruffian, thug, trouble-maker, vandal.

hoop band, circle, ring.

hop to bound, to jump, to leap, to skip, to spring.

hope 1 *Is there any hope of better weather?* likelihood, prospect. 2 *We hope that we'll win.* to have confidence, to have faith, to trust.

hopeful 1 *We're hopeful that we can win.* confident, optimistic. 2 *There are hopeful signs that we can do well.* encouraging, favourable, promising, reassuring.

hopefully 1 *The cat looked hopefully at the scraps left from dinner.* confidently, expectantly, optimistically. 2 (informal) *Hopefully, I'll be fit to play tomorrow.* all being well, probably.! Many people think that this is a wrong use of *hopefully.*

hopeless 1 *a hopeless situation.* desperate, impossible, incurable. 2 *a hopeless footballer.* feeble, incompetent, inefficient, poor, useless, weak, worthless. SEE ALSO **bad.**

horde *a horde of children from the other school.* band, crowd, gang, mob, swarm, tribe. SEE ALSO **group.**

horizontal *Is the snooker table horizontal?* flat, level. ! *Horizontal* is the opposite of *vertical.*

horrible *horrible weather, horrible food, etc.* awful, beastly, dreadful, ghastly, horrid, nasty, terrible. SEE ALSO **unpleasant.**

horrific *a horrific accident.* appalling, dreadful, frightful, gruesome, hair-raising, horrifying, shocking. ! You often use *horrible* to describe things that aren't important, but you use *horrific* to describe things that really horrify you.

horrify *The accident horrified us.* to appal, to frighten, to scare, to shock, to terrify.

horror dismay, dread, fear, terror.

horse 1 bronco, cart-horse, colt, foal, mare, mount, mule, nag, piebald, race-horse, stallion, steed. 2 ITEMS OF EQUIPMENT FOR HORSES: bridle, collar, girth, halter, harness, horseshoe, rein, saddle, spur, stirrups. 3 WAYS TO RIDE A HORSE: to amble, to canter, to gallop, to trot. 4 HORSE-RIDING EVENTS: gymkhana, hunting, pony-trekking, racing, riding, show-jumping, steeplechase.

hose *a water hose.* pipe, tube.

hospitable *The people we stayed with were very hospitable.* friendly, kind, sociable, welcoming.

hostage captive, prisoner.

hostile 1 *a hostile crowd.* aggressive, attacking, belligerent, pugnacious, unfriendly, warlike. 2 *hostile weather conditions.* adverse, contrary, opposing, unfavourable.

hot 1 *hot weather, a hot iron.* baking, blistering, boiling, burning, fiery, red-hot, roasting, scalding, scorching, sizzling, sweltering, warm. 2 *a hot temper.* angry, fierce, passionate, violent. 3 *a hot taste.* gingery, peppery, spicy.

hound 1 SEE **dog.** 2 *The wanted man was hounded by the police.* to chase, to hunt, to pursue, to track down.

house 1 *Come to my house.* abode, dwelling, home, lodgings, place, quarters, residence. 2 KINDS OF HOUSE: apartments, bungalow, chalet, cottage, council house, croft, detached house, farmhouse, flats, hovel, lodge, manor, manse, mansion, prefab, rectory, semi-detached house, shack, shanty, terrace house, thatched house, vicarage, villa. 3 ROOMS IN A HOUSE: attic, bathroom, bedroom, cloakroom, conservatory, corridor, dining-room, drawing-room, hall, kitchen, landing, larder, lavatory, living-room, loft, lounge, outhouse, pantry, parlour, passage, porch, scullery, sitting-room, study, toilet, WC. 4 ITEMS OF EQUIPMENT IN A HOUSE: air-conditioning, barometer, boiler, brush, central heating, clock, double-glazing, duster, fire, fire-extinguisher, freezer, Hoover, immersion heater, incinerator, iron, ironing-board, lighter, mangle, meter, mop, phone, plumbing, radiator, sanitation, scissors, spin-drier, step-ladder, thermometer, thermostat, tray, tumble-drier, vacuum-cleaner, washing-machine, wiring. FOR OTHER HOUSEHOLD EQUIPMENT SEE **bathroom, furniture, kitchen, tool.** 5 *to house someone.* to accommodate, to board, to lodge, to put up, to shelter.

house-trained *a house-trained dog.* clean in the house, domesticated.

hovel cottage, hut, shack, shanty.

hover 1 *The hawk hovered over its prey.* to float, to fly, to hang in the air. 2 *After the party, people hovered about for a while.* to hang about, to linger, to loiter, to wait about.

howler (informal) *to make a howler.* blunder, (informal) clanger, error, mistake, (informal) slip-up.

hubbub SEE **noise.**

huddle 1 *The sheep huddled in the corner of the field.* to cluster, to crowd, to flock, to gather, to herd, to press, to squeeze, to swarm, to throng. 2 *The children huddled together to keep warm.* to cuddle, to curl up, to nestle, to snuggle.

hue colour, shade, tinge, tint, tone.

hug *Dad hugged the baby.* to clasp, to cling to, to crush, to cuddle, to embrace, to hold, to snuggle, to squeeze.

huge *Elephants are huge animals.* colossal, enormous, gigantic, great, immense, large, mammoth, vast. SEE ALSO **big.**

hulking *The hulking wrestler towered above us.* bulky, clumsy, heavy, massive. SEE ALSO **big.**

human beings folk, humanity, mankind, mortals.

humane *Is it humane to kill animals for food?* benevolent, kind, kind-hearted, merciful, sympathetic, unselfish, warm-hearted.

humble 1 *humble behaviour.* lowly, meek, modest, unassuming. **2** *to humble someone.* to bring down, to disgrace, to humiliate, to shame.

humid *humid weather.* clammy, damp, dank, moist, muggy, steamy, sultry.

humiliate *They humiliated us by winning 14–0.* to disgrace, to humble, to make ashamed.

humorous *a humorous story.* amusing, comic, facetious, funny, hilarious, laughable, ridiculous, silly, witty.

humour *You seem to be in a good humour!* mood, state of mind, temper.

hump bulge, bump, lump, swelling.

hunch *I have a hunch that she broke that window.* feeling, guess, intuition.

hunger 1 *Did that meal satisfy your hunger?* appetite, desire, greed, longing. **2** *Hunger kills millions of people.* famine, malnutrition, starvation

hungry *He's always hungry!* famished, greedy, (informal) peckish, ravenous, starved, starving, underfed.

hunk *a hunk of cheese.* block, chunk, lump, mass, piece.

hunt 1 *to hunt animals.* to chase, to hound, to poach, to pursue, to stalk, to track down. **2** *We hunted for mum's keys.* to look for, to search for, to seek. **3** *Does the fox enjoy the hunt as much as the hounds do?* chase, pursuit, quest, search.

hunter predator.

hurdle barrier, fence, obstacle.

hurl *He hurled the sword into the lake.* to cast, to chuck, to fling, to pitch, to sling, to throw, to toss.

hurricane cyclone, storm, tempest, tornado, typhoon.

hurried *a hurried decision, hurried work, etc.* careless, cursory, hasty, impetuous, quick, rushed, speedy.

hurry 1 *I hurried home.* to dash, to hasten, to hurtle, to hustle, to rush, to speed, (informal) to zoom. **2** *If you want to finish you must hurry.* to accelerate, (informal) to buck up, to quicken, to work faster.

hurt 1 *That wasp sting hurts!* to ache, to be painful, to be sore, to smart, to sting, to throb. **2** *Did the attackers hurt her?* to afflict, to cripple, to damage, to disable, to distress, to harm, to injure, to maim, to misuse, to pain, to torment, to torture, to wound.

hurtle to dash, to race, to rush, to speed, (informal) to zoom.

hush 1 be quiet! be silent! shut up! **2** *We tried to hush it up, but everyone found out.* to conceal, to hide, to keep it quiet, to keep it secret.

husk covering, shell.

husky 1 *a husky voice.* croaking, gruff, harsh, hoarse, rasping, rough. **2** *a big, husky fellow.* beefy, big, brawny, bulky, hefty, hulking, muscular, strong.

hustle 1 *The gang hustled their victim into a car.* to jostle, to push, to shove. **2** *As we were late, they hustled us to our seats.* to hurry, to rush.

hut hovel, shack, shanty, shed, shelter.

hutch cage, coop, pen.

hygienic *You need hygienic conditions in hospital.* clean, disinfected, germ-free, healthy, sanitary, sterilized, unpolluted.

hypocritical *Is it hypocritical for a vegetarian to wear leather shoes?* false, inconsistent, insincere.

hysteria frenzy, madness, mania, panic.

hysterical 1 *The fans became hysterical when the group appeared.* delirious, demented, frantic, frenzied, mad, uncontrollable, wild. **2** *a hysterical joke.* comic, funny, hilarious, laughable, ridiculous, uproarious.

I

ice KINDS OF ICE: black ice, floe, glacier, iceberg, icicle.

icy 1 *icy weather.* bitter, cold, freezing, frosty, wintry. 2 *icy roads.* frozen, slippery.

idea 1 *I have an idea.* (informal) brainwave, concept, notion, plan, point, proposal, suggestion, thought. 2 *Have you any idea who will win?* attitude, belief, impression, inkling, opinion, view.

ideal *ideal conditions.* excellent, faultless, perfect, suitable.

identical *identical twins.* alike, equal, indistinguishable.

identify *Did the vet identify what was wrong with the cat?* to detect, to diagnose, to discover, to name, to recognize.

identity *Did you discover his identity?* name.

idiot ass, blockhead, booby, dope, dunce, fool, half-wit, ignoramus, imbecile, moron, nitwit, twerp. ! These words are mostly used informally and are often insulting.

idiotic *an idiotic mistake.* absurd, crazy, foolish, irrational, ludicrous, ridiculous, silly, stupid, unwise.

idle 1 *The machines were idle during the holiday.* inactive, not working, unemployed, unoccupied, unused. 2 *He lost his job because he was so idle.* lazy, slow, sluggish.

idol 1 *a pagan idol.* god, image, statue. 2 *a pop idol.* hero, star, superstar.

idolize *The children idolize their grandfather.* to adore, to love, to revere, to worship.

ignite 1 *The gas fire won't ignite.* to burn, to catch fire, to fire. 2 *I ignited the fire with a match.* to kindle, to light, to set fire to.

ignoramus SEE **idiot.**

ignorant 1 *ignorant of the facts.* unaware, uninformed. 2 *You'd be ignorant if you didn't go to school.* illiterate, uneducated. 3 (insulting) *He's just plain ignorant!* foolish, stupid, unintelligent.

ignore *He ignored the 'stop' sign.* to disobey, to disregard, to leave out, to miss out, to neglect, to omit, to overlook, to skip, to take no notice of.

ill 1 bedridden, diseased, feeble, indisposed, infirm, pasty, (informal) poorly, queer, sick, unhealthy, unwell. 2 ILL PEOPLE: invalid, out-patient, patient, sufferer, victim. 3 *ill effects.* bad, evil, harmful, unfavourable.

illegal *Cycling after dark without lights is illegal.* banned, criminal, forbidden, irregular, unauthorized, unlawful.

illegible *an illegible signature.* indecipherable, unreadable.

illegitimate *an illegitimate child*: bastard. ! Nowadays *bastard* is usually insulting.

illiterate ignorant, uneducated.

illness 1 affliction, ailment, attack, blight, (informal) bug, complaint, disease, disorder, infection, infirmity, injury, malady, sickness, wound. 2 VARIOUS ILLNESSES OR COMPLAINTS: abscess, allergy, amnesia, anaemia, appendicitis, arthritis, asthma, bilious attack, blister, boil, bronchitis, cancer, cataract, catarrh, chicken-pox, chilblain, chill, cholera, claustrophobia, cold, colic, coma, concussion, constipation, convulsion, corns, cough, cramp, dandruff, dermatitis, diabetes, diarrhoea, diphtheria, dysentery, earache, epilepsy, fever, fits, flu, frostbite, gastric flu, hay fever, headache, impetigo, indigestion, inflammation, influenza, insomnia, jaundice, leprosy, leukaemia, lumbago, malaria, measles, migraine, mumps, neuralgia, paralysis, phobia, plague, pneumonia, polio or poliomyelitis, rabies, rheumatism, scarlet fever, scurvy, seasickness, smallpox, spina bifida, stroke, sty, sunstroke, tonsilitis, toothache, tuberculosis, typhoid, typhus, ulcer, verruca, wart, whooping-cough.

illogical irrational, unreasonable.

illuminate to light up.

illusion *It didn't really happen: it was just an illusion.* conjuring trick, delusion, dream, fantasy, hallucination.

illustrate *The pictures illustrate how to do it.* to demonstrate, to depict, to explain, to picture, to portray, to show.

illustration 1 diagram, drawing, picture. 2 *The thesaurus gives illustrations of how words can be used.* case, example, instance.

image 1 *You can see your image in the mirror.* imitation, likeness, picture, reflection. 2 *The temple contained the god's image.* carving, figure, representation, statue.

imaginary *The unicorn is an imaginary beast.* fanciful, fictitious, invented, legendary, made-up, mythical, non-existent, unreal.

imaginative artistic, attractive, beautiful, clever, creative, ingenious, inspired, inventive, resourceful.

imagine 1 *Can you imagine what life was like 1000 years ago?* to conceive, to create, to dream up, to invent, to picture, to see, to think up, to visualize. 2 *I imagine you'd like something to eat.* to assume, to believe, to guess, to presume, to suppose, to think.

imbecile SEE **idiot.**

imitate to copy, to counterfeit, to echo, to duplicate, to impersonate, to mimic, to reproduce.

imitation *It isn't real: it's an imitation.* copy, counterfeit, dummy, duplicate, fake, forgery, likeness, replica, reproduction.

immature *immature behaviour.* babyish, childish, inexperienced, infantile, juvenile, young, youthful.

immediate 1 *I took immediate action.* instant, instantaneous, prompt, quick, speedy, swift. 2 *She talks to her immediate neighbour over the fence.* adjacent, closest, nearest, next.

immediately directly, forthwith, instantly, promptly.

immense colossal, enormous, gigantic, great, huge, large, massive, vast. SEE ALSO **big.**

immerse 1 *to immerse something in water.* to dip, to drench, to drown, to lower, to plunge, to submerge. 2 *immersed: immersed in your work.* absorbed, interested, preoccupied.

immigrate to settle.

immobile *The car was immobile in the mud.* fast, firm, fixed, immobilized, immovable, motionless, paralysed, secure, static, stationary.

immobilize *to immobilize a vehicle.* to cripple, to damage, to put out of action, to stop.

immoral *immoral behaviour.* base, corrupt, depraved, evil, sinful, villainous, wicked. SEE ALSO **bad.**

immortal *Some people believe that your soul is immortal.* endless, eternal, everlasting, undying.

immovable SEE **immobile.**

imp *a mischievous imp.* demon, devil, rascal, rogue, scamp, spirit.

impact 1 *Was the car damaged in the impact?* bump, collision, crash, smash. 2 *The pictures of the famine made a strong impact on us.* effect, impression, influence, shock.

impartial *an impartial referee.* detached, disinterested, fair, just, neutral, unbiased, uninvolved, unprejudiced.

impatient 1 *We were impatient to start.* anxious, eager. 2 *The horses were impatient.* edgy, fidgety, restless.

impede *A fallen tree impeded our progress.* to block, to check, to delay, to deter, to hinder, to obstruct, to slow down.

impenetrable *impenetrable forest.* dense, thick.

imperceptible *an imperceptible movement.* insignificant, invisible, microscopic, minute, negligible, slight, small, tiny, undetectable.

imperfect *If the goods are imperfect take them back to the shop.* defective, faulty, incomplete, unfinished.

imperfection blemish, defect, flaw, shortcoming, weakness.

impersonate to copy, to imitate, to mimic, to pose as, to pretend to be.

impertinent SEE **cheeky.**

impetuous *Our impetuous dash across the road almost caused an accident.* hasty, headlong, impulsive, quick, rash, reckless, speedy.

implement device, gadget, instrument, tool, utensil.

implore *She implored us to stay for tea.* to ask, to beg, to entreat, to plead, to request.

imply *Dad implied that we might have a treat at the weekend.* to hint, to indicate, to suggest.

impolite SEE **rude**.

important 1 *important facts, an important event, etc.* basic, big, chief, essential, fundamental, main, major, momentous, notable, pressing, primary, principal, serious, significant, urgent, weighty. 2 *an important person.* celebrated, distinguished, eminent, famous, great, influential, leading, notable, outstanding, prominent, renowned, well-known. 3 *to be important*: to matter.

impose *to impose a penalty.* to enforce, to inflict, to insist on.

imposing *an imposing castle.* big, grand, great, important, impressive, magnificent, majestic, stately, striking. SEE ALSO **splendid**.

impossible *It'd be impossible to swim the Atlantic.* impracticable, impractical, inconceivable, unimaginable.

impotent *I was impotent to help.* helpless, powerless, weak.

impoverished SEE **poor**.

impregnable *an impregnable castle.* invincible, strong, unconquerable.

impress *Did the film impress you?* to affect, to influence, to move.

impression 1 *I had the impression you were bored.* feeling, idea, opinion, view. 2 *The film made a big impression on us.* effect, impact, mark. 3 *Granny has clear impressions of her childhood.* memory, recollection.

impressive *an impressive occasion.* grand, great, imposing, magnificent, majestic, memorable, moving, spectacular, splendid, stately, striking.

imprison *to imprison a criminal.* to confine, to detain, to gaol, to intern, to lock up, to shut up.

improbable *an improbable story.* far-fetched, incredible, unbelievable, unconvincing, unlikely.

impromptu *an impromptu concert.* spontaneous, unplanned, unprepared, unrehearsed.

improper *improper language.* coarse, crude, inappropriate, indecent, rude, unbecoming, unsuitable, vulgar, wrong.

improve 1 *Your work has improved.* to advance, to develop, to move on, to progress. 2 *Has she improved since her illness?* to get better, to recover. 3 *Has he improved his behaviour?* to reform, to revise. 4 *to improve a house.* to make better, to modernize, to rebuild, to renovate, to touch up, to upgrade.

improvise 1 *We improvised a play.* to concoct, to invent, to make up. 2 *I didn't have all the ingredients, so I had to improvise.* to make do.

impudent SEE **cheeky**.

impulsive *When he thought about it, he regretted his impulsive action.* automatic, hasty, impetuous, impromptu, involuntary, rash, spontaneous, sudden, unconscious, unplanned, unthinking.

impure *impure water.* contaminated, dirty, filthy, foul, infected, polluted, unclean.

inaccessible *The South Pole is an inaccessible spot.* cut off, isolated, remote, unreachable.

inaccuracy error, fault, miscalculation, mistake, (informal) slip-up.

inaccurate *It was silly to give an inaccurate statement to the police.* false, incorrect, mistaken, untrue, wrong.

inactive *Hedgehogs are inactive in winter.* asleep, dormant, hibernating.

inadequate *an inadequate supply of food.* insufficient, unsatisfactory.

inanimate lifeless.

inappropriate *an inappropriate gift.* improper, incongruous, irrelevant, unsuitable, wrong.

incense *Our bad behaviour incensed her.* to anger, to enrage, to inflame, to infuriate, to madden, to provoke, to vex.

incentive *She gave us sweets as an incentive to work.* encouragement, stimulus.

incessant *The insects kept up an incessant buzzing.* ceaseless, chronic, constant, continual, continuous, everlasting, interminable, permanent, persistent, relentless, unending.

incident *The crash at the crossroads was a nasty incident.* affair, event, happening, occasion, occurrence.

incinerator SEE **fire.**

incite *Some trouble-makers incited the crowd to start fighting.* to arouse, to encourage, to excite, to provoke, to rouse, to stimulate, to stir up, to urge.

inclination *Grandad has an inclination to doze in the evening.* habit, instinct, leaning, readiness, tendency, trend.

incline **1** *That pillar inclines to the right.* to lean, to slant, to slope, to tilt, to tip. **2** *inclined to:* disposed to, liable to.

include *The packet includes everything you need to make a trifle.* to consist of, to contain, to cover, to incorporate, to involve.

incoherent *an incoherent message.* confused, disjointed, disorganized, garbled, jumbled, mixed up, muddled, rambling, unclear.

income earnings, pay, pension, salary, wages.

incompatible *What he said today is incompatible with what he said yesterday.* conflicting, contradictory, inconsistent.

incompetent *an incompetent workman.* bad, helpless, (informal) hopeless, incapable, inefficient, unqualified, untrained, useless.

incomplete imperfect, unfinished.

inconceivable *It's inconceivable that anyone could swim the Atlantic.* impossible, unimaginable.

incongruous *Granny thinks it might look incongruous if she wore a miniskirt.* inappropriate, odd, out of place, unsuitable.

inconsiderate *It is inconsiderate of them to park in front of our gate.* careless, negligent, rude, tactless, thoughtless, uncaring, unkind.

inconsistent **1** *Our performance has been inconsistent this season.* changeable, erratic, fickle, patchy, unpredictable, variable. **2** SEE **incompatible.**

inconvenient awkward, bothersome, troublesome.

incorporate *Our book incorporates the latest information.* to consist of, to contain, to include.

incorrect *an incorrect answer.* false, inaccurate, mistaken, untrue, wrong.

increase **1** *They've increased the number of police.* to add to, to boost, to build up, to enlarge, to expand, to strengthen, to swell. **2** *The traffic jam increased our journey by an hour.* to extend, to lengthen, to prolong. **3** *Dad increased my pocket-money.* to improve, to raise, to step up. **4** *Prices seem to increase every day.* to escalate, to go up, to grow, to multiply, to rise.

incredible *an incredible story.* extraordinary, far-fetched, improbable, miraculous, unbelievable, unconvincing, unlikely.

incredulous *She was incredulous when I said I'd won.* disbelieving, dubious, sceptical, unconvinced.

incriminate *He incriminated me to avoid taking all the blame.* to accuse, to blame, to involve.

incubate *The hen was incubating her eggs.* to brood, to hatch.

incurable *an incurable illness.* hopeless.

indecent *indecent language.* coarse, crude, dirty, foul, improper, obscene, offensive, rude, smutty, vulgar.

indecipherable *indecipherable handwriting.* illegible, unreadable.

indefinite *He was indefinite about how much it would cost.* confused, general, neutral, uncertain, unclear, undecided, unsure, vague.

indelible *indelible ink.* fast, fixed, permanent.

independence *Do animals in the zoo miss their independence?* freedom, liberty.

independent *an independent business.* free, private, self-governing.

indestructible *indestructible plastic.* durable, everlasting, unbreakable.

index *an index of library books.* alphabetical list, catalogue, directory, register.

indicate **1** *Indicate which way you are turning.* to make known, to point out, to register, to show. **2** *A red light indicates danger.* to be a sign of, to communicate, to convey, to mean, to stand for, to symbolize.

indication *The spots are an indication of measles.* clue, hint, omen, sign, signal, symptom, token, warning.

indifferent 1 *He seemed indifferent about the result.* cold, cool, half-hearted, unconcerned, uninterested. 2 *indifferent food.* commonplace, fair, mediocre, middling, moderate, ordinary, unexciting.

indignant angry, cross, furious, infuriated, irate, irritated, scornful, upset, vexed.

indirect *an indirect route.* devious, rambling, roundabout.

indispensable *A fishing rod is indispensable to an angler.* essential, necessary, vital.

indisposed *The teacher wasn't here because she was indisposed.* ill, (informal) poorly, sick, unwell.

indistinct 1 *an indistinct picture.* blurred, confused, dim, faint, fuzzy, hazy, misty, obscure, unclear. 2 *indistinct sounds.* deadened, dull, muffled.

indistinguishable *The twins are indistinguishable.* alike, identical.

individual 1 *She has her own individual style.* characteristic, different, distinct, distinctive, particular, peculiar, personal, private, separate, special, specific, unique.

indoctrinate to brainwash, to instruct, to teach, to train.

induce 1 *We couldn't induce granny to come to the disco.* to coax, to persuade, to tempt. 2 *What induced your cold?* to bring on, to cause, to lead to, to produce, to provoke.

indulgent *Mum says that grandpa is too indulgent.* easygoing, forgiving, genial, kind, lenient, patient, tolerant.

industrial *an industrial area.* industrialized, manufacturing.

industrious *an industrious worker.* busy, conscientious, diligent, earnest, enterprising, hard-working, involved, keen.

industry *Is there much industry in this town?* business, commerce, manufacturing, trade.

inedible *inedible food.* uneatable.

ineffective *an ineffective attempt to score.* feeble, futile, unsuccessful, useless.

inefficient 1 *an inefficient workman.* (informal) hopeless, incapable, incompetent. 2 *an inefficient use of resources.* extravagant, wasteful.

inevitable *Disaster was inevitable when the brakes failed.* certain, inescapable, sure, unavoidable.

inexcusable unforgivable, wrong.

inexhaustible never-ending.

inexpensive cheap, cut-price, economical, reasonable.

inexplicable *an inexplicable mystery.* baffling, insoluble, mysterious, puzzling, unaccountable.

infamous *an infamous crime.* disgraceful, evil, notorious, outrageous, scandalous, shocking, wicked.

infant baby, child.

infantile *infantile games.* babyish, childish, immature.

infatuation love, obsession, passion.

infect 1 to contaminate, to poison, to pollute. 2 *infected: an infected wound.* festering, inflamed, poisoned, putrid, septic.

infection *to catch an infection.* ailment, (informal) bug, blight, disease. SEE ALSO **illness.**

infectious *an infectious disease.* catching, contagious.

inferior 1 *an inferior rank.* junior, lower, subordinate. 2 *inferior quality.* cheap, poor-quality, shoddy, tawdry, tinny.

inferno blaze, conflagration, fire.

infested *infested with mice.* overrun, swarming.

infidelity 1 *infidelity to your team.* disloyalty, treachery, treason. 2 *infidelity to a wife or husband.* adultery, unfaithfulness.

infinite *Space is infinite.* boundless, endless, everlasting, immeasurable, interminable, limitless, unending, unlimited.

infirm bedridden, elderly, frail, ill, old, (informal) poorly, senile, unwell, weak.

infirmary clinic, health centre, hospital.

inflame 1 *to inflame someone's anger.* to arouse, to enrage, to excite, to incense, to infuriate, to madden, to provoke. 2 *inflamed: an inflamed wound.* festering, infected, poisoned.

inflammation abscess, boil, sore.

inflate *to inflate a tyre.* to blow up, to pump up.

inflexible 1 *an inflexible framework.* firm, hard, rigid, solid, unbending, unyielding. 2 *an inflexible attitude.* obstinate, strict, stubborn.

inflict *to inflict a punishment.* to administer, to impose.

influence 1 *Did the weather have any influence on the game?* effect, impact. 2 *Parents have influence over their children.* authority, control, power. 3 *Does TV violence influence you?* to affect, to control, to dominate, to impress, to modify, to move, to stir. 4 *Don't try to influence the referee.* to bribe, to persuade.

influential 1 *an influential person.* important, powerful. 2 *an influential idea.* convincing, persuasive.

inform 1 to advise, to notify, to tell. 2 *to inform against*: to complain about, to denounce, to report, to spy on, to tell of.

informal 1 *informal clothes.* casual, comfortable. 2 *an informal party.* easygoing, friendly, relaxed.

information 1 *Is there any information about our outing?* announcement, communication, message, news, report, statement. 2 *The police are collecting information.* data, evidence, facts, knowledge, statistics.

informer spy, tell-tale.

infrequent *The golden eagle is an infrequent sight in Britain.* occasional, rare, uncommon, unusual.

infringe *to infringe the law.* to break, to disobey, to disregard, to violate.

infuriate SEE **anger.**

ingenious *an ingenious plan.* artful, clever, crafty, cunning, imaginative, inventive, resourceful, shrewd, skilful.

ingot *a gold ingot.* lump, nugget.

ingredient component, element, part.

inhabit *We inhabit a council flat.* to dwell in, to live on, to occupy, to populate, to reside in.

inhabitant citizen, native, occupant, population, resident, tenant.

inhale *to inhale smoke.* to breathe in.

inheritance *He got a small inheritance from his uncle's will.* bequest, estate, fortune, legacy.

inherited *an inherited title.* hereditary.

inheritor heir.

inhospitable *an inhospitable welcome.* unfriendly, unwelcoming.

inhuman *inhuman cruelty.* bestial, bloodthirsty, cruel, heartless, merciless, pitiless, ruthless, savage, unfeeling.

initial *If you buy this on hire-purchase, the initial payment is £10.* earliest, first, opening, original, starting.

initiate *to initiate negotiations.* to begin, to commence, to embark on, to launch, to open, to start.

initiative *to take the initiative*: to begin, to commence, to open, to start.

injure to damage, to harm, to hurt. SEE ALSO **wound.**

inkling *I'd no inkling he was coming.* clue, hint, idea, indication.

inlet bay, creek, fiord.

inn hotel, pub, tavern.

innocent 1 *The trial proved he was innocent.* blameless, guiltless. 2 *Sleeping babies look innocent.* angelic, chaste, harmless, inoffensive, pure, virtuous.

innocuous *Grass-snakes are innocuous.* harmless, innocent, inoffensive, mild, safe.

innumerable *innumerable stars.* countless, numberless, untold.

inoffensive SEE **innocuous.**

inquest inquiry.

inquire to ask, to beg, to demand, to enquire, to entreat, to implore, to query, to question, to request.

inquiry inquest, investigation.

inquisitive *It's rude to be inquisitive.* curious, interested, nosey, prying.

insane *an insane idea, an insane person, etc.* crazy, demented, deranged, (informal) dotty, (informal) loony, lunatic, mad, unhinged.

insanitary dirty, unhealthy.

inscribe SEE **write**.

insect 1 VARIOUS INSECTS: ant, bee, beetle, blackbeetle, bluebottle, bumble-bee, butterfly, cockroach, crane-fly, cricket, daddy-long-legs, dragon-fly, drone, earwig, fly, glow-worm, gnat, grasshopper, hornet, ladybird, locust, louse, midge, mosquito, moth, nit, tsetse fly, wasp, woodworm. 2 OTHER FORMS OF AN INSECT: caterpillar, chrysalis, grub, larva, maggot. 3 OTHER CRAWLING CREATURES: centipede, earthworm, mite, slug, snail, spider, wood-louse, worm. ! These creatures are not proper insects.

insecticide pesticide.

insecure *an insecure foothold*. loose, precarious, rocky, shaky, unsafe, unsteady, wobbly.

insensible *I was insensible after the accident*. knocked out, senseless, unconscious.

insensitive *It was insensitive to joke about granny's operation*. callous, cruel, hard-hearted, heartless, tactless, thoughtless, unfeeling.

insert *Insert a coin*. to push in, to put in, to tuck in.

inside centre, core, heart, middle.

insignificant *an insignificant improvement*. imperceptible, minor, minute, negligible, small, trifling, trivial, unimportant.

insincere *an insincere compliment*. deceitful, dishonest, false, hypocritical.

insist 1 *She insists that she is innocent*. to assert, to emphasize, to maintain, to state, to stress. 2 *They insisted that I went to the police station*. to command, to demand, to enforce, to require.

insolent *an insolent stare*. arrogant, bold, cheeky, disrespectful, impertinent, impolite, impudent, insulting, presumptuous, rude.

insoluble *an insoluble problem*. baffling, inexplicable, mysterious, puzzling, unanswerable.

insomnia sleeplessness.

inspect *We inspected the damage*. to check, to examine, to investigate.

inspection check-up, examination, investigation, scrutiny.

inspire *The big crowd inspired us to play well*. to arouse, (informal) to egg on, to encourage, to prompt, to reassure, to stimulate, to support.

install *We installed central heating*. to establish, to put in, to set up.

instalment 1 *Have you paid all the instalments?* payment, rent. 2 *Did you see last week's instalment?* episode.

instance *Give me an instance of what you mean*. case, example, illustration, sample.

instant 1 *an instant reply*. immediate, instantaneous, prompt, quick, speedy, swift. 2 *The shooting star was gone in an instant*. flash, moment, second.

instantaneous immediate, instant.

instinct *Animals have an instinct to look after their young*. feeling, inclination, intuition, tendency.

institution 1 *a regular institution*. custom, habit, practice, routine. 2 *an institution for blind people*. establishment, organization.

instruct 1 to coach, to lecture, to teach, to train. SEE ALSO **educate**. 2 *He instructed us to wait*. to command, to direct, to order.

instructive *an instructive book*. educational, helpful, informative.

instructor coach, teacher, trainer.

instrument 1 *an instrument for measuring rainfall*. apparatus, device, equipment, gadget, implement, machine, tool, utensil. 2 *musical instruments*. SEE **music**.

insubordinate *The insubordinate soldier was punished*. defiant, disobedient, mutinous, rebellious.

insufficient *insufficient food*. inadequate, meagre, scanty, unsatisfactory.

insulate *to insulate pipes*. to lag.

insult 1 *Your chatter was an insult to our visitor*. cheek, impudence, rudeness. 2 *He didn't mean to insult her*. to abuse, to be rude, to mock, to offend, to snub.

intact *Did the glasses arrive intact?* complete, entire, perfect, undamaged, untouched, whole.

integer digit, figure, number.

integrate *to integrate two teams*. to amalgamate, to combine, to join, to merge, to put together, to unite.

integrity *You can trust his complete integrity.* fidelity, honesty, honour, principle, sincerity, virtue.

intellect ability, brains, cleverness, genius, intelligence, mind, reason, sense, understanding.

intellectual 1 *an intellectual student.* SEE **intelligent.** 2 *an intellectual book.* cultural, deep, educational, highbrow, improving.

intelligence 1 SEE **intellect.** 2 *Our intelligence discovered some enemy secrets.* espionage, spying.

intelligent *an intelligent student.* brainy, bright, clever, intellectual, wise.

intelligible *an intelligible message.* clear, comprehensible, logical, lucid, unambiguous, understandable.

intend *What do you intend to do?* to aim, to contemplate, to design, to mean, to plan, to plot, to propose, to scheme.

intense 1 *intense pain.* acute, extreme, keen, severe, sharp, strong, violent. 2 *intense feelings.* burning, deep, eager, earnest, passionate, profound, serious, vehement.

intent *intent on what you're doing.* absorbed, determined, eager, keen.

intention *What is your intention?* aim, ambition, goal, object, objective, plan, point, purpose, target.

intentional *an intentional foul.* conscious, deliberate, intended, premeditated, wilful.

intercept *We intercepted their gang before they got near our den.* to ambush, to attack, to cut off, to head off, to stop, to trap.

interchange *a motorway interchange.* crossroads, intersection, junction.

interest 1 *Did he show any interest?* attention, concern, curiosity, notice. 2 *What are your main interests?* hobby, pastime, pursuit. 3 *Astronomy interests me.* to appeal to, to attract, to fascinate, to intrigue. 4 *interested*: absorbed, curious, preoccupied.

interfere to be a busybody, to butt in, to interrupt, to intervene, to intrude, to meddle, to molest, to pry, to snoop, to tamper.

interlude *There will be an interlude before Part 2.* break, gap, intermission, interval, lull, pause.

intermediate *an intermediate position.* half-way, middle, neutral.

interminable SEE **endless.**

intermission SEE **interlude.**

intermittent *an intermittent fault.* occasional, on and off, spasmodic.

intern SEE **imprison.**

internal inner, inside, interior.

interpret *Can you interpret this old writing?* to decipher, to decode, to explain, to make clear, to translate.

interrogate *The police interrogated him.* to ask questions, to cross-examine, to examine, to question.

interrupt 1 *Please interrupt if you have questions.* to break in, to butt in, to cut in, to intervene, to intrude. 2 *A fire alarm interrupted the lesson.* to break off, to disrupt, to disturb, to interfere with.

interruption break, gap, pause.

intersect *Two motorways intersect.* to converge, to cross, to divide, to pass across.

intersection crossroads, interchange, junction.

interval 1 *an interval in time or space.* break, distance, gap, lapse, lull, opening, pause, respite, rest, space. 2 *We had an ice-cream in the interval.* break, interlude, intermission.

intervene *She intervened when we started quarrelling.* to butt in, to come between, to interfere, to interrupt, to intrude.

interview *A reporter interviewed the eyewitness.* to ask questions, to question.

intimate 1 *an intimate relationship.* affectionate, close, familiar, friendly, loving. 2 *intimate details.* confidential, personal, private, secret.

intimidate SEE **frighten.**

intolerable unbearable.

intolerant narrow-minded, prejudiced.

intoxicate 1 *intoxicated*: drunk, fuddled. 2 *intoxicating*: alcoholic.

intrepid *intrepid explorers.* bold, brave, courageous, daring, fearless, heroic, valiant.

intricate *intricate machinery.* complex, complicated, delicate, detailed, elaborate, involved.

intrigue 1 *Guy Fawkes took part in an intrigue against parliament.* conspiracy, plot, scheme. 2 *The parrot's swearwords intrigued us.* to appeal to, to arouse the curiosity of, to attract, to fascinate, to interest.

introduce 1 *Dad introduced me to his friend.* to make known, to present. 2 *The DJ introduced the next disc.* to announce. 3 *They introduced a new bus service.* to begin, to bring out, to create, to establish, to initiate, to set up, to start.

introduction *an introduction to a book.* preface, prelude, prologue.

intrude *Please don't intrude during the staff meeting.* to butt in, to interfere, to interrupt, to intervene.

intruder *The intruder ran away when the burglar alarm went off.* burglar, prowler, robber, thief, trespasser.

intuition *I had an intuition that you'd come.* feeling, instinct.

inundate *A tidal wave inundated the town.* to drown, to engulf, to flood, to submerge, to swamp.

invade to attack, to march into, to occupy, to overrun, to raid.

invalid 1 *an invalid who spends most of the time in bed.* patient, sufferer. 2 *an invalid passport.* out-of-date, unacceptable, unusable.

invaluable *Your help was invaluable.* precious, useful.

invariable *an invariable rule.* constant, reliable, unchangeable, unchanging, unvarying.

invasion attack, onslaught, raid.

invent to conceive, to concoct, to contrive, to create, to devise, to discover, to make up, to plan, to put together, to think up.

invention *a useful invention.* contraption, contrivance, device, discovery.

inventive *an inventive story-teller.* creative, enterprising, imaginative, ingenious, resourceful.

inventor creator, discoverer, originator.

invest *to invest money.* to save.

investigate *to investigate a topic.* to examine, to explore, to inquire into, to study.

investigation *an investigation into a crime.* examination, inquiry, inspection, research, scrutiny.

invigorating *an invigorating shower.* healthy, refreshing, stimulating.

invincible *We never scored: their defence was invincible.* impregnable, strong, unbeatable, unconquerable.

invisible *an invisible repair.* concealed, covered, hidden, imperceptible, inconspicuous, obscured, undetectable, unseen.

invite 1 *We invite you to join in.* to ask, to encourage, to request, to urge. 2 *inviting*: SEE **attractive**.

involuntary *Blinking is usually an involuntary movement.* automatic, impulsive, spontaneous, unconscious, unintentional, unthinking.

involve 1 *What does a policeman's job involve?* to contain, to include. 2 *The problem of feeding the world involves us all.* to affect, to concern, to interest. 3 *He tried to involve me in the crime.* to incriminate, to mix up. 4 *involved: involved in your work.* active, busy, employed, occupied. 5 *an involved story.* complex, complicated, confusing, elaborate, intricate.

irascible SEE **irritable**.

irate SEE **angry**.

iron 1 *They put convicts in irons.* chains, fetters, shackles. 2 *to iron clothes.* to flatten, to press, to smooth.

irrational *an irrational argument.* crazy, illogical, unreasonable.

irregular 1 *an irregular surface.* bumpy, rough, uneven. 2 *irregular intervals.* erratic, random, unequal, variable. 3 *It's irregular for this train to stop here.* abnormal, illegal, odd, peculiar, unauthorized, unusual.

irrelevant *Leave out the irrelevant details.* inappropriate, pointless, unconnected.

irrepressible *Our puppy is irrepressible.* boisterous, lively, uncontrollable.

irresistible *an irresistible temptation.* alluring, attractive, overpowering.

irresponsible *It is irresponsible to light fires during the dry weather.* careless, inconsiderate, negligent, reckless, unthinking, untrustworthy, wanton.

irreverent *irreverent behaviour in church.* blasphemous, disrespectful, sacrilegious.

irrigate to water.

irritable bad-tempered, edgy, grumpy, irascible, peevish, petulant, short-tempered, snappy, testy, touchy.

irritate 1 *Loud music irritates the neighbours.* (informal) to aggravate, to anger, to annoy, to bother, to exasperate, to make cross, to pester, to provoke, to upset, to vex, to worry. 2 *Cigarette smoke irritates my eyes.* to cause discomfort to, to cause itching in, to tickle.

Islam WORDS TO DO WITH ISLAM: Allah, imam, Koran, minaret, mosque, Muhammadan, Muslim, Ramadan.

island isle.

isolate 1 *They isolated the home supporters from the visitors.* to cut off, to segregate, to separate, to set apart. 2 *isolated: an isolated farmhouse.* desolate, inaccessible, lonely, private, remote, secluded, solitary.

issue 1 *Smoke issued from the chimney.* to appear, to come out, to emerge, to erupt, to flow out, to gush. 2 *The Post Office issued a special set of stamps.* to bring out, to circulate, to distribute, to give out, to print, to publish, to release, to send out. 3 *a political issue.* controversy, dispute, matter, problem, question, subject. 4 *an issue of a magazine.* edition, number, publication.

itch 1 *an itch inside my shoe.* irritation, tickle, tingle. 2 *an itch to be naughty.* desire, longing, urge, wish, yearning.

item *Have you any items for the jumble sale?* article, object, piece, thing.

J

jab to poke, to prod, to stab.

jackpot *to win the jackpot.* prize.

jaded *By the end of the day the class seemed jaded.* bored, (informal) done in, exhausted, tired out, weary.

jagged *a jagged edge.* rough, sharp, uneven.

jam 1 *It's illegal to jam so many people into a minibus.* to cram, to crowd, to crush, to pack, to squeeze. 2 *Cars jammed the street.* to block, to bung up, to congest, to fill, to obstruct, to overcrowd, to stop up. 3 *Jam the door open.* to stick, to wedge. 4 *Help me out of a jam!* difficulty, dilemma, plight, predicament, trouble.

jamboree carnival, celebration, festival, fête, party.

jar 1 *The collision jarred me.* to jerk, to jolt, to shake, to shock. 2 *jarring: a jarring noise.* grating, harsh, raucous, unpleasant.

jaunt *to go on a jaunt.* excursion, expedition, outing, tour, trip.

jaunty *a jaunty tune.* alert, bright, frisky, lively, perky, sprightly.

javelin lance, spear.

jealous *He's jealous because I won.* bitter, envious, grudging, resentful.

jeer *It was unkind to jeer at the losers.* to laugh at, to make fun of, to mock, to ridicule, to scoff at, to sneer at, to taunt.

jerk *If you jerk the lid it may come off.* to jolt, to pull, to tug, to twist, to twitch, to wrench.

jest to joke.

jester *the king's jester.* clown, comic, fool, wit.

jet *a jet of water.* fountain, gush, spray, spurt, squirt, stream.

jetty *A boat tied up at the jetty.* landing-stage, pier, quay, wharf.

Jew WORDS TO DO WITH THE JEWISH RELIGION: bar mitzvah, kosher food, Passover, rabbi, sabbath, scripture, synagogue, Yom Kippur.

jewel gem, precious stone.

jewellery 1 KINDS OF JEWELLERY: bangle, beads, bracelet, brooch, chain, clasp, ear-rings, locket, necklace, pendant, ring. 2 THINGS USED TO MAKE JEWELLERY: amber, coral, diamond, emerald, gold, ivory, jade, jet, opal, pearl, platinum, ruby, sapphire, silver.

jittery SEE **nervous**.

job 1 *Has your brother found a job yet?* employment, occupation, position, post, profession, trade, work. 2 *We do jobs in the house.* assignment, chore, duty, errand, function, task. 3 VARIOUS JOBS: accountant, air hostess, architect, artist (SEE **art**), astronaut, astronomer, banker, barber, barmaid or barman, barrister, blacksmith, bookmaker, brewer, bricklayer, builder, butler, caretaker, carpenter, cashier, caterer, chauffeur, chef, chemist, chimney-sweep, cleaner, clergyman, clerk, cobbler, commentator, composer, conductor, constable, cook, courier, curator, decorator, dentist, designer, detective, docker, doctor, driver, dustman, editor, electrician, engineer, entertainer (SEE **entertainment**), estate agent, executive, farmer, fireman, forester, gamekeeper, gardener, glazier, groom, groundsman, hairdresser, interpreter, joiner, journalist, labourer, lawyer, lecturer, librarian, life-guard, linguist, mannequin, manufacturer, mason, mechanic, midwife, milkman, miller, model, naturalist, night-watchman, nurse, optician, parson, photographer, physiotherapist, pilot, plasterer, plumber, policeman, politician, porter, postman, printer, probation officer, professor, programmer, publisher, radiographer, receptionist, reporter, salesman, saleswoman, scientist (SEE **science**), secretary, shepherd, shoemaker, signalman, social worker, solicitor, steeplejack, stunt man, surgeon, tailor, teacher, technician, test pilot, traffic warden, translator, typist, undertaker, usher or usherette, vet, waiter or waitress, warder, woodman. SEE ALSO **shopkeeper**.

jockey horseman, horsewoman, rider.

jog 1 *to jog someone's elbow.* to jolt, to knock, to nudge. 2 *to jog someone's memory.* to prompt, to refresh. 3 *to jog round the park.* to exercise, to run.

join 1 *to join things together.* to add, to amalgamate, to attach, to combine, to couple, to fasten, to fix, to link, to put together. 2 *Two rivers join here.* to come together, to converge, to merge. 3 *Are you going to join the youth club?* to enlist in, to enrol in, to participate in, to register for, to sign on for, to volunteer for. 4 *I can't see the join.* connection, joint, knot, link, mend, seam.

joiner carpenter.

joint 1 JOINTS IN YOUR BODY: ankle, elbow, hip, knee, knuckle, shoulder, vertebra, wrist. 2 *It was a joint effort: everyone helped.* common, communal, general, shared.

joist beam, girder, rafter.

joke 1 *I told a joke.* gag, jest, pun. 2 *I was joking.* to be facetious, to jest.

jolly *a jolly party.* bright, cheerful, happy, jovial, joyful, merry.

jolt 1 *The car jolted over the rough track.* to bounce, to bump, to jar, to jerk, to shake, to twitch. 2 *The shout jolted us into action.* to shock, to startle.

jostle *The big crowd jostled us.* to hustle, to push, to shove.

jot *I jotted down her phone number.* to note, to scribble, to write.

jotter exercise book, notebook, pad.

journal 1 *You find interesting journals in the library.* magazine, newspaper, paper, periodical. 2 *The captain wrote a journal describing the voyage.* account, diary, log, record.

journalist correspondent, reporter.

journey KINDS OF JOURNEY: cruise, drive, excursion, expedition, flight, hike, mission, outing, pilgrimage, ride, safari, sail, tour, trek, trip, voyage, walk.

jovial *a jovial man.* bright, cheerful, happy, jolly, joyful, merry.

joy bliss, delight, ecstasy, happiness, mirth, pleasure, rapture.

joyful cheerful, elated, exultant, glad, jolly, jovial, merry, overjoyed. SEE ALSO **happy**.

jubilee anniversary, celebration.

judge 1 *The headmaster is the chief judge at sports day.* adjudicator, arbitrator, referee, umpire. 2 *The referee judged that the ball was out.* to adjudicate, to conclude, to decide, to pass judgement, to rule. 3 *He was judged in a court of law.* to condemn, to convict, to punish, to sentence. 4 *Don't judge others.* to criticize, to rebuke, to scold. 5 *I judged that the eggs were cooked.* to believe, to consider, to guess, to reckon, to suppose.

judgement *Use your judgement.* discretion, good sense, reason, wisdom.

jumble 1 *Don't jumble those papers I've just sorted.* to confuse, to mix up, to muddle, to shuffle. 2 *My room is full of jumble.* chaos, clutter, confusion, disorder, mess, muddle.

jump 1 to bounce, to bound, to hop, to leap, to pounce, to skip, to spring. 2 *to jump a fence.* to clear, to vault. 3 *to jump about.* to caper, to dance, to frisk, to prance. 4 *The bang made me jump.* to flinch, to jerk, to start.

jumpy *Why are you so jumpy?* edgy, fidgety, jittery, nervous, restless, tense.

junction *a road junction.* corner, crossroads, interchange, intersection.

jungle forest, undergrowth, woods.

junior *junior rank.* inferior, lower, subordinate, younger.

junk *Throw away this junk.* garbage, litter, lumber, odds and ends, refuse, rubbish, scrap, trash, waste.

just *The decision to send him off was just.* fair, honest, impartial, lawful, legal, proper, rightful, right-minded, unbiased, unprejudiced.

justice fairness, the law, punishment, retribution, vengeance.

justify *Can you justify what you did?* to defend, to excuse, to explain, to support.

jut *A shelf juts out from the wall.* to overhang, to project, to protrude, to stick out.

juvenile 1 *juvenile behaviour.* childish, immature. 2 *juvenile novels.* adolescent, young, youthful.

K

keen 1 *He's keen to do well.* anxious, avid, eager, enthusiastic, fervent, interested. 2 *a keen pupil.* bright, clever, intelligent, quick, shrewd. 3 *keen eyesight.* acute, sharp. 4 *a keen frost.* extreme, intense, severe.

keep 1 *Keep it safe. Keep it for later.* to hang on to, to hold, to preserve, to put away, to retain, to save, to store, to stow away, to withhold. 2 *The farmer keeps sheep.* to care for, to cherish, to guard, to look after, to mind, to protect, to safeguard, to tend. 3 *Keep going!* to carry on, to continue, to persevere, to persist. 4 *Keep where you are!* to linger, to remain, to stay. 5 *How much does it cost to keep a family?* to feed, to maintain, to pay for, to provide for, to support. 6 *I won't keep you.* to delay, to detain, to hinder, to hold up, to obstruct. 7 *Keep to the rules!* to abide by, to be ruled by, to conform to, to

obey, to submit to. 8 *How long will this milk keep?* to be usable, to last.

keeper *a keeper in a zoo.* custodian, guard, guardian, warder.

keg barrel.

kernel nut.

key *the key to a problem.* clue.

keyboard KEYBOARD INSTRUMENTS: harmonium, harpsichord, organ, piano.

kick 1 to boot, to punt. 2 (informal) *to get a kick out of something.* adventure, excitement, stimulation, thrill.

kid 1 (informal) child, youngster. 2 (informal) *Don't try to kid me!* to bluff, to fool, to hoodwink, to lie to. SEE ALSO **deceive.**

kidnap to abduct, to carry off.

kill 1 to annihilate, to assassinate, (informal) to bump off, to destroy, to dispatch, to execute, to exterminate, to finish off, to martyr, to massacre, to murder, to put down, to put to death, to slaughter, to slay. 2 WAYS TO KILL: to behead, to choke, to crucify, to decapitate, to drown, to electrocute, to gas, to guillotine, to hang, to knife, to lynch, to poison, to shoot, to smother, to stab, to stifle, to stone, to strangle, to suffocate, to throttle. 3 *killing*: assassination, bloodshed, carnage, execution, homicide, manslaughter, massacre, murder, slaughter, suicide.

kind 1 *a kind of dog, a kind of butter, etc.* brand, breed, category, class, form, make, nature, set, sort, species, type, variety. 2 *a kind action, a kind person, etc.* affectionate, agreeable, amiable, attentive, benevolent, compassionate, considerate, encouraging, favourable, friendly, generous, genial, gentle, good-natured, good-tempered, helpful, humane, kind-hearted, kindly, merciful, mild, motherly, neighbourly, nice, obliging, pleasant, polite, public-spirited, soft-hearted, sympathetic, tender, thoughtful, unselfish, warm-hearted.

kindle to burn, to fire, to ignite, to light, to set fire to.

kingdom monarchy, realm.

kink *a kink in a rope.* loop, tangle, twist.

kiosk booth, stall, telephone-box.

kiss to caress, to embrace.

kit *games kit.* equipment, gear, rig, tackle.

kitchen THINGS YOU FIND IN A KITCHEN: baking tin, basin, blender, bowl, breadboard, bread-knife, carving-knife, casserole, chip pan, cooker, corkscrew, dish, dishrack, dishwasher, draining-board, extractor fan, freezer, fridge, frying-pan, glass, grill, jug, kettle, ladle, larder, lighter, microwave oven, mincer, mixer, oven, pan, pantry, paper towel, percolator, pot, range, refrigerator, rolling-pin, salt-cellar, saucepan, scales, sink, skewer, stove,

strainer, table-cloth, tea-cloth, teapot, thermos, tin-opener, toaster, tray, vacuum flask, whisk. SEE ALSO **crockery, cutlery.**

knack *You need a special knack to flush our toilet.* art, gift, skill, talent.

knapsack haversack, rucksack.

knave (old-fashioned) blackguard, rascal, rogue, scoundrel, villain.

kneel *He knelt to tie his shoe.* to bend, to bow, to crouch, to stoop.

knickers briefs, panties, pants, shorts, trunks, underpants.

knife 1 carving-knife, penknife, scalpel. 2 *to knife someone.* SEE **kill.**

knight warrior. SEE ALSO **fighter.**

knob 1 *a brass knob on his walking-stick.* handle. 2 bulge, bump, lump, swelling.

knock 1 *to knock against something.* (informal) to bash, to bump, to rap, to strike, to tap. SEE ALSO **hit.** 2 *knocked out*: insensible, unconscious.

knot 1 VARIOUS KNOTS: bow, granny-knot, reef-knot. 2 *to knot ropes together.* to bind, to join, to lash, to tie.

know 1 *Do you know who he is?* to discern, to distinguish, to perceive, to realize, to recognize, to remember, to see. 2 *I know a TV actor.* to be acquainted with, to be familiar with, to be a friend of. 3 *Do you know any French?* to appreciate, to comprehend, to understand.

know-all expert, genius, master-mind.

know-how *Have you got the know-how to sail a boat on your own?* ability, competence, knowledge, skill, talent, technique, training.

knowing *a knowing smile.* artful, crafty, cunning, sly, wily.

knowledge 1 *You need a lot of knowledge to do well in a quiz.* education, experience, facts, learning, wisdom. 2 *We've no knowledge of what happened to our uncle.* information, news.

knowledgeable educated, learned, well-informed.

L

label *Put a label on your suitcase.* sticker, tag, ticket.

laborious *a laborious climb.* arduous, difficult, exhausting, gruelling, hard, stiff, strenuous, tough, uphill.

labour *You deserve a reward for your labour.* drudgery, effort, exertion, slavery, toil, work.

labyrinth *a labyrinth of corridors.* maze.

lace *black shoes with red laces.* cord, string.

lack 1 *The game lacked excitement.* to be deficient in, to be short of, to need, to require, to want. 2 *They are dying for lack of food.* absence, need, scarcity, shortage, want.

lad boy, youngster, youth.

ladder fire-escape.

laden *laden with shopping.* burdened, loaded, weighed down.

lady woman.

ladylike *ladylike behaviour.* (informal) posh, refined. SEE ALSO **polite**.

lag 1 *to lag behind.* to dally, to dawdle, to fall behind, to hang about, to linger, to loiter, to straggle. 2 *to lag hot water pipes.* to insulate, to wrap up.

lair *an animal's lair.* den, hide-out, hiding-place.

lake pond, reservoir.

lame 1 *The lame man used a walking-stick.* crippled, disabled, limping, maimed. 2 *a lame excuse.* feeble, flimsy, poor, tame, unconvincing, weak.

lance javelin, spear.

land 1 *The refugees had to leave their own land.* country, nation, state, territory. 2 *The farmer ploughed the land.* earth, soil. 3 *He bought some land.* estate, ground. 4 *The ship reached land.* mainland. 5 *The plane landed.* to come down, to touch down. 6 *The sailors landed.* to disembark, to go ashore.

landing-stage berth, dock, harbour, jetty, port, quay, wharf.

landing-strip aerodrome, airfield, airstrip, runway.

landlady, landlord owner.

landscape *a painting of the landscape.* countryside, panorama, scene, scenery, view, vista.

lane SEE **road**.

language 1 *a foreign language.* tongue. 2 *a computer language.* code. 3 WORDS TO DO WITH LANGUAGE: accent, adjective, adverb, brogue, conjunction, consonant, dialect, grammar, informal language, noun, paragraph, phrase, plural, prefix, preposition, pronoun, sentence, singular, slang, spelling, suffix, swear-word, syllable, synonym, verb, vocabulary, vowel, word. SEE **punctuation**.

lanky *a lanky figure.* bony, long, lean, scraggy, skinny, tall, thin.

lantern SEE **light**.

lap *a lap of a race-track.* circuit.

lapse *We started training again after a lapse during the holidays.* break, gap, interval, pause.

larder food, cupboard, pantry.

large *a large building, large helpings, a large sum of money, etc.* ample, big, bold, bulky, colossal, considerable, enormous, extensive, fat, giant, gigantic, grand, great, hefty, high, huge, hulking, immeasurable, immense, incalculable, infinite, large, lofty, long, massive, mighty, monstrous, roomy, sizeable, spacious, substantial, tall, thick, towering, tremendous, vast, wide.

larva caterpillar, grub, maggot.

lash 1 *to lash someone with a whip.* to cane, to flog, to scourge, to thrash, to whip. SEE ALSO **hit**. 2 *to lash things together with string.* SEE **fasten**.

lass girl, (old-fashioned) damsel, (old-fashioned) maiden, youngster.

last 1 *This is your last chance.* closing, concluding, final, ultimate. 2 *Will this fine weather last?* to carry on, to continue, to keep on, to persist, to remain, to stay. 3 *When our dog was ill, the vet didn't think he'd last the night.* to endure, to linger, to live, to survive. 4 *lasting: a lasting friendship.* continuing, durable, permanent, stable.

latch *the latch on a door.* bolt, catch, fastening, lock.

late 1 *The bus is late.* behindhand, belated, delayed, overdue, slow, unpunctual. 2 *the late king.* dead, deceased.

lather *This soap makes a lot of lather.* bubbles, foam, froth, suds.

laugh 1 WAYS TO LAUGH: to beam, to chuckle, to giggle, to grin, to smile, to snigger, to titter. 2 *to laugh at:* to jeer, to mock, to ridicule, to scoff at, to smirk, to sneer at, to taunt, to tease.

laughter hysterics, laughing, mirth.

launch 1 *to launch a ship.* to float. 2 *to launch a rocket.* to fire, to set off. 3 *to launch a new business.* to begin, to embark on, to found, to initiate, to open, to set up, to start.

laundry *to do the laundry.* washing.

lavatory (informal) loo, toilet, water-closet, WC.

lavish *a lavish supply of food.* copious, extravagant, generous, liberal, luxurious, plentiful, sumptuous.

law 1 *the laws of a country, the laws of a game.* code, commandment, order, regulation, rule. 2 *a court of law.* justice. 3 WORDS TO DO WITH THE LAW: accusation, arrest, barrister, case, charge, coroner, court, court martial, defence, dock, evidence, inquest, judge, judgement, juror, jury, lawcourt, lawyer, magistrate, police, prosecution, prosecutor, sentence, sheriff, solicitor, to sue, summons, trial, verdict, witness. SEE ALSO **punishment.**

law-abiding *law-abiding citizens.* decent, honest, obedient, orderly, respectable, well-behaved. SEE ALSO **good.**

lawful 1 *It isn't lawful to steal.* allowed, authorized, just, permissible, permitted. 2 *Who is the lawful owner of this car?* legal, legitimate, proper, rightful, valid.

lawless *a lawless mob.* disorderly, riotous, rowdy, turbulent, undisciplined, unruly, wild.

lawlessness *The police try to stop lawlessness.* anarchy, chaos, disorder, rioting.

lay 1 *Lay your work on the table.* to deposit, to leave, to place, to position, to put down, to rest, to set down, to spread. 2 *We lay down to sleep.* SEE **lie.**

layer 1 *a layer of ice.* coating, film, sheet, skin. 2 *a layer of rock.* seam, stratum, thickness.

lazy idle, listless, slack, sluggish.

lead 1 *It's marvellous how the dog leads that blind person.* to conduct, to escort, to guide, to pilot, to steer. 2 *It's the captain's job to lead her team.* to be in charge of, to command, to direct, to head, to manage, to rule, to supervise. 3 *Who took the lead from my radio?* cable, flex, wire. 4 *a dog's lead.* leash.

leaf 1 *the leaves of a tree:* foliage, greenery. 2 *the leaves of a book.* page, sheet.

leaflet *an advertising leaflet.* booklet, brochure, pamphlet.

league *We combined with other chess teams to form a league.* alliance, association, club, group, society, union.

leak 1 *There's a leak in the bucket.* hole, opening, puncture. 2 *The water leaked out.* to drip, to escape, to ooze, to seep, to trickle.

lean 1 *a lean figure.* bony, gaunt, lanky, skinny, slender, slim, thin, wiry. 2 *The ship leaned dangerously to one side.* to bank, to heel over, to incline, to list, to slant, to slope, to tilt. 3 *I leaned against the fence.* to prop yourself, to rest, to support yourself.

leaning *She has a leaning towards subjects like maths.* inclination, instinct, readiness, tendency, trend.

leap 1 *The cat leapt into my lap.* to bound, to jump, to pounce, to spring, to vault. 2 *We leapt about for joy.* to caper, to dance, to frisk, to hop, to prance.

learn 1 *Where did you learn those rude words?* to discover, to find out, to gather, to grasp, to master, to memorize. 2 *We go to school to learn.* to be educated.

learner apprentice, beginner, L-driver.

leash *a dog's leash.* lead.

least slightest, smallest, tiniest.

leather hide, skin, suede.

leathery rubbery, tough.

leave 1 *The captain left his sinking ship.* to abandon, to desert, to evacuate, to forsake. 2 *We're ready to leave.* to depart, to go, to set off. 3 *Dad left his old job last summer.* to quit, to retire from, to withdraw from. 4 *Leave the empty milk bottles by the front door.* to deposit, to place, to position, to put down, to set down. 5 *to leave out: He was annoyed when we left him out of the team.* to drop, to eliminate, to omit, to reject. 6 *Dad's taking some leave from work.* holiday, time off, vacation.

lecture *The head gave us a lecture.* speech, talk.

lecturer instructor, professor, speaker, teacher, tutor.

ledge shelf, window-sill.

leg 1 PARTS OF YOUR LEG: ankle, calf, SEE **foot**, knee, kneecap, shin, thigh. 2 WORDS TO DESCRIBE PEOPLE'S LEGS: bandy-legged, bow-legged, knock-kneed.

legacy *She received a legacy from her grandmother's will.* bequest, inheritance.

legal 1 *It isn't legal to print your own £5 notes.* allowed, just, lawful, permissible. 2 *Who's the legal owner of this car?* authorized, legitimate, proper, rightful, valid.

legend CREATURES YOU READ ABOUT IN LEGENDS: brownie, dragon, dwarf, elf, fairy, giant, gnome, goblin, imp, mermaid, monster, nymph, ogre, troll, unicorn, vampire, witch, wizard.

legendary 1 *The unicorn is a legendary beast.* fictitious, invented, made-up, mythical. 2 *Presley is a legendary name for all pop fans.* celebrated, famous, historic, notable, renowned, well-known.

legible *legible handwriting.* clear, neat, plain, readable.

legitimate 1 *It isn't legitimate to copy someone's work.* allowed, just, permissible, permitted. 2 *Who is the legitimate owner of this car?* authorized, lawful, legal, proper, rightful.

leisure *Most people enjoy their leisure.* ease, recreation, relaxation, rest.

leisurely *a leisurely journey.* easy, peaceful, relaxing, slow, unhurried.

lend *Can you lend me a pen?* to loan.

length distance, measurement.

lengthen *The days lengthen in the spring. You can lengthen this ladder if you need to.* to draw out, to enlarge, to elongate, to extend, to get longer, to increase, to prolong, to stretch.

lengthy SEE **long.**

lenient *a lenient teacher.* easygoing, forgiving, indulgent, merciful, (informal) soft, tolerant.

lessen 1 *Please lessen the noise!* to cut, to reduce, to tone down. 2 *The noise lessened.* to decline, to decrease, to die, to slacken, to subside, to tail off.

lesson 1 lecture. 2 *This story teaches a lesson.* moral.

let 1 *Let the dog in.* to allow, to permit. 2 *The judge let him off.* to acquit, to excuse, to free, to liberate. 3 *a house to let.* to hire, to rent.

lethal *a lethal dose.* deadly, fatal, mortal, poisonous.

letter 1 *the letters of the alphabet.* character. 2 *to send someone a letter.* communication, correspondence, epistle, message, note, postcard. 3 *Have the letters come yet?* mail, post.

letter-box pillar-box, postbox.

level 1 *a level surface.* even, flat, horizontal, smooth. 2 *level scores.* equal, even. 3 *The lift takes you to the level you want.* floor, height, storey. 4 *She has reached a high level in gymnastics.* standard. 5 *We levelled the field to make a new pitch.* to even out, to flatten, to smooth. 6 *The earthquake levelled the whole town.* to demolish, to destroy, to knock down.

level-headed *You need a level-headed person to deal with a crisis.* calm, cool, reasonable, reliable, sedate, sensible.

lever *We had to lever open the jammed door.* to prize, to wrench.

liable *She is liable to do silly things.* disposed, inclined, likely, prone, willing.

liar (informal) fibber.

liberal 1 *a liberal supply of food.* abundant, ample, copious, generous, plentiful. 2 *a liberal attitude.* broadminded, easygoing, fair, lenient, tolerant, unprejudiced.

liberate *The prisoners were liberated.* to discharge, to emancipate, to free, to let out, to loose, to release, to rescue, to save, to set free, to untie.

liberty *to give people their liberty.* freedom, independence.

licence permit.

license *Our local shop is licensed to sell tobacco.* to allow, to authorize, to permit.

lick 1 *to lick a lollipop.* to suck. 2 (informal) *We licked the opposition last week.* SEE **defeat**.

lid *Where's the lid for the jam?* cap, cover, covering, top.

lie 1 *to tell a lie.* falsehood, (informal) fib, untruth. 2 *You can usually tell when someone is lying.* to bluff, (informal) to fib, (informal) to kid. 3 *Lie on the sofa.* to lean back, to recline, to sprawl. 4 *The house lies in a valley.* to be, to be located, to be situated.

life 1 *I wonder when life on earth began?* being, existence. 2 *Our dog is full of life.* energy, liveliness, sprightliness, vigour, vitality, zest. 3 *Have you read the life of Elvis Presley?* autobiography, biography.

lifeless 1 *a lifeless body.* dead, deceased, killed, motionless. 2 *a lifeless substance.* inanimate. 3 *a lifeless desert.* arid, barren, sterile.

lifelike *a lifelike statue.* authentic, natural, realistic.

lifelong 1 *a lifelong friendship.* constant, everlasting, permanent, steady, unchanging, unending. 2 *a lifelong illness.* chronic, persistent.

lift 1 *We need some strong people to lift the piano.* to carry, to elevate, to hoist, to jack up, to manhandle, to pick up, to pull up, to raise. 2 *The plane lifted off the ground.* to ascend, to rise, to soar.

light 1 KINDS OF LIGHT: beacon, bulb, candle, chandelier, daylight, electric light, floodlight, headlight, illuminations, lamp, lantern, moonlight, neon light, pilot-light, searchlight, spotlight, street light, sunlight, torch. 2 WAYS IN WHICH LIGHTS SHINE: to be bright, to be luminous, to be phosphorescent, to blaze, to blink, to burn, to dazzle, to flash, to flicker, to glare, to gleam, to glimmer, to glint, to glisten, to glitter, to glow, to shine, to spark, to sparkle, to twinkle, to wink. 3 *to light a fire.* to fire, to ignite, to kindle, to set fire to. 4 *The bonfire lit up the sky.* to brighten, to illuminate, to lighten. 5 *The big box was surprisingly light.* portable. 6 *a light sponge cake.* feathery. 7 *light work.* easy, effortless, painless.

light-hearted bright, carefree, cheerful, glad, jolly, merry, untroubled. SEE ALSO **happy**.

like 1 *Most of the class like their teacher.* to admire, to appreciate, to approve of, to be fond of, to love. 2 *Do you like ice-cream?* to enjoy, to be partial to. 3 *Would you like some ice-cream?* to fancy, to want, to wish for. 4 *How do you like this record?* to rate, to regard.

likelihood *Is there any likelihood of a change in the weather?* hope, possibility, probability, prospect.

likely 1 *It's likely that they will win.* plausible, possible, probable. 2 *She is a likely person to be captain.* appropriate, fitting, suitable. 3 *The others are likely to laugh at us.* disposed to, inclined to, liable to, willing to.

likeness *The painting is a good likeness of the headmaster.* copy, image, picture, portrait, resemblance, similarity.

limb VARIOUS LIMBS: arm, bough, flipper, leg.

limit 1 *the limit of a territory.* boundary, edge, frontier. 2 *the limit of your strength.* end, extreme, maximum. 3 *to limit someone's freedom.* to confine, to curb, to restrict.

limp 1 *to be lame, to hobble.* 2 *limp lettuce.* bendy, drooping, flabby, flexible, floppy, sagging, soft, wilting.

line 1 *Hold the end of this line.* cable, cord, flex, hawser, lead, rope, string, thread, wire. 2 *a dirty line round the bath.* band, dash, mark, streak, strip, stripe. 3 *lines on an old man's face.* crease, furrow, wrinkle. 4 *a line of police, a line of cars, etc.* chain, column, cordon, file, procession, queue, rank, row, series. 5 *a railway line.* route, service, track. 6 *Please line up.* to form a line, to queue.

linger 1 *The smell of burning lingered long after the fire was out.* to continue, to hang about, to last, to persist, to remain, to stay. 2 *Don't linger outside in this cold weather.* to dally, to delay, to hang about, to hover, to lag, to loiter, to wait about.

lingerie SEE **underclothes**.

link 1 *a link between two things.* bond, connection, join, joint, relationship. 2 *Can we link your computer to mine?* to attach, to connect, to couple, to join, to unite. 3 *The police are linking this robbery with the one last week.* to compare, to connect, to relate.

lip *the lip of a cup.* brim, brink, edge, rim.

liquid alcohol, alcoholic drink.

list 1 *a list of names.* catalogue, register. 2 *The ship listed to one side.* to heel, to lean, to slope, to tilt.

listen *Did you listen to what I said?* to hear, to eavesdrop, to overhear.

listless *It was a hot day, and everyone seemed listless.* feeble, lazy, poorly, sluggish, tired, uninterested, weak, weary.

literature VARIOUS KINDS OF LITERATURE: SEE **writing**.

litter 1 *Clear up the litter.* clutter, garbage, jumble, junk, refuse, rubbish, trash, waste. 2 *a litter of puppies.* family.

little 1 *a little book, a little dog, a little house, etc.* compact, concise, diminutive, miniature, minute, small, (informal) teeny, tiny, undersized, wee. 2 *We had a little chat.* brief, momentary, passing, short, temporary, transient. 3 *I only had a little bit to eat.* inadequate, meagre, measly, scanty, stingy. 4 *There has been little improvement in granny's health.* imperceptible, insignificant, negligible, slight. 5 *We had a little argument.* minor, petty, trifling, trivial, unimportant.

live 1 *It'd be amazing if we found a live dinosaur.* active, alive, existing, living. 2 *I wonder if our goldfish will live through the winter?* to continue, to exist, to remain, to survive. 3 *Which flat do you live in?* to dwell in, to inhabit, to occupy, to reside in. 4 *What do polar bears live on?* to eat, to feed on.

lively 1 *a lively baby, a lively game, etc.* active, agile, alert, energetic, frisky, jaunty, perky, playful, sprightly, vivacious. 2 *a lively party.* cheerful, gay, jolly, merry. 3 *a lively argument.* animated, enthusiastic, spirited.

livery uniform.

livid *I was livid when the cat misbehaved on the carpet.* angry, enraged, fuming, furious, incensed, infuriated, irate, mad, raging, raving, wrathful.

living-room drawing-room, lounge, sitting-room.

load 1 *a heavy load.* burden, weight. 2 *The plane carried a load of medical supplies.* cargo, freight. 3 *We helped to load the car.* to fill, to pack. 4 *loaded: loaded with gifts.* burdened, laden, weighed down.

loaf 1 bread. 2 *to loaf about.* to loiter, to lounge.

loam *Plant the seeds in good loam.* earth, ground, soil.

loan *Can you loan me 10p?* to lend.

loathe *Our dog loathes the snow.* to despise, to detest, to dislike, to hate.

loathsome *Some people find spiders loathsome.* detestable, disgusting, foul, obnoxious, odious, revolting.

lob *to lob a ball.* to bowl, to cast, (informal) to chuck, to fling, to pitch, to sling, to throw, to toss.

lobby *Wait for me in the lobby.* entrance hall, foyer, hall.

local *We buy our food from local shops.* near, nearby, neighbouring.

locality *There are several good shops in our locality.* area, district, neighbourhood, region, vicinity, zone.

locate 1 *Did you locate the book you wanted in the library?* to discover, to find, to search out, to track down, to unearth. 2 *They located the post office in the middle of town.* to place, to position, to situate, to station.

location 1 *Can you find our location on the map?* place, point, position, site, situation, spot. 2 *The best thing about the film was the beautiful locations.* scene, setting.

lock 1 *a lock on a door.* bolt, catch, latch, padlock. 2 *Please lock the door.* to bolt, to secure. SEE ALSO **fasten**. 3 *They locked him up as a punishment.* to confine, to gaol, to imprison, to shut in.

locomotive engine.

lodge 1 *They lodged the homeless families in a hostel.* to accommodate, to board, to house, to put up, to quarter. 2 *We lodged in a motel.* to reside, to stay. 3 *lodgings:* boarding house, quarters.

lodger *The lodgers were only allowed to stay for a few days.* boarder, guest, resident, tenant.

loft attic.

lofty *a lofty spire.* high, tall, towering.

log 1 timber, wood. 2 *The captain kept a log of the voyage.* diary, journal, record.

logical *a logical argument.* clear, coherent, intelligent, rational, reasonable, sensible.

loiter *You'll get left behind if you loiter.* to dally, to dawdle, to hang about, to linger, to loaf, to mess about, to straggle.

lonely 1 *I was lonely when my friends were away on holiday.* alone, desolate, forlorn, forsaken, friendless, neglected, solitary. 2 *a lonely farmhouse.* isolated, remote, secluded.

long 1 *a long journey.* endless, extended, interminable, lengthy, prolonged, slow, unending. 2 *I long for warmer weather.* to desire, to fancy, to hanker after, to pine for, to want, to wish for, to yearn for. 3 *Who was it who had a longing for toasted cheese?* appetite, craving, hunger, urge, wish, yearning.

long-playing record. album, LP.

long-winded *I fell asleep during the head's long-winded talk.* boring, dreary, dry, lengthy, long, tedious, uninteresting, wordy.

look 1 WAYS TO LOOK AT THINGS: to behold, to contemplate, to examine, to eye, to gape, to gaze, to glance, to glimpse, to observe, to peep, to peer, to regard, to scan, to see, to squint, to stare, to study, to survey, to view, to watch. 2 *Our house looks south.* to face, to overlook. 3 *You look pleased.* to appear, to seem. 4 *to look after something.* to attend to, to care for, to guard, to keep, to mind, to protect, to tend. 5 *to look down on someone.* to despise, to dislike, to scorn. 6 *to look for something.* to hunt, to nose about, to search, to seek. 7 *Give me a look.* sight. 8 *He has a friendly look.* appearance, countenance, expression, face.

looking-glass mirror.

look-out guard, sentinel, sentry, watchman.

loom *A castle loomed on the skyline.* to appear, to arise, to emerge, to stand out, to stick up, to tower.

loop 1 *a loop of rope.* noose. 2 *Loop the rope round the post.* to coil, to curl, to entwine, to turn, to twist, to wind.

loose 1 *loose stones, loose tiles.* insecure, movable, shaky, unsteady, wobbly. 2 *That rope is loose.* not tight, slack, unfastened, untied. 3 *The bull's loose!* free, unconfined. 4 *Someone loosed the bull.* to free, to let go, to liberate, to release, to set free, to untie.

loosen *Who loosened these guy ropes?* to ease off, to free, to loose, to relax, to release, to slacken, to undo, to unfasten, to untie.

loot 1 *The robbers ran off with their loot.* booty, contraband, plunder, (informal) swag, takings. 2 *The rioters looted the shops.* to plunder, to ransack, to rob, to steal from.

lop *to lop off a branch.* to chop, to sever. SEE ALSO **cut.**

lop-sided *The lop-sided load on the lorry looked dangerous.* asymmetrical, unbalanced, uneven.

lord aristocrat, noble, peer.

lose 1 *I lost my watch.* to mislay. 2 *He lost his way in the dark.* to miss, to stray from. 3 *Our team lost.* to be defeated, to fail.

lot *a lot of.* many, much, plenty of.

lotion ointment.

loud *a loud noise.* deafening, noisy, piercing, raucous, shrill.

lounge 1 drawing-room, living-room, sitting-room. 2 *We were lounging about.* to be idle, to be lazy, to loaf, to loiter, to relax, to slouch, to sprawl.

lousy (informal) *What lousy weather!* dreadful, nasty, rotten, terrible, unpleasant. SEE ALSO **bad.**

loutish *loutish behaviour.* bad-mannered, coarse, common, crude, discourteous, impolite, rude, uncouth, vulgar.

lovable *Teddy-bears are lovable toys.* appealing, attractive, charming, endearing, lovely.

love 1 *Giving flowers is a nice way to show your love for someone.* admiration, affection, desire, fondness, infatuation, passion. 2 *They love each other.* to admire, to adore, to be fond of, to cherish, to dote on, to idolize, to treasure, to value, to worship. 3 *to make love.* to court, to woo. SEE ALSO **mate.** 4 *loving*: affectionate, fond, friendly, kind, tender, warm.

lovely *a lovely day, a lovely view.* appealing, attractive, charming, enjoyable, fine, nice, pretty. SEE ALSO **beautiful, pleasant.**

lover beloved, boy-friend, darling, fiancé or fiancée, girl-friend, suitor, sweetheart, wooer.

low 1 *a low position.* inferior. 2 *a low whisper.* quiet, soft. 3 *a low note.* bass, deep. 4 *low spirits.* SEE **sad.** 5 *That was a low trick!* base, cowardly, mean, nasty, wicked.

lower 1 *We lowered our flag.* to dip, to drop, to let down, to take down. 2 *They lowered their prices.* to cut, to decrease, to lessen, to reduce. 3 *Lower your voice.* to quieten, to turn down.

lowly *a lowly position in life.* humble, meek, modest.

loyal *a loyal supporter.* constant, dependable, devoted, dutiful, faithful, patriotic, reliable, trustworthy.

LP album, disc, long-playing record.

lubricate to grease, to oil.

lucid *a lucid explanation.* clear, coherent, comprehensible, intelligible, understandable.

luck *I found my watch by luck.* accident, chance, coincidence, destiny, fate, fluke, fortune.

lucky 1 *a lucky discovery.* accidental, chance, happy, unintentional, unplanned. 2 *a lucky person.* fortunate.

ludicrous absurd, comic, crazy, foolish, funny, laughable, preposterous, ridiculous, silly, zany.

lug (informal) *How far have we got to lug this box?* to carry, to drag, to haul, to pull, to tug.

luggage baggage, bags, boxes, cases, suitcases, trunks.

lukewarm tepid, warm.

lull 1 *The song lulled him to sleep.* to calm, to pacify, to quieten, to soothe. 2 *a lull in a storm.* break, gap, interval, pause, respite, rest.

lumber 1 *The rhinoceros lumbered towards them.* to blunder, to move clumsily, to trudge. 2 *They are cutting lumber in the forest.* timber, wood. 3 *We cleared the lumber out of the garage.* junk, odds and ends, rubbish, trash.

luminous *a luminous clock.* glowing, phosphorescent, shining.

lump 1 *a lump of chocolate, a lump of metal, etc.* bar, bit, block, chunk, clot, dollop, hunk, ingot, mass, nugget, piece, slab. 2 *a lump on the head.* bulge, bump, hump, knob, swelling.

lunatic madman, maniac.

lunge *to lunge with a sword.* to stab, to thrust.

lurch *He lurched from side to side.* to lean, to pitch, to roll, to stagger, to totter.

lure *The poacher lured the animal into a trap.* to attract, to bait, to coax, to decoy, to entice, to persuade, to tempt.

lurid 1 *lurid colours.* bright, gaudy, startling, vivid. 2 *lurid details.* sensational, shocking, unpleasant, violent.

lurk *I imagined ogres lurking in the woods.* to hide, to lie low, to wait.

luscious *luscious peaches.* appetizing, delicious, juicy, sweet.

lust *a lust for power.* appetite, desire, greed, hunger, longing, passion.

luxurious *a luxurious palace, a luxurious banquet.* costly, expensive, grand, lavish, rich, sumptuous. SEE ALSO **splendid.**

luxury *a life of luxury.* comfort, ease, enjoyment, pleasure, relaxation.

M

machine apparatus, device, instrument, machinery, mechanism, tool.

machinery equipment, machines, plant.

mackintosh (informal) mac, sou'wester, waterproof.

mad 1 *mad behaviour.* berserk, crazy, delirious, demented, deranged, (informal) dotty, frantic, frenzied, hysterical, insane, (informal) loony, (informal) mental, (informal) potty, unbalanced, unhinged, wild. 2 *a mad person*: lunatic, madman, maniac.

madden *The noise maddened him.* to aggravate, to anger, to enrage, to exasperate, to incense, to inflame, to infuriate, to provoke, to vex.

madman lunatic, maniac.

magazine comic, journal, newspaper, paper, periodical.

maggot caterpillar, grub, larva.

magic 1 *Can witches do magic?* charm, enchantment, sorcery, spell, witchcraft, wizardry. 2 *A conjuror did some magic.* conjuring, illusions, trickery, tricks. 3 PEOPLE WHO ARE SUPPOSED TO DO MAGIC: conjuror, magician, sorcerer, witch, witch-doctor, wizard.

magician SEE **magic**.

magnificent *magnificent mountain scenery.* glorious, gorgeous, grand, impressive, majestic, marvellous, noble, superb, wonderful. SEE ALSO **beautiful, splendid.**

magnify to amplify, to enlarge, to exaggerate.

magnitude bulk, extent, importance, largeness, size, volume.

mail 1 *The knight wore chain-mail.* armour, protection. 2 *The postman brought the mail.* letters, parcels, post. 3 *The shop mailed the book to me.* to dispatch, to post, to send.

maim *He was maimed in an accident.* to cripple, to disable, to handicap, to injure, to mutilate.

main *the main ingredient. the main reason.* basic, chief, essential, foremost, fundamental, important, major, prevailing, primary, principal.

mainly chiefly, generally, mostly, predominantly, primarily, usually.

maintain 1 *Dad maintains his car in good order.* to keep, to preserve, to service, to take care of. 2 *How long can you maintain this speed?* to continue, to keep up. 3 *He maintained that he was innocent.* to assert, to claim, to declare, to insist, to proclaim, to state.

majestic *a majestic palace.* grand, imposing, impressive, lordly, magnificent, noble, regal, royal, stately. SEE ALSO **splendid.**

major *Birmingham is one of England's major cities.* chief, greater, important, larger, principal.

make 1 to create, to form, to invent, to originate, to produce, to shape, to think up. 2 VARIOUS WAYS TO MAKE THINGS: to assemble, to bake, to brew, to build, to carve, to cast, to compose, to construct, to cook, to cut, to erect, to knit, to manufacture, to mould, to mass-produce, to model, to mould, to sew, to weave, to write. 3 *Don't make trouble.* to bring about, to cause, to provoke, to result in. 4 *You can't make me do it.* to compel, to force, to oblige, to order, to require. 5 *The head made a speech.* to deliver, to pronounce, to speak, to utter. 6 *It's easy to make a P into a B.* to alter, to change, to convert, to modify, to transform, to turn. 7 *How can I make a fortune?* to earn, to gain, to get, to obtain, to receive. 8 *He would make a good player if he tried.* to become, to change into, to grow into, to turn into. 9 *Will I make the first team?* to achieve, to get to, to reach. 10 *Everyone knows that 2 and 2 make 4.* to add up to, to amount to, to come to, to total. 11 *I made an appointment.* to agree, to arrange, to decide on, to fix. 12 *Can you make out what is happening?* to decipher, to follow, to hear, to perceive, to see, to understand. 13 *I made up an excuse.* to concoct, to devise, to improvise, to invent, to plan, to think up. 14 *What make is your car?* brand, kind, sort.

make-believe *a make-believe story.* fanciful, fantasy, feigned, imaginary, pretended, unreal.

malady affliction, ailment, complaint, disease, disorder, infection, infirmity, sickness. SEE ALSO **illness.**

male MALE CREATURES: billy-goat, boar, buck, bull, cock, cockerel, drake, drone, gander, hog, ram, rooster, stag, stallion, tom-cat.

malefactor convict, criminal, crook, culprit, delinquent, offender, wrongdoer.

malevolent *a malevolent stare.* evil, malicious, nasty, revengeful, spiteful, vicious, villainous, wicked.

malicious *He hurt her with his malicious remarks.* bitter, catty, evil, malevolent, nasty, revengeful, sly, spiteful, vicious, vindictive.

malignant *a malignant disease.* dangerous, harmful, poisonous, spreading.

malnutrition famine, hunger, starvation.

man bachelor, (informal) bloke, (informal) chap, fellow, gentleman, (informal) guy, husband, widower.

manage 1 *The head teacher manages the school.* to administer, to be in charge of, to command, to control, to direct, to govern, to lead, to look after, to regulate, to rule, to run, to supervise. 2 *If £10 is too much, what can you manage?* to afford, to spare. 3 *Could you manage a lively horse like that?* to cope with, to deal with, to handle, to manipulate. 4 *See how much work you can manage before dinner.* to accomplish, to achieve, to carry out, to complete, to do, to finish, to perform, to succeed in, to undertake.

manager administrator, boss, chief, controller, director, governor, head, overseer, proprietor, ruler, supervisor.

mangle *He was off work because he mangled his hand in a machine.* to crush, to cut, to damage, to injure, to mutilate, to squash.

manhandle 1 *They had to manhandle the piano up the stairs.* to carry, to lift, to move. 2 *The muggers manhandled him brutally.* to beat up, to knock about, to treat roughly.

mania craze, enthusiasm, frenzy, hysteria, insanity, madness, obsession.

maniac lunatic, madman.

manipulate 1 *A good speaker can manipulate an audience.* to control, to feel, to handle, to manage. 2 *The trainer manipulated the injured player's leg.* to massage, to rub.

mankind human beings, men and women. SEE ALSO **person.**

manly masculine, virile.

man-made *Plastics are man-made substances.* artificial, manufactured, synthetic.

mannequin model.

manner 1 *Dad does jobs in a professional manner.* fashion, means, method, mode, style, way. 2 *I didn't like his cheeky manner.* attitude, behaviour, character, conduct, disposition.

manners *It's time he learned some manners.* good behaviour, civility, courtesy, politeness.

manoeuvre 1 *army manoeuvres.* exercise, operation, training. 2 *It was a clever manoeuvre to take his bishop.* move, plan, scheme, strategy, tactics, trick. 3 *He manoeuvred the van through the gate.* to guide, to move, to pilot, to steer.

mansion château, stately home.

manufacture 1 *What does this factory manufacture?* to assemble, to make, to mass-produce. 2 *manufacturing: a manufacturing town.* industrial. 3 *manufactured:* artificial, man-made, synthetic.

manure compost, dung, fertilizer, muck.

manuscript document, papers.

many countless, frequent, innumerable, numberless, numerous, untold.

map 1 chart, diagram, plan. 2 *a book of maps:* atlas.

mar *He marred his picture by spilling paint on it.* to blot, to damage, to deface, to disfigure, to spoil, to stain.

marauder buccaneer, invader, pirate, raider.

march *The soldiers marched into town.* to parade, to troop.

margin border, edge, frieze, verge.

marina *a marina for sailing-boats.* anchorage, harbour.

mariner sailor, seaman.

mark 1 *a dirty mark on your dress.* blemish, blot, dot, smear, spot, stain, streak, trace. 2 WAYS TO MARK SOMETHING: to brand, to bruise, to deface, to disfigure, to draw on, to mar, to scar, to scratch, to spot, to stain, to stamp, to streak, to tattoo, to write on. 3 *Teachers mark our work.* to assess, to correct. 4 *Mark what I say.* to attend to, to heed, to note, to notice, to observe, to take note of.

market 1 auction, bazaar, fair, sale. 2 *My uncle's firm markets furniture.* to retail, to sell, to trade.

maroon 1 *They marooned Ben Gunn on Treasure Island.* to abandon, to desert, to forsake, to leave, to strand. 2 *a marooned person:* castaway.

marquee tent.

marriage 1 *Granny and grandad have enjoyed 40 years of marriage.* matrimony. 2 *Today is the anniversary of their marriage.* wedding.

marsh bog, fen, quagmire, quicksands, swamp.

martial 1 *a martial figure.* belligerent, militant, pugnacious, war-like. 2 *martial law.* military. 3 *the martial arts*: judo, karate, kung fu.

marvel *We marvelled at the strange sight.* to admire, to be amazed by, to gape at, to wonder at.

marvellous 1 *The museum has some marvellous things.* admirable, excellent, fabulous, glorious, miraculous, sensational, splendid, wonderful. 2 *We had a marvellous time.* SEE **good.**

masculine male, manly, virile.

mash to crush, to grind, to mangle, to pound, to pulp, to smash, to squash.

mask *We planted a tree to mask the ugly building at the back.* to blot out, to camouflage, to cloak, to conceal, to cover, to disguise, to hide, to screen, to shroud.

masonry brickwork, stonework.

mass 1 *a mass of food.* chunk, dollop, heap, hunk, lump, mound, pile, quantity, stack. 2 *a mass of people.* crowd, large number, multitude, throng. SEE ALSO **group.** 3 *Do you go to mass on Sunday?* communion, service, worship.

massacre bloodshed, carnage, slaughter. SEE ALSO **kill.**

massage *The trainer massaged the injured player's leg.* to knead, to manipulate, to rub.

massive colossal, enormous, gigantic, heavy, huge, immense, mammoth, mighty, towering, vast, weighty. SEE ALSO **big.**

master 1 boss, captain, chief, head, ruler. 2 *a schoolmaster*: SEE **teacher.** 3 *a master at chess.* expert, genius, master-mind. 4 *Have you mastered the rules?* to grasp, to learn, to understand. 5 *You need courage to master a wild horse.* to conquer, to control, to govern, to overcome, to overpower, to quell, to subdue, to suppress.

masterful *a masterful personality.* bossy, domineering, forceful, strong.

masterly *I admire his masterly control of the ball.* accomplished, brilliant, clever, gifted, skilful, talented.

mastermind expert, genius, master.

masterpiece *That piece of music is a masterpiece.* classic.

mat carpet, matting, rug.

matador bullfighter, toreador.

match 1 *a boxing match.* bout, competition, contest, game, tie, tournament. 2 *Do these colours match?* to agree, to coincide, to compare, to correspond.

mate 1 *I went out with my mates.* chum, companion, comrade, friend, partner. 2 *Some birds take a mate for life.* husband, wife. 3 *Many birds mate in the springtime.* to copulate, to couple, to have intercourse, to make love, to unite.

material 1 *building materials.* matter, stuff, substance. 2 MATERIALS USED IN BUILDING, ETC.: asbestos, asphalt, brick, cement, concrete, creosote, fibreglass, glass, hardboard, lime, metal, mortar, nylon, paint, perspex, plaster, plastic, plywood, polystyrene, polythene, putty, PVC, rubber, slate, stone, tar, tiles, timber, veneer, vinyl, wood. 3 *I bought some material to make a skirt.* fabric, textile. SEE ALSO **cloth.**

materialize *A shape materialized out of the fog.* to appear, to come into existence, to emerge, to turn up.

maternal *maternal feeling.* motherly.

maternity motherhood, pregnancy.

mathematics, maths 1 WORDS USED IN MATHEMATICS: addition, algebra, angle, arithmetic, binary system, diagonal, diameter, division, equilateral, geometry, minus, multiplication, negative number, parallel, percentage, perpendicular, plus, positive number, radius, ratio, right angle, subtraction, sum, symmetry, tessellation, times. SEE ALSO **shape.** 2 MATHEMATICAL INSTRUMENTS: compasses, dividers, geo-board, protractor, ruler, set-square.

matrimony marriage.

matted *matted hair.* tangled.

matter 1 *We scooped a lot of filthy matter out of the drain.* material, stuff, substance. 2 *The headmaster will deal with this matter.* affair, business, concern, subject, thing, topic. 3 *What is the matter with the car?* difficulty, problem, trouble. 4 *Will it matter if I'm a bit late?* to be important.

matting carpet, mat, rug.

mature 1 *She is mature for her age.* adult, advanced, grown-up. 2 *mature fruit.* mellow, ready, ripe.

maul *The keeper was mauled by a lion.* to injure, to mangle, to mutilate.

maximum *maximum speed.* full, greatest, highest, most, top.

maybe perhaps, possibly.

maze *a maze of corridors.* labyrinth.

meadow field, pasture.

meagre *I got a meagre helping of pudding.* inadequate, mean, (informal) measly, (informal) mingy, scanty, small, sparse, stingy, thin.

meal 1 VARIOUS MEALS: banquet, barbecue, breakfast, buffet, dinner, feast, high tea, lunch, luncheon, picnic, snack, (informal) spread, supper, tea. 2 PARTS OF A MEAL: (informal) afters, course, dessert, main course, pudding, starter, sweet.

mean 1 *What does this sign mean?* to communicate, to convey, to express, to imply, to indicate, to say, to stand for, to suggest, to symbolize. 2 *What do you mean to do?* to intend, to plan, to propose. 3 *He's too mean to give a donation.* close, (informal) mingy, miserly, sparing, stingy. 4 *It was mean to take her last sweet.* base, cruel, nasty, sneaky, unkind.

meaning *What's the meaning of this word?* sense, significance.

means *What's the best means of getting to London?* fashion, manner, method, way.

measly SEE **meagre.**

measure 1 UNITS OF BREADTH, DEPTH, DISTANCE, GAUGE, HEIGHT, LENGTH OR WIDTH: centimetre, fathom, foot, furlong, inch, kilometre, light-year, metre, mile, millimetre, yard. 2 UNITS OF AREA: acre, hectare, square centimetre, etc. 3 UNITS OF TIME: day, hour, minute, month, second, week, year. 4 UNITS OF CAPACITY OR VOLUME: cubic centimetre, etc., gallon, litre, millilitre, pint, quart. 5 UNITS OF WEIGHT: gram, hundredweight, kilogram, milligram, ounce, pound, stone, ton, tonne. 6 UNITS OF SPEED OR VELOCITY: kilometre per hour, knot, mach number, mile per hour, (informal) ton. 7 UNITS OF QUANTITY: century, dozen, gross, score. 8 SCALES FOR MEASURING TEMPERATURE: Celsius, centigrade, Fahrenheit. (the unit is degree.) 9 INFORMAL MEASUREMENTS: armful, cupful, handful, mouthful, pinch, plateful, spoonful.

measurement *the measurements of a room.* dimensions, extent, size.

meat 1 flesh. 2 KINDS OF MEAT: bacon, beef, chicken, corned beef, game, gammon, ham, lamb, mutton, oxtail, pork, poultry, tripe, turkey, veal, venison. 3 WAYS OF SERVING MEAT: beefburger, chops, cutlets, hamburger, joint, mince, sausage, steak, stew.

mechanic *a motor mechanic.* engineer, technician.

mechanism apparatus, device, instrument, machine, machinery.

medal award, decoration, prize.

medallist winner.

meddle *Don't meddle in my affairs.* to butt in, to interfere, to intervene, to intrude, to pry, to snoop, to tamper.

media *the media*: magazines, newspapers, the press, radio, television. ! *Media* is a plural word, so you should talk about *the media,* not *a media.*

medicine 1 *medicine from the chemist's.* cure, dose, drug, prescription, remedy, treatment. 2 *Have you taken your medicine?* capsule, pastille, pellet, pill, tablet. 3 VARIOUS MEDICINES AND TREATMENTS: anaesthetic, antibiotic, antidote, antiseptic, aspirin, gargle, herbs, iodine, linctus, lotion, lozenge, morphia, narcotic, ointment, penicillin, the pill, sedative, tonic, tranquillizer. 4 PEOPLE WHO LOOK AFTER OUR HEALTH: dentist, doctor, midwife, nurse, oculist, optician, osteopath, physician, physiotherapist, psychiatrist, radiographer, sister, surgeon. 5 PLACES WHERE YOU GET MEDICAL TREATMENT: clinic, dispensary, health centre, hospital, infirmary, intensive care unit, nursing home, operating theatre, out-patients' department, surgery, ward. 6 OTHER WORDS TO DO WITH MEDICAL TREATMENT: bandage, dressing, first aid, forceps, hypodermic syringe, immunization, injection, inoculation, lint, plaster, plastic surgery, poultice, radiotherapy, scalpel, sling, splint, stethoscope, stretcher, syringe, therapy, thermometer, transfusion, transplant, tweezers, X-ray.

mediocre *There isn't much to say about a mediocre game.* commonplace, fair, middling, moderate, ordinary, passable, second-rate, unexciting.

meditate *I meditated quietly on what I had learned.* to brood, to consider, to contemplate, to ponder, to reflect, to think.

medium average, middle, middling, moderate, normal, ordinary, usual.

meek docile, gentle, humble, lowly, modest, obedient, patient, tame, unassuming.

meet 1 *The two roads meet here.* to come together, to converge, to intersect, to join, to merge. 2 *We met by accident.* to come across, to confront, to encounter, to face, to run into, to see. 3 *We all met in the hall.* to assemble, to come together, to congregate, to gather.

meeting 1 *a business meeting.* assembly, conference, congress, council, gathering. 2 *an unexpected meeting.* confrontation, encounter. 3 *We've arranged a meeting.* appointment, date, rendezvous.

melancholy dejected, depressed, gloomy, unhappy. SEE ALSO **sad.**

mellow *a mellow taste.* mature, pleasant, rich, ripe, soft.

melodious musical, tuneful.

melody air, theme, tune.

melt 1 *The sun melts the snow.* to soften, to thaw. 2 *The crowd melted away.* to disappear, to dissolve, to fade, to vanish.

member *to be a member*: to belong.

memorable unforgettable.

memorial monument.

memorize to learn, to remember.

memory *We've got happy memories of our holiday.* impression, recollection, reminder, souvenir.

menace *He shook his fist in a menacing gesture.* to frighten, to intimidate, to scare, to threaten.

mend 1 *The garage mended the car.* to fix, to put right, to renovate, to repair, to restore, to touch up. 2 *I mended my jeans.* to darn, to patch, to sew up, to stitch.

mention 1 *Did mum mention the broken window?* to allude to, to comment on, to refer to, to speak about. 2 *Dad mentioned that he might go out.* to observe, to remark, to say.

merchant *a timber merchant.* dealer, retailer, salesman, shopkeeper, stockist, supplier, trader.

merciful benevolent, compassionate, forgiving, humane, lenient, sympathetic, tolerant. SEE ALSO **kind.**

merciless callous, hard-hearted, heartless, inhumane, pitiless, ruthless, savage, unfeeling, vicious. SEE ALSO **cruel.**

mercury quicksilver.

mercy *The attackers showed no mercy.* clemency, compassion, forgiveness, grace, kindness, pity, sympathy.

merge 1 *Our school merged with the one down the road.* to amalgamate, to combine, to come together, to unite. 2 *The motorways merge here.* to converge, to join, to meet.

merit 1 *Do you think my painting has any merit?* importance, quality, value, worth. 2 *a certificate of merit.* credit, distinction. 3 *Her performance merited first prize.* to be entitled to, to deserve, to earn.

merry *a merry tune.* bright, cheerful, glad, jolly, jovial, joyful, spirited. SEE ALSO **happy.**

mesh net, netting, network, web.

mess 1 *Clear up this mess!* clutter, confusion, jumble, muddle, shambles, untidiness. 2 (informal) *You messed up this job!* to bungle, to spoil. 3 (informal) *We were messing about.* to loaf, to loiter, to play about.

message announcement, bulletin, communication, communiqué, dispatch, letter, note, notice, report, statement.

messenger dispatch-rider, herald, postman, runner.

messy *messy work.* careless, dirty, disorderly, filthy, (informal) mucky, slapdash, sloppy, slovenly, untidy.

metal 1 VARIOUS METALS: alloy, aluminium, brass, bronze, chromium, copper, galvanized iron, gold, iron, lead, mercury, nickel, pewter, platinum, quicksilver, silver, solder, stainless steel, tin, uranium, zinc. 2 *a lump of metal*: ingot, nugget.

method fashion, knack, manner, means, mode, procedure, process, routine, orderly, organized, painstaking, systematic.

metric *the metric system.* decimal.

microbe bacteria, (informal) bug, germ, virus. ! *Bacteria* is a plural word.

microscopic imperceptible, minute, tiny. SEE ALSO **small.**

middle 1 *the middle of the earth.* centre, core, heart, hub, inside, nucleus. 2 *the middle stump.* central, half-way, inner, intermediate, mid-way, neutral.

middling *She gave just a middling performance.* average, fair, indifferent, mediocre, ordinary.

midget dwarf, pigmy. ! These words are often insulting.

might *Push with all your might.* energy, force, power, strength, vigour.

mighty *He gave a mighty blow with his axe.* big, enormous, great, hefty, huge, powerful, strong.

migrate *Some birds migrate to other lands.* to travel. SEE ALSO **move.**

mild 1 *mild weather.* balmy, calm, peaceful, pleasant, soothing, warm. 2 *a mild flavour.* delicate, faint, subtle. 3 *a mild person.* gentle, good-tempered, harmless, kind.

mildew mould.

militant *a militant attitude.* aggressive, attacking, belligerent, hostile, pugnacious, warlike.

milk KINDS OF MILK: condensed, evaporated, pasteurized.

milky *a milky liquid.* cloudy, misty, unclear, whitish.

mimic *The parrot mimicked me.* to copy, to echo, to imitate, to impersonate.

mind 1 *Use your mind!* brain, cleverness, intellect, intelligence, mental power, sense, understanding. 2 *Mind the step.* to heed, to look out for, to note, to remember, to take notice of. 3 *Dad won't mind if I use his pen.* to bother, to care, to complain, to grumble, to object, to worry.

mine 1 *a coal-mine.* pit, quarry, shaft, working. 2 *to mine for gold.* to dig, to excavate.

mineral MINERALS FROM THE GROUND: metal, ore, rock.

mingle *Everyone mingled happily at the carnival.* to blend, to combine, to mix.

mingy (informal) *He's mingy with his money.* close, mean, miserly, stingy.

miniature diminutive, little, microscopic, minute, tiny. SEE ALSO **small.**

minimum *the minimum price.* bottom, least, lowest, smallest.

minor *a minor accident.* insignificant, little, petty, small, trivial, unimportant.

minstrel bard, singer.

mint *in mint condition.* new, perfect, unmarked, unused.

minute *The baby's ears are minute.* diminutive, little, microscopic, miniature, tiny, undersized. SEE ALSO **small.**

miracle marvel, mystery, wonder.

miraculous *a miraculous cure.* extraordinary, incredible, marvellous, mysterious, supernatural, unbelievable.

mirage *The oasis was a mirage.* delusion, hallucination, illusion, vision.

mirror looking-glass.

mirth gaiety, happiness, jollity, joy, laughter.

misadventure accident, calamity, mischance, misfortune, mishap.

misbehave to behave badly, to disobey, to err, to play up.

misbehaviour disobedience, mischief, misconduct, naughtiness.

miscalculate to err, to go wrong, to misjudge.

miscalculation error, inaccuracy, mistake, slip-up.

miscellaneous *miscellaneous odds and ends.* assorted, different, diverse, mixed, varied, various.

mischief *What mischief has that puppy been up to?* escapade, misbehaviour, misconduct, naughtiness, prank, scrape.

miser hoarder, miserly person.

miserable dejected, depressed, despondent, down-hearted, gloomy, heart-broken, melancholy, moping, unfortunate, unhappy, unlucky, wretched. SEE ALSO **sad.**

miserly close, mean, (informal) mingy, stingy.

misery distress, grief, hardship, sorrow, suffering, unhappiness.

misfortune accident, adversity, affliction, bad luck, calamity, disaster, mischance, mishap.

misgiving *I had misgivings about lending him money.* anxiety, doubt, qualm, uncertainty, worry.

misguided *It was misguided to lend him money.* foolish, mistaken, unwise.

mishap *We had a mishap on the motorway.* accident, difficulty, misadventure, mischance, misfortune.

mislay *Mum mislaid her bag.* to lose.

mislead 1 *Don't try to mislead us!* to bluff, to confuse, to deceive, to delude, to fool, to hoax, to hoodwink, to kid, to lie to, to muddle, to puzzle, to take in, to trick. 2 *misleading*: deceitful, deceptive, dishonest, unreliable.

miss 1 *We missed the bus.* to let go, to lose. 2 *Did we miss anything out?* to disregard, to forget, to ignore, to leave out, to neglect, to omit, to overlook, to skip. 3 *We missed mum while she was away.* to long for, to need, to pine for, to want.

misshapen deformed, disfigured, distorted, grotesque, twisted, ugly, warped.

mission expedition, exploration, journey.

mist fog, haze.

mistake 1 *I made a mistake.* blunder, error, (informal) howler, miscalculation, oversight, slip-up. 2 *I mistook your message.* to confuse, to misjudge, to misunderstand, to mix up.

mistrust *I mistrusted his promise.* to disbelieve, to distrust.

misty *misty windows.* blurred, clouded, dim, faint, fuzzy, hazy, indistinct, shadowy, steamy, unclear.

misunderstand *I misunderstood your message.* to misjudge, to mistake.

misuse 1 *Someone has misused my tape-recorder.* to damage, to harm, to hurt, to injure. 2 *She is careful not to misuse her money.* to fritter, to squander, to waste.

mix 1 *Mix the ingredients together.* to blend, to combine, to integrate, to mingle, to put together. 2 *I get things mixed up.* to confuse, to jumble, to muddle, to shuffle. 3 *mixed*: assorted, different, diverse, miscellaneous, varied, various.

mixture alloy, assortment, blend, collection, combination, compound, jumble, medley, variety.

moan (informal) *We moaned about the food.* to complain, to grouse, to grumble.

mob *an angry mob.* bunch, crowd, horde, pack, rabble, swarm, throng.

mobile *a mobile caravan.* movable, moving, travelling.

mobilize *to mobilize an army.* to assemble, to gather, to muster, to organize.

mock 1 to be sarcastic, to be satirical, to insult, to jeer, to laugh at, to make fun of, to ridicule, to scoff, to sneer, to taunt, to tease. 2 *mocking*: disparaging, rude, uncomplimentary.

model 1 *a model aircraft.* copy, dummy, imitation, replica, representation, toy. 2 *Our car is an old model.* design, type, version. 3 *We used his design as a model.* example, pattern, prototype. 4 *The models showed off the latest fashions.* mannequin.

moderate 1 *moderate prices.* average, fair, middle, middling, normal, ordinary, reasonable, usual. 2 *a moderate wind.* gentle, light, mild.

moderately fairly, pretty, rather.

modern *modern music, a modern house.* contemporary, current, fashionable, new, present, recent, stylish, (informal) trendy, up-to-date.

modernize *to modernize a house.* to improve, to rebuild, to renovate, to update.

modest 1 *a modest person.* bashful, coy, demure, humble, lowly, meek, shy, unassuming. 2 *a modest dress.* chaste, decent, plain, simple.

modify *After my model crashed, I modified the design.* to adapt, to adjust, to alter, to change, to convert, to transform, to vary.

moist clammy, damp, dank, humid, muggy, steamy, wet.

moisten to dampen.

mole (informal) *A mole must have discovered our secret plan.* secret agent, spy.

molest *The ruffians molested an old man.* to annoy, to assault, to attack, to bother, to harass, to interfere with, to pester, to set on.

molten *molten metal.* liquid, melted.

moment 1 *It was over in a moment.* flash, instant, second. 2 *This was an important moment.* occasion, opportunity, time.

momentary *A momentary loss of concentration caused the accident.* brief, passing, short, temporary, transient.

momentous *Going to a new school is a momentous step.* grave, important, serious, weighty.

monarchy kingdom, realm.

monastery abbey.

money 1 cash, change, cheque, coins, coppers, credit card, (informal) dough, notes, pocket-money, silver. 2 FORMS IN WHICH YOU MAY OWN OR EXCHANGE MONEY: assets, capital, currency, dowry, earnings, estate, funds, income, interest, investments, pay, pension, proceeds, profits, resources, revenue, riches, salary, savings, takings, taxes, wages, wealth, winnings.

money-box piggy-bank, safe, till.

monotonous boring, dreary, dull, flat, tedious, unexciting, uninteresting, wearisome.

monster beast, brute, giant, ogre.

monstrous 1 *monstrous helpings of food.* colossal, enormous, gigantic, huge, hulking, immense, mighty. SEE ALSO **big.** 2 *a monstrous crime.* dreadful, evil, gross, hideous, horrible, outrageous, repulsive, shocking, terrible, wicked.

monument memorial.

mood 1 *Is she in a good mood?* disposition, humour, state of mind, temper. 2 WORDS TO DESCRIBE VARIOUS MOODS: SEE **angry, happy, sad.**

moody bad-tempered, cross, depressed, disgruntled, gloomy, grumpy, irritable, melancholy, morose, snappy, sulky, sullen.

moon *to do with the moon*: lunar.

moor 1 *a windswept moor.* heath. 2 *to moor a boat.* to anchor, to berth, to tie up.

mope *He moped because he wasn't invited to the party.* to be unhappy, to brood, to grieve, to pine, to sulk.

moral 1 *a moral person.* chaste, good, honest, honourable, just, law-abiding, pure, right, trustworthy, truthful, upright, virtuous. 2 *a story with a moral.* lesson.

morale *The team's morale is good.* cheerfulness, confidence, spirit.

morbid *a morbid story about death.* brooding, gloomy, morose, pessimistic, unhappy, unhealthy.

more additional, extra, further.

moreover also, besides, furthermore, too.

morose *a morose expression.* bad-tempered, depressed, gloomy, moody, sullen, unhappy. SEE ALSO **sad.**

morsel *a morsel of food.* bite, mouthful, piece, taste, titbit.

mortal 1 *We are mortals.* human. SEE ALSO **person.** 2 *a mortal sickness.* deadly, fatal, lethal, terminal.

mostly chiefly, generally, mainly, predominantly, primarily, usually.

mother 1 mum, mummy. 2 *She likes to mother the toddlers.* to care for, to cherish, to fuss over, to love, to nurse.

motherly *a motherly person.* kind, loving, maternal.

motion movement.

motionless calm, immobile, lifeless, peaceful, stationary, still, unmoving.

motive *What was the motive for the crime?* purpose, reason.

motor 1 *an electric motor.* engine. 2 *We motored into town.* to drive, to go by car. SEE ALSO **travel.**

motor car automobile, car.

mottled *The snake had mottled skin.* blotchy, dotted, speckled, spotty.

motto proverb, saying, slogan.

mould 1 *There's mould on the cheese.* fungus, mildew. 2 *He moulded the clay to look like a face.* to cast, to form, to shape.

mouldy mildewed, musty.

mound *a mound of rubbish.* bank, heap, hill, pile, stack.

mount 1 *to mount upwards.* to ascend, to climb, to go up, to rise, to soar. 2 *My savings mounted up.* to grow, to increase. 3 *to mount a picture.* to frame. 4 *to mount a display.* to install, to set up.

mountain hill, peak, range, summit, volcano.

mountaineer climber.

mourn *He mourned for his dead dog.* to fret, to grieve, to lament, to mope, to pine, to weep.

mournful SEE **sad.**

moustache whiskers.

mouth *the mouth of a river.* opening, outlet.

mouthful bite, morsel.

move 1 *to move along*: to come, to cruise, to fly, to go, to jog, to journey, to make headway, to march, to pass, to proceed, to tour, to travel, to walk. 2 *to move along quickly*: to bolt, to canter, to career, to dart, to dash, to fly, to gallop, to hasten, to hurry, to hurtle, to hustle, (informal) to nip, to race, to run, to rush, to shoot, to speed, to stampede, to streak, to tear, (informal) to zoom. 3 *to move along slowly*: to amble, to crawl, to dawdle, to drift, to stroll. 4 *to move along gracefully*: to dance, to flow, to glide, to skate, to skim, to slide, to slip, to sweep. 5 *to move along awkwardly*: to dodder, to falter, to flounder, to lumber, to lurch, to pitch, to shuffle, to stagger, to stumble, to sway, to totter, to trip, to trundle. 6 *to move along stealthily*: to crawl, to creep, to edge, to slink, to slither. 7 *to move away*: to budge, to depart, to leave, to migrate, to quit. 8 *to move back*: to reverse, to withdraw. 9 *to move down*: to descend, to drop, to fall, to lower, to sink, to swoop. 10 *to move in*: to enter, to penetrate. 11 *to move round*: to circulate, to revolve, to roll, to rotate, to spin, to turn, to twirl, to twist, to wheel, to whirl. 12 *to move towards*: to advance, to approach, to proceed, to progress. 13 *to move up*: to arise, to ascend, to climb, to mount, to rise. 14 *to move restlessly*: to be agitated, to fidget, to flap, to roll, to shake, to stir, to swing, to toss, to tremble, to turn, to twist, to twitch, to wag, to waggle, to wave, to wiggle. 15 *to move things*: to carry, to shift, to ship, to transfer, to transplant, to transport. 16 *to move someone's feelings*: to affect, to influence, to stir, to touch. 17 *What will her next move be?* act, action, movement, shift. 18 *It's your move next.* chance, opportunity, turn.

movement action, activity, motion.

movie SEE **film.**

mow *to mow the grass.* to clip, to trim. SEE ALSO **cut.**

muck dirt, dung, filth, grime, manure, mud, rubbish, slime.

mucky SEE **dirty.**

mud dirt, (informal) muck, slime.

muddy caked, dirty, filthy, messy, (informal) mucky, soiled.

muddle 1 *My room is in a muddle.* clutter, confusion, jumble, mess, shambles. 2 *You'll muddle me if you talk so fast.* to bewilder, to confuse, to mislead, to perplex, to puzzle. 3 *Don't muddle the library books.* to jumble, to mix up.

muffle 1 *Muffle yourself up in this icy weather.* to cover, to wrap up. 2 *I tried to muffle my sneeze.* to deaden, to quieten, to soften, to stifle, to suppress.

mug 1 beaker, cup. 2 to assault, to attack, to molest, to rob, to set on.

mugger hooligan, robber, ruffian, thief, thug.

muggy *muggy weather.* close, humid, oppressive, steamy, stuffy, sultry, warm.

multiply *Mice multiply quickly.* to breed, to increase, to reproduce.

multitude *I have a multitude of things to do.* host, large number, mass. SEE ALSO **crowd.**

munch to bite, to chew, to crunch, to gnaw. SEE ALSO **eat.**

murder assassination, homicide. SEE ALSO **kill.**

murderer assassin, killer.

murderous *murderous bandits.* bloodthirsty, brutal, cruel, fierce, pitiless, ruthless, savage, vicious, violent.

murky *We couldn't see anything in the murky water.* cloudy, dark, dim, foggy, gloomy, sombre.

muscular *a muscular wrestler.* beefy, brawny, burly, strong, tough.

music 1 KINDS OF MUSICAL COMPOSITION: anthem, ballad, blues, calypso, carol, chamber music, chant, choral music, classical music, concerto, dirge, disco music, fanfare, folk music, hymn, improvisation, jazz, lullaby, march, opera, overture, pop music, reggae, rock, shanty, song, soul, spiritual, symphony. SEE ALSO **dance, sing.** 2 FOR FAMILIES OF MUSICAL INSTRUMENTS SEE **brass, keyboard, percussion, strings, woodwind.** 3 VARIOUS INSTRUMENTS: accordion, bagpipes, banjo, barrel-organ, bassoon, bugle, castanets, cello, clarinet, cornet, cymbals, double-bass, drum, fiddle, flute, glockenspiel, gong, guitar, harmonica, harmonium, harp, harpsichord, horn, kettledrum, lute, lyre, mouth-organ, oboe, organ, piano, piccolo, recorder, saxophone, sitar, tambourine, timpani, tom-tom, triangle, trombone, trumpet, tuba, tubular bells, tuning fork, viola, violin, xylophone, zither. **4** VARIOUS MUSICIANS: bass, bugler, cellist, clarinettist, composer, conductor, contralto, drummer, fiddler, flautist, guitarist, harpist, instrumentalist, oboist, organist, percussionist, performer, pianist, piper, player, soloist, soprano, tenor, timpanist, treble, trombonist, trumpeter, violinist, virtuoso, vocalist. **5** GROUPS OF MUSICIANS: band, choir, chorus, duet, ensemble, group, orchestra, quartet, quintet, trio. **6** OTHER MUSICAL WORDS: baton, chord, chromatic scale, clef, crotchet, discord, flat, harmony, key, melody, minim, natural, note, octave, pitch, quaver, scale, semibreve, semiquaver, sharp, stave, tempo, theme, tone, tune, unison.

muster *Can we muster a team for Saturday?* to assemble, to collect, to gather, to get together, to mobilize, to round up.

musty *The musty room needed airing.* damp, mildewed, mouldy, stale.

mute dumb, silent, speechless, tongue-tied.

mutilate *The soldier was mutilated in the explosion.* to cripple, to damage, to maim, to mangle. SEE ALSO **wound.**

mutinous *a mutinous crew.* defiant, disobedient, insubordinate, rebellious, unruly.

mutiny **1** *The starving crew organized a mutiny.* rebellion, revolt, rising. **2** *The crew mutinied.* to disobey, to rebel, to revolt, to rise up.

mutual *Friends usually have mutual interests.* common, joint, shared.

mysterious *a mysterious illness.* baffling, inexplicable, insoluble, puzzling, strange, unknown.

mystery **1** *Granny's sudden recovery was a mystery.* miracle. **2** *His disappearance is a mystery.* problem, puzzle, riddle.

mythical *mythical monsters.* fabulous, fictional, imaginary, legendary, non-existent.

N

nab (informal) *The head nabbed me before I could escape.* to arrest, to capture, to catch, to seize.

nag **1** SEE **horse. 2** *Mum nags me about the washing-up.* to keep complaining, to pester, to scold.

naked bare, nude, unclothed, uncovered, undressed.

name **1** *What's your name?* Christian name, first name, identity, nickname, surname, title. **2** *His parents named him Anthony.* to baptize, to call, to christen. **3** *What did you name your story?* to entitle. **4** *They named me as captain.* to appoint, to choose, to elect, to nominate.

nameless anonymous, unnamed.

nanny *a child's nanny.* nurse.

nap *to take a nap:* to doze, to nod off, to rest, to sleep, to snooze.

narcotic SEE **drug.**

narrate *to narrate a story.* to describe, to recount, to relate, to tell.

narration *Whose voice was doing the narration?* account, commentary, description, speaking, story-telling.

narrative *an exciting narrative.* account, story, tale, yarn.

narrow fine, slender, slim, thin.

narrow-minded intolerant, old-fashioned, prejudiced, prim, prudish.

nasty SEE **unpleasant.**

nation *the nations of the world.* civilization, community, country, land, people, race, society, state.

national *national customs.* ethnic, racial.

native 1 *I am a native of England.* citizen, inhabitant, resident. 2 *The early invaders fought the natives.* aboriginal, original inhabitant. ! Do not use *native* to mean *savage* or *uncivilized person.*

natural 1 *Many people say it's healthier to eat natural foods.* crude, raw, unprocessed, unrefined. 2 *a natural gift for music.* hereditary, inherited. 3 *a natural reaction.* normal, ordinary, regular, spontaneous. 4 *a natural pose.* authentic, realistic.

nature 1 *A naturalist loves nature.* natural environment, wildlife. 2 *He has a kind nature.* character, disposition, manner, personality, temperament. 3 *I collect coins, medals, and things of that nature.* kind, sort, type, variety.

naughty disobedient, impish, mischievous, troublesome, unruly. SEE ALSO **bad.**

nauseating *a nauseating mess.* disgusting, foul, revolting, sickening. SEE ALSO **unpleasant.**

nautical *nautical dress.* marine, naval, seafaring, seagoing.

navigate *The captain navigated his ship through the strait.* to direct, to guide, to pilot, to sail, to steer.

navy armada, convoy, fleet.

near adjacent to, close to.

nearly about, almost, around, not quite, practically.

neat 1 *a neat person.* clean, houseproud, tidy. 2 *a neat room.* orderly, shipshape, straight. 3 *neat clothes.* dainty, pretty, smart, spruce, trim.

necessary essential, important, indispensable, needed, required, unavoidable, vital.

need 1 *There's no need to shout.* necessity, obligation, requirement. 2 *The TV pictures made us aware of the need of the refugees.* poverty, suffering, want. 3 *What do you need?* to be short of, to lack, to require, to want. 4 *We need you to play in goal.* to depend on, to rely on.

needy *How can we help the needy?* destitute, deprived, impoverished, penniless, poor, poverty-stricken.

negative SEE **electricity, mathematics, photograph.** ! *Negative* is the opposite of *positive.*

neglect *Don't neglect your homework.* to disregard, to forget, to ignore, to miss, to overlook, to shirk, to skip.

negligent *negligent work.* careless, inattentive, reckless, sloppy, slovenly, thoughtless, uncaring.

negligible *a negligible amount of rain.* imperceptible, insignificant, slight, tiny, trifling, trivial, unimportant.

negotiate *to negotiate a price.* to arbitrate, to bargain, to discuss terms, to haggle.

neigh to whinny.

neighbourhood area, district, locality, place, region, vicinity, zone.

neighbouring adjacent, close, closest, near, nearest.

neighbourly *The people next door are a neighbourly crowd.* friendly, helpful, obliging. SEE ALSO **kind.**

nerve 1 *That steeplejack has some nerve!* bravery, courage, daring, (informal) guts, (informal) pluck, self-confidence. 2 (informal) *She's got a nerve, taking my pen!* cheek.

nervous anxious, apprehensive, edgy, fearful, fidgety, flustered, highly-strung, jittery, jumpy, shy, strained, tense, timid, uneasy, (informal) uptight, worried.

nestle *The baby nestled up to his mother.* to cuddle, to lie comfortably, to snuggle.

net criss-cross pattern, mesh, netting, network, web.

network 1 SEE **net.** 2 *a railway network.* organization, system.

neutral 1 *a neutral referee.* detached, disinterested, impartial, not involved, unbiased, unprejudiced. 2 *neutral colours.* indefinite, intermediate, middle.

new 1 *a new £5 note.* brand-new, clean, fresh, in mint condition, unused. 2 *a new invention.* modern, novel, recent, up-to-date.

news announcement, bulletin, communiqué, dispatch, information, message, notice, proclamation, report, statement, (old-fashioned) tidings.

newspaper journal, paper, the press.

next 1 *the next street.* adjacent, closest, nearest. 2 *the next bus.* following, subsequent, succeeding.

nibble SEE **eat.**

nice ! The word *nice* has many meanings. For some of the other words you can use SEE **beautiful, good, pleasant.**

nick 1 *I nicked my finger.* SEE **cut. 2** (informal) *I nicked some ice-cream out of the fridge.* to pilfer, (informal) to pinch, to steal, to take.

nickname SEE **name.**

nil SEE **nothing.**

nimble *nimble movements.* acrobatic, agile, deft, lively, quick-moving, swift.

nip *A dog nipped my leg.* to bite, to pinch, to snap at, to squeeze, to sting.

nipper SEE **child.**

nippy (informal) 1 *a nippy car.* fast, quick, rapid, speedy. 2 *nippy weather.* bitter, chilly, cold, frosty, icy, (informal) perishing, raw, wintry.

noble 1 *a noble family.* aristocratic, high-born, princely, royal, titled. 2 *a noble deed.* brave, chivalrous, courageous, gallant, glorious, heroic, honourable, virtuous, worthy. 3 *a noble building.* dignified, elegant, grand, imposing, majestic, stately. SEE ALSO **splendid.**

nod *to nod off:* to doze, to sleep, to snooze, to take a nap.

noise bedlam, clamour, commotion, din, hubbub, hullabaloo, pandemonium, racket, row, rumpus, uproar. FOR VARIOUS NOISES SEE **sound.**

noisy *a noisy class.* boisterous, deafening, rowdy, uproarious.

nomad *nomads in the desert.* gypsy, traveller, wanderer.

nominate *They nominated me as captain.* to appoint, to choose, to elect, to name, to select.

nondescript SEE **ordinary.**

non-existent *Unicorns are non-existent.* fictitious, imaginary, made-up.

nonplussed *The head was nonplussed when we cheered him.* amazed, dumbfounded, speechless, stumped, stunned, thunderstruck.

nonsense balderdash, bilge, drivel, gibberish, rubbish, tripe, twaddle. ! These words are usually used informally.

non-stop *He talks non-stop.* ceaselessly, constantly, continually, continuously, persistently.

noon midday.

noose *a noose in a rope.* loop.

normal *normal temperature.* accustomed, average, common, conventional, customary, habitual, ordinary, regular, routine, typical, usual.

nose 1 *the nose of a plane.* bow, front. 2 *to nose about.* to look, to pry, to search.

nosey curious, inquisitive, prying.

nostalgic romantic, sentimental.

notable 1 *a notable mistake.* conspicuous, extraordinary, noticeable, obvious, remarkable, striking. 2 *a notable visitor.* celebrated, distinguished, eminent, famous, important, noted, outstanding, prominent, renowned, well-known.

notch *a notch in a stick.* cut, nick.

note 1 *Write her a note.* communication, letter, message. 2 *an angry note in her voice.* feeling, sound, tone. 3 *Did you note what she was wearing?* to heed, to mark, to mind, to notice, to observe, to remark, to take notice of. 4 *Note this in your book.* to jot, to record, to scribble, to write.

notebook exercise book, jotter.

nothing nought, zero. *In cricket:* duck. *In tennis:* love. *In football:* nil.

notice 1 *Did you notice what we've got for dinner?* to detect, to discern, to discover, to feel, to find, to mark, to observe, to see, to spy. 2 *Did you see the notice on the door?* advertisement, announcement, leaflet, message, placard, poster, sign, warning. 3 *He didn't take any notice.* attention, heed, regard.

noticeable *a noticeable improvement in the weather.* detectable, evident, obvious, perceptible, pronounced, unmistakable.

notify *If you see anything suspicious, notify the police.* to advise, to inform, to tell, to warn.

notion *I had a notion that Father Christmas kept reindeer.* belief, concept, idea, opinion, theory, thought.

notorious *a notorious thief.* infamous, scandalous, well-known, wicked.

nought SEE **nothing**.

nourish 1 *Food nourishes us.* to feed, to strengthen. 2 *nourishing*: good for you, nutritious, wholesome.

nourishment SEE **food**.

novel *That's a novel way of doing it!* different, new, original, strange, uncommon, unusual.

novelist author, writer.

novice apprentice, beginner, learner.

nozzle spout.

nucleus centre, core, heart, middle.

nude bare, naked, unclothed, uncovered.

nugget *a gold nugget.* ingot, lump.

nuisance *Don't let the dog be a nuisance to you.* annoyance, bother, inconvenience, irritation, pest, trouble, worry.

numb *The cold numbed our fingers.* to deaden, to paralyse.

number 1 digit, figure, integer, numeral. 2 VARIOUS NUMBERS: century, dozen, gross, score. 3 *a large number.* amount, quantity, sum, total. 4 *a musical number.* item, piece, song. 5 *a number of a magazine.* edition, issue, publication. 6 *The crowd numbered a thousand.* to add up to, to total, to work out at.

numeral digit, figure, integer, number.

numerous countless, innumerable, many, numberless, plentiful, plenty of, untold.

nurse 1 *a child's nurse*: nanny. 2 *to nurse a sick person.* to care for, to cherish, to look after, to mother, to tend. 3 *to nurse a baby.* to feed.

nursery crèche.

nut 1 kernel. 2 KINDS OF NUT: almond, chestnut, coconut, hazel, peanut, walnut.

nutritious good for you, nourishing, wholesome.

O

oath 1 *He gave us his oath that he was telling the truth.* assurance, guarantee, pledge, promise, vow. 2 *He uttered some terrible oaths.* curse, exclamation, swear-word.

obedient *an obedient dog.* disciplined, docile, dutiful, law-abiding, well-behaved.

obey *Obey the rules.* to abide by, to be ruled by, to carry out, to conform to, to keep to, to submit to.

object 1 *What's that object you've found?* article, item, thing. 2 *What is the object of this exercise?* aim, goal, intention, objective, point, purpose, target. 3 *Mum objected because I got my feet wet.* to complain, to disapprove, to grouse, to grumble, to mind, to moan, to protest.

objection outcry, protest.

objectionable foul, nasty, offensive. SEE ALSO **unpleasant**.

objective 1 *The objective is to get the ball in the net.* aim, intention, object, purpose. 2 *Our objective was the top of the hill.* destination, goal, target.

obligation *You have an obligation to feed your pet.* duty, responsibility.

oblige 1 *obliged*: bound, certain, compelled, forced, required, sure. 2 *obliging*: accommodating, considerate, co-operative, helpful, kind, neighbourly, polite, thoughtful.

oblong rectangle.

obnoxious *an obnoxious taste.* disgusting, foul, loathsome, nasty, nauseating. SEE ALSO **unpleasant**.

obscene *obscene language.* coarse, crude, dirty, filthy, foul, improper, indecent, offensive, rude, smutty, vulgar.

obscure 1 *For some obscure reason he ran away.* dim, hidden, indistinct, puzzling, unclear, unheard of, unimportant, unknown. 2 *Mist obscured the view.* to cover, to conceal, to envelop, to hide, to mask, to shroud.

observant alert, astute, attentive, aware, careful, perceptive, shrewd, vigilant, watchful.

observation *Have you any observations?* comment, opinion, remark, statement.

observe 1 *We observed the eclipse.* to contemplate, to detect, to follow, to look at, to note, to notice, to see, to spy, to stare at, to view, to watch. 2 *I observed that it was a nice day.* to comment, to explain, to remark, to say. 3 *Do you observe Christmas?* to celebrate, to keep, to remember.

observer bystander, eyewitness, onlooker, spectator, witness.

obsession infatuation, mania, passion.

obsolete *an obsolete type of car.* antiquated, disused, old-fashioned, out-of-date.

obstacle *She put an obstacle in my way.* barricade, barrier, blockage, difficulty, hindrance, impediment, obstruction, problem, snag.

obstinate *He can be obstinate when he sets his heart on something.* defiant, dogged, inflexible, perverse, stubborn, unyielding, wilful.

obstreperous *We were rather obstreperous on the last day of term.* boisterous, disorderly, irrepressible, noisy, rough, rowdy, unruly.

obstruct *A fallen tree obstructed our progress.* to bar, to block, to deter, to halt, to hamper, to hinder, to impede, to interfere with, to stop.

obstruction barricade, barrier, blockage, obstacle.

obtain to acquire, to be given, to bring, to buy, to gain, to get, to get hold of, to procure, to purchase, to receive.

obtuse SEE **stupid.**

obvious *an obvious London accent.* clear, evident, notable, plain, prominent, pronounced, undisputed, unmistakable.

occasion 1 *A party is the occasion for a bit of fun.* chance, moment, opportunity, time. 2 *The wedding was a happy occasion.* ceremony, event, happening, incident, occurrence.

occasional *occasional showers.* infrequent, intermittent, rare, spasmodic, uncommon.

occupation activity, business, calling, employment, job, pastime, profession, trade, work.

occupy 1 *They won't allow six people to occupy a tiny flat like this.* to dwell in, to inhabit, to live in, to reside in. 2 *How do you occupy your time?* to fill, to take up, to use. 3 *The troops occupied the town.* to capture, to conquer, to invade, to take possession of. 4 *occupied:* active, busy, engaged.

occur 1 *When did the accident occur?* to befall, to come about, to happen, to take place. 2 *The same spelling mistake occurs throughout your story.* to appear, to arise, to be found, to crop up, to exist.

occurrence event, happening, incident, occasion, phenomenon.

ocean sea.

odd 1 *odd behaviour.* abnormal, (informal) cranky, curious, freak, funny, incongruous, irregular, peculiar, queer, strange, uncommon, weird. 2 *an odd sock.* left over, remaining, single, spare.

odious *We agreed that Nero was an odious person.* abominable, detestable, disgusting, hateful, loathsome, nasty, offensive, repulsive, revolting.

odour SEE **smell.**

offence *a criminal offence.* crime, misdeed, sin, wrongdoing.

offend 1 *I offended granny by not writing.* to anger, to annoy, to displease, to insult, to irritate, to upset, to vex. 2 *to be offended:* to take umbrage.

offender criminal, delinquent, malefactor, wrongdoer.

offensive *offensive behaviour, offensive language, etc.* antisocial, coarse, disagreeable, disgusting, disrespectful, foul, improper, indecent, nasty, objectionable, rude, vulgar. SEE ALSO **unpleasant.**

offer 1 *He offered me a cup of tea.* to extend, to give, to present. 2 *He offered to come with me.* to propose, to suggest. 3 *Dad made the garage an offer for the car.* bid, proposal, suggestion.

offering contribution, donation, gift, sacrifice.

office 1 bureau. 2 THINGS YOU FIND IN AN OFFICE: calculator, computer, copier, desk, diary, duplicator, enquiry desk, file, form, intercom, photocopier, stapler, stationery, switchboard, telephone, typewriter, word-processor. 3 PEOPLE WHO WORK IN AN OFFICE: cashier, clerk, receptionist, secretary, telephonist, typist.

officer 1 *an army officer.* SEE **rank.** 2 *an administrative officer.* SEE **official.** 3 *a police officer.* SEE **police.**

official 1 *an official document.* authorized, formal, proper. 2 *We spoke to an official.* authorized person, officer, responsible person.

officious *Dad hates that officious carpark attendant!* bumptious, (informal) cocky, interfering, self-important.

offspring baby, child, descendant, family, young.

often again and again, constantly, frequently, regularly, repeatedly.

ogre giant, monster.

oil *to oil your bike.* to grease, to lubricate.

oily *oily food.* fat, fatty, greasy.

ointment lotion.

old 1 *old exhibits in a museum.* ancient, antiquated, antique, early, prehistoric, primitive, venerable. 2 *old people.* aged, elderly. 3 *old ruins.* decrepit, dilapidated. 4 *an old style.* former, old-fashioned, out-of-date. 5 *old bread.* stale.

old-fashioned 1 SEE **old.** 2 *old-fashioned ideas.* narrow-minded, prim, proper, prudish.

omen *They thought the thunder was an omen of some terrible event.* indication, premonition, sign, warning.

ominous *an ominous sound of thunder.* forbidding, grim, menacing, sinister, threatening, unlucky.

omit 1 *Why was I omitted from the team?* to drop, to eliminate, to exclude, to ignore, to leave out, to reject. 2 *Don't omit to sign your passport.* to fail, to neglect, to overlook, to skip.

omnipotent almighty.

oncoming *oncoming cars.* approaching.

one-sided 1 *a one-sided referee.* biased, prejudiced, unfair. 2 *a one-sided match.* unbalanced, unequal, uneven.

onlooker *The accident horrified the onlookers.* bystander, eyewitness, observer, spectator, witness.

onslaught *a fierce onslaught.* assault, attack, blitz, bombardment, charge.

ooze *Oil oozed out of the crack.* to dribble, to leak, to seep, to trickle.

opaque *The muddy water was opaque.* cloudy, dark, murky, unclear.

open 1 *an open door.* ajar, unfastened, unlocked. 2 *an open space.* broad, empty, extensive, unfenced, wide, yawning. 3 *an open book.* spread out, unfolded. 4 *an open reply.* candid, frank, honest, outspoken, sincere, straightforward. 5 *an open insult.* blatant, obvious, unconcealed, undisguised. 6 *Open the door.* to undo, to unfasten, to unfold, to unlock, to unseal. 7 *The football season opens this week.* to begin, to commence, to start.

opening 1 *an opening in the fence.* breach, break, chink, crack, cut, gap, gash, hole, leak, mouth, outlet, rift, slit, slot, split, tear, vent. 2 *the opening of a concert.* beginning, commencement, start.

operate 1 *Do trains operate on Christmas Day?* to act, to function, to perform, to run. 2 *Can you operate this mowing-machine?* to deal with, to manage, to use, to work.

operation 1 *Granny had an operation.* surgery. 2 *a military operation.* action, campaign, manoeuvre.

opinion *I had my own opinion about who was guilty.* attitude, belief, comment, conclusion, conviction, guess, idea, judgement, thought, view.

opponent adversary, competitor, enemy, foe, opposition, rival.

opportunity *The weekend is a good opportunity to do some shopping.* chance, moment, occasion, time.

oppose to compete against, to contest, to contradict, to defy, to fight, to resist, to rival, to stand up to, to withstand.

opposite 1 *the opposite side of the road.* facing. 2 *opposite opinions.* conflicting, contradictory, different, incompatible, opposing.

oppress 1 *The owners oppressed the slaves.* to afflict, to depress, to exploit, to persecute, to trouble, to worry. 2 *oppressed*: downtrodden.

oppressive 1 *an oppressive ruler.* cruel, harsh, severe, tyrannical, unjust. 2 *oppressive weather.* close, hot, humid, muggy, stifling, sultry.

opt *We opted for rounders, and they opted for cricket.* to choose, to pick, to select, to settle on, to vote for.

optical OPTICAL INSTRUMENTS: bifocals, binoculars, field-glasses, glasses, lens, magnifying glass, microscope, periscope, spectacles, sun-glasses, telescope.

optimistic *We were optimistic about our chances.* cheerful, confident, expectant, hopeful.! *Optimistic* is the opposite of *pessimistic.*

option *We had the option of beans or peas.* alternative, choice.

optional voluntary.

oral *Instead of writing, we gave an oral report.* by mouth, spoken.

orbit *The spacecraft made an orbit of the earth.* circuit, revolution.

ordeal *The long trek across the ice was a terrible ordeal.* difficulty, suffering, test, trial.

order 1 *The boss gives the orders.* command, decree, instruction. 2 *The head restored order.* calm, control, discipline, good behaviour, law and order, obedience, peace. 3 *Is your bike in good order?* condition, state. 4 *Put the library books in order.* arrangement, sequence, series, tidiness. 5 *The teacher ordered us to be quiet.* to command, to compel, to direct, to instruct, to require. 6 *I ordered a new magazine.* to book, to reserve.

orderly 1 *orderly work.* careful, methodical, neat, organized, systematic, tidy, well-organized. 2 *orderly behaviour.* civilized, disciplined, law-abiding, well-behaved.

ordinary *ordinary people, ordinary things, etc.* accustomed, common, commonplace, conventional, customary, everyday, familiar, habitual, indifferent, mediocre, medium, middling, moderate, nondescript, normal, orthodox, plain, reasonable, regular, routine, satisfactory, standard, typical, undistinguished, unexciting, uninteresting, usual, well-known.

organism creature, living thing.

organization *a business organization.* alliance, association, body, business, club, company, corporation, firm, group, league, network, party, society, union.

organize 1 *We organized the library books.* to arrange, to classify, to group, to put in order, to sort. 2 *We organized an American football team.* to create, to establish, to mobilize, to set up. 3 *organized*: careful, civilized, methodical, orderly, scientific, systematic.

orgy party, revelry.

origin *We discussed the origin of life on earth.* beginning, birth, cause, commencement, creation, source, start.

original 1 *the original inhabitants of a country.* earliest, first, initial. 2 *an original idea, an original story.* creative, fresh, imaginative, inventive, new, novel, unique, unusual.

originate *How did the name 'America' originate?* to arise, to begin, to commence, to emerge, to start.

ornament adornment, decoration.

ornamental decorative, fancy.

ornithology bird-watching.

orthodox *Scientists are always questioning orthodox ideas.* accepted, conventional, official, ordinary, standard, traditional, usual.

outbreak *an outbreak of measles.* epidemic, plague.

outburst *an outburst of laughter.* eruption, explosion.

outcast exile, outlaw, refugee.

outcome *What was the outcome of your visit to the doctor?* consequence, effect, result, sequel.

outcry *There was an outcry when they stopped our bus service.* clamour, objection, protest.

outdo *She can outdo anyone at gymnastics.* to beat, to exceed, to excel, to surpass, to top.

outfit *a skin-diving outfit.* apparatus, clothing, costume, equipment, gear, kit, rig.

outhouse shed.

outing *an outing to the sea.* excursion, expedition, jaunt, tour, trip.

131 **owing**

outlaw 1 *The outlaws hid in the mountains.* bandit, criminal, deserter, desperado, fugitive, outcast, renegade. 2 *Smoking has been outlawed in many places.* to ban, to forbid, to prohibit.

outlet exit, mouth, opening, way out.

outline 1 *I sketched a quick outline.* diagram, drawing, framework, sketch, summary. 2 *We saw the outline of someone passing the window.* figure, form, profile, shadow, shape.

outlook 1 *My window has a pleasant outlook.* prospect, scene, sight, view. 2 *The outlook for tomorrow is good.* forecast, prediction.

outlying *They travel by bus from outlying areas.* distant, remote.

outrage atrocity, crime, disgrace, scandal, sensation.

outrageous *outrageous behaviour.* disgraceful, infamous, monstrous, notorious, offensive, scandalous, shocking, wicked.

outside covering, exterior, shell, skin, surface.

outsider *Make outsiders feel welcome.* alien, foreigner, immigrant, visitor.

outskirts *the outskirts of the town.* edge, fringe, suburbs.

outspoken *Our trainer was outspoken about our terrible performance.* blunt, candid, direct, frank, honest, plain, straightforward.

outstanding 1 *an outstanding player.* conspicuous, distinguished, dominant, eminent, excellent, exceptional, great, notable, prominent, well-known. 2 *outstanding bills.* due, overdue, owing, unpaid.

outward *outward appearances.* exterior, external, outer, outside.

outwit *I was glad that the fox outwitted the hounds!* to cheat, to dupe, to fool, to hoodwink, to take in, to trick. SEE ALSO **deceive.**

overcast cloudy, dull, gloomy.

overcome to beat, to conquer, to master, to overthrow, to overwhelm, to quell, to subdue, to suppress. SEE ALSO **defeat.**

overcrowd *The room was overcrowded.* to cram, to crush, to fill.

overdue 1 *The bus is overdue.* belated, delayed, late, unpunctual. 2 *The gas bill is overdue.* outstanding, owing, unpaid.

overflow *The lavatory cistern overflowed.* to brim over, to flood, to pour over, to run over, to spill.

overgrown *an overgrown garden.* tangled, uncut, unkempt, untidy, untrimmed, wild.

overhang *My book-shelf overhangs my bed.* to jut out, to project, to protrude, to stick out.

overhaul 1 *The garage overhauled our car.* to renovate, to repair, to service. 2 *The fast train overhauled a goods train.* to catch up with, to overtake, to pass.

overhear *to overhear a conversation.* to eavesdrop, to listen in.

overjoyed delighted, ecstatic, elated, joyful. SEE ALSO **happy.**

overlook 1 *We mustn't overlook small details.* to disregard, to forget, to ignore, to leave out, to miss, to neglect, to omit, to pay no attention to. 2 *My window overlooks the pie factory.* to face, to look at.

overpower 1 *She overpowered her attacker.* to beat, to keep off, to master, to overcome, to overwhelm. SEE ALSO **defeat.** 2 *overpowering:* irresistible.

overrun *A plague of mice overran the farm.* to infest, to invade, to march into, to occupy, to swarm over, to take over.

overseas abroad.

oversight *It wasn't deliberate, just an oversight.* blunder, error, mistake, slip-up.

overtake to catch up with, to overhaul, to pass.

overthrow SEE **overcome.**

overturn 1 *The boat overturned.* to capsize, to turn over, to turn turtle. 2 *The cat overturned the milk.* to spill, to tip over, to topple, to upset.

overweight chubby, dumpy, fat, flabby, gross, heavy, plump, podgy, portly, stout, tubby.

overwhelm 1 *We overwhelmed the opposition.* to beat, to conquer, to crush, to overcome, to overpower, to overthrow, to rout. SEE ALSO **defeat.** 2 *A tidal wave overwhelmed the town.* to drown, to engulf, to inundate, to submerge, to swamp.

owing 1 *You must pay whatever is owing.* due, outstanding, overdue, unpaid. 2 *owing to:* because of, thanks to.

own 1 *Who owns a catapult?* to have, to hold, to possess. 2 *I owned up.* to acknowledge, to admit, to confess.

owner 1 *the owner of a dog.* possessor. 2 *the owner of a business.* boss, proprietor.

P

pace 1 *Move forward two paces.* step, stride. 2 *The front runner set a quick pace.* movement, rate, speed, velocity. 3 SEE **walk.**

pacify *We pacified the baby by giving him some toys.* to appease, to calm, to quieten, to soothe.

pack 1 *a pack of biscuits.* box, bundle, package, packet, parcel. 2 *a pack of wolves.* SEE **group.** 3 *Pack your things in a box.* to fill, to load, to put, to stow. 4 *They packed us into the minibus.* to cram, to crowd, to huddle, to jam, to squeeze, to stuff.

package bale, bundle, pack, packet, parcel.

pact *We made a pact with our rivals.* agreement, alliance, armistice, bargain, contract, deal, peace, settlement, treaty, truce, understanding.

pad 1 *a pad to kneel on.* cushion, padding, wad. 2 *a writing pad.* jotter, notebook. 3 *We padded the seat with soft material.* to cover, to fill, to protect, to stuff. 4 *padding:* upholstery.

paddle *We paddled in the sea.* to wade.

paddock field, meadow, pasture.

padlock lock. SEE ALSO **fasten.**

pagan atheist, heathen. ! *Pagan* and *heathen* often sound insulting.

page *a page of a book.* leaf, sheet.

pageant parade, procession.

pageantry *The royal wedding was conducted with great pageantry.* ceremony, formality, grandeur, pomp, ritual, spectacle.

pail bucket.

pain ache, agony, anguish, hurt, ordeal, pang, soreness, spasm, sting, suffering, throb, torment, torture, twinge.

painful 1 *a painful wound.* agonizing, excruciating, inflamed, raw, sore. 2 *to be painful:* to ache, to hurt, to smart, to sting, to throb.

painless *My visit to the dentist was quite painless.* comfortable, easy, effortless.

paint 1 KINDS OF PAINT: emulsion, enamel, gloss paint, lacquer, matt paint, oil-colour, pastel, varnish, water-colour, white-wash. 2 *We painted the front room.* to decorate.

painter artist.

painting SEE **picture.**

pair brace, couple.

pal (informal) *Be a good pal and lend me £1!* chum, friend, (informal) mate.

palace castle, château, mansion, stately home.

pale 1 *a pale face.* colourless, pasty, wan, whitish. 2 *pale colours.* dim, faint, light.

paling fence, railway, stockade.

pamper *Grandad pampers his dog.* to humour, to indulge, to spoil.

pamphlet *a pamphlet about road safety.* booklet, brochure, catalogue, leaflet.

pan SEE **container.**

panda car police car.

pandemonium *There was pandemonium when my rats escaped.* bedlam, chaos, commotion, confusion, disorder, hubbub, hullabaloo, racket, riot, row, rumpus, tumult, turmoil, uproar.

pane glass, window.

panel *a group of experts.* committee, group, jury, team.

pang *a pang of toothache.* ache, throb, twinge. SEE ALSO **pain.**

panic *If a fire starts, we don't want any panic!* alarm, fear, horror, hysteria, stampede, terror.

panorama *We saw a beautiful panorama from the top of the hill.* landscape, prospect, scene, view, vista.

pant 1 *to gasp, to puff, to wheeze.* 2 *panting:* breathless, exhausted, puffed, tired out.

panties briefs, knickers, pants.

pantry food cupboard, larder.

pants briefs, knickers, panties, shorts, trousers, trunks, underpants.

paper 1 KINDS OF PAPER: card, cardboard, newspaper, notepaper, papyrus, parchment, postcard, stationery, tissue-paper, toilet-paper, wallpaper, wrapping-paper, writing-paper. 2 *She keeps important papers in a file.* certificates, deeds, documents, forms, records. 3 *We papered the front room.* to decorate.

parade *a fancy dress parade.* cavalcade, march, pageant, procession.

paradise heaven.

paralyse 1 *The shock paralysed him.* to deaden, to numb, to petrify. 2 *paralysed:* immobile, immovable, paraplegic, rigid. SEE ALSO **handicap.**

paraphernalia equipment, gear, tackle.

paraplegic SEE **handicap.**

parcel bale, bundle, package, packet.

parched 1 *Plants won't grow in parched ground.* arid, barren, dry, lifeless, sterile. 2 *(informal) I'm parched!* (informal) gasping, thirsty.

pardon 1 *The government issued a pardon for all prisoners.* amnesty, reprieve. 2 *The judge pardoned him.* to excuse, to forgive, to let off, to overlook, to reprieve, to set free, to spare.

park KINDS OF PARK: car-park, gardens, recreation ground, safari park.

parry *to parry a blow.* to fend off, to push away, to repel, to repulse, to ward off.

parson clergyman, minister, pastor, preacher, priest, vicar.

part 1 *Which part of the chicken do you prefer?* bit, fraction, fragment, particle, piece, portion, share. 2 *They sell computers in another part of the shop.* branch, department, division, section, sector. 3 *Did the garage get the parts for the car?* component, unit. 4 *Which part of the country do you come from?* district, region. 5 *It would be terrible if the caravan parted from the car.* to detach, to disconnect, to divide, to separate, to split.

partial 1 *Our play was only a partial success.* imperfect, incomplete, unfinished. 2 *to be partial to:* to be fond of, to enjoy, to like.

participate *to participate in a game.* to be involved, to join, to share, to take part.

particle *a particle of dust.* atom, bit, crumb, fraction, fragment, grain, piece, scrap, shred, speck.

particular 1 *She has a particular way of writing.* distinct, individual, personal, special, specific. 2 *Our cat's particular about food.* (informal) choosey, fastidious, finicky, fussy. 3 *in particular: Are you writing to anyone in particular?* important, notable, outstanding. 4 *particulars: Give me the particulars.* details, facts, information.

partition panel, room-divider, screen, wall.

partner accomplice, ally, assistant, collaborator, confederate.

party KINDS OF PARTY: ball, banquet, barbecue, birthday party, celebration, Christmas party, dance, disco, feast, function, gathering, orgy, picnic, reception, social, wedding.

pass 1 *We watched the traffic pass.* to go by, to move along, to proceed. 2 *We passed a lot of other cars.* to cross, to overhaul, to overtake. 3 *The time passed.* to elapse. 4 *The pain soon passed.* to disappear, to fade, to vanish. 5 *Please pass the books around.* to circulate, to deal out, to deliver, to give, to hand over, to offer, to present, to share, to submit, to supply. 6 *a mountain pass.* defile, gorge, ravine, valley. 7 *a bus pass.* permit, ticket.

passable 1 *The food was passable.* acceptable, adequate, all right, mediocre, ordinary, satisfactory, tolerable. 2 *The snow has gone and the road is passable again.* clear, open.

passage 1 corridor, hall. 2 *a secret passage.* tunnel. 3 *We read an exciting passage from the book.* episode, extract, piece, quotation, scene, section.

passenger traveller.

passer-by bystander.

passion *a passion for adventure, sexual passion.* appetite, desire, emotion, enthusiasm, infatuation, love, lust, thirst, urge.

passionate 1 *passionate love.* burning, emotional, fervent, hot, intense, lustful, sexy. 2 *a passionate interest in something.* avid, eager, enthusiastic.

paste adhesive, glue, gum.

pastime *My favourite pastime is water-skiing.* activity, amusement, diversion, entertainment, game, hobby, occupation, recreation.

pasture field, meadow, paddock.

pasty *She looked pasty after having flu.* anaemic, colourless, ill, pale, (informal) poorly, unwell, wan.

pat to caress, to dab, to slap, to stroke.

patch *I patched a hole in my jeans.* to darn, to mend, to repair, to sew up, to stitch up.

patchy *The fog was patchy.* changeable, erratic, inconsistent, uneven, unpredictable, variable.

paternal fatherly.

path alley, footpath, pathway, pavement, towpath, track. SEE ALSO **road**.

pathetic *It was pathetic to see how badly the dog had been treated.* moving, piteous, pitiful, touching, tragic. SEE ALSO **sad**.

patience *The people in the queue showed great patience.* calmness, endurance, restraint, self-control.

patient 1 *a patient animal.* calm, docile, easygoing, quiet, serene, tolerant. 2 *a patient worker.* determined, persevering, persistent, untiring. 3 *a patient at a hospital.* out-patient, sufferer.

patio terrace.

patrol guard, look-out, sentinel, sentry, watchman.

pattern 1 *Is there a pattern I can copy?* example, guide, model, prototype. 2 *There are nice patterns in my wallpaper.* decoration, design, figure, shape.

pauper beggar, tramp, vagrant.

pause 1 *We had a pause for a drink.* break, delay, gap, interruption, interval, lull, rest, stop. 2 *We paused for a drink.* to halt, to hang back, to hesitate, to rest, to stop, to wait.

pavement SEE **path**.

paw foot.

pay 1 *How much did you pay?* to give, to hand over, to spend. 2 *Did you pay his dad for the broken window?* to compensate, to recompense, to repay. 3 *How much pay do you get?* earnings, income, salary, wages.

payment *We make a payment to the wildlife fund every month.* contribution, cost, deposit, expenditure, fee, instalment, subscription, toll.

peace 1 *After the war there was a period of peace.* agreement, concord, friendliness, harmony, order. 2 *The two sides agreed on terms for peace.* alliance, armistice, pact, treaty, truce. 3 *We enjoy the peace of the countryside.* calmness, quiet, serenity, stillness, tranquillity.

peaceful *a peaceful evening, peaceful music.* balmy, calm, easy, gentle, placid, pleasant, quiet, serene, soothing, still, tranquil, untroubled.

peak 1 *snowy peaks.* hill, mountain, summit, tip, top. 2 *The music rose to a peak.* climax, crisis, height, pinnacle.

peasant farm worker, labourer.
! *Peasant* refers to a poor worker in certain countries.

pebbles cobbles, gravel, stones.

peckish (informal) *I'm feeling peckish.* famished, hungry, ravenous, starving.

peculiar *He has a peculiar way of writing.* abnormal, curious, different, distinctive, funny, individual, odd, particular, queer, special, strange, uncommon, unique, unusual, weird.

pedestrian walker.

pedigree *Do you know the dog's pedigree?* ancestry, family history.

peel 1 *orange peel.* rind, skin. 2 *to peel the covering off something.* to skin, to strip.

peep SEE **look.**

peer 1 SEE **look.** 2 aristocrat, lord, noble, nobleman, noblewoman, peeress.

peevish *a peevish mood.* bad-tempered, cross, grumpy, irritable, petulant, snappy, testy.

pellet ball, pill.

pelt 1 *The monkeys pelted us with peanuts.* to bombard. 2 *They pelted peanuts at us.* SEE **throw.**

pen 1 ball-point, felt-tipped pen, fountain pen. 2 *a pen for animals.* cage, compound, coop, enclosure, fold, run.

penalize *He was penalized for a foul.* to punish.

penalty *We have to pay the penalty for doing wrong.* fine, forfeit, punishment.

penetrate *Dad's drill couldn't penetrate the concrete.* to bore through, to enter, to pierce, to probe, to puncture.

penitent *I was penitent after breaking the window.* apologetic, regretful, remorseful, repentant, sorry.

penniless *a penniless beggar.* destitute, impoverished, needy, poor, poverty-stricken.

pensive *You look pensive: what are you thinking about?* dreamy, grave, philosophical, reflective, serious, thoughtful.

people folk, human beings, humanity, individuals, mankind, mortals, persons. SEE ALSO **person.**

perceive 1 *We perceived a dim shape on the horizon.* to detect, to discern, to notice, to recognize, to see. 2 *At last I began to perceive what she meant.* to feel, to know, to sense, to understand.

perceptible *a perceptible drop in temperature.* noticeable.

perceptive *a perceptive judge of character.* astute, clever, observant, shrewd.

perch *a bird's perch.* roost.

percussion PERCUSSION INSTRUMENTS: castanets, cymbal, drum, glockenspiel, gong, kettledrum, tambourine, timpani, tom-tom, triangle, tubular bells, xylophone.

perfect 1 *a perfect performance.* excellent, faultless, ideal. 2 *a perfect example.* in mint condition, pure, undamaged. 3 *a perfect fit.* accurate, correct, exact, precise. 4 (informal) *perfect chaos.* absolute, complete.

perforate *If you perforate a groundsheet the damp comes through.* to bore through, to penetrate, to pierce, to puncture.

perform 1 *to perform your duty.* to accomplish, to achieve, to carry out, to commit, to complete, to do, to execute, to finish. 2 *to perform on the stage.* to act, to appear, to dance, to play, to present, to produce, to sing.

performance 1 *We did a special performance for the parents.* ballet, concert, matinée, opera, play, première, preview, production, show. 2 *He isn't ill: he's only putting on a performance.* act, deception, pretence.

performer FOR VARIOUS PERFORMERS SEE **entertainment, music, theatre.**

perfume aroma, fragrance, odour, scent, smell, whiff.

perhaps maybe, possibly.

peril *Sailors face the perils of the sea.* danger, hazard, risk, threat.

perimeter *the perimeter of a field.* border, boundary, circumference, edge.

period age, era, interval, phase, season, session, spell, stretch, term, while.

periodical journal, magazine, paper.

perish 1 *Many birds perish in the cold weather.* to die, to expire, to fall, to pass away. 2 *Soft fruit perishes if it isn't used quickly.* to decay, to decompose, to disintegrate, to go bad, to rot.

perky *I felt perky again after I had a sleep.* alert, animated, frisky, jaunty, lively, playful, sprightly, vivacious.

permanent *The unfortunate woman suffers from a permanent headache.* chronic, constant, continual, continuous, enduring, everlasting, incessant, lasting, lifelong, perpetual, persistent, stable, unending.

permissible *Did he have a permissible excuse?* allowable, lawful, legal, permitted, proper, right, valid.

permission *We had the head's permission to go home.* approval, authority, consent.

permit 1 *Have you got a permit to fish here?* authorization, licence, pass, permission, ticket, warrant. 2 *Dad never permits smoking in the house.* to agree to, to allow, to approve of, to authorize, to consent to, to license, to tolerate.

perpetual *I hate their perpetual chattering.* ceaseless, chronic, constant, continual, continuous, endless, eternal, everlasting, incessant, interminable, non-stop, permanent, persistent, recurrent, unending.

perplex *The mystery of the missing money perplexed us.* to baffle, to bewilder, to confuse, to muddle, to puzzle, to stump.

persecute *People are sometimes persecuted for their religious beliefs.* to bully, to intimidate, to oppress, to terrorize, to torment, to victimize.

persevere *You'll succeed in the end if you persevere.* to be diligent, to be patient, to carry on, to continue, to endure, to persist.

persist 1 *You'll succeed in the end if you persist.* SEE **persevere.** 2 *How long is this snow going to persist?* to go on, to keep on, to last.

persistent 1 *a persistent cold.* ceaseless, chronic, constant, continuous, endless, eternal, everlasting, incessant, interminable, lasting, permanent, perpetual, recurrent, unending. 2 *a persistent worker.* determined, dogged, patient, resolute, stubborn, unwavering.

person adolescent, adult, baby, boy, child, gentleman, girl, human being, individual, infant, lad, lady, lass, man, mortal, teenager, toddler, woman, youngster, youth. SEE ALSO **people.**

personal 1 *personal characteristics.* distinct, distinctive, individual, particular, private, special, unique. 2 *personal details.* confidential, intimate, private, secret.

personnel *The boss issued an announcement for all personnel in the factory.* employees, people, workers.

perspire to sweat.

persuade 1 *We persuaded him to play in goal.* to coax, to entice, to induce, to tempt, to urge. 2 *She persuaded me that she was right.* to convince, to win over.

persuasion *It took a lot of persuasion to convince him.* argument, brain-washing, conditioning, propaganda.

persuasive *a persuasive argument.* convincing, eloquent, influential.

perturb *The bad news perturbed us.* to alarm, to distress, to disturb, to excite, to frighten, to scare, to shake, to upset, to worry.

perverse *It's perverse of you to buy hot dogs when we want ice-cream.* contrary, disobedient, obstinate, rebellious, stubborn, tiresome, unreasonable.

pervert *He was accused of trying to pervert a witness.* to bribe, to corrupt, to lead astray.

pessimistic *I'm afraid I'm pessimistic about our chances.* despairing, gloomy, hopeless, morbid, unhappy.! *Pessimistic* is the opposite of *optimistic.*

pest 1 *Ants can be a pest in the garden.* annoyance, nuisance. 2 *pests:* vermin.

pester *Don't pester me while I'm busy!* to annoy, to bait, to bother, to harass, to molest, to nag, to plague, to torment, to trouble, to worry.

pesticide SEE **poison.**

pet 1 CREATURES KEPT AS PETS: budgerigar, canary, cat, dog, ferret, fish, gerbil, goldfish, guinea-pig, hamster, mouse, parrot, pigeon, rabbit, rat, tortoise. 2 *Who's teacher's pet, then?* darling, favourite. 3 *The dog loves you to pet him.* to caress, to fondle, to stroke.

petition *We organized a petition against the ending of our bus service.* appeal, entreaty, plea, request.

petrify *The scream petrified me!* to appal, to paralyse, to scare stiff, to terrify. SEE ALSO **frighten**.

petrol (informal) gas, gasoline.

petty *5p is a petty amount to quarrel over!* insignificant, minor, small, trifling, trivial, unimportant.

petulant *a petulant mood.* bad-tempered, cross, grumpy, irritable, peevish, snappy, sulky, sullen, testy.

phantom SEE **ghost**.

phase period, stage, step, time.

phenomenal *The winner of the quiz had a phenomenal memory.* amazing, exceptional, extraordinary, fantastic, incredible, notable, remarkable, singular, unbelievable.

phenomenon *An eclipse is a rare phenomenon.* event, happening, occurrence.

philosophical *Mum was philosophical about losing her purse.* calm, patient, reasonable, resigned, thoughtful.

phone *I phoned granny.* to call, to dial, to ring, to telephone.

phoney (informal) *a phoney Welsh accent.* artificial, bogus, faked, false, synthetic, unreal.

phosphorescent glowing, luminous, shining.

photocopy to copy, to duplicate, to print, to reproduce.

photograph KINDS OF PHOTOGRAPH: enlargement, film, negative, photo, print, slide, snap, snapshot, transparency.

photography WORDS TO DO WITH PHOTOGRAPHY: camera, cine-camera, to develop, exposure, to focus, Polaroid, to print, reflex camera, telephoto lens, zoom lens. SEE ALSO **photograph**.

physical 1 *Do ghosts have a physical existence?* solid, tangible. 2 *physical exercise.* bodily.

physician doctor.

pick 1 *Pick a partner.* to choose, to decide on, to elect, to name, to nominate, to opt for, to prefer, to select, to settle on, to vote for. 2 *to pick flowers, to pick strawberries.* to collect, to cut, to gather, to harvest, to pull off, to take.

pickle *to pickle onions.* to preserve.

picture 1 KINDS OF PICTURE: cartoon, collage, doodle, drawing, engraving, graffiti, illustration, landscape, likeness, mosaic, mural, oil-painting, painting, photograph, portrait, print, self-portrait, sketch, slide, transfer, transparency. 2 WAYS OF MAKING A PICTURE: to depict, to draw, to illustrate, to paint, to photograph, to portray, to represent, to sketch. 3 *Can you picture what the world will be like in 100 years?* to conceive, to dream up, to imagine, to think up, to visualize.

picturesque *picturesque scenery.* attractive, charming, pretty, quaint. SEE ALSO **beautiful**.

piece 1 *a piece of cake, a piece of wood, etc.* bar, bit, bite, block, chip, chunk, crumb, division, dollop, fraction, fragment, grain, helping, hunk, lump, morsel, part, particle, portion, scrap, section, segment, share, slab, slice, snippet, speck, stick, tablet. 2 *a piece of machinery.* component, element, unit. 3 *a piece of good news.* case, example, instance, specimen. 4 *a piece of music.* composition, item, number, passage, work.

pier jetty, landing-stage.

pierce 1 *The needle pierced the skin.* to bore, to drill, to go through, to penetrate, to perforate, to prick, to puncture, to stab. 2 *piercing: a piercing scream.* deafening, loud, sharp, shrill.

pig hog, sow, swine.

piggy-bank money-box.

pigmy dwarf, midget.! These words sometimes sound insulting.

pile 1 *a pile of rubbish.* heap, mass, mound, stack. 2 *Pile everything in the corner.* to accumulate, to assemble, to bring together, to collect, to gather, to heap up, to mass, to stack up.

pilfer *He was caught pilfering goods from a shop.* (informal) to nick, (informal) to pinch, to steal, to take.

pilgrim traveller.

pill capsule, pellet.

pillar

pillar column, pile, post, prop, shaft, support.

pillow bolster.

pilot 1 DIFFERENT KINDS OF PILOT: airman, coxswain, guide, helmsman. 2 *He piloted us back to safety.* to drive, to fly, to guide, to navigate, to steer.

pimples boils, rash, spots.

pinafore apron.

pinch 1 *You hurt me when you pinched my arm.* to nip, to squeeze. 2 (informal) *Who pinched my pencil?* SEE **steal**.

pine 1 *The dog pined when his master died.* to mope, to mourn, to waste away. 2 *In the winter I pine for some warm sunshine.* to hanker after, to long for, to miss, to yearn for.

pinnacle *the pinnacle of his career.* climax, height, peak, summit, top.

pioneer discoverer, explorer, settler.

pip *an orange pip.* seed, stone.

pipe *a water pipe.* hose, pipeline.

pirate buccaneer. SEE ALSO **criminal**.

pit 1 *a deep pit.* abyss, chasm, crater, hole. 2 *The miners work in a pit.* mine, quarry, shaft, working.

pitch 1 tar. 2 *pitch-black*: SEE **black**. 3 *to pitch a tent.* to erect, to put up, to set up. 4 *I pitched a stone into the pond.* to bowl, to cast, (informal) to chuck, to fling, to hurl, to lob, to sling, to throw, to toss. 5 *The boat pitched about in the storm.* to lurch, to plunge, to rock, to roll, to toss about.

piteous SEE **pitiful**.

pitfall danger, trap.

pitiful 1 *The injured animal was a pitiful sight.* heart-breaking, pathetic, piteous, touching. SEE ALSO **sad**. 2 *He made a pitiful attempt to stop the ball.* contemptible, miserable, useless, worthless.

pitiless *a pitiless attack.* bloodthirsty, callous, heartless, relentless, ruthless. SEE ALSO **cruel**.

pity *The muggers showed no pity.* compassion, feeling, kindness, mercy, sympathy.

placard *an advertising placard.* bill, notice, poster, sign.

place 1 *Mark the place on the map.* location, point, position, site, situation, spot. 2 *What is your favourite place for a holiday?* area, country, district, locality, neighbourhood, region, town. 3 *Let's meet at your place.* SEE **house**. 4 *The hall has places for 90 people.* chair, seat. 5 *Place your things on the table.* to arrange, to deposit, to lay, to locate, to position, to put down, to rest, to set down, to situate, to stand, to station.

placid 1 *a placid lake.* calm, peaceful, quiet, tranquil, untroubled. 2 *a placid character.* cool, level-headed, mild, sensible, unexcitable.

plague 1 epidemic, outbreak. SEE ALSO **illness**. 2 *The flies plagued us.* to annoy, to bother, to disturb, to irritate, to molest, to pester, to trouble, to vex, to worry.

plain 1 *She gave a plain signal.* apparent, certain, clear, definite, distinct, evident, obvious, unmistakable. 2 *She wore a plain dress.* austere, simple, undecorated. 3 *She looked quite plain until she smiled.* ordinary, unattractive. 4 *He did some plain speaking.* blunt, candid, direct, frank, honest, outspoken, straight-forward.

plaintive *a plaintive tune.* doleful, melancholy, mournful, sorrowful. SEE ALSO **sad**.

plan 1 *Our plan was to buy food for a picnic.* aim, idea, intention, method, plot, policy, project, proposal, scheme, strategy. 2 *We drew a plan of the town.* chart, design, diagram, map. 3 *We planned to go to the seaside.* to aim, to contemplate, to intend. 4 *We planned a way to defeat the opposition.* to arrange, to design, to devise, to organize, to plot, to prepare, to scheme, to think up. 5 *planned*: premeditated. 6 *planning*: forethought.

plane SEE **aircraft**.

plank board, timber.

plant 1 *plants*: greenery, growth, undergrowth, vegetation. 2 KINDS OF PLANT: annual, cactus, grass, lichen, moss, perennial, seedling. SEE ALSO **bulb, cereal, climber, flower, fungus, herb, shrub, tree, vegetable, water plant, weed**. 3 PARTS OF A PLANT: bloom, blossom, bud, flower, leaf, petal, pod, root, seed, shoot, stalk, stem, trunk, twig. 4 *to plant seeds.* to set out, to sow.

plate-glass glass, pane, window.

platform stage.

plausible *a plausible excuse.* believable, credible, likely, reasonable.

play 1 *The kittens played happily.* to amuse yourself, to caper, to frisk, to have fun, to mess about, to romp. 2 *Can you play on Saturday?* to join in, to take part. 3 *Who are we playing on Saturday?* to compete against, to oppose. 4 *My sister played Mary in the nativity play.* to act, to pretend to be. 5 *I can play the piano.* to perform on. 6 *We were punished for playing up.* to be disobedient, to be naughty, to misbehave. 7 *We saw a good play on TV.* drama, production.

player 1 competitor, contestant, sportsman, sportswoman. 2 actor, musician, performer.

playful *a playful puppy.* active, frisky, lively, spirited, sprightly, vivacious.

playing-field recreation ground.

playwright SEE **writer.**

plea *a plea for mercy.* appeal, entreaty, petition, request.

plead *He pleaded to be let off.* to appeal, to beg, to entreat, to implore, to request.

pleasant *pleasant food, pleasant weather, etc.* agreeable, amiable, attractive, balmy, charming, decent, delicious, delightful, enjoyable, excellent, fine, friendly, genial, gentle, heavenly, hospitable, kind, likeable, lovely, mellow, mild, nice, peaceful, pleasing, pretty, relaxed, satisfying, soothing, sympathetic, warm, welcome.! *Pleasant* has many meanings. The words given here are only some of the other words you can use. SEE ALSO **beautiful, good,** etc.

please 1 *Did the present please her?* to amuse, to content, to delight, to entertain, to make happy, to satisfy. 2 *pleased: You look pleased!* complacent, content, grateful, satisfied, thankful. SEE ALSO **happy.** 3 *pleasing:* SEE **pleasant.**

pleasure 1 *He smiled with pleasure.* bliss, delight, ecstasy, enjoyment, gladness, happiness, joy, rapture, satisfaction. 2 *What are your favourite pleasures?* amusement, diversion, entertainment, fun, luxury, recreation.

pleat crease, fold.

pledge 1 *He gave me his pledge that he would do what I wanted.* assurance, guarantee, oath, pact, promise, vow, word. 2 *She pledged her support.* to agree, to promise, to swear, to vow.

plentiful *a plentiful supply of food.* abundant, ample, bountiful, copious, generous, lavish, liberal, profuse.

pliable *pliable wire.* bendable, flexible, springy, supple.

plight *We were in a terrible plight when we lost our money.* condition, difficulty, dilemma, jam, predicament, problem, situation, state.

plod SEE **walk.**

plot 1 *Guy Fawkes led a plot to blow up Parliament.* conspiracy, intrigue, plan, scheme. 2 *This novel has a complicated plot.* narrative, outline, story. 3 *a vegetable plot.* allotment, garden, patch. 4 *We plotted to ambush their gang.* to conspire, to design, to plan, to scheme.

pluck 1 (informal) *She's got a lot of pluck.* SEE **courage.** 2 *to pluck fruit.* to gather, to harvest, to pick, to pull off. 3 *The mugger plucked the handbag out of her hand.* to grab, to seize, to snatch.

plug 1 *Put a plug in the hole!* bung, cork, stopper. 2 *to plug a hole.* to block up, to close, to fill, to jam, to seal, to stop up. 3 (informal) *They keep on plugging that record on the radio.* to advertise, to mention frequently, to promote.

plumage feathers, plumes.

plump *a plump figure.* chubby, dumpy, fat, overweight, podgy, portly, squat, stout, tubby.

plunder 1 *The rioters plundered the shops.* to loot, to raid, to ransack, to ravage, to rob, to steal. 2 *They ran off with their plunder.* booty, contraband, loot, (informal) swag, takings.

plunge 1 *She plunged into the water.* to dive, to drop, to fall, to leap, to pitch. 2 *He plunged the red-hot steel into water.* to dip, to lower, to immerse, to submerge. 3 *He plunged the spear into the animal's side.* to force, to push, to thrust.

poach *He was arrested for poaching.* to hunt, to steal.

pocket-money allowance.

pod *a pea pod.* shell.

podgy *a podgy figure.* chubby, dumpy, fat, plump, portly, squat.

poem 1 poetry, rhyme, verse. 2 KINDS
OF POEM: ballad, epic, haiku, limerick,
lyric, nursery-rhyme, ode. 3 WORDS TO
DO WITH POETRY: line, rhyme, rhythm,
stanza.

poet bard.

poetry SEE **poem.**

point 1 *the point of a spear.* prong, spike,
tip. 2 *a decimal point.* dot, spot. 3 *Mark
the exact point on the map.* location,
place, position, situation. 4 *What is the
point of this game?* aim, idea, intention,
object, purpose. 5 *She pointed out the
way.* to indicate, to show. 6 *Can you
point us in the right direction for the
castle?* to aim, to direct, to guide, to
lead, to steer.

pointless 1 *As the train had gone, it was
pointless to wait.* fruitless, futile,
inappropriate, irrelevant. 2 *a pointless
remark.* meaningless, senseless, useless,
worthless.

poise *A gymnast needs poise.* balance,
calmness, equilibrium, self-confidence,
self-control, steadiness.

poison 1 venom. 2 KINDS OF POISON:
arsenic, insecticide, pesticide. 3 *The
chemicals poisoned the lake.* to
contaminate, to infect, to pollute.
4 *poisoned: a poisoned wound.* festering,
infected, septic.

poisonous *a poisonous snake-bite.*
deadly, fatal, lethal, mortal, toxic,
venomous.

poke 1 *He poked me in the ribs.* to dig, to
jab, to prod. 2 *I poked a bit of wood into
the hole.* to stick, to thrust.

pole *a long pole.* column, post, rod,
stick.

police constable, (informal) cop or
copper, detective, inspector, officer,
policeman, policewoman.

policy *Our school's policy is to let us
have two trips out each year.* plan,
procedure, strategy, tactics.

polish 1 *That table's got a lovely polish!*
brightness, gloss, lustre, sheen, shine,
smoothness. 2 *polished:* bright,
burnished, gleaming, shiny.

polite *polite behaviour, a polite person.*
attentive, chivalrous, civil, considerate,
courteous, cultivated, diplomatic,
gallant, gentlemanly, ladylike,
(informal) posh, refined, respectful,
thoughtful, well-bred, well-mannered.

politics PEOPLE WITH VARIOUS
POLITICAL VIEWS: anarchist, Communist,
Conservative, Democrat, Green,
Labour supporter, Liberal, Marxist,
monarchist, nationalist, Nazi,
Republican, SDP supporter, Socialist,
Tory.

poll 1 *to go to the polls.* ballot, election,
vote. 2 *an opinion poll.* census,
referendum, survey.

pollute *Refuse pollutes the beach.* to
contaminate, to defile, to dirty, to foul,
to infect, to poison, to soil.

poltergeist SEE **ghost.**

pomp *The coronation was conducted
with great pomp.* ceremony, grandeur,
magnificence, pageantry, ritual,
solemnity, spectacle.

pompous *Important people don't have
to be pompous.* arrogant, haughty,
self-important, showy, snobbish,
(informal) stuck-up.

pond *a fish pond.* lake, pool.

ponder *We pondered about the
difficulty.* to brood, to consider, to
contemplate, to meditate, to reflect, to
study, to think.

ponderous *a ponderous load.* bulky,
burdensome, heavy, massive, unwieldy,
weighty.

pool lake, pond, puddle,
swimming-pool.

poor 1 *The poor woman couldn't afford
any food.* bankrupt, destitute, hard up,
homeless, needy, penniless,
poverty-stricken, underpaid. 2 *a poor
person:* beggar, pauper, tramp, vagrant.
3 *poor quality.* cheap, faulty, feeble,
inadequate, inferior, useless, worthless.
SEE ALSO **bad.** 4 *We were sorry for the
poor animals.* luckless, miserable,
pathetic, pitiable, unfortunate,
unhappy.

poorly (informal) *I felt poorly.* feeble,
frail, ill, indisposed, infirm, queer, sick,
unwell, wan, weak.

popular *a popular performer.*
celebrated, famous, favourite,
renowned, well-known, well-liked.

population citizens, inhabitants,
occupants, residents.

porcelain china, earthenware, pottery.
SEE ALSO **crockery.**

port *The ship entered port.* dockyard,
harbour. SEE ALSO **dock.**

portable *a portable tool-box.* compact, convenient, handy, light, small.

portion *Can I have a small portion of pie?* bit, fraction, helping, quota, section, segment, share, slice. SEE ALSO **piece.**

portly *a portly figure.* chubby, dumpy, fat, overweight, plump, podgy, stout, tubby.

portrait likeness, representation, self-portrait. SEE ALSO **picture.**

portray *The book portrays what life was like 1000 years ago.* to depict, to illustrate, to represent, to show. SEE ALSO **picture.**

pose **1** *to pose for a photograph.* to model. **2** *He is always posing.* to show off. **3** *The burglar posed as a gas man.* to impersonate, to pretend to be. **4** *to pose a question.* to ask, to put forward, to suggest.

posh (informal) *a posh party.* elegant, formal, smart, snobbish, stylish.

position **1** *Their house is in a nice position.* locality, location, place, point, site, situation, spot. **2** *I was in an awkward position because I had no money.* circumstances, condition, state. **3** *A referee takes a neutral position.* attitude, opinion, standpoint, view. **4** *Mum has a responsible position in the firm.* employment, job, rank, status, title. **5** *The captain positioned her players.* to arrange, to locate, to place, to situate, to station.

positive **1** *He was positive that he could come.* assured, certain, confident, convinced, definite, sure. **2** *The policeman gave some positive advice.* beneficial, constructive, helpful, practical, useful. ! *Positive* is the opposite of *negative.*

posse SEE **group.**

possess **1** *Do you possess a dishwasher?* to have, to own. **2** *Foreign invaders possessed the country.* to control, to dominate, to govern, to occupy, to rule.

possession *I have few possessions.* belongings, fortune, goods, property, wealth.

possible **1** *Would it be possible to swim the Atlantic?* conceivable, feasible, imaginable, practicable, viable, workable. **2** *a possible goalkeeper.* likely, potential.

possibility *There's a possibility of rain.* chance, danger, likelihood, risk.

possibly maybe, perhaps.

post **1** *Concrete posts support the fence.* column, pile, pillar, pole, prop, shaft, support. **2** *Mum has a post in a local business.* employment, occupation, position, work. **3** *Has the post come?* airmail, letter, mail, packet, parcel, postcard. **4** *Did you post my letter?* to dispatch, to mail, to send.

post-box letter-box, pillar-box.

poster *We put up a poster about sports day.* advertisement, bill, notice, placard, sign.

posterity descendants, heirs, offspring.

postpone *We postponed the match because of the snow.* to adjourn, to defer, to delay, to put off.! Compare *postpone* with *cancel.*

posy *a posy of flowers.* bouquet, bunch, spray.

pot *a cooking pot.* casserole, cauldron, pan, saucepan.

potent *a potent smell.* overpowering, powerful, strong.

potential *a potential Olympic gymnast.* likely, possible.

pot-hole cave, cavern, hole.

pottery china, earthenware, porcelain. SEE ALSO **crockery.**

potty SEE **mad.**

poultry KINDS OF POULTRY: bantam, chicken, cock, cockerel, duck, goose, hen, pullet, rooster, turkey.

pounce *The cat pounced on the mouse.* to ambush, to jump, to leap, to spring, to swoop.

pound *We pounded the clay until it was soft.* to batter, to beat, to crush, to grind, to mash, to pulp. SEE ALSO **hit.**

pour *Water poured through the hole.* to flow, to gush, to run, to stream.

poverty *The refugees lived in terrible poverty.* beggary, need, want.

powder **1** dust. **2** *powdered: powdered coffee.* ground.

power 1 *We have the power to win.* ability, competence, skill, talent. 2 *The referee has the power to send him off.* authority, control, influence, right. 3 *The waves have the power to knock you over.* energy, force, might, strength, vigour.

powerful *a powerful machine, a powerful player.* dynamic, forceful, influential, mighty, potent, strong.

powerless *We were powerless against their gang.* feeble, helpless, impotent, weak.

practicable *a practicable plan.* feasible, possible, practical, realistic, sensible, viable, workable.

practical 1 *a practical worker.* businesslike, capable, competent, efficient. 2 *a practical tool.* handy, usable, useful. 3 *a practical plan.* SEE **practicable.** 4 *a practical joke:* hoax, prank, trick.

practically almost, close to, nearly.

practice 1 *It's our practice to end the day with a story.* custom, habit, routine. 2 *We need more practice before we perform in public.* preparation, rehearsal, training.

practise *We must keep on practising.* to exercise, to rehearse, to train. ! Notice the different spellings of *practice* (noun) and *practise* (verb).

praise 1 *Everyone praised us for raising so much money.* to admire, to applaud, to commend, to congratulate, to honour, to marvel at, to pay tribute to. 2 *Praise God!* to adore, to worship.

praiseworthy *a praiseworthy effort.* admirable, commendable, creditable, deserving, worthy. SEE ALSO **good.**

pram push-chair.

prance *to prance about.* to caper, to dance, to frisk, to jump, to leap, to play, to romp, to skip.

prank *Don't get up to any pranks.* escapade, mischief, practical joke, scrape.

prattle to chatter. SEE ALSO **talk.**

preach SEE **talk.**

preacher clergyman, evangelist, minister, missionary, parson, pastor, priest, vicar.

precarious *The climber stood on a precarious ledge.* dangerous, insecure, perilous, rocky, shaky, unsafe, unsteady, wobbly.

precaution *What precautions can you take against flu?* defence, protection, safeguard.

precede *Christmas precedes Boxing Day.* to come before, to go before.

precious *precious jewels.* costly, dear, expensive, invaluable, priceless, valuable.

precipice *The climber fell down a precipice.* cliff, crag, rock.

precipitous *a precipitous drop.* sharp, sheer, steep, vertical.

precise 1 *the precise time.* accurate, correct, definite, exact, right, specific. 2 *precise work.* careful, meticulous.

predator hunter.

predecessor ancestor, forefather.

predicament *How did they get out of that predicament?* difficulty, dilemma, emergency, jam, plight.

predict *She predicted that I would win.* to forecast, to foretell, to prophesy, to tell fortunes.

predominantly *The people at the party were predominantly grown-ups.* chiefly, generally, mainly, mostly, primarily.

preface introduction, prelude, prologue.

prefer *Which flavour do you prefer?* to choose, to fancy, to like better, to pick out.

pregnant 1 *a pregnant woman.* expectant, expecting. 2 WORDS TO DO WITH PREGNANCY: abortion, birth, to conceive, conception, miscarriage, premature birth.

prehistoric *prehistoric remains.* ancient, early, old, primitive.

prejudice 1 *A referee is not supposed to show prejudice to either side.* bias, discrimination, favouritism, intolerance, unfairness. 2 *racial prejudice:* racialism, racism. 3 *prejudiced:* biased, intolerant, unfair.

preliminary *the preliminary rounds in a championship.* early, introductory, opening.

prelude *The first match was an exciting prelude to the series.* beginning, introduction, opening, preface, preparation, prologue.

premature *a premature baby.* early, too early, too soon.

premeditated *a premeditated crime.* calculated, deliberate, intentional, planned, wilful.

premonition *I had a premonition that something nasty would happen.* foreboding, indication, omen, warning.

preoccupied *He is preoccupied with plans for his holiday.* absorbed in, immersed in, interested in.

prepare *to prepare a display.* to arrange, to get ready, to organize, to plan, to process.

preposterous *The clown wore a preposterous costume.* absurd, farcical, grotesque, ludicrous, ridiculous, stupid, unconventional, weird, zany.

prescribe *What did the doctor prescribe?* to advise, to recommend, to suggest.

present 1 *Is everyone present?* here. 2 *Who's the present champion?* current, existing. 3 *She gave me a present.* contribution, donation, gift, offering. 4 *Who presented the cups?* to award, to give, to hand over, to offer. 5 *We presented our work to the parents.* to demonstrate, to display, to exhibit, to reveal, to show. 6 *Let me present our guest.* to introduce, to make known. 7 *We presented a play.* to act, to perform, to put on.

presentable *Is your room presentable?* acceptable, clean, decent, proper, respectable, tidy, worthy.

presently shortly, soon.

preserve 1 *We all want to preserve peace.* to defend, to guard, to keep, to look after, to maintain, to protect, to safeguard, to save. 2 WAYS TO PRESERVE FOOD: to can, to cure, to dehydrate, to dry, to freeze, to pickle, to refrigerate, to salt, to tin.

press 1 *If I press the clothes down I can close the suitcase.* to compress, to crowd, to crush, to push, to shove, to squash, to squeeze. 2 *He pressed his trousers.* to flatten, to iron, to smooth. 3 *They pressed me to stay.* to compel, to order, to persuade, to require, to urge. 4 *the press*: newspapers, magazines. SEE ALSO **media.**

pressing *pressing business.* essential, important, urgent.

pressure *the pressure in a tyre.* compression, force, might, power, stress.

prestige *If we lose again, our prestige will suffer.* fame, glory, good name, honour, renown, reputation.

presume 1 *I presume you'd like something to eat.* to assume, to believe, to guess, to imagine, to suppose, to think. 2 *He presumed to contradict the teacher.* to dare, to venture.

presumptuous *It was presumptuous to ask for more.* arrogant, bold, cheeky, forward, impertinent, impudent, insolent, shameless.

pretend 1 WAYS OF PRETENDING: to act, to bluff, to conjure, to counterfeit, to deceive, to disguise, to fake, to feign, to fool, to hoax, to hoodwink, to imitate, to impersonate, (informal) to kid, to lie, to make believe, to mislead, to perform, to play a part, to put on, to sham, to take someone in, to trick. 2 *I don't pretend that I play well.* to believe, to claim, to fancy, to imagine, to maintain, to suppose.

pretty 1 *a pretty dress, pretty flowers.* appealing, attractive, charming, dainty, lovely, pleasing. SEE ALSO **beautiful.** 2 (informal) *That's pretty good!* fairly, moderately, rather, somewhat.

prevailing *What's the prevailing colour in this year's fashions?* chief, common, current, dominant, general, main, normal, prevalent, principal, usual.

prevalent SEE **prevailing.**

prevent *The snow prevented us from travelling.* to check, to curb, to deter, to hamper, to hinder, to impede, to obstruct, to stop.

previously before, earlier.

prey 1 *The lion killed its prey.* victim. 2 *Owls prey on small animals.* to eat, to feed on, to hunt, to kill.

price *a reasonable price.* amount, charge, cost, fare, fee, payment, rate, sum, terms, toll, value.

priceless 1 *priceless jewels.* costly, dear, expensive, invaluable, precious, (informal) pricey, valuable. 2 (informal) *a priceless joke.* SEE **funny.**

prick *to prick your finger.* to pierce, to puncture.

prickly *a prickly bush.* spiky, thorny.

pride 1 *It injured his pride when he let in three goals.* arrogance, conceit, self-importance, self-satisfaction, vanity. 2 *The new car is her pride and joy.* happiness, pleasure, satisfaction.

priest clergyman, minister, parson, preacher, vicar.

prim *She's too prim to enjoy rude jokes!* narrow-minded, old-fashioned, proper, prudish.

primarily *Amusement arcades are used primarily by young people.* chiefly, firstly, generally, mainly, mostly, predominantly.

primary *In soccer, the primary aim is to score goals!* SEE **principal.**

primitive 1 *primitive tribes.* ancient, early, prehistoric, uncivilized, undeveloped. 2 *a primitive machine.* crude, rough, simple.

principal 1 *In soccer, the principal aim is to score goals!* basic, chief, dominant, first, foremost, fundamental, greatest, important, leading, main, major, outstanding, primary, prime, supreme. 2 *the Principal of a college.* SEE **head.**

principle 1 *Can you teach me the principles of chess?* law, rule, science, theory. 2 *He is a man of principle.* honesty, honour, integrity, standards, virtue.

print 1 *to print a book.* to issue, to publish. 2 *Print your name clearly.* SEE **write.** 3 *We saw the prints of huge feet in the sand.* mark, stamp. 4 *It's not an original painting: it's a print.* copy, duplicate, reproduction.

priory abbey, monastery.

prison Borstal, cell, detention centre, dungeon, gaol.

prisoner captive, convict, hostage.

private 1 *private property.* individual, personal, special. 2 *private information.* confidential, intimate, secret. 3 *a private hide-out.* hidden, isolated, quiet, secluded.

privilege *Club members enjoy the privilege of cheap refreshments.* advantage, benefit, right.

prize 1 *I never win a prize!* award, jackpot, reward. 2 *Mum prizes the ring she got from granny.* to appreciate, to approve of, to cherish, to esteem, to like, to rate, to regard, to value. 3 *I lost the key so I had to prize the lid off.* to lever, to wrench.

probable likely, possible.

probe *The police probed deeply into the problem.* to examine, to explore, to inquire into, to investigate, to penetrate.

problem 1 *a problem to solve.* conundrum, mystery, puzzle, question, riddle. 2 *Life has its problems.* burden, complication, difficulty, dilemma, predicament, set-back, snag, trouble, worry.

procedure *a procedure for doing something.* method, process, system, technique.

proceed *After a break, we proceeded on our way.* to advance, to carry on, to continue, to go on, to move forward, to progress.

proceedings events, happenings.

proceeds *What were the proceeds from our OXFAM collection?* income, profit, takings.

process 1 *a manufacturing process.* method, procedure, system, technique. 2 *They have to process crude oil to make petrol.* to change, to convert, to prepare, to refine, to transform, to treat.

procession *a procession of soldiers.* cavalcade, line, march, pageant, parade.

proclaim *The head proclaimed that we would have an extra holiday.* to announce, to assert, to declare, to decree, to make known, to pronounce.

procure *How did you procure tickets for the Cup Final?* to acquire, to buy, to get, to get hold of, to obtain, to purchase.

prod *He prodded me in the back.* to dig, to jab, to poke, to push. SEE ALSO **hit.**

prodigal *a prodigal waste of money.* extravagant, lavish, wasteful.

produce 1 *produce from the garden.* crop, harvest, output, yield. 2 WAYS TO PRODUCE THINGS: to bear, to breed, to cause, to compose, to create, to cultivate, to form, to generate, to give birth to, to grow, to invent, to make, to manufacture, to originate, to provoke, to raise, to rear, to think up, to yield. 3 *The conjuror produced a rabbit from a hat.* to bring out, to disclose, to display, to exhibit, to present, to reveal, to show.

productive 1 *a productive factory.* busy, creative, effective, profitable, useful. 2 *a productive garden.* fertile, fruitful, lush, prolific.

profession *Nursing is an important profession.* business, calling, career, employment, job, occupation, trade, work.

professional 1 *professional advice.* expert, qualified, skilled, trained. 2 *a professional player.* paid. ! *Professional* is the opposite of *amateur.*

professor lecturer, tutor.

proficient *a proficient worker.* able, capable, competent, effective, qualified, skilled, trained.

profile outline, shape.

profit 1 *Did you make any profit?* advantage, benefit, gain. 2 *Did you profit from the sale?* to earn, to gain, to make money.

profitable *a profitable business deal.* advantageous, beneficial, fruitful, productive, rewarding, useful, worthwhile.

profound 1 *profound sympathy.* deep, sincere. 2 *a profound discussion.* intellectual, learned, serious, thoughtful, wise.

profuse *profuse apologies.* abundant, ample, copious, plentiful.

programme 1 *a programme for sports day.* plan, schedule, timetable. 2 *a television programme.* SEE **television**.

progress 1 *He has made progress with his swimming this year.* development, improvement. 2 *Our plans are progressing.* to advance, to develop, to improve, to make headway, to move forward, to proceed.

progression *We had a progression of disasters!* row, sequence, series, string, succession.

prohibit *They prohibit smoking in food shops.* to ban, to bar, to censor, to forbid, to make illegal, to outlaw, to prevent, to veto.

project 1 *The shelf projects from the wall.* to extend, to jut out, to overhang, to protrude, to stick out. 2 *The candle projected a flickering light.* to cast, to throw. 3 *We did a history project at school.* activity, assignment, task, work. 4 *There is a project to build a bypass.* plan, proposal, scheme.

prolific fertile, fruitful, productive.

prologue beginning, introduction, preface, prelude.

prolong *The game was prolonged by a number of injuries.* to draw out, to extend, to increase, to lengthen, to make longer, to stretch out.

prominent 1 *prominent teeth.* bulging, jutting out, large, protruding, sticking out. 2 *a prominent landmark.* conspicuous, noticeable, obvious, pronounced. 3 *a prominent politician.* celebrated, distinguished, eminent, famous, outstanding, renowned, well-known.

promise 1 *She gave me her promise.* assurance, guarantee, oath, pledge, vow. 2 *You promised me that you would pay.* to agree, to assure, to consent, to give your word, to guarantee, to pledge, to swear, to undertake, to vow.

promote 1 *She was promoted to a more responsible job.* to move up, to raise. 2 *A local firm promoted our sports festival.* to back, to boost, to encourage, to help, to sponsor, to support. 3 *We saw posters promoting the new film.* to advertise, to make known, (informal) to plug.

prompt 1 *a prompt reply.* immediate, instantaneous, on time, punctual, quick, speedy, swift. 2 *She prompted me to join the youth club.* to egg on, to encourage, to inspire, to stimulate, to urge. 3 *He forgot his lines until I prompted him.* to jog the memory, to remind.

prone *He lay prone on the floor.* face down, flat.

prong *the prong of a fork.* point, spike.

pronounce 1 *How do you pronounce this word?* to say, to speak, to utter. 2 *The doctor pronounced me fit again.* to announce, to declare, to make known, to proclaim. 3 *pronounced*: conspicuous, definite, distinct, noticeable, obvious, prominent.

proof *The police have proof of his guilt.* evidence, facts, grounds, testimony.

prop 1 crutch, post, support. 2 *She propped her bike against the wall.* to lean, to rest, to stand. 3 *The wall was propped up by some big timbers.* to hold up, to reinforce, to support.

propel to drive, to force, to push, to spur, to urge.

proper 1 *We always use proper language when auntie is here.* becoming, decent, dignified, formal, grave, modest, polite, respectable, serious, solemn, tasteful. 2 *I think £5 is the proper price.* advisable, appropriate, correct, deserved, fair, fitting, just, lawful, legal, right, suitable, valid.

property *I don't own much property.*
belongings, estate, fortune, possessions,
wealth.

prophecy *Her prophecy came true.*
forecast, prediction.

prophesy *She prophesied that I would
become rich.* to forecast, to foresee, to
foretell, to predict, to tell fortunes.
! Notice the difference in spelling
between *prophecy* (noun) and *prophesy*
(verb).

prophet forecaster, fortune-teller.

proportion 1 *What is the proportion of
girls to boys in your class?* balance, ratio.
2 *A large proportion of the audience
cheered.* fraction, part, piece, quota,
section, share. 3 *She's a lady of large
proportions.* dimensions,
measurements, size.

proposal *A big firm made a proposal to
build a supermarket.* bid, offer, plan,
project, scheme, suggestion.

propose *They propose to visit us on
Saturday.* to aim, to intend, to offer, to
plan, to suggest.

proprietor *the proprietor of a shop.*
boss, manager, owner.

prosecute *They prosecuted him for
dangerous driving.* to accuse, to charge,
to sue.

prospect 1 *There's a lovely prospect
from the top of the hill.* outlook,
panorama, scene, sight, view, vista. 2 *to
prospect for gold.* to explore, to search.

prospectus *The school sent us their
prospectus.* brochure, leaflet, pamphlet.

prosper *He's happy now that his
business is prospering.* to be successful,
to do well, to flourish, to grow, to
strengthen, to succeed, to thrive.

prosperous *He must be prosperous
with a big car like that!* affluent,
prospering, rich, successful, thriving,
well-off, well-to-do.

protect 1 *Parents protect their young.* to
care for, to cherish, to look after, to
mind, to watch over. 2 *The police
protected her when the crowd surged
forward.* to defend, to escort, to guard,
to harbour, to keep safe, to safeguard,
to screen, to shield.

protest 1 *We made a protest against the
referee's decision.* complaint, objection,
outcry. 2 *There was a big protest in the
square.* (informal) demo, demonstration,
march, rally. 3 *Why don't you protest?* to
complain, to demonstrate, to grouse, to
grumble, to march, to moan, to object.

protrude *His teeth protrude.* to bulge,
to jut out, to stick out, to swell.

proud 1 *We are proud of you.* delighted
with, happy with, pleased with. 2 *She
was too proud to ask for help.* dignified,
honourable, self-respecting. 3 *Don't get
too proud of yourself!* arrogant, boastful,
bumptious, cocky, conceited, disdainful,
haughty, (informal) stuck-up, vain.

prove *We did an experiment to prove that
plants need light.* to confirm, to
demonstrate, to establish, to explain, to
show, to verify.

proverb motto, saying.

provide *We'll provide the food if you
provide the drinks.* to afford, to allot, to
allow, to contribute, to donate, to equip,
to furnish, to give, to grant, to lay on, to
spare, to supply.

provisions food, rations, stores,
supplies.

provoke 1 *He provoked us with his
stupidity.* (informal) to aggravate, to
anger, to annoy, to enrage, to
exasperate, to incense, to infuriate, to
irritate, to tease, to torment, to upset, to
vex, to worry. 2 *Our play provoked a lot
of laughter.* to arouse, to bring about, to
cause, to excite, to incite, to produce, to
stimulate, to stir up.

prowess 1 *prowess in battle.* bravery,
courage, spirit, valour. 2 *The dancers
showed off their prowess.* ability,
accomplishment, cleverness,
competence, skill, talent.

prowl SEE **walk.**

prowler intruder.

prudent *It's prudent to keep some
money in the bank.* advisable, careful,
discreet, proper, sensible, thoughtful,
wise.

prudish *Granny isn't at all prudish.*
easily shocked, narrow-minded,
old-fashioned, prim, strict.

prune *to prune a rose bush.* SEE **cut.**

pry 1 *Don't pry into my affairs.* to
interfere, to meddle, to nose about, to
snoop. 2 *prying:* curious, inquisitive,
nosey.

psychic *Do you believe that some people have psychic powers?* supernatural, telepathic.

pub bar, inn, (informal) local, public house, saloon, tavern.

puberty *You reach puberty in your teens.* adolescence, growing-up.

public 1 *a public place.* common, general, open, shared. 2 *public knowledge.* familiar, known, unconcealed. 3 *the public*: the community, people, society.

publication FOR KINDS OF PUBLICATION SEE **book, magazine, record.**

publicity 1 SEE **advertisement.** 2 *TV stars get a lot of publicity.* attention, fame, notoriety.

public-spirited *Some public-spirited person tidied up the classroom.* generous, kind, unselfish.

publish 1 *to publish a magazine.* to bring out, to issue, to print, to produce, to release. 2 *When will they publish details of the new season?* to announce, to broadcast, to declare, to disclose, to divulge, to make known, to proclaim, to reveal.

puddle pool.

puff 1 *a puff of wind.* blast, gust. 2 *By the end of the race I was puffing.* to blow, to gasp, to pant, to wheeze. 3 *The sails puffed out.* to rise, to swell.

pugnacious *a pugnacious expression.* aggressive, belligerent, hostile, militant, warlike.

pull 1 *A locomotive pulls a train.* to drag, to draw, to haul, to lug, to tow, to trail. 2 *You nearly pulled my arm off!* to jerk, to tug, to wrench. 3 *to pull up*: to draw up, to halt, to stop.

pulp to crush, to mash, to pound, to smash, to squash.

pulse *a regular pulse.* beat, throb.

pump *The fire brigade pumped the water out of the cellar.* to empty, to force, to raise.

pun double meaning, joke.

punch to beat, (informal) to clout, to cuff, to jab, to poke, to prod, to slog, to strike, to thump. SEE ALSO **hit.**

punctual *The bus is punctual today.* on time, prompt.

punctuation PUNCTUATION MARKS: apostrophe, asterisk, brackets, colon, comma, dash, exclamation mark, full stop, hyphen, question mark, quotation marks or speech marks, semicolon.

puncture *A nail punctured my tyre.* to penetrate, to pierce, to prick.

punish to penalize.

punishment VARIOUS PUNISHMENTS: Borstal, the cane, capital punishment, confiscation, corporal punishment, detention, fine, flogging, forfeit, gaol, a hiding, imposition, penalty, prison, probation, the stocks, torture, whipping. SEE ALSO **execute.**

punt *to punt a ball.* to boot, to kick.

puny *a puny child.* feeble, frail, (informal) poorly, sickly, tiny, weak, (informal) weedy.

pupil learner, scholar, schoolboy, schoolchild, schoolgirl, student.

puppet dummy.

purchase to acquire, to buy, to get, to obtain, to pay for.

pure 1 *a pure person.* chaste, good, innocent, modest, virtuous. 2 *pure water.* clean, clear, undiluted, unpolluted. 3 *pure nonsense.* absolute, complete, perfect, sheer, total, utter.

purify *We purified the water before we drank it.* to clean, to disinfect, to refine, to sterilize.

purpose *Have you a particular purpose in mind?* aim, goal, intention, motive, object, objective, plan.

purposely deliberately, intentionally.

purse handbag, wallet.

pursue *How far did they pursue the robbers?* to chase, to follow, to hound, to hunt, to seek, to shadow, to tail, to track down.

pursuit 1 *The hounds dashed off in pursuit of the fox.* chase, hunt. 2 *What are your favourite pursuits?* hobby, interest, pastime.

push 1 *The gangsters pushed him into a car.* to drive, to force, to press, to propel, to thrust. 2 *Push everything into a suitcase.* to cram, to crush, to pack, to squeeze. 3 *The mob pushed forward.* to crowd, to force a way, to hustle, to jostle, to shove. 4 *Push a coin in the slot.* to insert, to put in.

push-chair pram.

put 1 *Put the books on the shelf.* to arrange, to deposit, to hang, to lay, to leave, to locate, to place, to position, to rest, to set down, to situate, to stand, to station. 2 *Put your question politely.* to express, to say. 3 *Dad put in new sparking-plugs.* to insert, to install. 4 *We put off our visit.* to adjourn, to defer, to delay. 5 *They put out the fire.* to extinguish, to quench. 6 *Can granny put us up?* to accommodate, to house, to lodge, to quarter. 7 *We put up the tent.* to build, to construct, to erect, to pitch, to raise, to set up. 8 *They put up their prices.* to increase, to raise, to step up.

putrid *putrid flesh.* bad, decayed, decomposing, festering, foul, rotten, smelly, tainted.

putt SEE **hit.**

puzzle 1 *Can you solve this puzzle?* conundrum, dilemma, mystery, problem, question, riddle. 2 *His bad mood puzzled us.* to baffle, to bewilder, to confuse, to nonplus, to perplex, to stump. 3 *puzzling:* inexplicable, insoluble, mysterious, strange, unanswerable.

Q

quadrangle courtyard.

quagmire *My wellingtons got stuck in the quagmire.* bog, fen, marsh, quicksand, swamp.

quail *I quailed when I heard the monster roar!* to cower, to cringe, to flinch, to show fear, to shrink, to tremble, to wince.

quaint *a quaint thatched cottage.* antiquated, charming, old-fashioned, picturesque, unusual.

quake *to quake with fear.* to quaver, to quiver, to shake, to shudder, to tremble.

qualification 1 *Has she got proper qualifications?* certificate, degree, diploma, examinations. 2 *Has she got any qualifications?* ability, experience, knowledge, skill.

qualify 1 *He qualifies for the senior race next birthday.* to be eligible. 2 *qualified:* equipped, skilled, trained.

quality 1 *Our butcher sells best-quality meat.* class, grade, standard, value. 2 *What qualities do you look for in a captain?* characteristics, feature.

qualm *Have you any qualms about climbing?* anxiety, doubt, hesitation, misgiving, uncertainty, worry.

quantity *a large quantity, a small quantity.* amount, measurement, number, sum, total, volume.

quarantine isolation.

quarrel 1 *a quarrel between two people.* argument, controversy, disagreement, dispute, feud, scene, vendetta. 2 *They often quarrel.* to argue, to differ, to disagree, to fall out, to fight, to squabble.

quarry mine, working.

quarter 1 *The troops were quartered in the town.* to lodge, to put up. 2 *quarters:* boarding house, lodgings.

quaver *He quavered when he heard an angry shout.* to quake, to quiver, to shake, to shudder, to tremble, to waver.

quay berth, dock, jetty, landing-stage, pier, wharf.

queasy *I felt queasy on the ship.* bilious, sick.

queer 1 *a queer shape, a queer smell.* abnormal, curious, funny, odd, peculiar, strange, uncommon, unusual, weird. 2 *I felt queer after six ice-creams.* ill, poorly, sick, unwell.

quell *The police quelled the riot.* to control, to master, to overcome, to subdue, to suppress.

quench 1 *to quench your thirst.* to satisfy. 2 *to quench a fire.* to extinguish, to put out.

query SEE **question.**

quest *a quest for treasure.* hunt, search.

question 1 *Can you answer this question?* conundrum, enquiry, problem, puzzle, query, riddle. 2 *There is some question about whether he is fit.* doubt, uncertainty. 3 *The police questioned me about the accident.* to ask, to cross-examine, to examine, to interrogate, to interview. 4 *We questioned the referee's decision.* to ask about, to dispute, to doubt, to enquire or inquire about, to query.

queue 1 *a queue of cars.* column, file, line, row. 2 *Please queue at the door.* to line up.

quick 1 *a quick journey.* fast, (informal) nippy, rapid, speedy, swift. 2 *quick movements.* agile, animated, brisk, deft, lively, nimble. 3 *a quick end.* abrupt, hasty, immediate, instant, prompt, sudden. 4 *a quick pupil.* apt, bright, clever, intelligent, quick-witted, sharp, shrewd, smart.

quicken to accelerate, to go faster, to hasten, to speed up.

quicksand *He sank into the quicksand!* bog, marsh, quagmire, swamp.

quicksilver mercury.

quiet 1 *a quiet engine.* noiseless, silent, soundless. 2 *a quiet voice.* low, soft. 3 *a quiet evening.* calm, peaceful, placid, serene, tranquil, untroubled.

quieten 1 *Please quieten the baby!* to calm, to hush, to pacify, to silence, to soothe, to subdue. 2 *A silencer quietens the noise of the engine.* to deaden, to muffle, to soften, to stifle, to suppress, to tone down.

quit 1 *to quit your job.* to abandon, to depart from, to desert, to forsake, to leave, to resign from. 2 (informal) *Quit pushing!* to cease, to give up, to stop.

quite 1 *Yes, I have quite finished.* absolutely, altogether, completely, entirely, totally, utterly, wholly. 2 *It was quite good, but nothing special.* fairly, moderately, pretty, rather. ! Take care how you use *quite*, as the two meanings are almost opposite.

quiver *He quivered with cold.* to quake, to shake, to shudder, to tremble.

quiz competition, test.

quota *The explorers shared out their daily quota of food.* portion, proportion, ration, share.

quotation *a quotation from a book.* excerpt, extract, reference.

quote *She often quotes poetry.* to mention, to refer to, to repeat.

R

rabble *a noisy rabble.* crowd, gang, horde, mob, swarm. SEE ALSO **group**.

race 1 *a race of people.* breed, nation, people, tribe. 2 COMPETITIVE RACES: cross-country, heat, horse-race, hurdles, marathon, motor-race, regatta, relay race, rowing, scramble, speedway, sprinting, steeplechase, stock car race, swimming. 3 *to race along.* SEE **rush**.

race-course, race-track circuit, lap.

racial *racial characteristics.* ethnic.

racialism, racism bias, discrimination, intolerance, prejudice.

rack *a plate rack.* stand, support.

racket 1 *I couldn't sleep because of the racket!* clamour, commotion, din, hub-bub, hullabaloo, noise, pandemonium, row, rumpus, uproar. 2 (informal) *Their business is a racket!* crime, dishonest business.

radiant bright, brilliant, gleaming, shining. SEE ALSO **beautiful, happy**.

radiate *The fire radiates heat.* to emit, to give out, to glow, to send out, to transmit.

radio set, transistor, wireless.

rafter beam, girder, joist.

rag *rags:* bits and pieces, cloths, scraps, shreds, tatters.

rage 1 *She couldn't hide her rage.* anger, exasperation, fury, tantrum, temper, wrath. 2 *She shouted and raged for ages.* to be angry, to be violent, to fume, to lose your temper, to rave, to seethe.

ragged *ragged clothes.* frayed, old, patched, shabby, tattered, tatty, torn, worn out.

raid 1 *We planned a raid on their hide-out.* assault, attack, blitz, invasion, onslaught. 2 *We raided their hide-out.* to attack, to invade, to plunder, to pounce, to ravage, to storm, to swoop down on.

rail bar, railing, rod.

railings barrier, fence.

railway WORDS TO DO WITH RAILWAYS: bogie, booking-office, buffer, buffet, carriage, coach, corridor, coupling, cutting, departure, diesel, driver, electric train, engine, express, fireman, footplate, freight, gauge, goods, guard, level crossing, locomotive, passenger, platform, points, porter, rail, shunter, siding, signal, signalbox, signalman, sleeper, sleeping-car, station, steam-engine, tender, terminus, ticket-office, timetable, track, train, wagon, waiting-room.

rain 1 *We had some rain.* deluge, downpour, drizzle, raindrops, shower. 2 *It's raining.* to drizzle, to pour, to teem.

raise 1 *A crane raised the wreck.* to elevate, to erect, to heave, to hoist, to lift, to pick up, to put up. 2 *A farmer raises animals and crops.* to breed, to cultivate, to grow, to produce, to rear. 3 *The forecast raised our hopes of a fine day.* to arouse, to boost, to build up, to enlarge, to excite, to improve, to increase, to stimulate. 4 *He raised £15 for charity.* to collect, to get, to make, to receive.

rally 1 *Granny rallied after her illness.* to get better, to recover, to revive. 2 *a political rally.* (informal) demo, demonstration, march, meeting, protest.

ram *The car rammed the garage door.* to bump, to collide with, to smash into, to strike. SEE ALSO **hit.**

ramble to amble, to hike, to roam, to rove, to stroll, to wander. SEE ALSO **walk.**

ramp slope.

rampage *Hooligans rampaged through the town.* to go berserk, to go wild, to rush about.

ramshackle *a ramshackle old hut.* broken down, decrepit, dilapidated, rickety, ruined, shaky, tumbledown.

ranch farm.

random *a random selection.* accidental, chance, haphazard, irregular, unplanned.

range 1 *a range of mountains.* chain, line, series. 2 *a wide range of goods.* selection, variety. 3 *I'm afraid that's outside my range.* area, field, limit, reach, scope. 4 (old-fashioned) *a kitchen range.* cooker, oven, stove. 5 *Prices range between £10 and £15.* to differ, to vary. 6 *The sheep range over the hills.* to roam, to rove, to stray, to travel, to wander.

rank 1 *The soldiers lined up in three ranks.* column, file, line, row. 2 *to have a high or low rank.* class, grade, level, position, status, title. 3 OFFICERS AND OTHER RANKS IN THE ARMY: brigadier, captain, colonel, corporal, general, lieutenant, major, private, sergeant.

ransack 1 *We ransacked the house looking for mum's keys.* to comb, to rummage through, to scour, to search. 2 *Rioters ransacked the shop.* to loot, to plunder, to ravage, to rob, to wreck.

rap *I rapped on the door.* to knock, to strike, to tap. SEE ALSO **hit.**

rape assault.

rapid brisk, fast, (informal) nippy, quick, speedy, swift.

rapids cataract, waterfall.

rapier sword.

rapture *The dog greeted us with rapture.* bliss, delight, ecstasy, happiness, joy, pleasure.

rapturous SEE **happy.**

rare *A white blackbird is a rare sight!* abnormal, curious, exceptional, infrequent, occasional, odd, peculiar, scarce, singular, special, strange, uncommon, unusual.

rascal blackguard, imp, knave, rogue, scamp, scoundrel, trouble-maker, villain.

rash 1 *a rash decision.* careless, hasty, impetuous, impulsive, incautious, reckless, thoughtless. 2 *a rash on your skin.* spots.

rasher *a rasher of bacon.* slice.

rasping *a rasping voice*. croaking, grating, harsh, hoarse, husky, rough.

rate 1 *We started at a fast rate*. pace, speed, velocity. 2 *The hotel charges reasonable rates*. amount, charge, cost, fare, fee, payment, price. 3 *How did you rate the game on Saturday?* to like, to prize, to regard, to value.

rather 1 *I was rather ill*. fairly, moderately, (informal) pretty, quite, somewhat. 2 *I'd rather have an apple than an orange*. preferably, sooner.

ratio proportion.

ration 1 *He ate my ration of sweets!* allowance, portion, quota, share. 2 *rations*: food, provisions, stores, supplies. 3 *We rationed out the sweets*. to allot, to distribute fairly, to share out.

rational *a rational discussion*. intelligent, logical, reasonable, sane, sensible.

raucous *raucous laughter*. harsh, grating, jarring, shrill.

ravage *The army ravaged the countryside*. to damage, to destroy, to devastate, to loot, to plunder, to raid, to ransack, to ruin, to wreck.

rave 1 *The head raved about our bad behaviour*. to be angry, to be mad, to fume, to rage. 2 *She raves about her new record*. to be enthusiastic.

ravenous SEE **hungry**.

ravine *a deep ravine*. canyon, defile, gorge, pass, valley.

raw 1 *raw food*. uncooked. 2 *raw materials*. crude, natural, unprocessed, unrefined. 3 *a raw wind*. SEE **cold**. 4 *a raw place on your skin*. grazed, inflamed, red, sore.

ray *a ray of light*. beam, shaft.

raze *Vandals razed the building to the ground*. to demolish, to destroy, to dismantle, to knock down.

reach 1 *Reach out your hand*. to extend, to stretch. 2 *Can you reach the handle?* to grasp, to get hold of, to touch. 3 *Have we reached the end?* to achieve, to arrive at, to get to. 4 *The shops are in easy reach*. distance, range, scope.

react *How did dad react when you asked for £10?* to answer, to reply, to respond, to retort.

read 1 *Can I read your story?* to glance at, to scan, to skim, to study. 2 *Can you read grandpa's handwriting?* to decipher, to interpret, to make out, to understand.

readable 1 *a readable story*. enjoyable, interesting, well-written. 2 *readable handwriting*. clear, legible, plain, understandable.

ready 1 *Are you ready for your holiday?* prepared, organized. 2 *She is always ready to help people*. disposed, eager, inclined, liable, likely, willing. 3 *He usually has a ready reply*. immediate, prompt, quick, speedy. 4 *Keep your tickets ready*. available, handy, obtainable.

real 1 *a real diamond*. actual, authentic, genuine. 2 *a real story*. factual, true. 3 *a real friend*. honest, sincere, trustworthy.

realistic 1 *a realistic statue*. authentic, lifelike, natural. 2 *a realistic plan*. feasible, possible, practicable, practical, viable, workable.

realize *Do you realize how expensive clothes are?* to appreciate, to comprehend, to grasp, to know, to see, to sense, to understand.

really *Was he really sorry?* actually, certainly, genuinely, honestly, truly.

realm country, kingdom, monarchy.

reap *to reap corn*. to gather in, to harvest, to mow.

rear 1 *the rear of the train*. back, end. 2 *Our dog nipped the intruder in the rear*. backside, behind, bottom, rump. 3 *Birds rear their chicks*. to bring up, to care for, to feed. 4 *Farmers rear cattle*. to breed, to produce, to raise.

reason 1 *Did he have a good reason for his behaviour?* argument, cause, excuse, explanation, grounds, justification, motive, occasion, pretext. 2 *Use your reason!* intelligence, judgement, sense, understanding, wit. 3 *He reasoned it out for himself*. to consider, to judge, to think, to work out. 4 *I tried to reason with her*. to argue, to debate, to discuss.

reasonable 1 *a reasonable person*. intelligent, logical, rational, sane, sensible. 2 *a reasonable price*. cheap, fair, moderate, ordinary.

reassure 1 to comfort, to encourage 2 *reassuring*: favourable, hopeful, promising.

rebel *The workers rebelled because of their bad conditions*. to disobey, to mutiny, to revolt, to rise up.

rebellion mutiny, revolt, revolution, rising.

rebellious *a rebellious mob.* defiant, disobedient, insubordinate, mutinous, quarrelsome, unruly.

rebound *The ball rebounded off the goalpost.* to bounce, to ricochet.

rebuild *They rebuilt the rooms which were damaged in the fire.* to modernize, to reconstruct, to renovate, to transform.

rebuke *The referee rebuked me for arguing.* to blame, to censure, to criticize, to reprimand, to reproach, to scold, (informal) to tell off, (informal) to tick off.

recall 1 *The garage recalled the faulty cars.* to call back, to withdraw. 2 *Do you recall what happened?* to recollect, to remember.

recede *The flood gradually receded.* to ebb, to go back, to retreat.

receipt *Did the shopkeeper give you a receipt?* account, bill.

receive 1 *We received lots of goods for the jumble sale.* to acquire, to get, to obtain. 2 *I received £1 for washing the car.* to accept, to earn, to take. 3 *We got ready to receive our visitors.* to entertain, to greet, to meet, to welcome.

recent contemporary, fresh, modern, new, up-to-date.

receptacle SEE **container.**

reception 1 *They gave us a friendly reception.* greeting, welcome. 2 *a wedding reception.* SEE **party.**

recital concert.

recite *to recite a poem.* to deliver, to perform, to repeat, to speak.

reckless 1 *reckless driving.* careless, inattentive, irresponsible, rash, thoughtless. 2 *reckless criminals.* desperate, violent, wild.

reckon 1 *He reckoned up how much I owed him.* to assess, to calculate, to compute, to count, to estimate, to figure out, to total, to work out. 2 *I reckon it's going to rain.* to believe, to consider, to judge, to think.

reclaim *to reclaim some derelict land.* to recover, to restore.

recline *to recline on a sofa.* to lean back, to lie, to rest, to sprawl.

recognize 1 *I hardly recognized you.* to identify, to know, to recall, to recollect, to remember. 2 *We recognized a familiar landmark.* to discern, to distinguish, to perceive, to see. 3 *I recognize that you've been working hard.* to accept, to acknowledge, to be aware, to understand.

recoil *I recoiled when I saw the blood.* to flinch, to jerk back, to shrink, to spring back, to wince.

recollect *Do you recollect that I lent you £5?* to recall, to remember.

recommend *I recommend that film.* to approve of, to commend, to praise.

recompense *Did she recompense you for the trouble you took to find her dog?* to compensate, to pay back, to refund, to repay, to reward.

reconcile *to reconcile people who have quarrelled.* to bring together, to reunite.

reconstruct *They reconstructed the remains of the dinosaur.* to rebuild, to repair.

record 1 *We recorded what we saw in our books.* to note, to register, to write down. 2 *We kept a record of what we saw.* account, description, diary, document, narrative, note, register, report. 3 *recording:* KINDS OF RECORDING: album, cassette, compact disc, digital recording, disc, long-playing record, LP, mono recording, single, stereo recording, tape, video, videotape.

record-player SEE **audio equipment.**

recount *He recounted his adventures.* to describe, to narrate, to relate, to tell.

recover 1 *Granny recovered slowly after her illness.* to get better, to heal, to improve, to mend, to pull through, to rally, to recuperate. 2 *I never recovered my lost watch.* to find, to get back, to reclaim, to regain, to retrieve, to salvage, to trace, to track down.

recreation 1 *You deserve a bit of recreation after working so hard.* amusement, diversion, enjoyment, entertainment, fun, games, hobby, leisure, pastime, play. 2 *recreation ground:* park, playing-field.

rectangle oblong.

rectify *She rectified the fault in the car.* to correct, to cure, to put right, to remedy, to repair.

recuperate 1 *Granny took a long time to recuperate after her operation.* to get better, to heal, to improve, to recover. 2 *recuperating:* convalescent.

recur *This problem keeps recurring.* to come again, to reappear, to return.

recurrent *recurrent illness.* chronic, constant, frequent, incessant, perpetual, persistent, repeated, unending. SEE ALSO **continual.**

recycle to use again.

red SEE **colour.**

redden to blush, to colour, to flush, to glow.

red-hot fiery.

reduce 1 *Reduce the quantity.* to cut, to decrease, to diminish, to halve, to lessen. 2 *Our supplies gradually reduced.* to contract, to dwindle, to shrink. 3 *Reduce the liquid by boiling.* to concentrate, to condense, to thicken.

reduction *You get a reduction if you're under 16.* concession, discount.

redundant *redundant workers.* superfluous, too many, unnecessary, unwanted.

reel 1 *a reel of film.* spool. 2 *I reeled after that knock on the head.* to rock, to stagger, to totter. 3 *reeling:* dizzy.

refer 1 *I hope dad won't refer to the broken window.* to allude to, to comment on, to mention. 2 *If I can't spell a word I refer to my dictionary.* to consult, to turn to. 3 *If I can't spell a word my teacher refers me to my dictionary.* to direct, to send.

referee adjudicator, arbitrator, judge, umpire.

referendum SEE **poll.**

refine *to refine oil.* to process, to purify, to treat.

refined *refined behaviour.* cultivated, elegant, dignified, ladylike, polite, (informal) posh, tasteful, well-bred.

reflect 1 *Glass reflects light.* to mirror, to send back. 2 *Give yourself time to reflect before you start your story.* to brood, to consider, to contemplate, to meditate, to ponder, to think.

reflection *a reflection in a mirror.* image, likeness.

reform *to reform your behaviour.* to change, to correct, to improve.

refrain 1 *We all sang the refrain.* chorus. 2 *Please refrain from smoking.* to abstain from, to do without.

refresh 1 *Let me refresh your memory.* to jog, to prompt, to stimulate. 2 *The drink refreshed us.* to cool, to invigorate, to quench the thirst, to revive.

refreshments snack. SEE ALSO **drink, food.**

refrigerate to chill, to freeze.

refuge *The climber found refuge from the blizzard.* asylum, cover, haven, hiding-place, protection, retreat, safety, sanctuary, shelter.

refugee exile, fugitive, outcast.

refund *to refund money.* to pay back, to repay.

refuse 1 *to refuse an invitation.* to decline, to turn down. 2 *to refuse someone their rights.* to deny, to deprive of.

regain *to regain something you've lost.* to find, to get back, to recover, to retrieve, to win back.

regal *a regal figure.* majestic, royal, stately.

regard 1 *The policeman regarded us closely.* to contemplate, to eye, to gaze at, to look at, to stare at, to view, to watch. 2 *We regard her as our best swimmer.* to consider, to judge, to reckon. 3 *We should have regard for others.* attention, care, concern, consideration, heed, notice, respect, thought.

regarding about, concerning, connected with, involving.

region *The Arctic is a cold region.* area, district, locality, neighbourhood, territory, vicinity, zone.

register 1 *She keeps our names in a register.* catalogue, directory, index, list. 2 *Grandad registered in the army in 1939.* to enlist, to enrol, to join, to sign on. 3 *The official registered our complaint.* to record, to write down. 4 *The speedometer registered 100 mph.* to indicate, to show.

regret *I regret being rude.* to be ashamed of, to be sad about, to be sorry for, to repent.

regretful *a regretful smile.* apologetic, penitent, remorseful, repentant, sorry. SEE ALSO **sad.**

regrettable *a regrettable accident.*
deplorable, reprehensible, unfortunate.
SEE ALSO **bad.**

regular 1 *a regular player.* consistent,
dependable, reliable. 2 *regular
breathing.* even, rhythmic, steady. 3 *a
regular habit.* accustomed, customary,
habitual, normal, traditional, usual. 4 *a
regular sight.* common, commonplace,
everyday, familiar, frequent, ordinary,
repeated.

regulate 1 *The police regulate the traffic.*
to control, to direct, to govern, to
manage, to supervise. 2 *Can you regulate
the central heating?* to adjust, to alter, to
change, to vary.

regulation *Obey the regulations.*
by-law, law, rule.

rehearse *to rehearse a play.* to practise,
to prepare.

reign to be king or queen, to govern, to
rule.

reinforce 1 *to reinforce a wall.* to
fortify, to hold up, to prop up, to
strengthen, to toughen. 2 *to reinforce an
army.* to assist, to help, to support.

reject 1 *I had no room in my cupboard,
so I rejected my old jeans.* to discard, to
disown, to eliminate, to renounce, to
scrap, to throw away. 2 *We rejected their
invitation.* to decline, to dismiss, to
refuse, to turn down.

rejoice to be happy, to celebrate, to
revel.

relapse *He behaved well for a while, but
then relapsed again.* to fall back, to
return, to slip back.

relate 1 *We related our adventures.* to
describe, to narrate, to recount, to
report, to tell. 2 *Her comments related to
work we did yesterday.* to be relevant, to
compare, to connect, to link.

relations SEE **family.**

relationship *a close relationship.* bond,
connection, link, tie.

relatives SEE **family.**

relax 1 *Mum relaxed in front of the TV.*
to be comfortable, to be easy, to feel at
home, to rest, to unbend, to unwind.
2 *He relaxed his grip.* to ease off, to
loosen, to slacken. 3 *relaxed: a relaxed
atmosphere.* casual, comfortable,
easygoing, friendly, informal, restful.

relay to broadcast, to pass on, to send
out, to televise, to transmit.

release 1 *to release prisoners.* to allow
out, to dismiss, to free, to let go, to
liberate, to rescue, to save, to set free,
to set loose, to unfasten, to untie. 2 *to
release a new record.* to distribute, to
issue, to make available, to publish, to
send out.

relent *He was cross at first, but later he
relented.* to be merciful, to show pity.

relentless 1 *a relentless rhythm.* SEE
continual. 2 *a relentless attack.* SEE
cruel.

relevant *Is your comment relevant to
what we are discussing?* connected,
linked, related.

reliable *a reliable player.* consistent,
constant, dependable, devoted,
efficient, faithful, level-headed, loyal,
regular, responsible, safe, sound,
steady, trustworthy, unchanging.

relic *a relic from the past.* reminder,
remnant.

relief *The pills gave some relief from the
pain.* aid, assistance, comfort, ease,
help, relaxation, respite.

relieve *The medicine relieved the pain.* to
calm, to comfort, to console, to ease, to
lessen, to soothe.

religion 1 *Which religion do you belong
to?* belief, creed, cult, denomination,
faith. 2 PEOPLE OF VARIOUS RELIGIONS:
Buddhist, Christian (SEE **church**),
Hindu, Jew (SEE **Jew**), Muhammadan or
Muslim (SEE **Islam**), Sikh. SEE ALSO
worship. ! There are many more
religions than are given here. 3 LEADERS
OR TEACHERS IN VARIOUS RELIGIONS:
Druid, guru, imam, minister, priest,
prophet, rabbi.

religious 1 *a religious ceremony.*
divine, holy, sacred. 2 *a religious
believer.* committed, dedicated, devout.

relish *She relishes a challenge.* to
appreciate, to delight in, to enjoy, to
like, to love.

reluctant *I was reluctant to pay £1.*
disinclined, hesitant, unwilling.

rely 1 *You can rely on him to do his best.*
to bank on, to count on, to depend on, to
trust. 2 *Dad relies on the car to get to
work.* to need.

remain 1 *How many people remained at
the end?* to be left, to survive. 2 *The
sentry remained at his post.* to carry on,
to continue, to endure, to keep on, to
linger, to live on, to persist, to stay.

remains 1 *the remains of an animal.* body, carcass, corpse. 2 *the remains of a building.* debris, fragments, rubble, ruins, wreckage. 3 *the remains of the coffee.* dregs.

remark 1 *rude remarks.* comment, observation, opinion, statement. 2 *He remarked that he was bored.* to comment, to mention, to note, to observe, to say.

remarkable amazing, exceptional, extraordinary, notable, phenomenal, special, surprising, (informal) terrific, (informal) tremendous, uncommon, unusual.

remedy 1 *Mum remedied the fault in the car.* to correct, to cure, to heal, to mend, to put right, to rectify. 2 *Is there any remedy for a cold?* cure, medicine, therapy, treatment.

remember 1 *Do you remember your great-uncle?* to recall, to recollect. 2 *It's a good idea to remember your phone number.* to learn, to memorize.

remind *Remind me to buy some potatoes.* to jog the memory, to prompt.

remnant *We put the remnants of the bread out for the birds.* fragment, piece, relic, scrap.

remorse *to show remorse.* grief, guilt, regret, shame.

remorseful apologetic, ashamed, guilty, penitent, regretful, repentant, sorry.

remote *a remote farmhouse.* desolate, distant, far-away, inaccessible, lonely, outlying, solitary.

remove 1 *The police removed the intruders.* to eject, to evict, to expel, to get rid of, (informal) to kick out, to throw out, to turn out. 2 *Remove your things from the table.* to carry away, to convey, to move, to take away, to transfer, to transport. 3 *He removed the fuse from the bomb.* to detach, to disconnect, to part, to separate, to undo, to unfasten. 4 *He had to remove what he wrote on the wall.* to delete, to dispose of, to erase, to get rid of, to wash off, to wipe out. 5 *The dentist removed my tooth.* to draw out, to extract, to pull out, to take out. 6 *The nurse removed the bandage.* to peel off, to strip off, to take off.

rend to rip, to split, to tear.

render 1 *to render a song.* to give, to perform, to recite, to sing. 2 *The shock rendered her speechless.* to make.

rendezvous *The lovers arranged a rendezvous.* appointment, date, meeting, meeting-place.

renegade deserter, fugitive, outlaw, traitor.

renew 1 *Dad renewed the car tyres.* to change, to replace. 2 *We renewed the paint.* to repair, to restore.

renounce 1 *The duke renounced his title.* to abandon, to abdicate, to give up, to resign. 2 *Don't renounce your friends.* to disown, to forsake, to reject.

renovate *It'll be nice when they renovate the bus station.* to improve, to mend, to modernize, to overhaul, to renew, to repair, to restore.

renown *The actor's renown spread far and wide.* distinction, fame, honour, importance, prestige, reputation.

renowned *renowned throughout the world.* eminent, famous, noted, popular, well-known.

rent 1 *Dad forgot to pay the rent for the TV.* instalment, regular payment, rental. 2 *We rented a caravan for our holiday.* to charter, to hire.

repair 1 *Mum repaired the car.* to fix, to mend, to overhaul, to put right, to rebuild, to rectify, to renovate, to restore, to service. 2 *He repaired his jeans.* to darn, to patch, to sew up.

repay *Did they repay you for those bad eggs?* to compensate, to pay back, to recompense, to refund.

repeat 1 *Don't repeat everything I say!* to echo, to quote, to say again. 2 *repeated*: SEE **continual**.

repel 1 *The defenders repelled the attack.* to check, to fend off, to parry, to push away, to repulse, to ward off. 2 *The smell repelled us.* to disgust, to nauseate, to offend, to revolt, to sicken.

repent to be ashamed, to be sorry, to regret.

repentant *He was repentant when he saw what he'd done.* apologetic, ashamed, penitent, regretful, remorseful, sorry.

replace 1 *Replace the books on the shelf.* to put back, to restore, to return. 2 *Who is likely to replace the present prime minister?* to come after, to follow, to substitute, to succeed, to take over from. 3 *It's time we replaced those tyres.* to change, to renew.

replica *We saw a replica of a lunar module.* copy, duplicate, imitation, model, reconstruction, reproduction.

reply to answer, to react, to respond, to retort.

report 1 *We reported that we'd been successful.* to announce, to communicate, to declare, to inform, to proclaim, to publish, to reveal, to state. **2** *Report to reception when you arrive.* to announce yourself, to introduce yourself, to make yourself known, to present yourself. **3** *I reported him to the police.* to complain about, to denounce, to inform against, to tell of. **4** *a report in a newspaper.* account, announcement, description, narrative, record, statement, story. **5** *the report of a gun.* bang, blast, explosion, noise.

reporter *a newspaper reporter.* correspondent, journalist.

repose *a moment of repose before we went on working.* calm, comfort, ease, peacefulness, relaxation, rest.

reprehensible *reprehensible behaviour.* deplorable, immoral, regrettable, shameful, unworthy, wicked. SEE ALSO **bad.**

represent *The paintings represented scenes from history.* to depict, to describe, to illustrate, to paint, to picture, to portray, to show, to stand for, to symbolize.

representation *The statue was a representation of Peter Pan.* figure, image, imitation, likeness, model, picture, statue.

representative 1 *a sales representative.* agent, salesman, traveller. **2** *a government representative.* ambassador, consul, diplomat. **3** *She couldn't come, so she sent a representative.* deputy, stand-in, substitute.

reprieve *to reprieve a prisoner.* to forgive, to let off, to pardon, to set free, to spare.

reprimand *Mum reprimanded him for being rude.* to censure, to condemn, to criticize, to disapprove of, to rebuke, to reproach, to scold, (informal) to tell off, to tick off.

reprisal retaliation, revenge, vengeance.

reproach SEE **reprimand.**

reproduce 1 *to reproduce a document.* to copy, to counterfeit, to duplicate, to imitate, to mimic, to photocopy, to print. **2** *Rabbits reproduce quickly.* to breed, to increase, to multiply.

reproduction *It's a reproduction, not the original picture.* copy, duplicate, fake, forgery, imitation, likeness, print, replica.

reptile SOME REPTILES: alligator, crocodile, lizard, snake, tortoise, turtle.

repulse *The defenders repulsed the attack.* to drive back, to fend off, to push away, to repel, to resist, to ward off.

repulsive disgusting, hideous, nauseating, odious, offensive, repellent, revolting, ugly, unsightly.

reputation *These cars have a good reputation.* fame, name, prestige, renown.

request 1 *We requested help.* to appeal for, to ask, to beg, to claim, to demand, to entreat, to implore, to invite. **2** *Dad didn't listen to our request.* appeal, entreaty, petition, plea, question.

require 1 *We required 3 runs to win.* to be short of, to lack, to need, to want. **2** *The policeman required dad to show his licence.* to command, to compel, to direct, to order.

rescue 1 *Robin Hood rescued the prisoners.* to free, to liberate, to release, to save, to set free. **2** *We managed to rescue our things after the flood.* to recover, to retrieve, to salvage.

research inquiry, investigation, searching, study.

resemblance likeness, similarity.

resemble *The twins resemble each other.* to be similar to, to look like, to take after.

resent *He resented her success.* to begrudge, to be jealous, to envy, to feel bitter about.

resentful bitter, envious, jealous.

reserve 1 *We reserved some of our rations to eat later.* to hold, to keep, to preserve, to save. **2** *We reserved tickets for the play.* to book, to order. **3** *Who are the reserves for Saturday's game?* deputy, stand-in, substitute. **4** *a wild life reserve:* game park, safari park.

reserved *quiet and reserved.* bashful, distant, reticent, secretive, self-conscious, shy, stand-offish, timid, withdrawn.

reservoir lake, pond.

reside *to reside in*: to dwell in, to inhabit, to live in, to lodge in, to occupy.

residence SEE **house.**

resident 1 inhabitant, occupant. 2 *a temporary resident*: guest, lodger, visitor.

resign 1 *to resign from your job.* to abdicate, to give up, to leave, to quit, to renounce. 2 *resigned: He seemed resigned about his troubles.* calm, patient, philosophical, reasonable.

resist *He made things worse by resisting the police.* to defy, to fight, to oppose, to stand up to, to withstand.

resolute SEE **determined.**

resolve *We resolved to have a camping holiday.* to conclude, to decide, to determine, to elect, to opt, to settle.

resound *Our voices resounded in the cave.* to echo, to reverberate.

resourceful *Ask him how to do it: he's very resourceful.* clever, imaginative, ingenious, inventive.

resources 1 *We pooled our resources.* assets, funds, money, wealth. 2 *Oil and coal are valuable resources.* materials, raw materials.

respect 1 *We stayed silent for a minute as a sign of respect.* admiration, awe, consideration, honour, liking, love, regard, reverence, tribute. 2 *My work isn't perfect in all respects.* aspect, detail, feature, point. 3 *We respected him for owning up.* to admire, to honour, to pay homage, to think well of.

respectable 1 *respectable people.* decent, honest, honourable, law-abiding, worthy. 2 *respectable clothes.* clean, modest, presentable, proper.

respite *It rained without respite.* interval, lull, pause, relief, rest.

resplendent SEE **splendid.**

respond *to respond to a question.* to answer, to react, to reply.

responsible 1 *The teacher is responsible for the class.* in charge of. 2 *Who's responsible for the damage?* guilty of. 3 *We need a responsible person to keep the money.* concerned, conscientious, dependable, diligent, dutiful, honest, law-abiding, loyal, reliable, trustworthy.

rest 1 *We had a rest.* break, interlude, interval, lull, pause. 2 *On Mother's Day we give mum the rest she deserves.* comfort, ease, leisure, quiet, relaxation, repose. 3 *He made a rest for his telescope.* stand, support. 4 *We rested on the lawn.* to lie, to lounge, to recline, to relax, to sprawl. 5 *Grandad rests in the evening.* to doze, to nod off, to sleep, to snooze, to take a nap. 6 *Rest the ladder against the wall.* to lean, to place, to prop, to stand, to support. 7 *We can't eat all the food: what shall we do with the rest?* extra, remainder, surplus.

restaurant café, cafeteria, canteen, snack-bar.

restless *The class was restless.* agitated, excitable, fidgety, impatient, jittery, jumpy, nervous, unsettled.

restore 1 *I restored what I had borrowed.* to give back, to put back, to return. 2 *They are restoring the old station.* to mend, to renew, to renovate, to repair, to touch up.

restrain *Please restrain your dog.* to check, to control, to curb, to hold back, to keep back, to stop, to subdue.

restrict 1 *The use of cheap tickets is restricted to weekends.* to confine, to keep within, to limit. 2 *The prisoners were restricted in their cells.* to enclose, to shut in.

result 1 *One result of the cold weather is that I have chilblains!* consequence, effect, outcome. 2 *the result of a trial.* decision, judgement, verdict. 3 *the result of a game.* score. 4 *What resulted from your interview with the head?* to arise, to come about, to follow, to happen, to occur, to take place, to turn out. 5 *to result in: I hope it doesn't result in tears!* to bring about, to cause, to give rise to, to lead to, to provoke.

resume *We resumed after a break.* to begin again, to carry on, to continue, to proceed.

retail SEE **sell.**

retain *Please retain your ticket.* to hang on to, to hold, to keep.

retaliate *He retaliated because she hurt him.* to pay back, to seek retribution, to take revenge.

reticent *a reticent person.* quiet, reserved, shy, timid.

retire *to retire from work.* to give up, to leave, to quit, to resign.

retort SEE **reply**.

retreat 1 *The army retreated.* to back away, to fall back, to leave, to move back, to retire, to run away, to withdraw. 2 *The floods retreated.* to ebb, to flow back, to recede. 3 *They made a quick retreat.* escape, flight. 4 *The outlaws found a retreat in the hills.* asylum, hiding-place, refuge, sanctuary, shelter.

retribution *to seek retribution.* justice, punishment, retaliation, revenge, vengeance.

retrieve *Did you retrieve that watch you dropped in the river?* to fetch, to find, to get back, to recover, to regain, to rescue, to salvage, to trace, to track down.

return 1 *When are you likely to return?* to come back, to go back, to reappear. 2 *Can you return the money I lent you?* to give back, to repay, to send back, to take back.

reveal 1 *Dad revealed his knobbly knees.* to air, to bare, to display, to expose, to show, to uncover, to unmask. 2 *to reveal the truth.* to announce, to communicate, to declare, to disclose, to divulge, to make known, to produce, to publish.

revel *We revelled in the sunshine.* to be happy, to celebrate, to delight, to enjoy, to love, to rejoice.

revelry celebration, merry-making, orgy, party.

revenge 1 *His heart was set on revenge.* reprisal, retaliation, retribution, vengeance, vindictiveness. 2 *to take revenge*: to retaliate.

revenue SEE **money**.

reverberation echo, rumble, vibration.

revere *She reveres grandad.* to admire, to adore, to honour, to idolize, to praise, to respect, to worship.

reverie *lost in a reverie.* daydream, dream, fantasy, meditation, thought.

reverse 1 *What is on the reverse side?* back, contrary, opposite, rear. 2 *What would happen if we reversed the batting order?* to invert, to turn round. 3 *to reverse a car.* to back, to go backwards.

review 1 *a record review.* criticism. 2 *We reviewed the evidence.* to consider, to examine, to inspect, to study, to survey. 3 *He reviewed the new records.* to criticize, to write about.

revise 1 *We revised our articles for the magazine.* to adapt, to alter, to correct, to edit, to improve, to rewrite. 2 *to revise work for an exam.* to go over, to learn, to study.

revive 1 *He revived slowly after being knocked out.* to rally, to recover, to rouse. 2 *A cold drink revived us.* to invigorate, to refresh.

revolt 1 *The people revolted against the dictator.* to disobey, to mutiny, to rebel, to rise up. 2 *The cruel treatment of the animals revolted us.* to disgust, to nauseate, to repel, to sicken. 3 *revolting*: SEE **unpleasant**.

revolution 1 *The king was killed in a revolution.* mutiny, rebellion, revolt, rising. 2 *The satellite made a revolution of the earth.* circuit, orbit, turn.

revolve *The wheels revolved.* to rotate, to spin, to swivel, to turn, to twirl, to whirl.

revulsion *a feeling of revulsion.* aversion, disgust, dislike, hatred, loathing.

reward 1 *She received a reward for bravery.* award, decoration, medal, payment, prize. 2 *She was rewarded for her bravery.* to decorate, to honour. 3 *He rewarded us for our hard work.* to compensate, to pay, to recompense.

rewrite to edit, to revise.

rhyme SEE **poem**.

rhythm beat, pulse, throb.

rhythmic *a rhythmic beat.* regular, repeated, steady.

ribbon band, braid, strip, tape.

rich 1 *a rich person.* affluent, prosperous, wealthy, well-off, well-to-do. 2 *rich furnishings.* costly, expensive, luxurious, splendid, sumptuous. 3 *riches*: SEE **money**.

rick haystack.

rickety *a rickety old building.* decrepit, dilapidated, frail, ramshackle, ruined, shaky, tumbledown, unsteady.

ricochet to bounce, to rebound.

rid *to get rid of*: to dispense with, to eject, to evict, to expel, to remove, to throw out.

riddle 1 *Can you solve this riddle?* conundrum, mystery, problem, puzzle, question. 2 *She sifted the soil in a riddle.* sieve.

ride SEE **travel**.

ridge *We had a good view from the top of the ridge.* bank, edge, embankment, hill.

ridicule *It is cruel to ridicule people because of their appearance.* to be sarcastic about, to be satirical about, to jeer at, to laugh at, to make fun of, to mock, to scoff at, to sneer at, to taunt, to tease.

ridiculous *What a ridiculous thing to do!* absurd, amusing, comic, crazy, eccentric, farcical, foolish, funny, grotesque, illogical, irrational, laughable, ludicrous, mad, preposterous, senseless, silly, stupid, unreasonable, weird, zany.

rift *We noticed a rift in their friendship.* break, crack, split.

rig equipment, gear, kit, tackle.

right 1 *the right decision.* fair, good, honest, just, lawful, moral, virtuous. 2 *the right answer.* accurate, correct, exact, factual, precise, true. 3 *Is this paint the right colour?* appropriate, apt, fitting, proper, suitable. 4 *The head has the right to give orders.* authority, influence, position, power.

righteous good, law-abiding, moral, upright, virtuous.

rightful *Who is the rightful owner of this car?* authorized, lawful, legitimate, proper.

rigid 1 *a rigid substance.* firm, hard, inflexible, solid, stiff, unbending, wooden. 2 *a rigid disciplinarian.* harsh, stern, strict, stubborn, unkind, unyielding.

rim *the rim of a cup.* brim, brink, edge.

rind *cheese rind, the rind of an orange.* crust, peel, skin.

ring 1 *Draw a ring.* band, circle, hoop, loop. 2 *a boxing ring.* arena. SEE ALSO **sport.** 3 *The police ringed the area.* to circle, to encircle, to enclose, to surround. 4 *The bell rang.* to chime, to peal, to tinkle, to toll. SEE ALSO **sound.** 5 *I must ring to see how granny is.* to call, to phone, to telephone.

rinse *Rinse the things in clean water.* to bathe, to clean, to swill, to wash.

riot 1 *The police quelled the riot.* anarchy, commotion, confusion, disorder, disturbance, hubbub, mutiny, pandemonium, revolt, rioting, rumpus, turmoil, unrest, uproar. 2 *Why did the people riot?* to mutiny, to rampage, to rebel, to revolt.

riotous SEE **rowdy.**

rip *He ripped his jeans.* to rend, to slit, to split, to tear.

ripe *ripe fruit.* mature, mellow, ready to use.

ripen *These pears need to ripen.* to age, to develop, to mature.

ripple *The wind rippled the surface of the water.* to agitate, to disturb, to make waves, to ruffle.

rise 1 *He rose at 7.30.* to get up. 2 *Prices have risen.* to go up, to grow, to increase. 3 *The balloon rose into the air.* to ascend, to climb, to mount. 4 *My sponge cake didn't rise.* to puff up, to swell. 5 *A cliff rose above us.* to loom, to stand out, to stick out, to tower. 6 *He pushed his bike up the rise.* ascent, bank, hill, incline, ramp, slope.

rising SEE **revolution.**

risk 1 *a risk of frost.* chance, danger, possibility. 2 *He risked a lot of money starting his business.* to dare, to gamble, to venture.

risky *It's risky cycling on icy roads.* chancy, dangerous, hazardous.

rite SEE **ritual.**

ritual *a religious ritual.* ceremony, rite, service.

rival 1 *We beat our rivals from the other school.* adversary, competitor, enemy, opponent, opposition. 2 *The new shop tries to rival the shop down the road.* to compare with, to compete with, to contend with, to contest, to oppose, to struggle with.

rivalry competition, competitiveness.

river stream, tributary.

road 1 KINDS OF ROAD AND PATH: alley, avenue, bypass, causeway, cul-de-sac, drive, footpath, highway, lane, motorway, one-way street, path, pathway, ring road, route, sliproad, street, thoroughfare, towpath, track, trunk road, way. 2 WORDS TO DO WITH ROADS: bridge, camber, flyover, footbridge, ford, hairpin bend, junction, lamp-post, lay-by, level-crossing, roundabout, service area, signpost, traffic lights, underpass, U-turn, viaduct, zebra crossing. 3 SURFACES FOR ROADS AND PATHS: asphalt, cobbles, concrete, crazy paving, flagstones, gravel, paving stones, tarmac, tiles.

roam *The sheep roam over the hills.* to ramble, to range, to rove, to stray, to travel, to wander.

roar SEE **sound.**

roast SEE **cook.**

rob 1 *to rob a shop.* to loot, to pilfer, to plunder, to ransack. 2 *to rob someone.* to deprive, to steal from, to take from.

robber burglar, highwayman, mugger, pickpocket, shoplifter, thief.

robust *a robust person.* hardy, healthy, strong, sturdy, tough.

rock 1 boulder, crag, stone. 2 KINDS OF ROCK: chalk, clay, flint, granite, gravel, lava, limestone, marble, ore, pumice-stone, sandstone, slate. 3 *I rocked the baby.* to move gently, to sway, to swing. 4 *The ship rocked in the storm.* to lurch, to pitch, to reel, to roll, to shake, to toss, to totter.

rod bar, baton, cane, pole, rail, stick, wand.

rogue blackguard, knave, rascal, scoundrel, villain. ! These words are rather old-fashioned.

role *a role in a play.* character, part.

roll 1 *a bread roll.* SEE **bread.** 2 *Add your name to the roll.* list, register. 3 *The wheels began to roll.* to revolve, to rotate, to spin, to turn. 4 *Roll up the carpet.* to curl, to twist, to wind. 5 *We rolled the cricket pitch.* to flatten, to level out, to smooth. 6 *The ship rolled in the storm.* to lurch, to pitch, to reel, to sway, to toss, to totter.

romance love story.

romantic *a romantic story.* emotional, nostalgic, sentimental.

romp *We romped in the garden.* to caper, to dance, to frisk, to leap about, to play, to prance, to run about.

roof THINGS ROOFS ARE MADE OF: corrugated iron, slates, thatch, tiles.

room 1 cell, chamber. 2 *Give me a bit more room.* freedom, space.

roomy *a roomy car.* large, spacious.

rope cable, cord, hawser, line.

rot *Wood rots. Iron rots.* to corrode, to decay, to decompose, to disintegrate, to go bad, to perish, to spoil.

rotten 1 *rotten iron, rotten wood.* corroded, decayed, disintegrating. 2 *rotten food.* decomposed, foul, mouldy, perished, putrid, smelly.

rough 1 *a rough surface.* bumpy, irregular, jagged, rugged, uneven. 2 *a rough crowd.* boisterous, disorderly, rowdy. 3 *rough weather.* stormy, turbulent, violent, wild. 4 *rough skin.* bristly, coarse, hairy, harsh, scratchy. 5 *a rough voice.* grating, gruff, hoarse, husky, unpleasant. 6 *rough manners.* bad-tempered, crude, impolite, rude, surly, unfriendly. 7 *rough work.* careless, clumsy, hasty, unfinished, unskilful.

roughly about, approximately, around, close to, nearly.

round 1 *a round shape.* circular, spherical. 2 *a round in a competition.* bout, contest, game. 3 *to round a corner.* to turn. 4 *to round off:* to close, to compete, to conclude, to end, to finish. 5 *to round up:* to assemble, to collect, to gather, to group, to herd, to mass.

roundabout *a roundabout route.* devious, indirect, rambling.

round-shouldered hunchbacked.

rouse 1 *It takes ages to rouse me in the mornings.* to arouse, to awaken, to call, to wake up. 2 *The group roused the audience to a frenzy.* to excite, to incite, to provoke, to stimulate, to stir up.

rout *We completely routed the opposition.* to conquer, to crush, to defeat, to overwhelm.

route *Which route shall we take?* course, direction, road, way.

routine *a normal routine.* custom, habit, method, practice, procedure, system, way.

rove *In the safari park the animals rove about freely.* to prowl, to range, to roam, to stray, to wander.

row 1 *Stand in a row.* column, cordon, file, line, queue, rank. 2 *Arrange them in a row.* chain, sequence, series, string. 3 *to row a boat.* to move, to propel.

rowdy *a rowdy crowd.* badly-behaved, boisterous, disorderly, irrepressible, lawless, noisy, obstreperous, riotous, rough, turbulent, undisciplined, unruly, violent, wild.

royal 1 *a royal palace.* majestic, regal, stately. 2 ROYAL PEOPLE: consort, Her or His Majesty, Her or His Royal Highness, king, monarch, prince, princess, queen, regent, sovereign. 3 WORDS TO DO WITH ROYALTY: abdication, accession, coronation, crown, throne.

rub 1 *The dog likes you to rub his chest.* to massage, to stroke. 2 *to rub clean:* to polish, to scour, to scrape, to scrub, to wipe. 3 *to rub out:* to blot out, to delete, to erase, to remove, to wipe out.

rubbish 1 *Throw away that rubbish.* garbage, junk, litter, (informal) muck, refuse, rubble, scrap, trash, waste. 2 *Don't talk rubbish!* balderdash, bilge, drivel, gibberish, nonsense, tripe, twaddle. ! Most of these words are used informally.

rubble *The building collapsed into a pile of rubble.* debris, fragments, remains, ruins, wreckage.

rucksack haversack.

ruddy *a ruddy face.* flushed, fresh, healthy, red, rosy, sunburnt.

rude 1 *rude language, a rude person.* abusive, bad-mannered, bad-tempered, blasphemous, cheeky, coarse, common, crude, discourteous, disparaging, disrespectful, foul, impertinent, impolite, improper, impudent, inconsiderate, indecent, insolent, insulting, loutish, mocking, offensive, saucy, uncomplimentary, uncouth, vulgar. 2 *to be rude to:* to abuse, to insult, to offend, to snub.

rueful *a rueful expression.* dejected, downcast, down-hearted, regretful, sorrowful. SEE ALSO **sad.**

ruffian criminal, desperado, gangster, hooligan, lout, mugger, scoundrel, villain.

ruffle *The breeze ruffled the water.* to agitate, to disturb, to ripple, to rumple, to stir.

rug 1 *Wrap yourself in a rug.* blanket. 2 *We put a rug on the floor.* mat.

rugby WORDS USED IN RUGBY: pack, scrum, tackle, touch-down, touch-line, try.

rugged *Ordinary vehicles can't cross this rugged country.* bumpy, irregular, rough, uneven.

ruin 1 *The loss of our money meant the ruin of our plans.* collapse, destruction, downfall, end, fall. 2 *ruins:* debris, remains, rubble, wreckage. 3 *The gale ruined our runner beans.* to demolish, to destroy, to devastate, to flatten, to spoil, to wreck.

rule 1 *Obey the rules.* code, law, regulation. 2 *As a rule we have gravy with meat.* convention, custom, practice, routine. 3 *Who rules the country?* to administer, to command, to control, to direct, to govern, to manage, to run. 4 *Victoria ruled for many years.* to be king or queen, to reign. 5 *The umpire ruled that the batsman was out.* to adjudicate, to decide, to decree, to judge.

ruler VARIOUS RULERS: dictator, emperor, empress, king, monarch, president, queen, sultan, tyrant.

rumble SEE **sound.**

rummage *I rummaged through the cupboard looking for my hat.* to comb, to ransack, to scour, to search.

rumour *The story was only a rumour.* gossip, prattle, scandal.

rump behind, bottom, buttocks, rear.

rumple *Don't rumple the bedclothes.* to agitate, to crease, to crumple, to disturb, to ruffle.

rumpus SEE **commotion.**

run 1 WAYS TO RUN: to canter, to dash, to gallop, to jog, to race, to rush, to scamper, to scuttle, to speed, to sprint, to trot. 2 *Do the buses run on Sundays?* to go, to operate, to travel. 3 *The car runs well.* to behave, to function, to perform, to work. 4 *The blood ran down his leg.* to dribble, to flow, to gush, to pour, to stream, to trickle. 5 *The government is supposed to run the country.* to administer, to control, to direct, to govern, to look after, to maintain, to manage, to rule, to supervise. 6 *to run away:* SEE **escape.** 7 *to run into:* SEE **collide.** 8 *a run of bad luck.* sequence, series. 9 *a chicken run.* compound, enclosure, pen.

runny *It was so hot that the ice-cream went runny.* creamy, flowing, fluid, liquid, sloppy, smooth, thin, watery, wet.

runway airstrip, landing-strip.

rural rustic.

ruse SEE **trick**.

rush 1 to dash, to gallop, to hasten, to hurry, to race, to run, to scramble, to speed, (informal) to zoom. 2 *a rush of water*. cataract, flood, gush, spate. 3 *a rush of people*. panic, stampede.

rust *Iron rusts*. to corrode, to rot.

rustic *rustic surroundings*. rural.

rustle SEE **sound**.

rusty *rusty iron*. corroded, rotten.

rut *to stick in a rut*. furrow, groove.

ruthless *a ruthless attack*. SEE **cruel**.

S

sabotage damage, destruction.

sack 1 *bag, pouch*. 2 *to sack someone from a job*. to dismiss, to fire.

sacred *The Bible and the Koran are sacred books*. blessed, consecrated, divine, hallowed, holy, religious.

sacrifice *She sacrificed her weekend to train for the competition*. to give up, to offer up, to surrender.

sacrilegious *I think it's sacrilegious to play about in church*. blasphemous, irreverent, wicked.

sad *a sad expression, a sad story, etc.* careworn, cheerless, crestfallen, dejected, depressed, desolate, despairing, desperate, despondent, disappointed, disconsolate, discontented, discouraged, disgruntled, dismal, dissatisfied, distressed, doleful, down, downcast, down-hearted, dreary, forlorn, gloomy, glum, grave, grieving, grim, guilty, heart-broken, heavy, hopeless, joyless, low, lugubrious, melancholy, miserable, moping, morbid, morose, mournful, pathetic, penitent, pessimistic, pitiful, plaintive, regretful, rueful, sombre, sorrowful, sorry, tearful, touching, tragic, troubled, unhappy, wistful, woeful, wretched.

sadden *The dog's death saddened us*. to depress, to dishearten, to dismay, to grieve.

sadistic SEE **cruel**.

safe 1 *Are your belongings safe from burglars?* defended, protected, secure. 2 *We got home safe in spite of the storm*. undamaged, unharmed, unscathed. 3 *Is he safe with our money?* dependable, reliable, trustworthy. 4 *Is that dog safe?* docile, harmless, innocuous, tame. 5 *a safe aircraft*. airworthy. 6 *a safe ship*. seaworthy.

safeguard *Insurance safeguards us against unforeseen disasters*. to defend, to guard, to look after, to protect, to shield.

safety protection, security.

safety-belt seat-belt.

sag *The rope sags in the middle*. to be limp, to droop, to flop, to slump.

sail *to sail a boat*. to navigate.

sailor VARIOUS SAILORS: able seaman, admiral, boatswain, captain, cox or coxswain, crew, helmsman, mariner, mate, navigator, pilot, rower, seaman.

saintly blessed, holy, religious. SEE ALSO **good**.

sake *Do it for your own sake*. advantage, benefit, good, welfare.

salad THINGS YOU EAT IN SALAD: beetroot, celery, cress, cucumber, lettuce, mustard and cress, onion, potato, tomato, watercress.

salary *a salary of £10,000 a year*. earnings, income, pay, wages.

sale KINDS OF SALE: auction, bazaar, fair, jumble sale, market.

salvage *They salvaged the wrecked ship*. to recover, to rescue, to retrieve, to save.

same *She wore the same dress as her friend*. corresponding, equal, equivalent, identical, similar.

sample *Show me a sample of your work*. example, illustration, instance, specimen.

sanctuary *The escaping prisoner sought sanctuary in a church.* asylum, haven, refuge, retreat, safety, shelter.

sand grit.

sane *They said he was crazy, but he seems sane to me.* normal, rational, reasonable.

sanitary *You must have sanitary conditions in a hospital.* clean, germ-free, healthy, hygienic, sterilized, unpolluted.

sanitation drainage, drains, lavatories, sewers, WC.

sap *The long climb sapped our energy.* to exhaust, to tire, to weaken, to wear out.

sarcastic *His sarcastic jokes hurt me.* disparaging, hurtful, mocking, satirical.

satchel bag.

satellite moon, planet.

satirical *satirical comments.* disparaging, mocking, sarcastic.

satisfactory *She said my work was only just satisfactory.* acceptable, adequate, all right, fair, good enough, passable, sufficient, tolerable.

satisfy 1 *Will sandwiches satisfy you?* to content, to make happy, to please. 2 *Will £10 satisfy your needs?* to fulfil, to meet. 3 *to satisfy your thirst.* to quench.

saturate 1 *The rainstorm saturated the ground.* to drench, to soak, to wet. 2 *saturated:* waterlogged.

sauce KINDS OF SAUCE: custard, dressing, gravy, ketchup, mayonnaise, mint sauce, salad cream.

saucepan cauldron, pan, pot.

saucy *a saucy joke.* cheeky, impertinent, impudent, rude.

sauna bath.

savage 1 *a savage attack.* atrocious, barbaric, beastly, bloodthirsty, bloody, brutal, callous, cold-blooded, cruel, ferocious, fierce, heartless, inhuman, merciless, murderous, pitiless, ruthless, sadistic, uncivilized, unfeeling, vicious, violent. 2 *The explorers were attacked by savages.* barbarian, cannibal, heathen, pagan. ! Nowadays we do not use *savage* to describe people from developing countries.

save 1 *Robin Hood saved the prisoners.* to free, to liberate, to release, to rescue, to set free. 2 *Save something for later.* to hold on to, to keep, to preserve, to reserve, to safeguard, to store up, to take care of. 3 *to save money.* to deposit, to hoard, to invest, to scrape together, to set aside. 4 *to save fuel.* to economize on. 5 *to save a wrecked ship.* to recover, to retrieve, to salvage.

savings *Have you got any savings?* capital, funds, investments, riches.

say to comment, to communicate, to convey, to express, to mention, to pronounce, to remark, to speak, to state, to utter. SEE ALSO **talk.**

saying expression, motto, phrase, proverb, remark, slogan.

scab scar.

scabbard sheath.

scaffold gallows.

scale 1 *the scale of a map.* proportion, size. 2 *to scale a ladder.* to ascend, to climb, to mount.

scales *a pair of scales.* balance, weighing-machine.

scamp imp, knave, rascal, rogue.

scamper *The dog scampered home.* to dash, to hasten, to hurry, to run, to rush, to scuttle.

scan 1 *The castaway scanned the horizon.* to examine, to eye, to gaze at, to look at, to stare at, to study, to view, to watch. 2 *I scanned the newspaper.* to glance at, to read quickly, to skim.

scandal 1 *It's a scandal that so much food is wasted.* disgrace, embarrassment, notoriety, outrage, sensation, shame. 2 *I heard a bit of scandal.* gossip, rumour.

scandalous *What a scandalous waste of money!* disgraceful, infamous, notorious, outrageous, shameful, shocking, wicked.

scanty *The provisions were scanty.* inadequate, insufficient, meagre, (informal) measly, scarce, small, sparse, thin.

scar 1 *The wound left a scar.* mark, scab. 2 *The wound scarred his face.* to damage, to deface, to disfigure, to mark, to spoil.

scarce *Vegetables were scarce during the cold weather.* insufficient, rare, scanty, sparse, uncommon.

scarcely barely, hardly.

scare 1 *The explosion scared us.* to alarm, to dismay, to shock, to startle. 2 *Their gang tried to scare us.* to bully, to frighten, to intimidate, to make afraid, to menace, to persecute, to terrorize, to threaten.

scary (informal) *It was scary in the dark.* creepy, eerie, frightening, ghostly, spooky, uncanny, weird.

scatter 1 *The wind scattered leaves over the road.* to disperse, to shed, to spread, to sprinkle, to throw about. 2 *scattered:* dispersed, strewn.

scatterbrained absent-minded, careless, disorganized, forgetful, muddled, silly, thoughtless, unsystematic, vague.

scene 1 *the scene of a crime.* location, place, setting, site. 2 *He made a scene because he didn't get a prize.* argument, fuss, quarrel. 3 *a beautiful scene.* landscape, outlook, panorama, picture, view, scenery, sight, spectacle, view, vista.

scenic *a scenic drive.* attractive, beautiful, lovely, picturesque, pretty.

scent *the scent of flowers.* aroma, fragrance, odour, perfume, smell, whiff.

sceptical *I was sceptical when he said he would do all the clearing up.* disbelieving, doubting, dubious, incredulous, questioning, suspicious, unconvinced.

schedule *a schedule of events.* list, programme, timetable.

scheme 1 *a scheme to make a lot of money.* conspiracy, design, intrigue, manoeuvre, plan, plot, project, ruse. 2 *The two boys schemed together.* to conspire, to intrigue, to plan, to plot.

school 1 KINDS OF SCHOOL: academy, boarding-school, coeducational school, comprehensive school, high school, infant school, junior school, kindergarten, nursery school, playgroup, prep school, primary school, secondary school. 2 WORDS TO DO WITH SCHOOL: assembly, audio-visual aids, blackboard, chalk, classroom, cloakroom, desk, display, dormitory, exercise book, homework, laboratory, lesson, library, monitor, notice-board, peripatetic teacher, playground, playing-field, playtime, prefect, prep, project, register, satchel, staff, syllabus, textbook, truant, uniform, workcard. SEE ALSO **head, pupil, teacher.**

schoolchild SEE **pupil.**

schoolteacher SEE **teacher.**

science VARIOUS SCIENCES: anatomy, astronomy, biology, botany, chemistry, electronics, geology, meteorology, physics, psychology, technology, zoology.

scientific *a scientific investigation.* methodical, organized, systematic.

scoff SEE **scorn.**

scold *Mum scolded me for being late.* to blame, to censure, to criticize, to rebuke, to reprimand, to reproach, (informal) to tick off.

scoop 1 *an ice-cream scoop.* ladle, shovel, spoon. 2 *We scooped out a hole in the sand.* to dig, to gouge, to hollow, to shovel.

scope extent, limit, range, reach.

scorch SEE **burn.**

score 1 *What was your score?* mark, result, total. 2 *We scored the polished floor when we moved the piano.* to mark, to scrape, to scratch.

scorn *They scorned our cooking and bought some chips.* to be contemptuous of, to despise, to disdain, to dislike, to hate, to insult, to jeer at, to laugh at, to look down on, to make fun of, to mock, to ridicule, to scoff at, to sneer at, to taunt.

scoundrel blackguard, knave, rascal, rogue, ruffian, villain. ! These words sound rather old-fashioned.

scour 1 *to scour a saucepan.* to clean, to polish, to rub, to scrape, to scrub, to wash. 2 *We scoured the house looking for mum's keys.* to comb, to ransack, to rummage through, to search.

scourge crop, lash, whip.

scout *You wait here while I scout round.* to get information, to look about.

scowl to frown, to glower.

scraggy *a weak, scraggy animal.* bony, emaciated, gaunt, lean, skinny, thin.

scramble 1 *I scrambled up the cliff.* to clamber, to climb, to crawl. 2 *We scrambled to get some food before it all went.* to fight, to scuffle, to struggle, to tussle. 3 *We scrambled into our places at the last minute.* to dash, to hasten, to rush.

scrap 1 *a pile of useless scrap.* junk, litter, refuse, rubbish, waste. 2 *a scrap of food.* bit, crumb, fragment, particle, piece, snippet, speck. 3 *Two dogs had a scrap.* SEE **fight.** 4 *We had to scrap our plan.* to abandon, to discard, to drop, to give up, to throw away.

scrape 1 *I scraped my knuckles.* to graze, to scratch. 2 *The dog scratched at the door.* to claw. 3 *a scratch on the surface.* groove, line.

scrawl SEE **write.**

scream to cry, to howl, to screech, to shriek, to squeal, to wail, to yell.

scree stones.

screech SEE **sound.**

screen 1 *We closed the screen.* blind, curtain, partition. 2 *We planted a bush to screen the manure heap.* to camouflage, to conceal, to cover, to disguise, to hide, to mask, to protect, to shade, to shield.

scribble to doodle, to jot, to write.

scrounge *The stray cat scrounged for scraps.* to beg, to cadge.

scrub *to scrub the floor.* to brush, to clean, to rub, to scour, to wash.

scruffy *a scruffy appearance.* bedraggled, dirty, dishevelled, scrappy, shabby, tatty, untidy.

scrupulous 1 *a scrupulous worker.* diligent, honest. 2 *scrupulous attention to detail.* careful, meticulous, painstaking, systematic, thorough.

scrutiny *She subjected my work to close scrutiny.* examination, inspection, investigation.

scuffle SEE **fight.**

sculpture carving, figure, image, statue.

scum foam, froth.

scuttle 1 *to scuttle a ship.* to sink. 2 *A crab scuttled away when we moved the stone.* to shuffle, to run.

sea 1 ocean. 2 *of or on the sea:* marine, nautical, naval, seafaring, seagoing.

seal 1 *the royal seal.* crest, emblem, sign, stamp, symbol. 2 *to seal a lid.* to fasten, to lock, to secure, to shut. 3 *to seal an envelope.* to close, to stick. 4 *to seal a leak.* to plug, to stop up.

seam 1 *He sewed up the seam of his jeans.* join, stitching. 2 *a seam of coal.* layer, stratum, thickness.

seaman SEE **sailor.**

search 1 *We searched for a decent snackbar.* to explore, to hunt, to look, to nose about, to prospect, to seek. 2 *We searched the house for mum's keys.* to comb, to ransack, to rummage through, to scour. 3 *The search took ages.* hunt, look, quest.

seashore SEE **shore.**

seaside WORDS TO DO WITH THE SEASIDE: beach, breaker, breakwater, cliff, coast, dune, esplanade, life-guard, pier, promenade, resort, sand-dune, sands, seashell, seashore, seaweed, skin-diving, sunbathing, sunburn, surf, surf-riding, swimming, tide, water-skiing, wave.

season period.

seasoning flavouring.

seat KINDS OF SEAT: armchair, bench, chair, couch, deck-chair, pouffe, rocking-chair, settee, sofa, stool, throne.

seat-belt safety-belt.

seaworthy *a seaworthy ship.* safe.

secluded *We were the only people on the secluded beach.* inaccessible, isolated, lonely, private, remote, solitary.

second 1 *The pain only lasted a second.* flash, instant, moment. 2 *I seconded my friend in our classroom debate.* to back, to help, to side with, to support.

second-hand *a second-hand car.* used.

second-rate *We were disappointed by her second-rate performance.* commonplace, mediocre, middling, ordinary, unexciting.

secret 1 *secret information.* confidential, hushed up, intimate, personal, private. 2 *a secret hide-out.* concealed, hidden.

secretive *He was secretive about where he found the money.* furtive, mysterious, reserved, reticent, shifty, uncommunicative.

section bit, compartment, branch, division, fraction, part, portion, sector, segment.

sector *a sector of a town.* area, district, division, part, section, zone.

secure 1 *Is the house secure against burglars?* defended, protected, safe. 2 *During the storm we remained secure indoors.* snug, unharmed, unscathed. 3 *Is that hook secure?* fast, firm, fixed, immovable, solid, steady, tight, unyielding.

sedate *The procession moved at a sedate pace.* calm, cool, dignified, grave, level-headed, sensible, serious, sober.

sedative sleeping-pill, tranquillizer.

sediment *sediment at the bottom of a bottle.* deposit, dregs, remains.

seductive *a seductive dress, seductive music, etc.* alluring, appealing, bewitching, captivating, enticing, irresistible, (informal) sexy, tempting.

see 1 *Did you see anything interesting?* to behold, to discern, to distinguish, to look at, to make out, to notice, to observe, to perceive, to recognize, to sight, to spot, to spy, to witness. 2 *Do you see what I mean?* to appreciate, to comprehend, to follow, to grasp, to know, to realize, to understand. 3 *The refugees saw much misery.* to endure, to experience, to go through, to suffer, to undergo. 4 *Guess who I saw in town!* to encounter, to face, to meet, to run into, to visit. 5 *Shall I see you home?* to accompany, to conduct, to escort. 6 *I can't see granny going to a disco.* to conceive, to imagine, to picture, to visualize.

seed pip, stone.

seek to hunt for, to look for, to pursue, to search for.

seem *The weather seems better today.* to appear, to feel, to look.

seep *Water seeped through the crack.* to dribble, to drip, to flow, to leak, to ooze, to run, to trickle.

segment division, fraction, part, piece, portion, section.

segregate *They segregated the visitors from the home supporters.* to cut off, to isolate, to keep apart, to separate, to set apart.

seize 1 *The police seized a suspect.* to arrest, to capture, to catch, to detain, (informal) to nab, to take prisoner. 2 *I seized the end of the rope.* to clutch, to grab, to grasp, to hold, to pluck, to snatch. 3 *The police seized the stolen property.* to confiscate, to take away.

seldom infrequently, rarely.

select *They selected me as captain.* to appoint, to choose, to decide on, to elect, to nominate, to opt for, to pick, to prefer, to settle on, to vote for.

selection *Make your selection.* choice, pick.

self-confident *You need to be self-confident to be a good captain.* assertive, assured, bold, fearless, positive, sure of yourself.

self-conscious *I used to be self-conscious in front of an audience.* bashful, embarrassed, reserved, shy.

self-control *He showed great self-control when she was teasing him.* calmness, patience, restraint.

self-explanatory *a self-explanatory diagram.* apparent, clear, evident, obvious.

self-important SEE **bumptious.**

selfish grasping, greedy, mean, miserly, stingy, thoughtless, worldly.

self-righteous, self-satisfied SEE **smug.**

sell 1 *What does the shop at the corner sell?* to deal in, to market, to retail, to trade in. 2 PEOPLE WHO SELL THINGS: dealer, merchant, retailer, salesman, saleswoman, shopkeeper, stockist, supplier, trader, tradesman.

send 1 *We sent a parcel to grandad.* to convey, to dispatch, to post, to transmit. 2 *They sent a rocket to the moon.* to launch, to shoot. 3 *to send away:* to banish, to dismiss, to exile, to expel. 4 *to send out:* to belch, to broadcast, to emit. 5 *to send round:* to circulate, to distribute, to issue, to publish.

senile decrepit, infirm, old.

senior *a senior position.* chief, older, superior.

sensation 1 *It was so cold that I had no sensation in my fingers.* awareness, feeling, sense. 2 *It was a sensation when news of the robbery got out.* excitement, outrage, scandal, thrill.

sensational 1 *We won by the sensational score of 13–0.* amazing, exciting, extraordinary, fabulous, fantastic, great, marvellous, spectacular, superb, thrilling, wonderful. ! These words are usually informal. 2 *a sensational murder.* lurid, shocking, startling, violent.

settle

sense 1 YOUR FIVE SENSES: hearing, sight, smell, taste, touch. 2 *I had a sense that something awful was happening.* awareness, feeling, sensation. 3 *Haven't you got any sense?* brains, gumption, intellect, intelligence, judgement, reason, reasoning, understanding, wisdom, wit. 4 *I can't make sense of this.* meaning, significance. 5 *I sensed that he was bored.* to be aware, to detect, to discern, to feel, to perceive, to realize, to understand.

senseless 1 *a senseless thing to do.* SEE **absurd.** 2 *knocked senseless.* SEE **unconscious.**

sensible 1 *a sensible person.* calm, cool, level-headed, reasonable, thoughtful, wise. 2 *a sensible decision.* advisable, logical, prudent.

sensitive 1 *a sensitive skin.* delicate, soft, tender. 2 *a sensitive nature.* emotional, touchy.

sentence *The judge sentenced him.* to condemn, to convict, to pass judgement.

sentiment *What are your sentiments about experiments on animals?* attitude, emotion, feeling, opinion, thought, view.

sentimental *I get sentimental when I look at old family photographs.* emotional, nostalgic, romantic, soft-hearted, tearful, tender.

sentinel, sentry guard, look-out, watchman.

separate 1 *Keep the two sides separate.* apart, divided, isolated, segregated. 2 *The infants are in a separate part of the school.* detached, different, distinct. 3 *The police separated the two gangs.* to break up, to cut off, to detach, to isolate, to part, to segregate, to set apart, to split. 4 *Our paths separated.* to diverge, to divide, to fork. 5 *Their parents separated.* to divorce, to split up.

septic *a septic wound.* festering, infected, inflamed, poisoned.

sequel *Was there a sequel to the row you had with the neighbours?* consequence, outcome, result.

sequence SEE **series.**

serene *a serene mood.* calm, peaceful, placid, tranquil, untroubled.

series *a series of events.* chain, course, cycle, line, order, progression, range, row, sequence, string, succession.

serious 1 *a serious expression.* dignified, earnest, grave, sedate, sober, solemn. 2 *a serious accident.* appalling, awful, calamitous, dreadful, frightful, ghastly, hideous, horrible, nasty, severe, shocking, terrible, (informal) terrific, unfortunate, unpleasant, violent. 3 *a serious worker.* careful, conscientious, diligent, earnest, hard-working, sincere.

serpent snake.

servant VARIOUS SERVANTS: attendant, butler, chauffeur, cook, footman, house-keeper, maid, page, slave, steward, stewardess.

serve 1 *to serve the community.* to assist, to help, to look after, to work for. 2 *to serve at table.* to wait.

service 1 *He did me a service by posting my letter.* assistance, favour, help. 2 *a religious service.* ceremony, meeting, worship. 3 *Dad services his own car.* to maintain, to mend, to overhaul, to repair.

serviceable *a pair of strong serviceable shoes.* durable, hard-wearing, lasting, strong, tough.

serviette napkin.

session *When does the next session start at the baths?* period, time.

set 1 *Set the things down on the table.* to arrange, to deposit, to lay, to leave, to place, to position, to put, to rest, to stand. 2 *They set the gatepost in concrete.* to embed, to fix. 3 *Has the concrete set?* to harden, to stiffen. 4 *to set off on a journey.* SEE **depart.** 5 *to set off an explosion.* to detonate, to explode, to let off. 6 *to set on someone.* SEE **attack.** 7 *to set on fire:* to ignite, to kindle, to light. 8 *a set of people, a set of tools, etc.* batch, bunch, category, class, collection, group, kind, sort.

set-back *I did well at first, but then I had a set-back.* complication, difficulty, obstacle, problem, snag.

settee couch, sofa.

settle 1 *When did you settle in this country?* to immigrate, to make your home, to move, to stay. 2 *A robin settled on the fence.* to come to rest, to land, to pause, to rest. 3 *Wait until the dust settles.* to go down, to subside. 4 *Have you settled what to do?* to agree, to choose, to decide, to establish, to fix. 5 *Mum settled the bill.* to pay.

sever SEE **cut**.

severe 1 *a severe ruler.* austere, cruel, hard, harsh, stern, strict. 2 *a severe frost, severe flu, etc.* acute, bad, drastic, extreme, intense, keen, serious, sharp, violent.

sew 1 *I sewed up the hole in my jeans.* to darn, to mend, to repair, to stitch, to tack. 2 *sewing:* embroidery, needlework.

sewage waste.

sewers drainage, drains, sanitation.

shabby *shabby clothes.* dowdy, drab, frayed, ragged, scruffy, tattered, tatty, threadbare, unattractive, worn.

shack hovel, hut, shanty.

shackles *The prisoners wore shackles on their legs.* bonds, chains, fetters, irons.

shade 1 *the shade of a tree.* shadow, shelter. 2 *a pale shade of blue.* colour, hue, tinge, tint, tone. 3 *The sun was so bright I had to shade my eyes.* to darken, to mask, to protect, to screen, to shield.

shadow 1 *I won't get a good photo if you stand in shadow.* darkness, shade. 2 *The low sun cast long shadows on the ground.* outline, shape. 3 *The detective shadowed the suspect.* to follow, to hunt, to pursue, to stalk, to tag onto, to tail, to track, to trail.

shady 1 *a shady spot under a tree.* dark, dim, gloomy, shaded, shadowy. 2 *a shady character.* disreputable, dubious, suspicious, untrustworthy.

shaft 1 *a wooden shaft.* column, pillar, pole, post, rod. 2 *a mine shaft.* mine, pit, working. 3 *a shaft of light.* beam, ray.

shaggy *a shaggy beard.* bushy, fleecy, hairy, rough, woolly.

shake 1 *I shook with fear!* to quiver, to shiver, to shudder, to tremble. 2 *The earthquake made the buildings shake.* to quake, to sway, to throb, to vibrate, to wobble. 3 *Grandad shook his umbrella.* to brandish, to flourish, to twirl, to wag, to waggle, to wave, to wiggle. 4 *The terrible news shook us.* to alarm, to distress, to frighten, to perturb, to shock, to startle.

shaky *The bench was so shaky we didn't dare sit down.* flimsy, frail, insecure, precarious, ramshackle, rickety, rocky, unsteady, weak, wobbly.

shallow not deep.

sham SEE **pretend**.

shambles 1 slaughterhouse. 2 *My bedroom is in a shambles.* chaos, confusion, disorder, mess, muddle.

shame 1 *We'll never live down the shame of losing 14–0.* disgrace, dishonour, embarrassment, guilt, humiliation, remorse. 2 *It's a shame to treat a dog so badly!* outrage, pity, scandal.

shameful SEE **bad**.

shameless *shameless boasting.* bold, brazen, impudent, insolent, rude, unashamed.

shanty hovel, hut, shack.

shape 1 *I saw the shape of a bird against the sky.* figure, form, outline. 2 FLAT SHAPES: circle, diamond, ellipse, hexagon, oblong, octagon, oval, pentagon, quadrilateral, rectangle, semicircle, square, triangle. 3 THREE-DIMENSIONAL SHAPES: cone, cube, cylinder, hemisphere, prism, pyramid, sphere. 4 *The sculptor shaped the clay.* to carve, to cast, to cut, to form, to mould.

share 1 *We gave everyone a fair share of the food.* allowance, bit, division, fraction, helping, part, piece, portion, quota, ration. 2 *We shared the food equally.* to allot, to deal out, to distribute, to divide, to halve, to split. 3 *If we all share in the work we'll finish quickly.* to be involved, to join, to participate, to take part.

sharp 1 *a sharp knife, etc.* cutting, fine, keen, pointed. 2 *a sharp mind.* acute, astute, bright, clever, cute, intelligent, quick, shrewd, smart. 3 *a sharp taste.* acid, sour, tangy, tart. 4 *a sharp drop, a sharp rise.* abrupt, precipitous, steep, sudden. 5 *a sharp frost, a sharp pain, etc.* extreme, intense, serious, severe, violent. 6 *a sharp sound.* high, piercing, shrill.

sharpen *to sharpen a knife.* to grind.

shatter *The explosion shattered the window. The window shattered.* to break up, to burst, to disintegrate, to explode, . to smash, to splinter.

shave SEE **cut**.

sheaf *a sheaf of papers.* bunch, bundle.

shear *to shear sheep.* to clip, to cut.

sheath scabbard.

shore

shed 1 *a garden shed.* hut, outhouse, shack, shelter. 2 *A lorry shed its load.* to discard, to drop, to let fall, to scatter, to spill, to throw off.

sheen *A rub with polish gives the furniture a nice sheen.* brightness, gloss, lustre, polish, shine.

sheep ewe, lamb, ram.

sheepish *a sheepish look.* bashful, coy, embarrassed, guilty, self-conscious, shy, timid.

sheer 1 *sheer nonsense.* absolute, complete, pure, total, utter. 2 *a sheer cliff.* precipitous, vertical.

sheet 1 *a sheet of paper.* leaf, page. 2 *a sheet of glass.* pane, plate. 3 *a sheet of ice on a pond.* coating, film, layer, skin. 4 *a sheet of water.* area, expanse.

shelf ledge.

shell 1 *an outer shell.* case, covering, crust, exterior, husk, outside, pod. 2 *They shelled the battleship.* to attack, to bombard, to fire at, to shoot at.

shellfish VARIOUS SHELLFISH: barnacle, clam, cockle, crab, limpet, lobster, mussel, oyster, prawn, shrimp, whelk, winkle.

shelter 1 *We sought shelter from the storm.* asylum, cover, haven, protection, refuge, safety, sanctuary. 2 *The fence sheltered us from the wind.* to defend, to guard, to protect, to shield. 3 *Is it wrong to shelter a criminal?* to give asylum, to give refuge to, to harbour.

shield 1 *The fence acts as a shield against the wind.* defence, guard, protection, safeguard, screen. 2 *Parents try to shield their young from danger.* to defend, to guard, to keep safe, to protect, to safeguard, to shelter. 3 *The umbrella shielded us from the sun.* to cover, to screen, to shade.

shift *He refused to shift. Please shift your things.* to budge, to change, to move, to transfer.

shifty *I didn't trust his shifty expression.* crafty, deceitful, furtive, secretive, sly, tricky, untrustworthy, wily.

shine to gleam, to glimmer, to glow, to radiate.

shingle *shingle on the beach.* gravel, pebbles, stones.

shiny bright, burnished, gleaming, glossy, polished, shining.

ship 1 SEE **vessel.** 2 *They ship a lot of goods to foreign countries.* to carry, to convey, to export, to ferry, to move, to transport.

shipshape *We tidied up and made everything shipshape.* clean, neat, orderly, tidy, trim.

shirk *to shirk the washing-up.* to avoid, to dodge, to evade, to get out of, to neglect, (informal) to skive.

shiver *to shiver with cold.* to quake, to quaver, to quiver, to shake, to shudder, to tremble, to vibrate.

shock 1 *It was a shock to learn that the head was leaving.* bombshell, surprise. 2 *When the plane crashed we felt the shock.* blow, collision, impact, jolt. 3 *The bad news shocked us.* to alarm, to amaze, to astound, to daze, to dismay, to frighten, to scare, to stagger, to startle, to stun, to surprise. 4 *The bad language shocked granny.* to appal, to disgust, to horrify, to offend, to repel, to revolt. 5 *shocking:* SEE **outrageous.**

shoddy 1 *shoddy goods.* cheap, inferior, nasty, poor-quality. 2 *shoddy work.* careless, messy, negligent, sloppy, slovenly, untidy.

shoe KINDS OF SHOE: boot, bootee, brogue, clog, gumboot, plimsoll, pump, sandal, slipper, trainer, wellington.

shoemaker cobbler.

shoot 1 *to shoot a gun.* to aim, to discharge, to fire. 2 *to shoot at:* to bombard, to shell, to snipe at. 3 *The plants shoot up in the spring.* to grow, to spring up, to sprout.

shop VARIOUS SHOPS AND BUSINESSES: baker, bank, barber, betting shop, bookmaker, bookshop, boutique, building society, butcher, chemist, dairy, delicatessen, department store, DIY store, draper, electrician, estate agent, fishmonger, florist, furniture store, greengrocer, grocer, hairdresser, hardware store, insurance office, ironmonger, jeweller, launderette, market, newsagent, off-licence, pawnbroker, post office, radio and TV shop, shoemaker, supermarket, tailor, tobacconist.

shopkeeper merchant, retailer, salesman, saleswoman, stockist, supplier, trader, tradesman. SEE ALSO **shop.**

shore bank, beach, coast, sands, sea-shore, shingle.

short 1 *a short book, a short remark.* brief, compact, concise, terse. 2 *a short person.* diminutive, little, small, squat. 3 *a short pause, a short visit.* cursory, momentary, passing, quick, temporary, transient. 4 *During the drought water was short.* deficient, lacking, scarce, wanting. 5 *He was short with me when I asked for a loan.* abrupt, bad-tempered, cross, curt, grumpy, irritable, snappy, testy.

shortage *a shortage of water.* deficiency, lack, scarcity, want.

shortcoming SEE **fault**.

shorten *We shortened our play because it was too long.* to abbreviate, to abridge, to compress, to condense, to cut short, to reduce, to telescope.

shortly *The post should arrive shortly.* directly, presently, soon.

short-tempered SEE **cross**.

shout to bawl, to bellow, to call, to cheer, to cry, to roar, to shriek, to yell.

shove *They shoved me into the water.* to crowd, to hustle, to jostle, to push.

shovel *We shovelled the snow off the path.* to dig, to scoop.

show 1 *We showed our work to the parents.* to display, to exhibit, to present, to produce, to reveal. 2 *My knee showed through the hole in my jeans.* to appear, to be seen, to be visible, to emerge, to materialize, to stand out. 3 *She showed me the way to the station.* to direct, to guide, to indicate, to point out. 4 *The photo shows us swimming in the sea.* to depict, to illustrate, to picture, to portray, to represent. 5 *She showed us how to do it.* to describe, to explain, to instruct, to make clear, to teach, to tell. 6 *The experiment showed that plants need light.* to demonstrate, to prove. 7 *to show off*: to boast, to brag, (informal) to crow, to gloat, (informal) to swank.

shower *A passing bus showered us with rainwater.* to spatter, to splash, to spray, to sprinkle.

showy *You couldn't miss her showy clothes.* bright, conspicuous, flashy, gaudy, lurid, striking.

shred 1 to grate, to tear. 2 *The barbed wire tore her jeans to shreds.* bits, rags, strips, tatters.

shrewd *a shrewd plan.* artful, astute, clever, crafty, cunning, ingenious, intelligent, knowing, sly, wise.

shriek SEE **sound**.

shrill *a shrill voice.* harsh, high, piercing, sharp.

shrink 1 *The river shrank during the drought.* to contract, to decrease, to diminish, to dwindle, to lessen, to reduce, to shrivel. 2 *The dog shrank back when the cat spat at him.* to cower, to cringe, to flinch, to hang back, to quail, to recoil, to wince, to withdraw.

shrivel *The plants shrivelled in the heat.* to droop, to dry up, to shrink, to wilt, to wither.

shroud *Mist shrouded the top of the mountain.* to cloak, to conceal, to cover, to envelop, to hide, to mask, to wrap up.

shrub 1 bush. 2 VARIOUS SHRUBS: broom, gorse, heather, lavender, lilac, privet, rhododendron.

shudder *I shuddered when I thought of the monster.* to quake, to quiver, to shake, to tremble.

shuffle *I shuffled the cards.* to jumble, to mix.

shut 1 *Shut the door.* to close, to fasten, to lock, to replace, to seal, to secure. 2 *to shut in*: to confine, to detain, to enclose, to imprison, to keep in. 3 *to shut out*: to ban, to bar, to exclude, to keep out, to prohibit. 4 *Shut up!* be quiet! be silent! hush! silence!

shutter *Close the shutters.* blind, curtain.

shy *He was too shy to call out.* bashful, coy, modest, nervous, reserved, self-conscious, timid, timorous.

sick 1 *She was away for a week because she was sick.* bedridden, diseased, ill, indisposed, infirm, poorly, queer, unwell. 2 *to be sick*: (informal) to throw up, to vomit.

sicken *Their cruelty sickened us.* to disgust, to nauseate, to repel, to revolt.

sickly *a sickly child.* delicate, feeble, frail, unhealthy, weak. 2 *a sickly sweet taste.* nasty, nauseating, obnoxious, unpleasant.

side 1 *A cube has six sides.* face, surface. 2 *the side of the road.* edge, margin, verge. 3 *A game of hockey is played by two sides.* team.

siege blockade.

sieve 1 riddle. 2 *Sieve out the lumps.* to filter, to sift, to strain.

sight 1 *the power of sight.* eyesight, vision. 2 *I had a sight of the castle between the trees.* appearance, look, view. 3 *The procession was an impressive sight.* display, scene, spectacle. 4 *The look-out sighted a ship.* to discern, to make out, to notice, to observe, to recognize, to see, to spot.

sightseer *The castle was full of sightseers.* tourist, visitor.

sign 1 *I gave them the sign to begin.* cue, gesture, hint, indication, reminder, signal. 2 *A yawn is a sign of tiredness.* clue, symptom. 3 *The flowers were a sign of our love.* token. 4 *We painted a sign for the sweet stall.* advertisement, notice, placard, poster, publicity. 5 *Do you recognize the British Rail sign?* badge, emblem, symbol. 6 *I signed that I was turning right.* to gesture, to indicate, to signal. 7 *Sign your name.* to autograph, to write. 8 *Our team signed a new goalkeeper.* to enrol, to register, to take on. 9 *He signed on in the army.* to enlist, to join up, to volunteer.

signal 1 *I gave him a clear signal.* cue, gesture, indication, sign. 2 *He signalled that he was turning right.* to gesture, to indicate, to sign.

signature autograph.

significance *What's the significance of wearing a red poppy?* importance, meaning, sense.

significant *a significant amount of rain.* big, considerable, important, sizeable.

silage fodder.

silence to gag, to quieten.

silent 1 *a silent engine.* inaudible, noiseless, quiet, soundless. 2 *a silent person.* dumb, mute, reserved, speechless, tongue-tied.

silky *The cat has a silky coat.* sleek, smooth, soft.

silly *Why did he do such a silly thing?* absurd, crazy, foolish, grotesque, illogical, irrational, laughable, ludicrous, mad, preposterous, ridiculous, senseless, stupid, unreasonable.

similar 1 *The twins are similar in their habits.* akin, alike, related. 2 *They are similar to each other.* like, resembling. 3 *They wear similar clothes.* corresponding, matching.

similarity likeness, matching.

simmer to boil, to stew.

simple 1 *a simple dress.* austere, plain. 2 *a simple problem.* easy, elementary, uncomplicated. 3 *a simple explanation.* clear, understandable.

sin blasphemy, evil, immorality, sacrilege, vice, wickedness, wrongdoing.

sincere *a sincere opinion, a sincere person.* candid, earnest, frank, genuine, honest, open, real, straightforward, truthful.

sincerity honesty, honour, integrity, truthfulness.

sinful *sinful behaviour.* bad, blasphemous, evil, immoral, sacrilegious, wicked, wrong.

sing 1 to chant, to croon, to hum. 2 SINGERS: bass, choir, chorus, contalto, soloist, soprano, tenor, treble, vocalist. 3 KINDS OF MUSIC YOU SING: anthem, ballad, blues, calypso, carol, chant, descant, folksong, hymn, lullaby, opera, pop, reggae, rock, shanty, song, soul, spiritual.

singe to burn, to char, to scorch.

single 1 *There wasn't a single sandwich left!* one, sole, solitary. 2 *a single person.* SEE **unmarried.**

single-handed *You can't shift the piano single-handed.* unaided.

singular *It's a singular sight to see snow so late in the spring.* abnormal, curious, extraordinary, odd, peculiar, remarkable, uncommon, unusual.

sinister *The giant in the pantomime was a sinister character.* evil, forbidding, frightening, menacing, ominous, threatening, villainous.

sink 1 *The sun sinks in the west.* to descend, to drop, to fall, to go down. 2 *to sink a ship.* to scuttle, to submerge, to swamp.

sip *I sipped a little water.* to drink, to taste.

sit to be seated, to perch, to rest, to squat.

site *a site for a new building.* location, place, position, situation, spot.

sitting-room drawing-room, living-room, lounge.

situated *Where is your house situated?* located, placed.

situation 1 *Their house is in a pleasant situation.* location, place, position, site, spot. 2 *We were in an awkward situation when the referee didn't turn up.* circumstances, condition, position.

size amount, area, bulk, capacity, dimensions, extent, largeness, magnitude, volume.

sizeable *sizeable helpings.* considerable, generous. SEE ALSO **big**.

skate to glide, to skim, to slide.

skeleton bones, frame, framework.

sketch 1 description, design, diagram, drawing, picture. 2 *to sketch with crayons.* to depict, to draw, to portray, to represent.

skid *I skidded on the ice.* to glide, to slide, to slip.

skilful *a skilful carpenter, a skilful player, etc.* able, accomplished, apt, artful, brilliant, capable, clever, competent, crafty, cunning, deft, experienced, expert, gifted, ingenious, proficient, qualified, shrewd, skilled, smart, talented, trained, versatile.

skill *the skill of a carpenter, the skill of a tennis-player, etc.* ability, accomplishment, aptitude, art, cleverness, craft, gift, handicraft, knack, prowess, talent, workmanship.

skilled SEE **skilful**.

skim 1 *I skimmed over the ice.* to glide, to skate, to slide. 2 *I skimmed through the book.* to look through, to read quickly, to scan.

skin 1 VARIOUS WORDS FOR SKIN: coat, coating, exterior, film, husk, outer layer, outside, peel, rind, shell, surface. 2 *an animal's skin.* fur, hide. 3 *to skin an orange.* to peel, to strip.

skinny *a skinny person.* emaciated, lanky, scraggy, thin.

skip 1 *The lambs skipped about the field.* to bound, to caper, to dance, to frisk, to hop, to jump, to leap, to prance, to spring. 2 *He skips the boring parts of a book.* to forget, to ignore, to leave out, to miss out, to neglect, to overlook.

skipper captain.

sky *The balloon rose into the sky.* air, atmosphere, space, stratosphere.

skylight window.

slab *a slab of chocolate.* block, chunk, hunk, piece.

slack 1 *He was dropped from the team because of his slack attitude.* idle, lazy, listless, sluggish. 2 *The tent flapped about because the guy ropes were slack.* loose.

slacken 1 *I slackened the tension in the guy ropes.* to ease off, to loosen, to relax, to release. 2 *The pace of the game slackened in the second half.* to decrease, to lessen, to lower, to reduce.

slam *to slam the door.* to bang, to shut.

slant *My handwriting slants backwards.* to incline, to lean, to slope, to tilt.

slap SEE **hit**.

slapdash *slapdash work.* careless, hasty, messy, shoddy, slovenly, untidy.

slash *to slash with a knife.* to chop. SEE ALSO **cut**.

slaughter 1 *The prisoners were brutally slaughtered.* to annihilate, to kill, to massacre, to murder, to slay. 2 *a terrible scene of slaughter.* bloodshed, carnage, killing, massacre, murder.

slaughterhouse shambles.

slave *We slaved away all day.* to exert yourself, to labour, to toil, to work.

slay to assassinate, (informal) to bump off, to dispatch, to execute, to finish off, to martyr, to massacre, to murder, to put down, to put to death, to slaughter. SEE ALSO **kill**.

sledge sleigh, toboggan.

sleek *The cat has a sleek coat.* glossy, silky, smooth, soft.

sleep 1 to doze, to nod off, to rest, to slumber, to snooze, to take a nap. 2 *sleeping*: asleep, dormant, hibernating, resting.

sleepy drowsy, tired, weary.

sleigh sledge, toboggan.

slender *a slender figure, a slender thread.* fine, lean, narrow, slight, slim, thin, wiry.

slide 1 *The toboggan slid over the snow.* to glide, to skate, to skid, to skim, to slip. 2 *Dad takes slides with his camera.* transparency.

slight 1 *a slight improvement.* imperceptible, insignificant, negligible, small, tiny, trivial, unimportant. 2 *a slight figure.* delicate, flimsy, frail, weak. SEE ALSO **slim**.

slim *a slim figure.* fine, lean, narrow, slender, slight, thin, wiry.

slime muck, mud, ooze.

sling *I slung the rubbish on the tip.* to cast, (informal) to chuck, to fling, to hurl, to lob, to throw, to toss.

slink *The naughty dog slunk into the corner.* to creep, to edge, to slither, to sneak.

slip 1 *I slipped on the ice.* to glide, to skid, to slide. 2 *to slip away:* to abscond, to elope, to escape, to run away. 3 *The detective noticed the suspect's slip.* blunder, error, inaccuracy, miscalculation, mistake.

slippery *Take care: the floor is slippery.* greasy, icy, oily, slithery, smooth.

slit 1 *a slit in your jeans, a slit in a tyre, etc.* breach, break, chink, crack, cut, gap, gash, hole, opening, rift, slot, split, tear, vent. 2 *to slit something with a knife.* SEE **cut.**

slither *The snake slithered away.* to creep, to glide, to slide, to slink, to slip, to worm.

slog SEE **hit.**

slogan *an advertising slogan.* motto, saying.

slop *I slopped my tea into the saucer.* to spatter, to spill, to splash.

slope 1 *It's hard work cycling up the slope.* ascent, bank, hill, incline, ramp, rise. 2 *The beach slopes gently into the sea.* to shelve. 3 *The leaning tower slopes to one side.* to incline, to lean, to slant, to tilt, to tip.

sloppy 1 *a sloppy mixture.* liquid, runny, wet. 2 (informal) *sloppy work.* SEE **slovenly.**

slot *Put a coin in the slot.* groove, slit.

slouch *Don't slouch about in that slovenly way.* to droop, to loaf, to lounge.

slovenly *slovenly work.* careless, hasty, messy, shoddy, slapdash, (informal) sloppy, thoughtless, untidy.

slow 1 *a slow change in the weather.* gradual, moderate, steady, unhurried. 2 *a slow learner.* backward, dense, dim, obtuse, stupid. 3 *a slow worker.* idle, lazy, sluggish. 4 *slow progress.* careful, cautious, deliberate, painstaking. 5 *The bus is slow.* delayed, late. 6 *to be slow:* SEE **dawdle.** 7 *Please slow down!* to brake, to go slower.

sluggish *Wake up: you're sluggish today!* idle, lazy, listless, slow.

slumber *Grandad slumbered in his chair.* to doze, to nod off, to rest, to sleep, to snooze, to take a nap.

slump 1 *He slumped unconscious to the ground.* to be limp, to flop, to sag. 2 *Our spirits slumped when we saw how far we had to go.* to decline, to droop, to drop, to sink.

sly *I didn't trust his sly expression.* artful, catty, crafty, cunning, deceitful, devious, furtive, sneaky, tricky, wily.

smack to slap. SEE ALSO **hit.**

small 1 *a small baby.* diminutive, little, minute, (informal) teeny, tiny, undersized, wee. 2 *a small book.* brief, compact, concise, short. 3 *a small TV set.* miniature, portable. 4 *small helpings.* inadequate, meagre, (informal) measly, microscopic, scanty, stingy. 5 *a small problem.* insignificant, minor, negligible, petty, slight, trifling, trivial, unimportant.

smart 1 *You look smart!* clean, fashionable, neat, (informal) posh, spruce, stylish, tidy, trim. 2 *That was a smart thing to do!* artful, astute, bright, clever, crafty, cute, intelligent, shrewd. 3 *We set off at a smart pace.* brisk, fast, quick, rapid, speedy, swift. 4 *My cut smarts when you touch it.* to ache, to be painful, to be sore, to hurt, to sting, to throb.

smash 1 *to smash an egg.* to crumple, to crush, to demolish, to destroy, to shatter, to squash. SEE ALSO **break.** 2 *to smash into a wall.* to bang, to bash, to batter, to bump, to collide, to hammer, to knock, to pound, to ram, to slam, to strike, to thump, to wallop. SEE ALSO **hit.**

smear 1 *a smear of dirt.* mark, smudge, streak. 2 *I smeared fat over the pan.* to rub, to smudge, to spread, to wipe.

smell aroma, fragrance, incense, odour, perfume, reek, scent, stench, stink, whiff.

smile to beam, to grin, to smirk. SEE ALSO **laugh.**

smirk SEE **smile.**

smith blacksmith.

smoke 1 *clouds of smoke.* exhaust, fumes, gas, steam, vapour. 2 VARIOUS THINGS WHICH PEOPLE SMOKE: cigar, cigarette, (informal) fag, pipe, tobacco. 3 *The fire was smoking.* to smoulder.

smooth 1 *a smooth sea.* calm, even,
flat, level, peaceful, placid, quiet,
restful, steady. **2** *The cat has a smooth
coat.* silky, sleek, soft, velvety. **3** *Mix the
ingredients to a smooth mixture.* creamy,
runny. **4** *Can we smooth this crumpled
paper?* to flatten, to iron, to press.

smother to choke, to stifle, to strangle,
to suffocate, to throttle.

smoulder *The ashes were still
smouldering.* to smoke.

smudge 1 *I smudged the ink.* to smear,
to streak. **2** *I smudged the paper.* to blot,
to mark, to stain.

smug *He looked so smug when he won
that prize!* complacent, pleased,
self-righteous, self-satisfied, superior.

snack refreshments.

snack-bar buffet, café, cafeteria.

snag *I'd like to come, but the snag is that
I haven't any money.* complication,
difficulty, hindrance, obstacle, problem,
set-back.

snake VARIOUS SNAKES: adder, boa
constrictor, cobra, grass-snake, python,
rattlesnake, viper.

snap 1 *The dog snapped at me.* to bite,
to nip. **2** *A twig snapped.* to crack.
3 *holiday snaps.* SEE **photograph.**

snare ambush, booby-trap, trap.

snatch *The muggers snatched her
handbag.* to catch, to clutch, to grab, to
pluck, to seize, to take.

sneak *I sneaked in without anyone
seeing.* to creep, to move stealthily, to
prowl, to slink, to stalk, to steal.

sneaky (informal) *It was sneaky to copy
my answer.* crafty, deceitful, devious,
furtive, mean, sly, treacherous.

sneer 1 *Some people sneered, but he'd
done his best.* to boo, to hiss, to hoot, to
jeer, to mock, to ridicule, to scoff, to
taunt. **2** *sneering:* contemptuous,
scornful.

snigger *They sniggered at the rude joke.*
to chuckle, to giggle, to titter. SEE ALSO
laugh.

snip SEE **cut.**

snipe *A gunman sniped at them from the
roof.* to fire, to shoot.

snippet *We collected every little snippet
of information.* fragment, morsel,
particle, piece, scrap.

snivel *He snivelled when he didn't get his
own way.* to blubber, to cry, to grizzle,
to grovel, to sob, to weep, to whine.

snobbish *Rich people aren't always
snobbish.* disdainful, haughty, pompous,
posh, presumptuous, (informal)
stuck-up, superior.

snoop *Don't snoop into my affairs!* to
interfere, to intrude, to meddle, to nose
about, to pry.

snooze *The dog was snoozing in the
sun.* to doze, to nod off, to sleep, to
slumber, to take a nap.

snout *an animal's snout.* face, nose.

snub *He snubbed me by ignoring my
question.* to be rude to, to disdain, to
insult, to offend, to scorn.

snuff *to snuff a candle.* to extinguish, to
put out.

snug *It's nice to be snug in bed on a cold
night.* comfortable, cosy, relaxed, safe,
secure, soft, warm.

snuggle *The baby snuggled against his
mother.* to be comfortable, to cuddle, to
huddle, to nestle.

so accordingly, therefore.

soak 1 *The rain soaked us.* to drench, to
saturate, to wet thoroughly. **2** *soaked:*
sodden, soggy, sopping, wet through.
3 *A sponge soaks up water.* to absorb, to
take up.

soap detergent.

soar *An eagle soared overhead.* to fly, to
glide, to hover, to rise.

sob to blubber, to cry, to gasp, to snivel,
to wail, to weep.

sober 1 not drunk. **2** *a sober occasion.*
dignified, grave, sedate, serious,
solemn.

soccer football.

sociable *a sociable crowd of people.* friendly, hospitable, welcoming.

social 1 *Human beings are supposed to be social creatures.* civilized, friendly, organized. 2 *We organized a social at Christmas.* ball, dance, disco, gathering, party, reception.

society 1 *We are all members of society.* civilization, community, nation, the public. 2 *I enjoy the society of my friends.* company. 3 *a secret society.* association, club, group, organization, union.

sodden *My clothes were sodden after the rainstorm.* drenched, saturated, soaked, soggy, sopping, wet through.

sofa couch, settee.

soft 1 *soft rubber.* flexible, floppy, limp, pliable, spongy, springy, supple. 2 *a soft bed.* comfortable, cosy. 3 *soft material.* silky, sleek, smooth, velvety. 4 *a soft breeze.* delicate, gentle, mild, tender. 5 *soft music.* low, peaceful, quiet, restful. 6 (informal) *a soft teacher.* easygoing, kind, lenient.

soften *Please soften the noise.* to deaden, to quieten, to subdue, to tone down.

soft-hearted *I'm soft-hearted where animals are concerned.* emotional, romantic, sentimental, tender. SEE ALSO **kind.**

soggy 1 *a soggy towel.* drenched, saturated, soaked, sodden, sopping, wet through. 2 *soggy cake.* heavy, stodgy.

soil 1 *I raked the soil before planting the seeds.* earth, ground, loam. 2 *Don't soil your hands with that filthy stuff.* to contaminate, to defile, to make dirty, to stain. 3 *soiled:* SEE **dirty.**

soldier cavalryman, commando, gunner, infantryman, marine, paratrooper, sentry. SEE ALSO **fighter, rank.**

sole *The weather was so cold that I was the sole person swimming.* one, only, single, solitary.

solemn *The funeral was a solemn occasion.* dignified, earnest, formal, grave, important, sedate, serious, sober, thoughtful.

solid 1 *solid rock.* dense, firm, hard, rigid, sound, unyielding. 2 *solid evidence.* physical, real, tangible.

solitary 1 *a solitary person.* alone, friendless, lonely. 2 *a solitary place.* desolate, isolated, remote. 3 *There was a solitary potato in the dish.* one, only, single, sole.

solo *to perform solo.* alone.

solution *the solution to a problem.* answer, explanation.

solve *Can you solve a riddle?* to answer, to explain, to work out.

sombre 1 *sombre colours.* cheerless, dark, dismal, drab, dull. 2 *a sombre expression.* gloomy, grave, mournful, serious.

somewhat fairly, moderately, pretty, rather.

son SEE **family.**

song SEE **sing.**

soon presently, quickly.

sooner 1 *I wish you'd come sooner.* before, earlier. 2 *I'd sooner have an apple than sweets.* preferably, rather.

soot dirt, grime.

soothe 1 *Quiet music soothes your nerves.* to appease, to calm, to comfort, to ease, to pacify, to relieve. 2 *soothing:* balmy, gentle, healing, mild, peaceful, pleasant, relaxing.

sophisticated 1 *a sophisticated argument, sophisticated machinery.* advanced, complicated, elaborate, ingenious, intricate, involved, subtle. 2 *sophisticated clothes.* adult, fashionable, grown-up, stylish.

sopping SEE **sodden.**

sorcerer, sorcery SEE **magic.**

sordid *a sordid story, sordid surroundings.* dirty, filthy, foul, (informal) mucky, squalid. SEE ALSO **unpleasant.**

sore 1 *a sore wound.* aching, hurting, inflamed, painful, raw, tender. 2 *They put ointment on his sores.* abscess, boil, inflammation, wound.

sorrow depression, grief, misery, regret, remorse, sadness, unhappiness.

sorry 1 *He was sorry for what he did.* apologetic, penitent, regretful, remorseful, repentant. 2 *We were sorry for the girl who came last.* compassionate, merciful, pitying, understanding.

sort 1 *What sort of food do you like?* brand, category, form, group, kind, make, set, type, variety. 2 *What sort of dog is that?* breed, class, species. 3 *We sorted the books in the library.* to arrange, to classify, to group, to put in order. 4 *to sort out: Can you sort out this problem?* to attend to, to cope with, to deal with, to grapple with, to handle, to manage, to tackle.

soul *your immortal soul.* spirit.

sound 1 *The dog is in a sound condition.* healthy, robust, strong, sturdy, well. 2 *She is a sound player.* dependable, reliable, safe, solid, trustworthy. 3 *We couldn't find a flaw in his sound argument.* coherent, convincing, logical, reasonable, sensible. 4 *I heard a sound.* noise. 5 VARIOUS SOUNDS: bang, bark, bawl, bay, bellow, blare, bleat, bleep, boo, boom, bray, buzz, cackle, chime, chink, chirp, clang, clank, clap, clash, clatter, click, clink, cluck, coo, crack, crackle, crash, creak, croak, crooning, crowing, crunch, cry, drone, echo, grating, groan, growl, grunt, gurgle, hiccup, hiss, hoot, howl, hum, jabber, jangle, jingle, lowing, miaow, moan, moo, murmur, neigh, patter, peal, ping, plop, pop, purr, quack, rattle, reverberation, ring, roar, rumble, rustle, scream, screech, shout, shriek, sigh, sizzle, slam, snap, snarl, sneeze, sniff, snore, sob, splutter, squawk, squeak, squeal, swish, throb, thud, thunder, tick, tinkle, twang, twitter, wail, warble, whimper, whine, whinny, whistle, whiz, whoop, yap, yell, yelp, yodel.

soup broth, stock.

sour 1 *sour fruit.* acid, sharp, tangy, tart. 2 *a sour temper.* bad-tempered, bitter, grumpy, peevish, snappy, testy, unpleasant.

source 1 *the source of a rumour.* beginning, cause, origin, starting-point. 2 *the source of a river:* spring.

souvenir *a souvenir of a holiday.* reminder.

sow *to sow seeds.* to plant.

space 1 *I need more space.* freedom, room. 2 *Leave an empty space.* area, break, distance, gap, hole, opening, place. 3 *The rocket sped away into space.* emptiness, stratosphere, vacuum. 4 WORDS TO DO WITH TRAVEL IN SPACE: blast-off, capsule, extraterrestrial beings, module, orbit, probe, re-entry, retro-rocket, rocket, satellite, spacecraft, spaceship, space shuttle, spacesuit.

spacious *a spacious house.* large, roomy, sizeable. SEE ALSO **big.**

span *The bridge spans the river.* to cross, to pass over, to reach over, to stretch over.

spank to slap, to smack.

spare 1 *The judge would not spare the violent criminal.* to be merciful to, to forgive, to free, to let off, to pardon, to reprieve, to save. 2 *Can you spare something for our collection?* to afford, to give, to manage, to provide. 3 *a spare tyre.* additional, extra, odd, unused.

sparing *He's sparing with his money.* economical, mean, miserly, stingy, thrifty.

spark *a spark of light.* flash, sparkle.

sparkle 1 to flash, to spark. SEE ALSO **light.** 2 *sparkling: sparkling drinks.* bubbly, effervescent, fizzy, foaming.

sparse *Grass for the cows was sparse during the drought.* inadequate, meagre, scanty, scattered, thin.

spasm *a violent spasm of coughing.* attack, convulsion, fit, seizure.

spasmodic *We've got a spasmodic fault on our TV.* intermittent, occasional, on and off.

spate *a spate of water.* cataract, flood, gush, rush.

spatter *The bus spattered us with water as it went by.* to shower, to slop, to splash, to spray, to sprinkle.

speak 1 *Please speak to me!* to communicate, to express yourself. SEE ALSO **say, talk.** 2 *Can you speak French?* to pronounce, to talk, to utter. 3 *The vicar spoke to us in assembly.* to address, to lecture, to make a speech.

spear harpoon, javelin, lance, pike.

special 1 *A birthday is a special event.* important, infrequent, notable, rare, unusual. 2 *Petrol has a special smell.* characteristic, distinctive, unique. 3 *The baby has a special cup.* individual, particular, personal. 4 *a special tool for cutting glass.* proper, specialized, specific.

specialist *a specialist on foreign stamps.* authority, expert, professional.

species *a species of animal.* breed, class, race.

specific *I need specific information, not rumours.* definite, detailed, exact, particular, precise.

specimen *Give me a specimen of your handwriting.* example, illustration, instance, model, sample.

speck *a speck of dirt.* bit, dot, grain, mark, particle, spot.

speckled *a speckled pattern.* blotchy, dotted, mottled, spotty.

spectacle 1 *a colourful spectacle.* display, exhibition, scene, show, sight. 2 *the spectacle of a coronation.* ceremony, grandeur, pageantry, pomp.

spectacles bifocals, glasses.

spectacular SEE **impressive**.

spectator 1 bystander, eyewitness, observer, onlooker, viewer, watcher, witness. 2 *spectators*: audience, crowd.

spectre *The spectre is supposed to appear at midnight.* apparition, ghost, phantom, spirit, (informal) spook.

speech 1 *the power of speech.* speaking. SEE ALSO **speak**. 2 *to give a speech.* lecture, talk.

speechless dumb, dumbfounded, mute, nonplussed, silent, tongue-tied.

speed 1 *What speed were you going?* pace, quickness, rate, velocity. 2 *He sped along.* to bolt, to career, to dart, to dash, to fly, to gallop, to hasten, to hurry, to hurtle, to race, to run, to rush, to shoot, to streak, to tear, (informal) to zoom.

speedy 1 *a speedy journey.* fast, quick, rapid, swift. 2 *a speedy reply.* hasty, immediate, instant, prompt, sudden.

spell 1 *We rested for a spell.* interval, period, phase, season, session, stretch, time. 2 *The witch cast a spell.* charm, enchantment.

spellbound *We were spellbound by the music.* bewitched, captivated, charmed, enchanted, entranced, fascinated.

spend 1 *How much did you spend?* to invest, to pay. 2 *We spent everything we had.* to consume, to exhaust, to squander, to use up.

sphere ball, globe.

spice SPICES INCLUDE: ginger, pepper.

spike point, prong.

spiky *a spiky bush.* bristly, prickly, thorny.

spill 1 *Water spilled over the edge.* to brim, to flow, to overflow, to run, to pour, to run, to slop. 2 *The lorry spilled its load.* to drop, to overturn, to scatter, to shed, to tip.

spin *A wheel spins on an axle.* to revolve, to rotate, to swirl, to turn, to twirl, to whirl.

spine 1 backbone. 2 *A hedgehog has sharp spines.* bristle, needle, point, spike.

spineless *a spineless coward.* cowardly, faint-hearted, feeble, helpless, timid, unheroic, weak, weedy.

spirit 1 soul. 2 *supernatural spirits.* apparition, demon, devil, ghost, imp, phantom, (informal) spook. 3 *The marathon runners had great spirit.* bravery, cheerfulness, confidence, courage, daring, determination, fortitude, heroism, morale, pluck, valour.

spirited 1 *a spirited game.* animated, frisky, lively, sprightly, vigorous. 2 *a spirited attempt.* brave, courageous, daring, gallant, intrepid, plucky.

spiteful *spiteful remarks.* bitter, catty, hateful, malevolent, malicious, resentful, revengeful, sour, vicious, vindictive.

splash *The dolphin splashed water all over us.* to shower, to slop, to spatter, to spill.

splendid *a splendid banquet, splendid clothes, etc.* admirable, beautiful, brilliant, dazzling, elegant, excellent, first-class, glittering, glorious, gorgeous, grand, great, handsome, imposing, impressive, lavish, luxurious, magnificent, majestic, marvellous, noble, (informal) super, superb, wonderful.

splinter 1 *a splinter of wood.* chip, flake, fragment. 2 *to splinter a piece of wood.* to chip, to crack, to fracture, to shatter, to smash, to split.

split 1 *We split the class into two.* to divide, to separate. 2 *The axe split the log.* to burst, to chop, to crack, to rend, to slice. 3 *The roads split here.* to branch, to diverge, to fork. 4 *a split in a plank.* break, crack, slit.

spoil 1 *Don't spoil that nice piece of work.* to blot, to bungle, to damage, to deface, to destroy, to disfigure, to mar, to mess up, to ruin, to stain, to undo, to wreck. 2 *The fruit will spoil if we don't eat it.* to go bad, to perish, to rot. 3 *Grandad spoils us.* to indulge, to make a fuss of, to pamper.

sponge *to sponge down:* to clean, to mop, to rinse, to swill, to wash.

sponsor 1 *Will you sponsor me in a charity race?* to back, to help, to promote, to subsidize, to support. 2 *Our team's sponsor gave us some new equipment.* backer, benefactor, donor, promoter.

spontaneous *a spontaneous performance.* automatic, impromptu, impulsive, involuntary, natural, unplanned, unprepared, unrehearsed.

spooky (informal) *The big house was spooky in the dark.* creepy, eerie, frightening, ghostly, scary, uncanny, weird.

spool *a spool of film.* reel.

spoor *an animal's spoor.* footprints, traces, tracks.

sport 1 VARIOUS SPORTS: aerobics, angling, athletics, badminton, baseball, basketball, billiards, bobsleigh, bowls, boxing, bullfighting, canoeing, climbing, cricket, croquet, cross-country, darts, decathlon, discus, fishing, football, gliding, golf, gymnastics, hockey, hurdling, ice-hockey, javelin, marathon, martial arts (SEE **martial**), mountaineering, netball, orienteering, pentathlon, (informal) ping-pong, pole-vault, polo, pool, pot-holing, quoits, racing (SEE **race,**) rock-climbing, roller-skating, rounders, rowing, rugby, running, sailing, shot, show-jumping, skating, skiing, skin-diving, sky-diving, snooker, soccer, sprinting, squash, surf-riding, swimming (SEE **swim**), table-tennis, tennis, tobogganing, trampolining, volley-ball, water polo, water-skiing, windsurfing, wrestling, yachting. 2 PLACES WHERE SPORTS TAKE

PLACE: arena, boxing-ring, circuit, course, court, field, golf-course, grandstand, ground, gymnasium, ice-rink, links, pavilion, pitch, playing-field, race-course, race-track, stadium, stand. 3 WORDS TO DO WITH SPORT: ball, bat, club, cue, cup-tie, final, forward, goal, linesman, match, racket, referee, score-board, scorer, semi-final, shuttlecock, touch-judge, umpire.

spot 1 *a dirty spot.* blemish, blot, blotch, dot, mark, speck, stain. 2 *a spot of water.* bead, blob, drop. 3 VARIOUS SPOTS ON THE SKIN: boil, freckle, impetigo, mole, pimple, rash, sty. 4 *a nice spot for a picnic.* location, place, point, position, site, situation. 5 *We spotted a rare bird.* SEE **see.**

spotless clean, hygienic, washed.

spotty *to be spotty.* to have a rash.

spout 1 *Water came out of the spout.* gargoyle, jet, nozzle, outlet. 2 *Water spouted out.* to flow, to gush, to pour, to spurt, to squirt, to stream.

sprawl *We sprawled on the lawn.* to lean back, to lie, to lounge, to recline, to relax, to slouch, to spread out, to stretch out.

spray 1 *a spray of water.* fountain, shower. 2 *a spray of flowers.* bouquet, bunch, posy. 3 *I accidentally sprayed paint on the carpet.* to scatter, to shower, to spatter, to splash, to sprinkle.

spread 1 *to spread out a map.* to lay out, to open out, to unfold, to unroll. 2 *to spread butter.* to apply. 3 *to spread news.* to disperse, to distribute, to scatter. 4 *to spread out in a line.* to straggle.

sprightly *Great-granny is sprightly for 90 years old!* animated, brisk, lively, playful, quick-moving, spirited, vivacious.

spring 1 *He sprang over the fence.* to bounce, to bound, to jump, to leap, to pounce, to vault. 2 *Our seeds are springing up.* to emerge, to germinate, to grow, to shoot up, to sprout. 3 *This clock is worked by a spring.* coil.

springy bendy, elastic, flexible, floppy, pliable, supple.

sprinkle *We sprinkled water on the plants.* to drip, to scatter, to spatter, to splash, to spray.

sprint SEE **run.**

sprout *The seeds began to sprout.* to develop, to emerge, to germinate, to grow, to shoot up, to spring up.

spruce *He looked spruce in his best clothes.* clean, neat, posh, tidy, trim, well-dressed.

spur *Our success spurred us to even greater efforts.* (informal) to egg on, to encourage, to prompt, to stimulate, to urge.

spurt *Water spurted out of the leak.* to flow, to gush, to jet, to pour, to spout, to squirt, to stream.

spy 1 informer, (informal) mole, secret agent, tell-tale, undercover agent. 2 *to spy on an enemy.* to inform, to tell tales. 3 *spying*: espionage, intelligence. 4 *We spied a ship in the distance.* SEE **see.**

squabble *We won't get much done if we squabble.* to argue, to fall out, to fight, to quarrel.

squalid *squalid surroundings.* dirty, filthy, foul, (informal) mucky, sordid, unpleasant.

squander *Don't squander your money.* to fritter, to misuse, to use up, to waste.

squash *Don't squash the strawberries!* to compress to crumple, to crush, to mangle, to mash, to press, to pulp, to smash, to squeeze.

squat 1 *a squat figure.* dumpy, plump, podgy, short, stocky. 2 *to squat on the ground.* to crouch, to sit.

squeamish *He's squeamish about touching slimy things.* (informal) choosey, fastidious, finicky, prim.

squeeze 1 *He squeezed my hand.* to clasp, to compress, to crush, to grip, to hug, to pinch, to press, to squash, to wring. 2 *They squeezed us into a little room.* to crowd, to push, to shove.

squint 1 to be cross-eyed. 2 *We squinted through a crack in the door.* to peep, to peer. SEE ALSO **look.**

squirm *The worm squirmed.* to turn, to twist, to wriggle, to writhe.

squirt *Water squirted out.* to gush, to jet, to spout, to spray, to spurt.

stab *to stab with a dagger.* to jab, to pierce, to stick, to wound.

stabilize to make steady, to settle.

stable 1 *Make sure the tripod is stable.* firm, fixed, solid, sound, steady. 2 *a stable marriage.* continuing, durable, lasting, permanent.

stack 1 *a stack of books.* heap, mound, pile. 2 *a stack of hay.* rick. 3 *Stack the books on the table.* to accumulate, to collect, to heap, to mass, to pile.

stadium arena.

staff 1 *the staff of a business.* assistants, crew, employees, personnel, workers. 2 THE STAFF OF A SCHOOL: caretaker, head teacher, secretary. SEE ALSO **teacher.**

stage 1 *We performed our play on the stage.* platform. 2 *I went through an unsettled stage.* period, phase, time.

stagger 1 *He staggered after getting a knock on the head.* to falter, to reel, to stumble, to totter. 2 *The price staggered us.* to alarm, to amaze, to astound, to dismay, to shock, to startle, to stun, to surprise.

stagnant *stagnant water.* motionless, stale, static.

stain 1 *The bath is stained with rusty marks.* to blot, to defile, to discolour, to make dirty, to mark, to smudge, to soil, to tarnish. 2 *We stained the wood an oak colour.* to colour, to dye, to paint, to tint. 3 *What's that stain on your shirt?* blemish, blot, blotch, mark, smear, spot.

stairs escalator, staircase, steps.

stake 1 *a wooden stake.* pole, post, stick. 2 *to put a stake on a horse.* bet, wager.

stale *stale bread, stale news.* dry, old, out-of-date.

stalk 1 stem, twig. 2 *The lion stalked its prey.* to follow, to hound, to hunt, to pursue, to shadow, to track, to trail. 3 *He stalked up and down.* to prowl, to rove.

stall 1 *a sweet stall.* booth, kiosk, stand. 2 *Stop stalling!* to delay, to hang back, to hesitate, to pause, to postpone, to put off, to stop.

stamp 1 *Don't stamp on the poor spider!* to crush, to trample, to tread. 2 *to stamp a mark on something.* to brand, to mark, to print. 3 *The king put his stamp on the document.* seal. 4 *I put a stamp on my letter.* postage stamp.

stampede *The cattle stampeded.* to bolt, to career, to dash, to panic, to rush.

stand 1 *We stand when a visitor comes in.* to get up, to rise. 2 *A statue stands in the square.* to be, to exist. 3 *I stood my books on a shelf.* to arrange, to deposit, to put up, to set up, to situate, to station. 4 *The offer I made yesterday still stands.* to be unchanged, to continue, to persist, to remain, to stay. 5 *She can't stand people who smoke.* to abide, to bear, to endure, to put up with, to tolerate. 6 *What do these initials stand for?* to be a sign for, to indicate, to mean, to represent, to symbolize. 7 *The church spire stands out.* to be obvious, to be prominent, to show, to stick out. 8 *to stand up to:* to clash with, to confront, to defy, to face up to, to oppose, to resist, to withstand. 9 *to stand up for:* to defend, to help, to protect, to shield, to speak up for, to support. 10 *a stand for a telescope.* base, support, tripod. 11 *a newspaper stand.* booth, kiosk, stall.

standard 1 *a standard procedure, a standard size.* accustomed, common, conventional, customary, everyday, familiar, habitual, normal, ordinary, orthodox, regular, routine, typical, usual. 2 *The regiment flew its standard.* banner, colours, ensign, flag. 3 *a high standard of work.* achievement, grade, level. 4 *By what standard are you judging us?* ideal, measurement.

stand-in deputy, reserve, substitute.

stand-offish SEE **unfriendly.**

standpoint *Can you understand my standpoint?* attitude, belief, opinion, position, view.

standstill *to come to a standstill.* halt, stop.

stare *What are you staring at?* to contemplate, to examine, to gape, to gaze, to study, to watch. SEE ALSO **look.**

start 1 *We start our holiday on Saturday.* to begin, to commence, to embark on. 2 *to start a business, to start a process.* to activate, to create, to found, to initiate, to introduce, to open, to originate, to set up. 3 *A loud bang made me start.* to flinch, to jerk, to jump, to twitch, to wince.

startle *The explosion startled us.* to alarm, to frighten, to jolt, to scare, to shake, to shock, to surprise, to upset.

starvation *to die of starvation.* famine, hunger, malnutrition.

starve 1 *to starve yourself:* to fast, to go without. 2 *starving:* emaciated, famished, hungry, ravenous, underfed.

state 1 *He was in a terrible state!* condition, fitness, health, situation. 2 *It's important for a state to have a good government.* country, nation. 3 *The head stated that we'd raised £500.* to announce, to assert, to comment, to communicate, to declare, to proclaim, to remark, to report, to say.

stately *a stately palace.* dignified, grand, imposing, majestic, noble, regal, royal. SEE ALSO **splendid.**

statement *an official statement.* announcement, comment, communication, communiqué, declaration, message, notice, proclamation, report.

static motionless, stagnant, stationary.

station 1 *a radio station.* channel, wavelength. 2 *We stationed a look-out at the door.* to locate, to place, to position, to put, to situate, to stand.

stationary *stationary cars.* immobile, motionless, static, still, unmoving. ! Notice the difference in spelling between *stationary* and *stationery*.

stationery paper, writing materials.

statistics data, figures, numbers.

statue carving, figure, image, sculpture.

status *high status, low status.* class, level, position, rank, title.

stay 1 *Stay here.* to carry on, to continue, to endure, to keep on, to last, to linger, to live on, to persist, to remain, to survive, to wait. 2 *Will you stay with us?* (old-fashioned) to abide, to be accommodated, to be housed, to board, to dwell, to live, to lodge, to reside, to visit.

steady 1 *a steady foundation.* fast, firm, immovable, secure, solid, stable. 2 *a steady supply of food.* consistent, constant, continuous, dependable, regular, reliable. 3 *a steady rhythm.* even, invariable, repeated, rhythmic, unchanging. 4 *a steady friend.* devoted, faithful, loyal. 5 *Baby is steady on her feet now.* balanced, confident, poised. 6 *We steadied the rocking boat.* to hold, to secure, to stabilize.

steal 1 to loot, (informal) to nick, to pilfer, (informal) to pinch, to rob, to sneak, (informal) to swipe, to take. 2 *I stole quietly upstairs.* to creep, to move stealthily, to slink.

stealthy *stealthy movements.* furtive, quiet, secretive, shifty, sneaky, sly.

steam condensation, smoke, vapour.

steamy 1 *steamy windows.* cloudy, hazy, misty. 2 *a steamy atmosphere.* close, damp, humid, moist, muggy.

steed horse.

steep *a steep cliff.* abrupt, precipitous, sharp, sheer, sudden, vertical.

steer *to steer a vehicle.* to control, to drive, to guide, to pilot.

stem stalk, trunk, twig.

stench *the stench of rotting meat.* odour, reek, smell, stink, whiff.

step 1 *I took a step forward.* pace, stride. 2 *I climbed up the steps.* stair, stepladder. 3 *Starting at a new school is an important step.* phase, stage. 4 *Don't step in the mud!* to trample, to tread, to walk. 5 *The rioters stepped up the violence.* to escalate, to increase.

sterile 1 *sterile land.* arid, barren, dry, infertile, lifeless, unproductive. 2 *sterile bandages.* SEE **sterilize.**

sterilize 1 to disinfect, to purify. 2 *sterilized: sterilized bandages.* clean, disinfected, germ-free, hygienic, pure, sterile.

stern 1 *The head was stern when he told me off.* austere, forbidding, grim, hard, harsh, severe, strict. 2 *the stern of a ship.* back, rear.

stew 1 *We stewed some apples.* to boil. 2 *We had stew for dinner.* goulash, hash, hot-pot.

steward 1 *a steward on a ship.* attendant, waiter. 2 *a steward at a race-course.* officer, official.

stick 1 *We collected sticks for firewood.* branch, stalk, twig. 2 OTHER KINDS OF STICK: bar, baton, cane, club, pole, rod, staff, walking-stick, wand. 3 *A thorn stuck into my tyre.* to jab, to pierce, to puncture, to stab, to thrust. 4 *The pages stuck together.* to adhere, to glue. 5 *The door stuck.* to jam, to wedge. 6 *He stuck at his work.* to continue, to remain, to stay, to stop. 7 *I hit my head on a shelf which stuck out.* to jut, to overhang, to project, to protrude. 8 *The spire sticks up above the other buildings.* to loom, to rise, to stand out, to tower.

sticky *sticky tape.* adhesive, gluey, gummed, tacky.

stiff 1 *stiff clay.* firm, heavy, solid, thick, unyielding. 2 *stiff cardboard.* hard, inflexible, rigid, unbending. 3 *stiff joints.* immovable, paralysed, tight, wooden. 4 *a stiff task.* difficult, hard, severe, tough, uphill. 5 *stiff opposition.* powerful, strong.

stifle 1 to choke, to smother, to strangle, to suffocate, to throttle. 2 *We stifled our giggles.* to deaden, to muffle, to silence, to suppress. 3 *stifling*: SEE **stuffy.**

still 1 *a still evening.* calm, noiseless, peaceful, placid, quiet, serene, silent, tranquil, untroubled. 2 *Keep still!* immobile, motionless, static, stationary, unmoving.

stimulate *to stimulate interest.* to arouse, to excite, to incite, to inspire, to invigorate, to prompt, to provoke, to rouse, to stir up, to urge.

stimulus encouragement, incentive, inspiration.

sting 1 *Some insects sting.* to bite, to nip. 2 *These ant bites do sting!* to ache, to hurt, to throb, to tingle.

stingy 1 *a stingy miser.* close, mean, (informal) mingy, miserly. 2 *stingy helpings.* inadequate, meagre, (informal) measly, scanty, small.

stink *a nasty stink.* odour, reek, stench, whiff. SEE ALSO **smell.**

stir 1 *Stir the ingredients thoroughly.* to agitate, to beat, to mix, to whisk. 2 *Stir yourself!* SEE **move.** 3 *The music stirred us.* to affect, to arouse, to excite, to impress, to inspire, to move, to rouse, to stimulate, to touch.

stitch *He stitched the hole in his jeans.* to darn, to mend, to repair, to sew, to tack.

stock 1 *We keep a stock of crisps.* store, supply. 2 *We boiled the bones to make stock.* broth, soup. 3 *The farmer bought some new stock.* animals, livestock. 4 *Our local shop stocks most things.* to keep, to sell, to supply.

stockade fence, paling, palisade, wall.

stockist merchant, retailer, shopkeeper, supplier.

stocky *a stocky figure.* dumpy, short, squat, sturdy.

stodgy 1 *a stodgy pudding.* firm, heavy, lumpy, soggy, solid, starchy. 2 *a stodgy lecture.* boring, dull, tedious, uninteresting.

stomach abdomen, belly, (informal) tummy.

stone 1 VARIOUS STONES: boulders, cobbles, gems, gravel, jewels, pebbles, rocks, scree. SEE ALSO **jewellery, rock. 2** *a plum stone.* pip, seed.

stony 1 *a stony beach.* pebbly, rocky, rough, shingly. **2** *a stony expression.* cold, hard, heartless, indifferent, uncaring, unfeeling, unfriendly.

stool SEE **seat.**

stoop to bend, to bow, to crouch, to kneel, to lean.

stop 1 *The referee stopped the game. The music stopped.* to break off, to cease, to cut off, to discontinue, to end, to finish, to halt, to terminate. **2** *An accident stopped the traffic.* to bar, to block, to check, to curb, to delay, to hamper, to hinder, to immobilize, to impede. **3** *Wait for the bus to stop.* to draw up, to halt, to pull up. **4** *Stop the thief!* to arrest, to capture, to catch, to detain, to hold, to seize. **5** *We came to a stop.* halt, standstill.

stopper *Put the stopper in the bottle.* bung, cork, plug.

store 1 *a store of supplies.* cache, depot, reserve, stock, supply. **2** *a grocery store.* supermarket. SEE ALSO **shop. 3** *We store food in the pantry.* to accumulate, to keep, to preserve, to put away, to reserve, to save, to stock, to stow away.

storey *The building has six storeys.* floor, level. ! Don't confuse this word with *story.*

storm 1 KINDS OF STORM: blizzard, cyclone, deluge, gale, hurricane, rainstorm, tempest, thunderstorm, tornado, typhoon, whirlwind. **2** *The army stormed the castle.* to assault, to attack, to charge, to raid.

story *the story of my life.* account, narration, narrative, report, tale, yarn.

stout 1 *stout rope.* sound, strong, sturdy, thick. **2** *a stout gentleman.* chubby, fat, heavy, overweight, plump, portly, stocky, tubby. **3** *a stout fighter.* bold, brave, courageous, fearless, gallant, heroic, intrepid, plucky, spirited, valiant.

stove boiler, cooker, oven.

stow 1 *We stowed our camping things in the attic.* to put away, to store. **2** *We stowed our luggage in the car.* to load, to pack.

straggle 1 *Some of the runners straggled behind.* to dawdle, to fall behind, to lag, to loiter. **2** *straggling:* scattered, spread out.

straight 1 *a straight line.* direct, unswerving. **2** *Put the room straight.* neat, orderly, tidy. **3** *a straight answer.* SEE **straightforward.**

straightforward 1 *a straightforward question.* easy, simple, uncomplicated. **2** *a straightforward answer.* blunt, candid, frank, honest, plain, straight, truthful.

strain 1 *The sailors strained at the ropes.* to pull, to stretch, to tighten. **2** *He strained to escape from the monster's grasp.* to attempt, to exert yourself, to make an effort, to strive, to struggle, to try. **3** *Don't strain yourself.* to exhaust, to tire out, to weaken, to wear out, to weary. **4** *I strained a muscle during training.* to damage, to hurt, to injure. **5** *I strained the lumps out of the gravy.* to filter, to sieve, to sift. **6** *Mum has been under a lot of strain lately.* anxiety, difficulty, hardship, pressure, stress, tension, worry.

strait *the Straits of Gibraltar.* channel.

strand 1 *a strand of cotton.* fibre, thread. **2** *The pirates stranded Ben Gunn on the island.* to abandon, to desert, to forsake, to maroon. **3** *stranded: a stranded ship.* aground, helpless.

strange 1 *a strange event.* abnormal, curious, extraordinary, funny, irregular, odd, peculiar, queer, singular, unaccustomed, uncommon, unnatural, unusual, weird. **2** *strange behaviour.* (informal) cranky, eccentric, unconventional, weird. **3** *a strange problem.* baffling, inexplicable, insoluble, mysterious, puzzling. **4** *a strange appearance.* alien, foreign, new, novel, unfamiliar.

stranger *I'm a stranger here.* alien, foreigner, outsider, visitor.

strangle to choke, to suffocate, to throttle.

strap belt.

strategy *We worked out a strategy to beat the opposition.* manoeuvre, method, plan, plot, policy, scheme, tactics.

stratum *a stratum of rock.* layer, seam, thickness.

straw corn, stalks, stubble.

stray *It's dangerous to stray in the hills.* to get lost, to go astray, to range, to roam, to rove, to wander.

streak 1 *The rocket left a streak of smoke in the sky.* band, line, stripe. 2 *The rain streaked the new paint.* to smear, to smudge.

stream 1 *We had to cross a stream.* brook, burn, river. 2 *A stream of water poured through the hole.* cataract, current, flood, jet, rush, spate, tide, torrent. 3 *Water streamed through the hole.* to flow, to gush, to pour, to spout, to spurt, to squirt.

streamer banner, flag.

street SEE **road.**

strength 1 *You need good food to build up your strength.* condition, fitness, health, vigour. 2 *Have you got the strength to lift that weight?* energy, force, might, power.

strengthen 1 *to strengthen your muscles.* to build up, to fortify, to make stronger, to toughen. 2 *to strengthen a fence.* to prop up, to reinforce, to support.

strenuous 1 *strenuous work.* arduous, difficult, exhausting, gruelling, laborious, stiff, tough, uphill. 2 *strenuous efforts.* active, determined, dynamic, energetic, firm, powerful, resolute, vigorous.

stress 1 *a time of stress.* anxiety, difficulty, hardship, pressure, strain, tension, worry. 2 *The trainer stressed that we must keep fit.* to assert, to emphasize, to insist, to underline.

stretch 1 *to stretch elastic.* to draw out, to elongate, to lengthen, to pull out. 2 *to stretch out your arms.* to extend, to reach, to spread. 3 *a stretch in prison.* period, spell, time. 4 *a stretch of road.* distance, length.

strict 1 *strict discipline.* austere, firm, harsh, severe, stern. 2 *a strict rule.* hard, inflexible, unchangeable. 3 *the strict truth.* accurate, correct, exact, precise, right, true.

stride 1 *He strode along the road.* SEE **walk.** 2 *Take two strides forward.* pace, step.

strife SEE **conflict.**

strike 1 *I struck my head.* SEE **hit.** 2 *The employees had a strike.* industrial action, stoppage.

striking *striking colours.* conspicuous, impressive, noticeable, obvious, prominent, showy, unmistakable.

string 1 *We tied it up with string.* cord, line, rope, twine. 2 *a string of coincidences.* chain, progression, row, sequence, series.

strings MUSICAL INSTRUMENTS WITH STRINGS: banjo, cello, double-bass, fiddle, guitar, harp, lute, lyre, sitar, viola, violin, zither.

stringy *stringy meat.* tough.

strip 1 *Strip off your clothes.* to peel off, to remove, to take off. 2 *Strip to the waist.* to bare, to expose, to uncover, to undress. 3 *a strip of carpet down the stairs.* band, line, ribbon, stripe.

stripe *Our football shirts have red and white stripes.* band, line, strip.

stroke 1 *He scored six with his first stroke.* action, blow, hit, knock, movement. 2 *Stroke the cat.* to caress, to pat, to pet.

stroll SEE **walk.**

strong 1 *a strong person.* athletic, beefy, brawny, burly, hardy, hefty, mighty, muscular, sturdy, tough, wiry. 2 *a strong attack.* forceful, powerful, severe, vehement, vigorous, violent. 3 *a strong fortress.* impregnable, invincible, unconquerable. 4 *strong shoes.* durable, robust, sound, well-made. 5 *strong rope.* stout, thick, unbreakable. 6 *a strong smell.* noticeable, obvious, prominent, pronounced, unmistakable. 7 *strong drink.* alcoholic, concentrated, potent, undiluted. 8 *strong evidence.* clear, evident, plain, solid, undisputed. 9 *a strong interest.* eager, earnest, enthusiastic, fervent, keen, zealous.

stronghold castle, citadel, fort, fortress, garrison.

structure building, construction, edifice, framework.

struggle 1 *to struggle to achieve something.* to endeavour, to exert yourself, to make an effort, to strain, to strive, to try, to work hard. 2 *to struggle with an enemy.* to clash, to compete, to conflict, to contend, to fight, to grapple, to oppose, to rival, to wrestle. 3 KINDS OF STRUGGLE: battle, bout, brawl, combat, competition, conflict, confrontation, contest, duel, feud, hostilities, quarrel, rivalry, row, scrap, scuffle, squabble, tussle, war. 4 *We struggled through the mud.* to flounder, to wallow.

strut SEE **walk.**

stubborn *The stubborn animal refused to move.* defiant, disobedient, dogged, inflexible, obstinate, rigid, unmanageable, unyielding, wilful.

stuck-up arrogant, bumptious, cocky, conceited, proud, self-important.

student learner, pupil, scholar, undergraduate.

studious *a studious pupil.* academic, brainy, intellectual.

study 1 *The jury studied the evidence.* to analyse, to consider, to enquire into, to examine, to investigate, to learn about, to read about, to think about. 2 *to study for an examination.* to learn, to read, (informal) to swot.

stuff 1 *What's that stuff in the jar?* matter, substance. 2 *Mum bought some stuff to make a skirt.* cloth, fabric, material, textile. 3 *That's my stuff in that drawer.* articles, belongings, possessions, things. 4 *I stuffed everything into a suitcase.* to cram, to fill, to jam, to pack, to squeeze, to tuck.

stuffy *a stuffy room.* airless, close, humid, muggy, oppressive, steamy, stifling, warm.

stumble to blunder, to falter, to hesitate, to stagger, to totter, to trip, to tumble.

stump *The riddle stumped us.* to baffle, to bewilder, to perplex, to puzzle.

stun 1 *The blow stunned him.* to daze, to knock out, to make unconscious, to numb. 2 *The terrible news stunned us.* to amaze, to astonish, to astound, to bewilder, to dumbfound, to shock.

stunt exploit, feat, trick.

stupendous amazing, exceptional, extraordinary, incredible, miraculous, notable, phenomenal, remarkable, singular, special, unbelievable.

stupid 1 *a stupid decision.* absurd, crazy, foolish, idiotic, irrational, silly, unintelligent. 2 *a stupid person.* dense, dim, dull, obtuse, slow, (informal) thick.

sturdy 1 *a sturdy person.* burly, hardy, healthy, hefty, robust, sound, stocky, strong, tough. 2 *a sturdy pair of shoes.* durable, well-made.

stutter to stammer.

style *the latest style of dancing.* fashion, manner, method, mode, way.

stylish *stylish clothes.* contemporary, fashionable, modern, (informal) posh, smart, sophisticated, (informal) trendy, up-to-date.

subdue 1 *We subdued the opposition.* to beat, to conquer, to defeat, to master, to overcome. 2 *Subdue your excitement!* to check, to control, to curb, to hold back, to quell, to restrain, to suppress. 3 *subdued: a subdued mood, subdued music.* grave, hushed, peaceful, placid, quiet, soft, solemn, soothing, toned down.

subject 1 *a subject for discussion.* affair, issue, matter, theme, topic. 2 SUBJECTS WHICH STUDENTS STUDY: anatomy, archaeology, architecture, art, astronomy, biology, botany, business, chemistry, computing, craft, drama, ecology, economics, education, electronics, engineering, English, environment, geography, geology, heraldry, history, languages, Latin, law, literature, mathematics, mechanics, medicine, meteorology, music, ornithology, philosophy, physics, politics, psychology, religious studies, science, scripture, social work, sport, surveying, technology, theology, zoology.

submerge 1 *The submarine submerged.* to dive, to go under, to subside. 2 *The flood submerged the whole village.* to cover, to drown, to engulf, to flood, to immerse.

submit 1 *to submit to an opponent.* to capitulate, to give in, to surrender, to yield. 2 *to submit to a decision.* to conform to, to keep to, to obey. 3 *to submit entries for a competition.* to give in, to hand in, to offer, to present.

subordinate *subordinate rank.* inferior, junior, lower.

subscription *a club subscription.* contribution, fee, payment.

subsequent *I came last in the first race, but subsequent races went better.* following, later, next, succeeding.

subside 1 *The flood gradually subsided.* to decline, to diminish, to dwindle, to go down, to lessen, to melt away, to shrink. 2 *I subsided into a comfortable chair.* to rest, to settle, to sink.

subsidize *Our parents subsidized the cost of our trip.* to aid, to back, to sponsor, to support.

substance material, matter, stuff.

substantial 1 *a substantial door.* strong, well-made. 2 *a substantial amount of money.* big, considerable, large, significant, sizeable.

substitute 1 *They sent on a substitute.* deputy, replacement, reserve, stand-in. 2 *I substituted an apple for the chocolate.* to change, to exchange, to replace, to swop.

subtle 1 *a subtle argument.* clever, ingenious, sophisticated. 2 *a subtle flavour.* delicate, faint, gentle, mild.

subtract to deduct, to take away.

suburb outskirts.

subway tunnel, underpass.

succeed 1 *If you work hard you will succeed.* to be successful, to do well, to flourish, to grow, to prosper, to thrive. 2 *Did your plan succeed?* to be effective, to work. 3 *Elizabeth II succeeded George VI.* to come after, to follow, to replace, to take over from.

success 1 *We were pleased with the success of our plan.* accomplishment, achievement, attainment, prosperity. 2 *The plan was a success.* triumph, victory.

successful 1 *a successful business.* flourishing, fruitful, prosperous, well-off. 2 *a successful team.* victorious, winning.

succession *a succession of disasters.* line, progression, sequence, series, string.

successor *the successor to the throne.* heir, replacement, substitute.

sudden 1 *a sudden decision, a sudden rainstorm.* abrupt, hasty, quick, sharp, swift, unexpected. 2 *a sudden illness.* acute.

suds bubbles, foam, froth, lather.

sue to prosecute.

suede leather.

suffer 1 *to suffer pain.* to bear, to cope with, to endure, to experience, to go through, to put up with, to stand, to tolerate, to undergo. 2 *suffering:* SEE **pain**.

sufficient *Have we got sufficient food?* adequate, enough.

suffocate to choke, to smother, to stifle, to strangle, to throttle.

sugar 1 KINDS OF SUGAR: castor, demerara, granulated, icing, lump. 2 OTHER FORMS OF SUGAR: sweets, syrup, treacle.

sugary sweet.

suggest 1 *Which brand did the shopkeeper suggest?* to advise, to offer, to propose, to recommend. 2 *The closed curtains suggest they are still in bed.* to hint, to imply, to indicate, to mean.

suit *That colour suits you.* to become, to be suitable for, to fit.

suitable *a suitable present for granny.* acceptable, appropriate, apt, becoming, convenient, fitting, handy, proper, timely.

suitor lover, sweetheart, wooer.

sulk *He sulked because he lost.* to be sulky, to brood, to mope.

sulky *a sulky look.* bad-tempered, cross, disgruntled, moody, sad. sullen.

sullen 1 *a sullen expression.* bad-tempered, moody, sulky. 2 *a sullen sky.* dark, dismal, gloomy, sombre.

sultry *sultry weather.* close, hot, humid, muggy, oppressive, steamy, stifling, stuffy, warm.

sum *Add up the sum.* amount, number, total, whole.

summarize *The judge summarized the evidence.* to sum up.

summary outline.

summit *the summit of a mountain.* head, peak, top.

summon *The head summoned me to his office.* to call, to send for.

sumptuous *a sumptuous banquet.* costly, grand, lavish, luxurious, magnificent, rich, splendid, superb.

sunburn sunstroke, sun-tan.

sunless *a sunless day.* cloudy, dull, grey, overcast.

sunny *a sunny day.* bright, clear, fine.

sunrise dawn, day-break.

sunset dusk, evening, twilight.

sun-tan sunburn, tan.

super, superb SEE **splendid.**

superficial *a superficial wound.* not deep, shallow, slight, trivial, unimportant.

superfluous *Why not give away your superfluous possessions?* excessive, redundant, unnecessary, unwanted.

superintendent officer, supervisor.

superior 1 *superior quality.* better, greater. 2 *a superior rank.* higher, senior. 3 *a superior attitude.* arrogant, haughty, self-important, smug, snobbish, (informal) stuck-up.

supernatural *Witches are supposed to have supernatural powers.* magical, miraculous, mysterious, psychic, spiritual.

superstar idol, star.

supervise *We need an adult to supervise our swimming party.* to administer, to control, to direct, to look after, to manage, to run, to watch over.

supple *Gymnasts look so supple.* flexible, graceful, pliable, soft.

supplement *You pay a supplement if you travel first class.* addition, bonus, extra.

supplementary *a supplementary fare.* additional, auxiliary, extra.

supplier SEE **shopkeeper.**

supply 1 *A local firm supplied our new sports equipment.* to contribute, to donate, to equip, to furnish, to give, to provide. 2 *a supply of sweets.* reserve, stock, store. 3 *supplies:* equipment, food, provisions, rations.

support 1 *Those pillars support the roof.* to bear, to carry, to hold up, to prop up. 2 *The lame man supported himself on a crutch.* to lean, to rest. 3 *My friend supported me in the debate.* to aid, to defend, to encourage, to reassure, to speak up for, to stand up for. 4 *Is there any evidence to support your story?* to explain, to justify, to verify. 5 *It costs a lot to support a family.* to feed, to keep, to maintain, to pay for, to provide for. 6 *Which team do you support?* to back, to be interested in, to follow. 7 *Thank you for your support.* aid, assistance, backing, co-operation, help.

supporter *a football supporter.* enthusiast, fan, follower.

suppose *I suppose you want some food?* to assume, to believe, to fancy, to guess, to imagine, to judge, to presume, to think.

suppress *The soldiers suppressed the rebellion.* to crush, to overcome, to put an end to, to quell, to subdue.

supreme best, greatest, highest.

sure 1 *He's sure to come.* bound, certain, compelled, obliged, required. 2 *I'm sure I'm right.* assured, confident, convinced, definite, positive. 3 *He's a sure ally.* dependable, faithful, loyal, reliable, safe, steady, trustworthy, undoubted.

surf breakers, waves.

surface 1 *It looks nice on the surface.* coat, covering, crust, exterior, outside, shell, skin. 2 *A cube has six surfaces.* face, side. 3 *The submarine surfaced.* to come up, to emerge.

surge *The crowd surged forward.* to move, to push, to rush.

surgery *They can cure appendicitis by surgery.* operation.

surly *a surly temper.* bad-tempered, cross, gruff, grumpy, irascible, peevish, rude, sulky, sullen, unfriendly.

surpass *The success of the sale surpassed our expectations.* to beat, to do better, to exceed, to excel, to outdo, to top.

surplus *If you've got too many sandwiches, give the surplus to me!* excess, extra, remainder.

surprise 1 *The news was a complete surprise.* bombshell, shock. 2 *The news surprised us.* to alarm, to amaze, to astonish, to astound, to dismay, to dumbfound, to shock, to startle, to stun. 3 *We surprised him writing rude words on the wall.* to catch, to catch out, to discover, to take unawares. 4 *surprising:* accidental, sudden, unexpected, unforeseen, unplanned.

surrender *After a long fight, they surrendered.* to capitulate, to give in, to submit, to yield.

surround *The police surrounded the area.* to besiege, to encircle, to ring.

surroundings environment.

survey 1 *a survey of local facilities.* examination, investigation, look, study. 2 *to survey a house.* to examine, to inspect, to investigate, to look over, to view.

survive *You can't survive without water.* to carry on, to continue, to endure, to keep going, to last, to live, to persist, to remain.

suspect 1 *I suspect his promises.* to distrust, to doubt, to mistrust. 2 *I suspect that he's lying.* to guess, to imagine, to presume, to suppose, to think.

suspend 1 *We suspended a rope from a branch.* to dangle, to hang, to swing. 2 *We had to suspend the meeting.* to adjourn, to break off, to defer, to delay, to interrupt, to postpone, to put off.

suspense *We were full of suspense as we wondered who had first prize.* drama, excitement, tension, uncertainty.

suspicion *I had a suspicion that she was lying.* distrust, doubt, feeling, misgiving, uncertainty.

suspicious 1 *There's no need to be so suspicious!* disbelieving, distrustful, incredulous, sceptical, unconvinced, wary. 2 *a suspicious character.* disreputable, dubious, shady, unreliable, untrustworthy.

swag (informal) *robber's swag.* booty, loop, plunder, takings.

swallow 1 SEE **drink, eat.** 2 *The ship was swallowed up in the fog.* to enclose, to engulf.

swamp 1 *Don't sink into the swamp!* bog, fen, marsh, quagmire, quicksands. 2 *A tidal wave swamped the town.* to deluge, to engulf, to flood, to inundate, to overwhelm, to submerge.

swan *a young swan:* cygnet.

swank to boast, to brag, (informal) to crow, to gloat, to show off.

swarm *Ants were swarming over the sugar.* to infest, to overrun, to teem.

swarthy *a swarthy skin.* brown, dark, tanned.

sway to rock, to swing.

swear 1 *He swore that he wasn't lying.* to give your word, to pledge, to promise, to take an oath, to testify, to vow. 2 *swearing:* bad language, blasphemy, curses, foul language, obscenity, swear-words.

sweat to perspire.

sweep *Sweep the floor.* to brush, to clean.

sweet 1 SWEET THINGS: saccharine, sweets, syrup. SEE ALSO **sugar.** 2 VARIOUS SWEETS: acid drop, barley sugar, boiled sweet, bull's eye, butterscotch, candy, candy-floss, chewing-gum, chocolate, fruit pastille, fudge, humbug, liquorice, lollipop, marzipan, mint, nougat, peppermint, rock, toffee. 3 *We had jelly as a sweet.* dessert, pudding.

sweetheart beloved, boy-friend, darling, fiancé, fiancée, girl-friend, lover, suitor, wooer.

swell 1 *The balloon swelled as it filled with air.* to billow, to blow up, to bulge, to distend, to enlarge, to grow, to increase, to puff up. 2 *the swell of the ocean.* waves.

swelling *a painful swelling.* bulge, hump, knob, lump.

sweltering *a sweltering summer day.* baking, boiling, hot, oppressive, scorching, sizzling, steamy, stifling, sultry.

swerve *The car swerved to avoid the hedgehog.* to change direction, to dodge about, to turn, to veer, to wheel.

swift *a swift journey.* brisk, fast, (informal) nippy, quick, rapid, speedy.

swill *Swill the plates in clear water.* to bathe, to clean, to rinse, to wash.

swim 1 to bathe, to dive in, to float, to go swimming, to take a dip. 2 VARIOUS SWIMMING STROKES: backstroke, breast-stroke, butterfly, crawl.

swimming-pool baths, pool.

swindle *He swindled us by charging too much.* to cheat, to deceive, to defraud, to dupe, to fool, to hoax, to hoodwink, to trick.

swine hog, pig.

swing *to swing to and fro.* to dangle, to flap, to rock, to sway, to swivel, to turn, to wave.

swirl *The water swirled round.* to eddy, to spin, to twirl, to whirl.

switch *Will you switch places?* to change, to exchange, to replace, to substitute, to swop.

swivel *a swivelling chair.* to revolve, to rotate, to swing, to turn.

swoop   188

swoop 1 *The owl swooped down.* to
dive, to drop, to fly, to plunge, to
pounce. 2 *The police swooped on the
thieves' headquarters.* to raid.

swop SEE **exchange.**

swot (informal) to learn, to read, to
study, to work.

symbol 1 *We designed a symbol for our
club.* badge, emblem, sign. 2 *The
formula used symbols that I didn't
understand.* character, letter.

symbolize *Easter eggs symbolize the
renewing of life.* to be a sign for, to
communicate, to indicate, to represent,
to stand for.

symmetrical balanced, even.

sympathetic benevolent,
compassionate, friendly, humane,
merciful, pitying, sorry, tolerant,
understanding.

sympathize *We sympathized with
grandad when his dog died.* to be sorry
for, to comfort, to console, to feel for, to
pity.

sympathy compassion, consideration,
feeling, kindness, mercy, pity,
understanding.

symptom *Spots are a symptom of
measles.* indication, sign.

synthetic *Nylon is a synthetic material.*
artificial, man-made, manufactured,
unnatural.

system 1 *a railway system.* network,
organization. 2 *a system for doing
something.* method, procedure, process,
routine, technique.

systematic orderly, organized,
planned, scientific.

T

tablet 1 *a tablet of soap.* bar,
block, chunk, piece, slab. 2 *The
doctor prescribed some tablets.*
capsule, pellet, pill.

table-tennis (informal) ping-pong.

tack 1 *to tack down a carpet.* to nail,
to pin. 2 *to tack up the hem of a
garment.* to sew, to stitch.

tackle 1 *fishing tackle.* apparatus,
equipment, gear, kit, paraphernalia,
rig. 2 *to tackle a problem.* to attend
to, to cope with, to deal with, to
grapple with, to handle, to manage,
to sort out, to undertake.

tacky *The new paint was still tacky.*
gluey, sticky.

tactful *a tactful reminder.*
considerate, diplomatic, discreet,
polite.

tactics *We planned our tactics for
tomorrow's game.* manoeuvre, plan,
policy, scheme, strategy.

tactless *It's tactless to say that you
don't like the food.* impolite,
inconsiderate, insensitive,
undiplomatic, unwise.

tag *a price tag.* label, sticker,
ticket.

tail 1 back, end, rear. 2 *The police
tailed our car.* to follow, to pursue,
to shadow, to stalk, to track, to
trail. 3 *to tail off:* to decline, to
lessen, to reduce, to slacken, to
subside.

take 1 *Take my hand.* to clutch, to
grab, to grasp, to hold, to pluck, to
seize, to snatch. 2 *The soldiers took
prisoners.* to arrest, to capture, to
catch, to corner, to detain, to
seize. 3 *Who took my pen?* to move,
(informal) to nick, to pick up, to
pilfer, (informal) to pinch, to
remove, to sneak, to steal,
(informal) to swipe. 4 *The bus takes
you to the shopping centre.* to bring,
to carry, to convey, to transport. 5
I took granny round the garden. to
conduct, to guide, to lead. 6 *Take
your medicine.* to consume, to have,
to swallow, to use. 7 *He wouldn't
take any money.* to accept, to
receive. 8 *It took a lot of effort to
move the piano.* to need, to require,
to use up. 9 *to take away:* to deduct,
to subtract. 10 *to take in:* SEE
deceive. 11 *to take place:* to come about,
to happen, to occur.

takings *The shopkeeper added up her
takings.* income, proceeds, profits.

tale *She told us her tale.* account, narrative, story, yarn.

talent *musical talent.* ability, accomplishment, aptitude, genius, gift, know-how, prowess, skill.

talented *a talented musician.* able, accomplished, artistic, brilliant, expert, gifted, intelligent, skilful, skilled, versatile. SEE ALSO **clever.**

talk **1** *She talked all through the lesson. Can you talk in French?* to address someone, to communicate, to express yourself, to speak. SEE ALSO **say.** **2** WAYS OF TALKING: to babble, to bawl, to bellow, to blurt out, to call out, to chat, to chatter, to croak, to cry, to drone, to exclaim, to gabble, to gossip, to grunt, to harp, to howl, to jabber, to jeer, to lisp, to moan, to mumble, to murmur, to mutter, to prattle, to pray, to preach, to rave, to recite, to roar, to scream, to screech, to shout, to shriek, to snap, to snarl, to speak in an undertone, to splutter, (informal) to spout, to squeal, to stammer, to stutter, to utter, to wail, to whimper, to whine, to whisper, to yell. **3** *I had a talk with granny.* chat, conversation, dialogue, discussion. **4** *We heard an interesting talk about engineering.* address, lecture, speech.

talkative **1** chatty, communicative. **2** *a talkative person:* chatterbox.

tall *a tall tower.* high, lofty, towering. SEE ALSO **big.**

talon claw.

tame **1** *a tame animal.* docile, domesticated, gentle, meek, obedient, safe. **2** *a tame story.* boring, dull, feeble, tedious, unexciting, uninteresting.

tamper *Don't tamper with the TV set.* to interfere, to meddle, to play about, to tinker.

tan **1** sun-tan. **2** *tanned:* brown, sunburnt, weather-beaten.

tangible *tangible evidence.* physical, real, solid.

tangle **1** *Don't tangle the guy ropes.* to confuse, to entangle, to muddle, to twist. **2** *tangled: tangled hair.* dishevelled, knotted, matted, unkempt.

tangy SEE **tart.**

tank *fish tank:* aquarium.

tantalize *The delicious smell tantalized us.* to entice, to tease, to tempt, to torment.

tantrum *Baby had a tantrum when we took her sweets.* hysterics, rage, temper.

tap *I tapped on the door.* to knock, to rap.

tape *I tied the parcel with tape.* band, braid, ribbon, strip.

target *Our target was to raise £100.* aim, goal, objective.

tarnish *The chemicals tarnished the metal.* to blacken, to corrode, to discolour.

tart *Lemons have a tart taste.* acid, sharp, sour, tangy.

task activity, assignment, chore, duty, errand, job, work.

taste **1** *Taste a bit of this!* to nibble, to sip, to try. SEE ALSO **drink, eat. 2** *I like the taste of this.* character, flavour, quality. **3** *Can I have a taste?* bit, morsel, piece, titbit. **4** WORDS USED TO DESCRIBE TASTE: acid, appetizing, bitter, creamy, delicious, fresh, fruity, hot, luscious, meaty, mellow, peppery, rancid, salt, salty, savoury, sharp, sour, spicy, stale, sugary, sweet, tangy, tart, tasty.

tasteful *tasteful clothes.* attractive, dignified, elegant, fashionable, smart, stylish.

tasty SEE **taste.**

tattered *tattered clothes.* frayed, ragged, tatty, torn, worn out.

tatters rags, shreds.

tatty *tatty clothes.* frayed, old, patched, ragged, scruffy, shabby, tattered, torn, untidy, worn out.

taunt *They taunted him cruelly when he missed an easy goal.* to boo, to hiss, to hoot at, to jeer at, to laugh at, to mock, to ridicule, to scoff at, to sneer at.

taut *Make sure the rope is taut.* stretched, tense, tight.

tavern bar, inn, pub, public house.

tawdry cheap, fancy, flashy, gaudy, showy.

tax VARIOUS TAXES: customs, duty, rates.

taxi cab.

teach to coach, to indoctrinate, to inform, to instruct, to lecture, to train.

teacher VARIOUS TEACHERS: coach, guru, headteacher, instructor, lecturer, master, mistress, preacher, professor, schoolmaster, schoolmistress, schoolteacher, trainer, tutor.

team club, side.

tear 1 *He tore his jeans.* to rip, to shred, to slit, to split. 2 *The lion tore its prey apart.* to claw, to rend. 3 *There's a tear in his jeans.* cut, gash, hole, slit, split.

tearful SEE **sad.**

tease *The cat scratches if you tease her!* (informal) to aggravate, to annoy, to irritate, to laugh at, to make fun of, to pester, to ridicule, to tantalize, to torment, to vex.

technique *the technique of a craftsman.* art, craft, dodge, knack, know-how, method, procedure, routine, skill, system, trick, workmanship.

tedious *a tedious journey.* boring, dreary, dull, long-winded, monotonous, slow, tiresome, tiring, unexciting, uninteresting, wearisome.

teem 1 *The pond teemed with tadpoles.* to be full of, to be infested with, to be overrun by, to swarm with. 2 *The rain teemed down.* to pour.

teenager adolescent, juvenile, youngster, youth.

teeny SEE **small.**

teetotaller abstainer.

telegram cable, wire.

telepathic psychic.

telephone 1 *Telephone us if you can't come.* to call, to dial, to phone, to ring. 2 WORDS TO DO WITH TELEPHONES: dial, kiosk, receiver, telegraph pole, telephone box, switchboard.

televise *They televise a lot of snooker these days.* to broadcast, to relay, to send out, to transmit.

television 1 *a television set*: monitor, receiver, (informal) telly, (informal) the box, (informal) the small screen, video. 2 TELEVISION PROGRAMMES: cartoon, chat show, comedy, commercial, documentary, drama, film, interview, movie, news, panel game, play, quiz, serial, series, sport.

tell 1 *Tell us what happened.* to describe, to disclose, to divulge, to explain, to make known, to reveal. 2 *Tell us a story.* to narrate, to recount, to relate. 3 *He told me it would cost less than £10.* to advise, to assure, to inform, to promise. 4 *The teacher told us to stop.* to command, to direct, to instruct, to order. 5 *Can you tell who wrote this?* to discover, to discriminate, to distinguish, to identify, to recognize. 6 (informal) *to tell someone off*: to censure, to condemn, to criticize, to rebuke, to reprimand, to reproach, to scold, (informal) to tick off.

temper 1 *Mum's in a good temper.* disposition, humour, mood, state of mind. 2 *a bad temper*: anger, fury, rage, tantrum. SEE ALSO **angry.**

temperament *a melancholy temperament.* character, disposition, nature, personality.

temperamental *a temperamental person.* changeable, fickle, inconsistent, irritable, moody, touchy, unpredictable, variable.

temperature 1 SCALES FOR MEASURING TEMPERATURE: Celsius, centigrade, Fahrenheit. 2 FOR WORDS TO DO WITH TEMPERATURE SEE **cold, hot, weather.** 3 *to have a temperature*: to be feverish, to have a fever.

tempest cyclone, gale, hurricane, storm, tornado, typhoon, whirlwind.

tempo *the tempo of a piece of music.* pace, rhythm, speed.

temporary 1 *a temporary pause.* brief, momentary, passing, short, transient. 2 *a temporary captain.* acting.

tempt 1 *We tempted the mouse with a bit of cheese.* to bait, to bribe, to coax, to entice, to lure. 2 *tempting*: SEE **attractive.**

tenant *a tenant of a flat.* inhabitant, lodger, occupant, resident.

tend 1 *A shepherd tends sheep.* to attend to, to guard, to look after, to mind, to protect, to watch. 2 *Nurses tend their patients.* to care for, to cherish, to nurse, to treat. 3 *Dad tends to fall asleep in the evenings.* to be disposed to, to be inclined to, to be liable to, to have a tendency to.

tendency *Hedgehogs have a tendency to curl up when danger comes.* inclination, instinct, leaning, readiness, trend.

tender 1 *tender plants*. dainty, delicate, fragile. 2 *tender meat*. eatable, edible, not tough. 3 *tender care*. affectionate, compassionate, fond, kind, loving, merciful, soft-hearted, sympathetic, touching. 4 *a tender kiss*. gentle, soft. 5 *a tender wound*. painful, sensitive, sore.

tense 1 *With the scores equal, the competitors were tense*. anxious, edgy, excited, highly-strung, jittery, jumpy, nervous, strained, touchy, (informal) uptight. 2 *tense muscles*. stretched, taut, tight.

tension anxiety, suspense.

tent 1 KINDS OF TENT: marquee, tepee, wigwam. 2 PARTS OF A TENT: canvas, frame, groundsheet, guy rope, pole, tent-peg.

tepid lukewarm, warm.

term 1 *a term in prison*. period, session, spell, stretch. 2 *'Offside' is a term used in football*. expression, phrase, saying, word. 3 *We'll surrender if you agree to our terms*. conditions. 4 *The hotel's terms are reasonable*. charges, fees, prices, rates.

terminal *a terminal illness*. deadly, fatal, mortal.

terminate 1 *The head terminated our interview*. to close, to conclude, to end, to finish. 2 *The war terminated when the treaty was signed*. to cease, to stop.

terminus destination.

terrestrial *terrestrial beings*. earthly.

terrible *a terrible accident*. SEE **unpleasant**.

terrific (informal) 1 *It's a terrific size*. SEE **big**. 2 *We had a terrific time*. SEE **good**. 3 *It's a terrific problem*. SEE **serious**. ! *Terrific* once meant *terrifying*. Nowadays its meaning is usually rather vague.

terrify 1 to alarm, to appal, to dismay, to horrify, to make afraid, to petrify, to scare. SEE ALSO **frighten**. 2 *terrifying*: hair-raising, scary.

territory *enemy territory*. area, district, land, region, sector, zone.

terror alarm, dread, fear, fright, horror, panic.

terrorist assassin, gunman, hijacker.

terrorize *Their gang terrorized the infants*. to bully, to frighten, to intimidate, to persecute, to terrify, to threaten, to torment.

terse *a terse comment*. brief, concise, short.

test 1 *a maths test*. examination, quiz. 2 *a scientific test*. experiment, trial. 3 *The garage tested the steering*. to check, to examine, to inspect.

testify *The witness testified that she had been attacked*. to declare, to give evidence, to state on oath, to swear.

testimony evidence.

testy *a testy old gentleman*. bad-tempered, cross, disgruntled, grumpy, irascible, irritable, peevish, petulant, short-tempered, snappy.

tether 1 *They kept the goat on a tether*. chain, leash, rope. 2 *The goat was tethered*. to secure, to tie up.

textile fabric, material, stuff. SEE ALSO **cloth**.

thank to acknowledge, to show appreciation, to show gratitude.

thankful *I was thankful to be home*. appreciative, grateful, pleased.

thaw *The snow thawed*. to melt, to soften, to unfreeze.

theatre 1 THEATRICAL ENTERTAINMENTS: ballet, comedy, drama, farce, mime, nativity play, opera, pantomime, play. 2 KINDS OF PERFORMANCE: dress rehearsal, first night, matinée, première, preview, production, rehearsal, show. 3 PEOPLE WHO WORK IN A THEATRE: actor, actress, ballerina, dancer, director, producer, prompter, stage manager, understudy, usher or usherette. 4 PARTS OF A THEATRE: balcony, box-office, circle, dressing-room, foyer, gallery, stage, stalls. 5 OTHER WORDS TO DO WITH THEATRE: costume, curtain, footlights, lighting, make-up, programme, scenery, set, sound-effect, spotlight.

theft burglary, pilfering, robbery, shop-lifting, stealing.

theme 1 *the theme of a talk*. issue, matter, subject, topic. 2 *a musical theme*. air, melody, tune.

theology religious studies.

theoretical abstract.

theory 1 *I explained my theory*. argument, assumption, belief, explanation, guess, idea, notion, supposition, view. 2 *Do you understand the theory of how computers work?* laws, principles, rules, science.

therapy *He goes to hospital for therapy.* cure, healing, remedy, treatment.

therefore accordingly, consequently, so, thus.

Thermos vacuum flask.

thick 1 *thick snow.* deep. 2 *a thick book.* fat. 3 *thick rope.* stout, strong, sturdy. 4 *a thick crowd.* dense, impenetrable, solid. 5 *thick mud.* heavy, stiff. 6 (informal) *He must be thick if he doesn't understand!* SEE **stupid.**

thicken *to thicken a sauce.* to concentrate, to condense, to reduce, to stiffen.

thief bandit, burglar, highwayman, mugger, pickpocket, robber, shoplifter.

thin 1 *a thin layer.* emaciated, lanky, lean, scraggy, skinny, slender, slight, slim, wiry. 2 *a thin line.* fine, narrow. 3 *thin gravy.* runny, watery. 4 *a thin audience.* meagre, scanty, small, sparse. 5 *to thin paint.* to dilute, to water down, to weaken.

thing 1 *What's that thing in your hand?* article, item, object. 2 *I saw a funny thing this morning.* action, affair, deed, happening, occurrence. 3 *There are some things I want to discuss.* idea, thought.

think 1 *I thought about how to earn some money.* to brood, to consider, to contemplate, to meditate, to ponder, to reflect. 2 *I think he's right.* to accept, to admit, to believe, to conclude, to judge. 3 *I think it's about 12 o'clock.* to assume, to feel, to guess, to presume, to reckon, to suppose. 4 *If you think, you won't make mistakes.* to attend, to concentrate. 5 *to think up: I thought up a clever plan.* to conceive, to concoct, to devise, to imagine, to invent, to make-up.

thirst 1 *to have a thirst:* (informal) to be dry, (informal) to be parched. 2 *a thirst for knowledge.* appetite, craving, desire, hunger, itch, longing, love, lust, passion, urge, wish.

thorn *Gorse has sharp thorns.* needle, prickle, spike.

thorny 1 *a thorny bush.* prickly, scratchy, spiky. 2 (informal) *a thorny problem.* SEE **difficult.**

thorough *a thorough piece of work.* attentive, careful, conscientious, diligent, exhaustive, methodical, meticulous, observant, orderly, organized, painstaking, scrupulous, systematic, thoughtful, watchful.

thought 1 *deep in thought.* contemplation, day-dreaming, meditation, reflection, reverie. 2 *I had a sudden thought.* belief, concept, idea, notion, opinion. 3 *It was a nice thought to give granny flowers.* attention, consideration, kindness, thoughtfulness.

thoughtful 1 *It was thoughtful of you to wash up.* attentive, considerate, friendly, good-natured, helpful, obliging, public-spirited, unselfish. SEE ALSO **kind.** 2 *a thoughtful expression.* dreamy, grave, pensive, philosophical, reflective, serious, solemn. 3 *a thoughtful piece of work.* careful, conscientious, diligent, exhaustive, methodical, meticulous, observant, orderly, organized, painstaking, scrupulous, systematic, thorough, watchful.

thoughtless 1 *It was thoughtless to leave the shopping on the bus!* absent-minded, careless, forgetful, inattentive, irresponsible, negligent, scatterbrained. 2 *It was thoughtless to make fun of her family.* cruel, heartless, insensitive, selfish, tactless, uncaring, unfeeling.

thrash 1 *Teachers used to thrash naughty children.* SEE **hit.** 2 (informal) *We thrashed them 7–0.* SEE **defeat.**

thread 1 fibre, hair, strand. 2 THREADS USED IN SEWING AND WEAVING: cotton, silk, twine, wool, yarn.

threadbare *threadbare clothes.* frayed, ragged, shabby, tattered, tatty, thin, worn.

threat 1 *to make threats:* SEE **threaten.** 2 *a threat of snow.* danger, risk, warning.

threaten 1 *Their gang threatened us.* to bully, to frighten, to intimidate, to make threats, to menace. 2 *An avalanche threatened the town.* to endanger. 3 *threatening:* threatening storm-clouds. forbidding, grim, menacing, ominous, stern, unfriendly.

thrifty *thrifty with money.* careful, economical, sparing.

thrill 1 *the thrills of a fun-fair.* excitement, (informal) kicks, sensation, suspense. 2 *The music thrilled us.* to delight, to electrify, to excite, to rouse, to stimulate, to stir. 3 *thrilling:* extraordinary, sensational, spectacular.

thrive 1 *Our tomato plants are thriving.* to do well, to flourish, to grow, to prosper, to succeed. 2 *thriving:* prosperous, successful.

throb 1 *a throb of toothache.* ache, pang, twinge. SEE ALSO **pain.** 2 *the throb of music.* beat, pulse, rhythm.

throng *We pushed through the throng.* company, crowd, gathering, horde, mass, multitude, swarm.

throttle to choke, to smother, to stifle, to strangle, to suffocate.

throw 1 *to throw a ball, etc.* to bowl, to cast, (informal) to chuck, to fling, to heave, to hurl, to lob, to pelt, to pitch, to sling, to toss. 2 *to throw something away*: to cast off, to discard, to dispose of, to dump, to get rid of, to reject, to scrap, to shed.

thrust 1 *They thrust me to the front.* to drive, to force, to propel, to push, to send, to shove. 2 *to thrust with a dagger, etc.* to lunge, to plunge, to poke, to stab.

thug delinquent, hooligan, mugger, ruffian, trouble-maker, vandal.

thump *He thumped me in the back.* to bash, to beat, to bump, to butt, to clout, to hammer, to jab, to knock, to poke, to pound, to prod, to punch, to ram, to slog, to smack, to smash, to strike, to swipe, to wallop, to whack. SEE ALSO **hit.**

thunderstruck *I was thunderstruck when she gave me £10.* amazed, astonished, astounded, nonplussed, stunned.

thus accordingly, consequently, so, therefore.

tick (informal) *to tick someone off*: to censure, to condemn, to criticize, to rebuke, to reprimand, to reproach, to scold, (informal) to tell off.

ticket *Buy a ticket before you start fishing.* coupon, permit, voucher.

tickle 1 *I giggle if someone tickles me.* SEE **touch.** 2 *My throat tickles when I get a cold.* to itch, to tingle.

ticklish *a ticklish problem.* difficult, (informal) thorny, tricky.

tide *the tides of the sea.* current, ebb and flow, rise and fall.

tidings (old-fashioned) *good tidings.* information, news.

tidy 1 *Make yourselves tidy before dinner.* neat, presentable, smart, spruce, trim. 2 *Make your room tidy.* orderly, shipshape, spick and span, straight. 3 *tidy in the house*: house-proud.

tie 1 *to tie with string.* to bind, to hitch, to knot, to lash. 2 *to tie up a boat.* to anchor, to moor. 3 *to tie up an animal.* to secure, to tether. 4 *to tie in a game.* to be equal, to be level, to draw.

tight 1 *Make sure the screws are tight.* fast, firm, fixed, immovable, secure. 2 *I need a jar with a tight lid.* airtight, sealed, watertight. 3 *Pull the string tight.* stiff, stretched, taut, tense. 4 *It was a tight crowd in that small room.* close, crammed, crowded. 5 (informal) *He was tight after drinking several beers.* drunk, fuddled, intoxicated.

tiller helm.

tilt *The bike tilts when you go round a bend.* to incline, to lean, to slant, to slope, to tip.

timber KINDS OF TIMBER: beam, board, log, lumber, plank, post, tree trunk. SEE ALSO **wood.**

time 1 *What's the best time to call?* date, day, hour, moment, occasion, opportunity. 2 *We spent a long time in the museum.* session, spell, while. 3 *There was a time when I was captain.* phase, season, stretch, term. 4 *What was life like in the time of Elizabeth I?* age, era, period. 5 UNITS OF TIME: century, day, decade, eternity, fortnight, hour, instant, leap year, lifetime, minute, month, second, week, weekend, year. 6 TIMES OF THE DAY: afternoon, bedtime, dusk, evening, midday, midnight, morning, night, nightfall, noon, sunrise, sunset, twilight. 7 DEVICES FOR MEASURING TIME: calendar, clock, digital watch, hour-glass, stop-watch, sundial, watch. 8 SPECIAL TIMES OF THE YEAR: Advent, autumn, Boxing Day, Christmas, Easter, Good Friday, Hallowe'en, Hogmanay, Lent, midsummer, New Year, Palm Sunday, Passover, Ramadan, St Valentine's Day, spring, summer, Whitsun, winter, Yom Kippur, yuletide.

timely appropriate, apt, fitting, suitable.

timetable *a timetable of events for sports day.* programme, schedule.

timid *Don't be timid—jump in!* bashful, cowardly, coy, faint-hearted, fearful, nervous, reserved, sheepish, shy, timorous, unheroic.

tinge *The evening sky was tinged with red.* to colour, to dye, to paint, to stain, to tint.

tingle *I still tingle where I sat in the nettles.* to sting, to tickle.

tinker *Never tinker with the inside of a TV set.* to interfere, to mess about, to tamper.

tinny *a tinny old car.* cheap, inferior, poor-quality.

tint colour, dye, hue, shade, stain, tinge, tone.

tiny 1 *a tiny insect, etc.* diminutive, imperceptible, little, microscopic, miniature, minute, teeny, wee. SEE ALSO **small.** 2 *a tiny wound.* insignificant, minor, negligible, petty, slight, trifling, trivial, unimportant.

tip 1 *the tip of a pencil.* end, point. 2 *the tip of an iceberg.* peak, top. 3 *tips on safety in the water.* advice, clue, hint, suggestion, warning. 4 *We took the rubbish to the tip.* dump, rubbish-heap. 5 *A big wave nearly tipped the boat over.* to capsize, to knock over, to overturn, to topple, to turn over, to upset.

tire 1 *The long game tired us.* to exhaust, to wear out, to weary. 2 *tired:* bored, done in, drowsy, jaded, listless, sleepy.

titbit *Give the dog a few nice titbits.* morsel, piece, taste.

title 1 *the title of a story.* heading, name. 2 *a person's title.* position, rank, status. 3 *a titled person:* aristocrat, lord, nobleman, noblewoman, peer, peeress. 4 *titled:* aristocratic, highborn, noble. 5 TITLES YOU USE WHEN SPEAKING OR WRITING TO PEOPLE: Baron, Baroness, Count, Countess, Dame, Dr or Doctor, Duchess, Duke, Earl, Lady, Lord, Master, Miss, Mr, Mrs, Ms, Professor, Rev or Reverend, Sir. SEE ALSO **rank, royal.**

titter to chuckle, to giggle, to snigger. SEE ALSO **laugh.**

toadstool fungus, mushroom.

toboggan sled, sledge.

toddler baby, child, infant.

to-do SEE **commotion.**

toil drudgery, effort, exertion, labour, work.

toilet lavatory, (informal) loo, water-closet, WC.

token 1 *Please accept these flowers as a token of our love.* indication, mark, reminder, sign. 2 *You can get £1 off if you present this token.* counter, coupon, voucher.

tolerable *The food was just about tolerable.* acceptable, adequate, all right, passable, satisfactory.

tolerant *Grandad is tolerant when we are naughty.* easygoing, forgiving, indulgent, lenient, liberal, patient, sympathetic.

tolerate 1 *I can't tolerate this toothache!* to abide, to bear, to endure, to put up with, to stand. 2 *Mum won't tolerate smoking in the house.* to accept, to allow, to approve of, to permit.

toll *We had to pay a toll to cross the bridge.* charge, fee, payment.

tomb burial place, grave, gravestone, memorial, monument, tombstone.

tone 1 *There was an angry tone in her voice.* expression, note, sound. 2 *We chose some eerie music to set the tone for our play.* atmosphere, feeling, mood. 3 *The paint in my room has a pink tone.* colour, hue, shade, tinge, tint. 4 *Please tone down the noise!* to lessen, to quieten, to soften, to subdue.

tongue *He spoke a foreign tongue.* language.

tongue-tied *I don't explain things well because I get tongue-tied.* dumb, mute, speechless.

tonic SEE **medicine.**

tool 1 *Dad has tools for every job.* apparatus, contraption, device, gadget, hardware, implement, instrument, invention, machine, utensil. 2 VARIOUS TOOLS: axe, bellows, chisel, chopper, clamp, cramp, crowbar, cutter, drill, file, fretsaw, glass-paper, hack-saw, hammer, hatchet, jack, jigsaw, ladder, lever, mallet, oil-can, penknife, pick, pickaxe, pincers, plane, pliers, pocket-knife, sandpaper, saw, screwdriver, shears, shovel, sledgehammer, spanner, tape-measure, tongs, vice, wrench. FOR OTHER TOOLS SEE **house, farm, garden, kitchen.**

tooth 1 fang. 2 WORDS TO DO WITH TEETH: dental nurse, dental surgery, dentist, denture, extraction, filling, gums, toothache, toothbrush, toothpaste.

top 1 *the top of a mountain.* apex, crown, head, peak, summit, tip. 2 *the top of a jar.* cap, cover, covering, lid. 3 *Our collection for OXFAM topped last year's record.* to beat, to exceed, to excel, to outdo, to surpass.

topic *a topic for discussion.* issue, matter, subject, theme.

topical *You get topical news on TV.* contemporary, current, recent.

topple 1 *The gale toppled our TV aerial.* to knock down, to overturn, to throw down, to tip over, to upset. 2 *The vase toppled off the mantelpiece.* to fall, to tumble.

topsy-turvy chaotic, confused, disorderly, haphazard, higgledy-piggledy, jumbled, mixed up, muddled, upside-down.

toreador bullfighter, matador.

torment 1 *The wasps tormented us.* to afflict, to annoy, to bait, to distress, to pester, to vex, to worry. 2 *The bully tormented the infants.* to bully, to hurt, to intimidate, to persecute, to tease, to torture, to victimize. 3 *I hope you never experience the torment of bad sunburn.* agony, anguish, pain, suffering, torture.

torrent *a torrent of water.* cataract, deluge, downpour, flood, spate, stream.

torture 1 to afflict, to be cruel, to cause pain, to hurt, to inflict pain, to torment. 2 agony, pain, suffering.

toss 1 *I tossed a coin in the well.* to bowl, to cast, (informal) to chuck, to fling, to heave, to hurl, to lob, to pitch, to sling, to throw. 2 *The boat tossed about in the storm.* to bob, to pitch, to reel, to rock, to roll, to shake.

total 1 *Dad signed a cheque for the total amount.* complete, entire, full, whole. 2 *Our play was a total disaster.* absolute, perfect, sheer, utter. 3 *Add up the figures and tell me the total.* amount, answer, sum. 4 *Our shopping totalled £37.* to add up to, to amount to, to come to, to make.

totter *We tottered unsteadily off the ship.* to dodder, to falter, to reel, to rock.

touch 1 WAYS TO TOUCH THINGS OR PEOPLE: to caress, to contact, to cuddle, to dab, to embrace, to feel, to finger, to fondle, to handle, to kiss, to manipulate, to massage, to nuzzle, to pat, to paw, to pet, to rub, to stroke, to tickle. 2 *The sad story touched us.* to affect, to concern, to move, to stir. 3 *touching: a touching scene.* emotional, moving. 4 *Our speed touched 100 miles an hour.* to reach, to rise to.

touchy *Be careful what you say because he's a bit touchy.* edgy, emotional, irritable, jittery, jumpy, nervous, sensitive, snappy, temperamental, tense, (informal) uptight.

tough 1 *tough shoes.* durable, hardwearing, indestructible, lasting, unbreakable, well-made. 2 *a tough wrestler.* beefy, brawny, burly, hardy, muscular, robust, strong, sturdy, wiry. 3 *tough meat.* hard, gristly, leathery, rubbery. 4 *a tough climb.* arduous, difficult, gruelling, hard, laborious, stiff, strenuous, uphill.

toughen to reinforce, to strengthen.

tour 1 *a coach tour.* excursion, journey, outing, trip. 2 *Our class toured a local factory.* to go round, to visit.

tourist *The cathedral was full of tourists.* holiday-maker, sightseer, tripper, visitor.

tournament *a tennis tournament.* championship, competition, contest, series.

tow *Our car isn't powerful enough to tow a trailer.* to drag, to draw, to haul, to pull.

tower 1 *The castle towers above the village.* to loom, to rise, to stand out, to stick up. 2 *towering:* colossal, high, lofty, tall.

town 1 borough, city. 2 PLACES YOU FIND IN A TOWN: bank, café, cinema, college, concert hall, car-park, council-houses, disco, factory, filling-station, flats, garage, ghetto, hotel, leisure centre, library, museum, night-club, park, police-station, post office, pub, recreation ground, restaurant, school, shopping centre, slum, snack bar, sports centre, square, station, suburb, supermarket, theatre, warehouse. SEE ALSO **building, house, road, shop.**

toxic *toxic fumes.* deadly, lethal, poisonous.

toy VARIOUS TOYS: ball, doll, kaleidoscope, kite, rag doll, rattle, rocking-horse, scooter, teddy-bear, top, tricycle, water-pistol. SEE ALSO **game.** ! Many toys are models of real things, such as *aeroplanes, cars, cooking things, furniture, etc.* Many other toys have special names invented by the manufacturers. So there are lots of toys that are not listed here.

trace 1 *Did mum trace her lost keys?* to discover, to find, to get back, to recover, to retrieve. 2 *The hounds traced the fox across the field.* to follow, to hunt, to pursue, to track down, to trail. 3 *The criminals left no traces.* evidence, mark, sign, track, trail.

track 1 *a cycle track.* SEE **road.** 2 *animal tracks.* footprint, mark, trace, trail. 3 *a railway track.* line, rails. 4 *The hunters tracked the deer.* to chase, to follow, to hound, to hunt, to pursue, to stalk, to tail, to trail. 5 *The police tracked down the stolen property.* to discover, to find, to get back, to recover, to retrieve, to trace.

trade 1 *the clothing trade.* business, buying and selling, commerce, industry, traffic. 2 *I'm going to train for a trade when I leave school.* calling, employment, occupation, profession, work. FOR VARIOUS TRADES SEE **job.** 3 *Some shops trade on Sundays.* to do business. 4 *to trade in something*: to market, to retail, to sell. 5 *to trade something in*: to exchange, to swop.

trader dealer, merchant, retailer, salesman, shopkeeper, stockist, supplier, tradesman.

tradition *It's a tradition to have mince pies at Christmas.* convention, custom, habit, practice, routine.

traffic 1 *road traffic.* FOR KINDS OF TRAFFIC SEE **vehicle.** 2 *a traffic in drugs.* SEE **trade.**

tragedy *It was a tragedy when the dog was knocked over.* calamity, catastrophe, disaster, misfortune.

tragic *a tragic accident.* awful, calamitous, depressing, dire, disastrous, dreadful, fearful, pathetic, terrible, unfortunate, unlucky. SEE ALSO **sad.**

trail 1 *The hounds followed the trail.* evidence, mark, sign, trace, track. 2 *He trailed an old cart behind him.* to drag, to draw, to haul, to pull, to tow. 3 *He trailed him for miles.* to follow, to hunt, to pursue, to trace, to track down.

train 1 *Who trains your football team?* to coach, to educate, to instruct, to teach. 2 *Our team trains every evening.* to exercise, to practise.

trainer coach, instructor, teacher.

traitor *The traitor went over to the other side.* betrayer, deserter, renegade.

tramp 1 *The tramp had nowhere to live.* beggar, destitute person, homeless person, vagabond, vagrant. 2 *We tramped across the hills.* to hike, to march, to plod, to stride, to trudge. SEE ALSO **walk.**

trample *Don't trample on the flowers.* to crush, to flatten, to stamp on, to tread on, to walk over.

trance *to be lost in a trance.* day-dream, hypnotic state, unconsciousness.

tranquil *a tranquil lake.* calm, peaceful, placid, quiet, restful, serene, still, undisturbed, untroubled.

tranquillizer sedative.

transfer 1 *We transferred our luggage from the bus into the train.* to carry, to convey, to ferry, to take, to transport. 2 *They transferred me into the reserve team.* to change, to move.

transform *We transformed the attic into a games room.* to adapt, to alter, to change, to convert, to modify, to rebuild, to turn.

transient *Migrating birds are transient visitors to our country.* brief, momentary, passing, temporary.

translate *Can you translate these French words?* to interpret.

transmit 1 *Transmit this message to headquarters.* to convey, to dispatch, to pass on, to send. 2 *The satellite transmits radio signals.* to broadcast, to emit.

transparent *transparent glass.* clear.

transplant 1 *We transplanted some seedlings.* to move, to shift, to transfer. 2 *a heart transplant.* operation, surgery.

transport *to transport goods.* to carry, to convey, to move, to shift, to ship, to transfer.

trap 1 *The gamekeeper set a trap.* ambush, booby-trap, snare. 2 *to trap an animal, to trap a criminal.* to ambush, to arrest, to capture, to corner, to ensnare.

trash garbage, junk, litter, refuse, rubbish, waste.

travel 1 VARIOUS WAYS TO TRAVEL: to cruise, to cycle, to drive, to fly, to hitch-hike, to journey, to navigate, to paddle, to pedal, to punt, to ride, to row, to sail, to steam, to tour, to trek, to walk. 2 KINDS OF TRAVEL: cruise, drive, excursion, expedition, exploration, flight, hike, journey, mission, outing, pilgrimage, ride, safari, sail, tour, trek, trip, visit, voyage, walk. 3 METHODS OF TRANSPORT: bus, car, coach, horse, lorry, minibus, monorail, (old-fashioned) omnibus, metro, ship, taxi, tram, tube, underground, van. SEE ALSO **aircraft, cycle, railway, vehicle, vessel.** 4 KINDS OF TRAVELLER: driver, gipsy, holiday-maker, nomad, passenger, pedestrian, pilgrim, representative, stowaway, tourist, tramp, vagabond, vagrant, wayfarer.

treacherous 1 *a treacherous friend.* disloyal, false, sneaky, unfaithful, untrustworthy. 2 *treacherous weather conditions.* dangerous, deceptive, hazardous, misleading, unsafe.

treachery betrayal, disloyalty, treason.

tread *You trod on my foot!* to stamp, to step, to trample, to walk.

treason betrayal, disloyalty, treachery.

treasure 1 *a miser's treasure.* hoard, riches, wealth. 2 *Mum treasures the brooch granny gave her.* to appreciate, to cherish, to esteem, to love, to prize, to value.

treat 1 *Treat animals kindly.* to behave towards, to care for, to look after. 2 *How would you treat this problem?* to attend to, to deal with, to manage, to tackle. 3 *to treat an illness, to treat a wound.* to cure, to dress, to heal, to nurse, to tend. 4 *They treat milk to kill germs.* to process.

treatment SEE **medicine**.

treaty *a peace treaty.* agreement, alliance, armistice, pact.

tree 1 TYPES OF TREE: conifer, deciduous, evergreen. 2 VARIOUS TREES: ash, beech, birch, cedar, chestnut, cypress, elder, elm, eucalyptus, fir, gum-tree, hawthorn, hazel, holly, horse-chestnut, larch, lime, maple, oak, olive, palm, pine, plane, poplar, spruce, sycamore, willow, yew. 3 *a young tree*: sapling.

trek expedition, hike, journey.

tremble 1 *I trembled with fear.* to quake, to quaver, to shake, to shiver, to shudder, to vibrate. 2 *The candle flame trembled.* to flicker, to waver.

tremendous 1 *a tremendous explosion.* alarming, appalling, awful, fearful, fearsome, frightening, frightful, horrifying, shocking, terrible, (informal) terrific. 2 (informal) *a tremendous helping of potatoes.* SEE **big**. 3 (informal) *a tremendous party.* SEE **excellent**. 4 (informal) *a tremendous victory.* SEE **remarkable**. ! *Tremendous* originally meant *fearful*. When it is used informally, the meaning is rather vague.

tremor 1 *There was a tremor in his voice.* quiver, shaking, vibration. 2 *an earth tremor*: earthquake.

trench ditch.

trend 1 *There has been a trend towards eating health foods recently.* inclination, leaning, movement, shift, tendency. 2 *What's the latest trend in clothes?* fashion, style, way.

trendy (informal) *trendy clothes.* contemporary, fashionable, modern, stylish, up-to-date.

trespass *to trespass on someone's property.* to intrude.

trial 1 *They're doing trials on a new type of spacecraft.* experiment, test. 2 *Every maths lesson is a trial for me!* ordeal.

tribe *a tribe of warriors.* clan, family, group, horde, race.

tributary river, stream.

tribute *We paid tribute to her courage.* appreciation, compliment, honour, praise, respect.

trick 1 *a conjuring trick*: illusion, magic. 2 *a nasty trick*: cheat, deceit, deception, fraud, hoax, manoeuvre, pretence, ruse, scheme, stunt, trickery, wile. 3 *I know a trick for opening pop bottles.* dodge, knack, skill, technique. 4 *He tricked us into buying rubbish.* to bluff, to cheat, to deceive, to defraud, to dupe, to fool, to hoax, to hoodwink, (informal) to kid, to mislead, to outwit, to swindle.

trickle *Water trickled out of the crack.* to dribble, to drip, to flow, to leak, to ooze, to run, to seep.

tricky 1 *Watch him—he's a tricky player!* artful, crafty, cunning, deceitful, sly, wily. 2 *Backing the car into the drive is a tricky manoeuvre.* awkward, complicated, delicate, difficult.

trifling *a trifling scratch.* insignificant, minor, negligible, small, trivial, unimportant.

trim 1 *a trim garden.* neat, orderly, shipshape, tidy. 2 *to trim a hedge.* to clip, to cut.

trip 1 *I tripped on the step.* to fall over, to stagger, to stumble, to totter. 2 *a trip to the seaside.* excursion, expedition, journey, outing, visit.

tripod *a camera tripod.* stand, support.

triumph 1 *It was a triumph to beat our rival team!* achievement, conquest, success, victory. 2 *We triumphed in the end.* to be victorious, to succeed, to win.

trivial *The police thought that losing 10p was a trivial matter.* frivolous, insignificant, minor, negligible, petty, superficial, trifling, unimportant. SEE ALSO **small.**

troop 1 *a troop of circus performers.* band, company, gang, horde. SEE ALSO **group.** 2 *troops:* SEE **armed services.** 3 *We trooped along the road.* to march, to parade.

trophy 1 *a sports trophy.* award, cup, medal, prize, reward. 2 *The thieves hid their trophies.* booty, loot.

trouble 1 *We got into trouble.* misbehaviour, misconduct, naughtiness. 2 *The ship was in trouble during the storm.* adversity, difficulty, distress, hardship, misfortune. 3 *What's the trouble?* burden, grief, misery, problem, sadness, sorrow, unhappiness, worry. 4 *Grandad has some trouble with his eyes.* affliction, disease, illness, pain, suffering. 5 *He took a lot of trouble.* care, effort, exertion, labour, struggle, work. 6 *There was trouble in the crowd.* bother, commotion, disorder, disturbance, fighting, fuss, row, turmoil, violence. 7 *Will it trouble you if I open a window?* to annoy, to bother, to concern, to distress, to disturb, to upset, to vex, to worry. 8 *My toothache troubled me.* to afflict, to hurt, to pain, to torment.

trouble-maker culprit, delinquent, hooligan, offender, rascal, ruffian, vandal, wrongdoer.

troublesome 1 *In hot weather, insects can be troublesome.* annoying, inconvenient, irritating. 2 *a troublesome child.* badly-behaved, disobedient, naughty, unruly.

trousers KINDS OF TROUSERS: breeches, dungarees, jeans, jodhpurs, overalls, pants, shorts, slacks, trunks.

truant *to play truant:* (informal) to skive, to stay away.

truce *The two sides agreed on a truce.* armistice, pact, peace, treaty.

trudge *We trudged home tired out.* to lumber, to plod, to tramp, to trek. SEE ALSO **walk.**

true 1 *a true happening.* actual, authentic, factual, genuine, real. 2 *the true time.* accurate, correct, exact, proper, right. 3 *a true friend.* constant, dependable, faithful, honest, honourable, loyal, reliable, responsible, steady, trustworthy. 4 *Are you the true owner of this car?* authorized, legal, legitimate, rightful, valid.

trundle *A wagon trundled up the road.* to lumber, to lurch.

trunk 1 *a tree trunk.* stem. 2 *a person's trunk.* body. 3 *a clothes trunk.* box, chest. 4 *trunks:* briefs, shorts.

trust 1 *The team trusts the goalkeeper.* to bank on, to believe in, to be sure of, to count on, to depend on, to have faith in, to rely on. 2 *I trust you are well?* to assume, to expect, to hope, to presume. 3 *The dog has trust in his mistress.* belief, confidence, faith.

trustworthy *a trustworthy friend.* constant, faithful, honest, honourable, loyal, reliable, responsible, safe, steady, true.

truth *Tell the truth.* facts, reality.

truthful *a truthful answer.* accurate, correct, frank, honest, proper, right, sincere, straight, true.

try 1 *Try to do your best.* to aim, to attempt, to endeavour, to exert yourself, to make an effort, to strain, to strive. 2 *Dad tried a new car.* to experiment with, to test. 3 *He tries us with his continual chatter.* to annoy, to exasperate, to irritate, to trouble, to upset, to vex, to worry. 4 *Have a try!* attempt, effort, endeavour.

tub barrel, bath, butt, cask, drum, pot.

tubby *a tubby figure.* chubby, dumpy, fat, overweight, plump, podgy, portly, stout.

tube 1 *a rubber tube.* hose, pipe. 2 *a tube train.* underground.

tuck *Tuck your shirt into your jeans.* to cram, to insert, to push, to shove, to stuff.

tuft *a tuft of grass.* bunch, clump.

tug 1 *We tugged a cart behind us.* to drag, to draw, to lug, to tow. 2 *I tugged at the rope.* to jerk, to pull.

tumble *I tumbled into the water.* to collapse, to drop, to fall, to stumble, to topple.

tumbledown *a tumbledown cottage.* broken down, decrepit, derelict, dilapidated, ramshackle, rickety, ruined.

tumbler beaker, glass.

tummy (informal) *a pain in the tummy.* abdomen, belly, stomach.

tumult *The crowd went wild, and people were knocked over in the tumult.* bedlam, chaos, commotion, confusion, disorder, disturbance, hubbub, hullabaloo, pandemonium, riot, row, rumpus, turmoil, uproar.

tune air, melody, theme.

tuneful catchy, melodious.

tunnel 1 KINDS OF TUNNEL: burrow, hole, mine, passage, shaft, subway, underpass. 2 *The rabbit tunnelled under the fence.* to burrow, to dig, to excavate.

turbulent 1 *a turbulent crowd.* badly-behaved, disorderly, lawless, obstreperous, riotous, rowdy, undisciplined, unruly. 2 *turbulent weather.* rough, stormy, violent, wild, windy.

turf grass, lawn.

turmoil SEE **commotion.**

turn 1 *The wheel began to turn.* to revolve, to rotate, to spin, to twirl, to whirl. 2 *The car turned a corner.* to go round. 3 *I turned the wire round a stick.* to bend, to coil, to curl, to loop, to twist, to wind. 4 *Tadpoles turn into frogs.* to become, to change into. 5 *We turned the attic into a games room.* to change, to convert, to modify, to transform. 6 *The snake turned this way and that.* to squirm, to twist, to wriggle, to writhe. 7 *to turn down: I turned down the invitiation.* to decline, to refuse, to reject. 8 *to turn out: How did your party turn out?* to befall, to emerge, to happen, to result. 9 *to turn someone out:* to eject, to evict, to expel, (informal) to kick out, to remove, to throw out. 10 *to turn up:* to appear, to arrive, to come, to materialize. 11 *a turn in the road.* bend, corner, curve, hairpin-bend, junction, twist, U-turn. 12 *It's your turn to play.* chance, opportunity. 13 *I had a nasty turn today.* attack, bout, fit, illness.

turnstile entrance, exit, gate.

tussle *a friendly tussle.* battle, bout, brawl, clash, combat, conflict, contest, duel, encounter, feud, fight, quarrel, rivalry, row, scrap, scuffle, squabble, strife, struggle.

tutor SEE **teacher.**

twiddle *to twiddle your thumbs.* to fiddle with, to fidget with.

twig branch, stalk, stem, stick.

twilight dusk, evening, gloom, sunset.

twine *I tied up the parcel with twine.* cord, string, thread.

twinge *a twinge in your tooth.* ache, pain, pang, spasm, throb.

twinkle *Lights twinkled in the distance.* to blink, to flicker, to glimmer, to quiver, to tremble, to waver.

twirl 1 *The roundabout twirled faster and faster.* to revolve, to rotate, to spin, to turn, to whirl. 2 *She twirled her umbrella.* to brandish, to wave.

twist 1 *I twisted the string round my fingers.* to coil, to curl, to loop, to turn, to wind. 2 *The ropes became twisted.* to entangle, to entwine, to tangle. 3 *The road twisted up the mountain.* to bend, to curve, to zigzag. 4 *I twisted the lid off the jar.* to jerk, to wrench. 5 *The heat twisted the rails.* to buckle, to crumple, to distort, to warp.

twitch to fidget, to jerk, to jump, to start.

type *Pop songs are a type of music.* class, form, group, kind, set, sort, species, variety.

typhoon SEE **storm.**

typical 1 *a typical day.* average, normal, ordinary, usual. 2 *a typical Chinese meal.* characteristic, distinctive, particular, special.

tyrannical *a tyrannical ruler.* bossy, cruel, dictatorial, domineering, harsh, oppressive, unjust.

tyrant dictator. SEE ALSO **ruler.**

U

ugly *an ugly monster.* frightful, ghastly, grisly, grotesque, gruesome, hideous, monstrous, repulsive, unattractive, unsightly. **2** *ugly storm-clouds.* dangerous, forbidding, hostile, menacing, ominous, threatening.

ulcer boil, sore.

ultimate *We scored in the ultimate minutes of the game.* closing, concluding, extreme, final, last.

ultimately eventually, finally.

ultimatum *The gang gave us an ultimatum.* final demand.

umpire adjudicator, arbitrator, judge, referee.

---

un- ! There are many words beginning with the prefix *un-*, and only some of them can be given here. We give full entries for the words you are most likely to need help with, and we tell you where you can look for help with some of the others.

---

unaccountable SEE **inexplicable**.

unaccustomed SEE **strange**.

unaided single-handed, solo.

unanimous *a unanimous decision.* agreed, united.

unanswerable SEE **insoluble**.

unauthorized *The train made an unauthorized stop.* abnormal, illegal, irregular, unusual.

unavoidable **1** *an unavoidable accident.* certain, destined, fated, inescapable, inevitable, sure. **2** *an unavoidable payment.* compulsory, necessary, required.

unaware SEE **ignorant**.

unbalanced **1** *an unbalanced load.* asymmetrical, lop-sided, uneven. **2** *an unbalanced mind.* SEE **mad**.

unbearable intolerable.

unbelievable SEE **incredible**.

unbiased SEE **just**.

uncanny SEE **eerie**.

uncaring SEE **careless**.

uncertain SEE **doubtful**.

unchangeable SEE **invariable**.

uncivilized SEE **savage**.

unclean SEE **dirty**.

unclothed SEE **naked**.

uncomfortable **1** *an uncomfortable chair.* hard, lumpy. **2** *an uncomfortable feeling.* SEE **uneasy**.

uncommon SEE **rare**.

uncomplimentary SEE **rude**.

unconscious **1** *The boxer was unconscious.* insensible, knocked out, senseless. **2** *I was unconscious of his presence.* unaware. **2** *Blinking is an unconscious action.* automatic, impulsive, involuntary, spontaneous, unintentional, unthinking.

unconventional SEE **abnormal**.

uncover **1** *We were horrified when she uncovered her wound.* to bare, to disclose, to expose, to reveal, to strip, to undress. **2** *We uncovered the foundations of an ancient building.* to come across, to dig up, to discover, to locate, to unearth.

undamaged faultless, in mint condition, perfect.

undaunted SEE **brave, resolute**.

underclothes **1** undergarments, underwear. **2** VARIOUS UNDERGARMENTS: bra, briefs, corset, drawers, girdle, knickers, lingerie, panties, pants, panty-hose, petticoat, slip, tights, trunks, underpants, vest.

underdeveloped backward, slow, undeveloped.

underdone uncooked.

underfed famished, hungry, ravenous, starving.

undergo *to undergo an operation.* to bear, to endure, to experience, to go through, to put up with, to submit yourself to, to suffer.

undergraduate student.

undergrowth *We forced a way through the undergrowth*. bushes, plants, vegetation.

underhand SEE **dishonest**.

underline *She underlined the main facts*. to emphasize, to stress.

undermine 1 *to undermine a wall*. to burrow under, to dig under, to erode, to mine under, to tunnel under. 2 *to undermine someone's confidence*. to destroy, to ruin, to weaken.

underpass subway.

undersized *an undersized child*. diminutive, little, minute, small, teeny, tiny.

understand 1 *Do you understand what I mean?* to appreciate, to comprehend, to follow, to gather, to grasp, to know, to realize, to see. 2 *She quickly understood how to do it*. to learn, to master. 3 *Can you understand this French?* to decipher, to decode, to interpret.

understanding 1 *She has a good understanding of maths*. ability, awareness, grasp, knowledge. 2 *The shopkeeper and I reached an understanding about the price*. accord, agreement, arrangement, bargain, consent, contract, deal, pact, settlement, treaty. 3 *Our teacher showed great understanding when I was ill*. compassion, consideration, feeling, kindness, mercy, pity, sympathy.

undertake 1 *I undertook to organize a collection for OXFAM*. to agree, to consent, to promise. 2 *Dad undertook the task of building an extension*. to attend to, to begin, to cope with, to deal with, to grapple with, to handle, to manage, to tackle.

underwear SEE **underclothes**.

underworld hell.

undistinguished SEE **ordinary**.

undo 1 *to undo a fastening, to undo a knot, etc.* to detach, to disconnect, to divide, to part, to remove, to separate, to unfasten, to untie. 2 *to undo someone's work*. to destroy, to spoil, to wipe out, to wreck.

undress 1 to strip, to uncover yourself. 2 *undressed*: SEE **naked**.

unearth *The dog unearthed a bone*. to come across, to dig up, to discover, to excavate, to locate, to uncover.

unearthly SEE **eerie**.

uneasy *an uneasy feeling*. anxious, apprehensive, concerned, distressed, fearful, jittery, nervous, uncomfortable, worried.

unemployed on the dole, out of work.

unequal 1 *unequal treatment*. biased, prejudiced, unjust. 2 *an unequal contest*. one-sided, uneven, unfair.

uneven 1 *an uneven road*. bumpy, irregular, rough. 2 *an uneven edge*. bent, crooked, jagged, wavy. 3 *an uneven load*. asymmetrical, lop-sided, unbalanced. 4 *an uneven contest*. one-sided, unequal, unfair.

unexpected *an unexpected meeting*. accidental, sudden, surprising, unforeseen, unplanned.

unfair *an unfair decision, an unfair referee*. biased, one-sided, prejudiced, unjust, unreasonable.

unfaithful 1 disloyal, false, treacherous. 2 *unfaithfulness to your husband or wife*: adultery, infidelity.

unfamiliar SEE **strange**.

unfasten to detach, to disconnect, to divide, to part, to remove, to separate, to undo, to untie.

unfavourable 1 *unfavourable winds*. adverse, contrary, opposing. 2 *unfavourable comments*. attacking, critical, hostile, unfriendly.

unfinished imperfect, incomplete.

unfit 1 *A drunkard is unfit to drive a car*. inadequate, incompetent, unsuitable, unsuited. 2 *This stale bread is unfit to eat*. inappropriate, useless.

unforeseen SEE **unexpected**.

unforgettable memorable.

unfortunate SEE **unlucky**.

unfriendly 1 *an unfriendly welcome*. cool, distant, forbidding, indifferent, reserved, stand-offish, unenthusiastic. 2 *unfriendly behaviour*. aggressive, antisocial, disagreeable, hostile, nasty, obnoxious, offensive, rude.

unhappy SEE **sad**.

unhealthy 1 *unhealthy conditions*. dirty, insanitary. 2 *an unhealthy animal*. diseased, feeble, (informal) poorly, sick, unwell. SEE ALSO **ill**.

unidentified anonymous, nameless, unnamed, unrecognized.

unify to bring together, to unite.

unimportant SEE **insignificant**.

uninhabited *an uninhabited house.* deserted, empty, unoccupied, vacant.

uninterested bored. ! This does not mean the same as *disinterested*.

uninterrupted constant, continuous, non-stop.

union 1 *a union of youth clubs.* alliance, association, combination, league. **2** marriage.

unique *The speaking computer is a unique feature of this car.* distinctive, peculiar, singular.

unite 1 *We united the two teams.* to add together, to amalgamate, to bring together, to combine, to couple. **2** *united: a united decision.* unanimous.

universal *It would be wonderful to have universal peace.* general, global, international, widespread.

universe cosmos.

university college.

unjust *an unjust decision.* biased, one-sided, prejudiced, unfair, unreasonable, wrongful.

unkempt *an unkempt appearance.* bedraggled, dishevelled, scruffy, tangled, uncombed, untidy.

unkind *We hate unkind treatment of animals.* beastly, brutal, callous, cold-blooded, cruel, hard, harsh, heartless, inconsiderate, inhuman, insensitive, merciless, pitiless, relentless, ruthless, sadistic, savage, stern, thoughtless, uncaring, unfeeling, unfriendly, unsympathetic, vicious.

unlikely *an unlikely story.* far-fetched, improbable, incredible, unbelievable, unconvincing.

unlimited SEE **boundless**.

unload *We unloaded the cases at the station.* to drop off, to dump, to take off.

unlock SEE **open**.

unlucky *an unlucky mistake.* accidental, calamitous, disastrous, dreadful, tragic, unfortunate, unwelcome.

unmarried 1 single. **2** *an unmarried person*: batchelor, spinster.

unmistakable SEE **obvious**.

unnatural SEE **artificial**.

unnecessary excessive, extra, redundant, superfluous, surplus, uncalled-for, unwanted.

unoccupied SEE **uninhabited**.

unpleasant abhorrent, abominable, antisocial, appalling, awful, bad-tempered, beastly, bitter, coarse, crude, detestable, diabolical, dirty, disagreeable, disgusting, displeasing, distasteful, dreadful, fearful, fearsome, filthy, foul, frightful, ghastly, grisly, gruesome, harsh, hateful, hellish, hideous, horrible, horrid, horrifying, improper, indecent, loathsome, lousy, malevolent, malicious, (informal) mucky, nasty, nauseating, objectionable, obnoxious, odious, offensive, repellent, repulsive, revolting, rude, shocking, sickly, sordid, sour, spiteful, squalid, terrible, ugly, unattractive, uncouth, undesirable, unfriendly, upsetting, vexing, vicious, vile, vulgar.

unreal SEE **imaginary**.

unreasonable 1 *It's unreasonable to talk to plants!* SEE **absurd**. **2** *He was unreasonable when I asked him to help.* SEE **obstinate**. **3** *unreasonable prices.* SEE **excessive**.

unreliable *unreliable information.* false, inaccurate, misleading.

unruly SEE **disorderly**.

unscathed safe, unharmed.

unscrupulous SEE **dishonest**.

unseen SEE **invisible**.

unselfish SEE **generous**.

unsightly SEE **ugly**.

untidy 1 *untidy work.* careless, disorganized, messy, slapdash, (informal) sloppy, slovenly. **2** *untidy hair.* bedraggled, dishevelled, scruffy, tangled, uncombed, unkempt. **3** *an untidy room.* chaotic, confused, disorderly, jumbled, muddled, topsy-turvy.

untie SEE **undo**.

untold SEE **numerous**.

untrue SEE **false**.

unused *an unused videotape.* blank, clean, in mint condition, new.

unusual SEE **strange**.

unwanted SEE **unnecessary**.

unwell SEE **ill**.

unwieldy SEE **awkward**.

unwilling SEE **reluctant**.

unwise SEE **foolish.**

upbringing *the upbringing of children.* education, instruction, teaching, training.

update to modernize.

upgrade to improve, to make better.

upheaval change, commotion, disruption, disturbance, turmoil.

uphill *an uphill struggle.* arduous, difficult, exhausting, hard, laborious, stiff, strenuous, tough.

uphold *The judge upheld the verdict.* to support, to verify.

upholstery padding.

upkeep *The upkeep of the house is expensive.* maintenance, running.

upright 1 *Human beings walk upright.* erect, vertical. 2 *an upright judge.* fair, good, honest, honourable, just, moral, trustworthy.

uproar SEE **commotion.**

uproarious SEE **funny.**

uproot *to uproot plants.* to destroy, to dig up, to eliminate, to eradicate, to get rid of, to pull up, to remove.

upset 1 *I upset my tea.* to overturn, to spill, to tip over, to topple. 2 *The thunder upset the animals.* to agitate, to alarm, to bother, to distress, to disturb, to excite, to frighten, to perturb, to scare, to trouble, to worry. 3 *Bad language upsets granny.* to anger, to annoy, to displease, to grieve, to irritate, to offend, to vex. 4 *A sudden rainstorm upset our plans.* to affect, to alter, to change, to disrupt, to interfere with, to interrupt.

upside-down inverted, topsy-turvy.

uptight SEE **tense.**

up-to-date 1 *up-to-date technology.* advanced, current, modern, new, present, recent. 2 *up-to-date clothes.* contemporary, fashionable, stylish, (informal) trendy.

urge 1 *The jockey urged the horse on.* to compel, to drive, to force, to press, to propel, to push, to spur. 2 *Mum urged me to put my money into the bank.* to appeal to, (informal) to egg on, to encourage, to entreat, to invite, to persuade, to plead with, to prompt, to recommend, to stimulate. 3 *I had an urge to giggle.* desire, itch, longing, wish, yearning.

urgent *The car needs urgent repairs.* essential, immediate, important, necessary, pressing.

use 1 *I used all my strength.* to employ, to exercise, to exploit, to make use of, to utilize, to wield. 2 *Use some polish.* to administer, to apply, to spread. 3 *They say we should use less salt.* to consume. 4 *How do you use this tool?* to deal with, to manage, to operate, to work. 5 *used*: second-hand.

useful 1 *useful advice.* advantageous, beneficial, constructive, good, helpful, invaluable, positive, profitable, valuable, worthwhile. 2 *a useful tool.* convenient, effective, efficient, handy, powerful, practical, productive. 3 *a useful player.* capable, competent, proficient, successful.

useless 1 *a useless goalkeeper, a useless machine.* (informal) dud, incompetent, ineffective, ineffectual, unhelpful, unusable, worthless. 2 *a useless search.* fruitless, futile, pointless, unsuccessful.

usual 1 *We went by our usual route.* accustomed, conventional, customary, habitual, normal, ordinary, regular, routine, traditional. 2 *It was the usual sort of weather for December.* average, common, everyday, familiar, prevalent, typical, well-known, widespread. 3 *I got the usual reply when I asked for money.* accepted, expected, official, orthodox, standard.

utensil *kitchen utensils.* appliance, device, gadget, implement, instrument, machine, tool.

utilize SEE **use.**

utter 1 *The party was utter chaos!* absolute, complete, perfect, pure, sheer, total, unrestricted. 2 *I didn't utter a word.* SEE **say, talk.**

V

vacant 1 *a vacant house.* deserted, empty, uninhabited, unoccupied. 2 *a vacant space.* clear, free, open, unused. 3 *a vacant look.* blank, expressionless.

vacation holiday, leave, time off.

vacuum flask Thermos.

vagabond, vagrant beggar, destitute person, homeless person, tramp, wanderer, wayfarer.

vague 1 *vague remarks.* ambiguous, broad, confused, general, indefinite, uncertain, unclear, unsure, woolly. 2 *a vague person.* absent-minded, careless, forgetful, inattentive, thoughtless, scatter-brained.

vain 1 *He's vain about his appearance.* arrogant, boastful, cocky, conceited, haughty, proud, self-important, (informal) stuck-up. 2 *They made a vain attempt to rescue her.* fruitless, futile, ineffective, pointless, unsuccessful, useless.

valiant *a valiant struggle.* bold, brave, courageous, daring, fearless, gallant, heroic, intrepid, noble, plucky, spirited, undaunted.

valid *a valid excuse, a valid ticket.* allowed, authorized, genuine, lawful, legal, legitimate, official, permissible, permitted, proper, reasonable, rightful, suitable, usable.

valley KINDS OF VALLEY: canyon, chasm, dale, defile, glen, gorge, gully, hollow, pass, ravine, vale.

valour SEE **courage.**

valuable 1 *valuable jewellery.* costly, expensive, precious, priceless. 2 *valuable advice.* advantageous, beneficial, constructive, good, helpful, invaluable, positive, profitable, useful, worthwhile.

value 1 *This old chair may be of value to an antique dealer.* worth. SEE ALSO **price.** 2 *He knows the value of keeping fit.* advantage, benefit, importance, merit, significance, usefulness. 3 *She values her old brooch.* to appreciate, to care for, to cherish, to esteem, to love, to prize, to treasure.

vandal barbarian, delinquent, hooligan, looter, marauder, raider, ruffian, savage, thug, trouble-maker.

vanish *The mist vanished when the sun rose.* to clear, to disappear, to dwindle, to evaporate, to fade, to melt away, to pass.

vanity SEE **pride.**

vanquish SEE **conquer.**

vaporize *Petrol vaporizes quickly.* to dry up, to evaporate.

vapour fumes, gas, smoke.

variable *variable weather.* changeable, erratic, fickle, inconsistent, temperamental, unpredictable, unreliable.

variation *a variation from routine.* alteration, change, difference.

variety 1 *I like a bit of variety.* alteration, change, difference, diversity, variation. 2 *We bought a variety of things.* assortment, blend, combination, jumble, mixture. 3 *There are many varieties of flowers in the park.* form, kind, sort, type.

various *We made various suggestions.* assorted, contrasting, different, dissimilar, miscellaneous, mixed, varied.

vary *You can vary the temperature by turning the knob.* to adapt, to adjust, to alter, to change, to convert, to modify.

vast *a vast desert.* broad, enormous, extensive, great, huge, immense, large, wide. SEE ALSO **big.**

vault 1 *a wine vault.* basement, cellar, crypt. 2 *to vault a fence.* to bound over, to clear, to jump, to leap, to spring over.

veer *The car veered across the road.* to change direction, to dodge, to serve, to turn, to wheel.

vegetable VARIOUS KINDS OF VEGETABLE: asparagus, bean, beetroot, Brussels sprout, cabbage, carrot, cauliflower, celery, greens, kale, leek, marrow, onion, parsnip, pea, potato, pumpkin, runner bean, spinach, sugar-beet, swede, tomato, turnip. SEE ALSO **salad.**

vegetation foliage, greenery, growth, plants, undergrowth, weeds.

vehement *a vehement attack.* eager, excited, fierce, intense, strong, vigorous, violent.

vehicle 1 KINDS OF VEHICLE:
ambulance, articulated lorry,
automobile, bulldozer, bus, cab, car,
caravan, carriage, cart, chariot, coach,
double-decker, dustcart, estate car,
fire-engine, float, go-kart, hearse,
horsebox, jeep, juggernaut, lorry,
moped, motor car, motor cycle,
(old-fashioned) omnibus, panda car,
patrol car, pick-up truck, removal van,
rickshaw, saloon car, sidecar, sledge,
snowplough, sports car, stagecoach,
steamroller, tank, tanker, taxi, traction
engine, tractor, trailer, tram, trap,
trolley, trolley bus, truck, van, wagon,
wheelbarrow, wheelchair. SEE ALSO
cycle. 2 PARTS OF A MOTOR VEHICLE:
accelerator, axle, bonnet, brake,
bumper, carburettor, choke, clutch,
cylinder, exhaust, gear, headlight,
ignition, milometer, mudguard, piston,
plug, radiator, safety belt or seat-belt,
sidelight, silencer, sparking-plug,
speedometer, starter, steering-wheel,
tachograph, tail-light, throttle, tyre,
windscreen, windscreen-wiper, wing,
wheel.

velocity *It's hard to imagine the
enormous velocity of a spacecraft.*
movement, pace, rate, speed.

vendetta *a vendetta between two
families.* dispute, feud, quarrel.

venerable *The cathedral is a venerable
building.* aged, ancient, old, respected,
revered.

vengeance reprisal, retaliation,
retribution, revenge.

venom poison.

venomous *The adder has a venomous
sting.* deadly, lethal, poisonous, toxic.

vent *The smoke escaped through a vent in
the roof.* cut, gap, hole, opening, outlet,
slit.

ventilate *Ventilate the classroom.* to air,
to freshen.

venture 1 *I ventured a small wager.* to
gamble, to risk. 2 *I wouldn't venture out
in this weather.* to dare to go, to risk
going.

verge 1 *the verge of a road.* border,
edge, margin, side. 2 *I think I'm on the
verge of a discovery.* brink.

verify 1 *He verified that my story was
accurate.* to confirm, to establish, to
prove, to show. 2 *He verified my story.* to
support, to uphold.

vermin pests.

versatile *A versatile footballer plays
well in any position.* adaptable, gifted,
skilful, talented.

verse SEE **poem**.

version 1 *He gave his version of what
happened.* account, description, report,
story. 2 *We read from a modern version
of the Bible.* interpretation, translation.
3 *That car is a new version of the one we
used to have.* design, model, type.

versus against.

vertical 1 *a vertical position.* erect,
upright. 2 *a vertical drop.* precipitous,
sheer. ! *Vertical* is the opposite of
horizontal.

very enormously, especially,
exceedingly, extremely, greatly, most,
outstandingly, (informal) terribly, truly.

vessel 1 *There were many vessels in the
harbour.* boat, craft, ship. 2 KINDS OF
VESSEL: aircraft-carrier, barge,
battleship, canoe, catamaran, clipper,
cruiser, cutter, destroyer, dhow, dinghy,
dredger, ferry, frigate, galleon, galley,
gondola, gunboat, houseboat,
hovercraft, hydrofoil, hydroplane,
ice-breaker, junk, kayak, launch,
lifeboat, lightship, liner, merchant ship,
motor boat, oil-tanker, paddle-steamer,
pedalo, pontoon, power-boat, punt, raft,
rowing-boat, schooner, speedboat,
steamer, submarine, tanker, tramp
steamer, trawler, tug, warship, whaler.
3 PARTS OF A VESSEL: aft, amidships,
anchor, boom, bridge, conning tower,
crow's nest, deck, fo'c'sle or forecastle,
funnel, galley, helm, hull, keel, mast,
oar, paddle, poop, port, porthole,
propeller, prow, rigging, rudder, sail,
scull, starboard, stern, tiller. 4 WAYS TO
TRAVEL IN A VESSEL: to cruise, to
navigate, to paddle, to pilot, to punt, to
row, to sail, to steam.

veto *Dad vetoed our plan for a midnight
ramble.* to ban, to bar, to forbid, to
prohibit.

vex 1 *This cold weather is enough to vex
the most patient gardener!* (informal) to
aggravate, to anger, to annoy, to bother,
to displease, to exasperate, to irritate, to
offend, to provoke, to trouble, to try, to
upset, to worry. 2 *vexed*: SEE **angry**.

viable *a viable plan.* feasible, possible,
practicable, practical, realistic,
workable.

viaduct SEE **bridge**.

vibrate *The old bus began to vibrate as it speeded up.* to quake, to quiver, to shake, to shiver, to shudder, to throb, to tremble, to wobble.

vice 1 *Don't ever begin to lead a life of vice!* evil, immorality, sin, wickedness, wrongdoing. 2 *His worst vice is his continual chattering.* defect, failing, fault, imperfection, shortcoming, weakness.

vicinity area, district, locality, neighbourhood, region, sector, territory, zone.

vicious 1 *a vicious attack.* barbaric, beastly, bloodthirsty, brutal, callous, cruel, inhuman, merciless, murderous, pitiless, ruthless, sadistic, savage, unfeeling, violent. 2 *a vicious animal.* dangerous, ferocious, fierce, untamed, wild. 3 *a vicious character.* depraved, evil, heartless, immoral, malicious, nasty, spiteful, villainous, vindictive, wicked.

victim 1 *a victim of an accident.* casualty, fatality, injured person, wounded person. 2 *a victim of an illness.* sufferer. 3 *The cat pounced on her victim.* prey.

victimize *Don't victimize the little ones.* to bully, to intimidate, to oppress, to persecute, to terrorize, to torment, to treat unfairly.

victor champion, hero, winner.

victorious *We cheered the victorious team.* successful, triumphant, winning.

victory *We celebrated our team's victory.* achievement, conquest, success, triumph, (informal) walk-over, win.

view 1 *There's a lovely view from this window.* landscape, outlook, panorama, prospect, scene, scenery, vista. 2 *I had a good view of what happened.* look, sight. 3 *Mum has strong views about smoking.* attitude, belief, conviction, idea, opinion, thought. 4 *We viewed the scene.* to contemplate, to eye, to gaze at, to look at, to observe, to regard, to stare at, to watch.

vigilant *A look-out must be vigilant.* alert, attentive, awake, careful, observant, watchful.

vigorous *a vigorous game, a vigorous player.* active, dynamic, energetic, forceful, lively, spirited, strenuous.

vigour energy, force, liveliness, might, power, strength, vitality, zeal, zest.

vile *a vile crime.* disgusting, filthy, foul, horrible, loathsome, nasty, nauseating, obnoxious, offensive, odious, repulsive, revolting.

village hamlet, settlement.

villain (informal) baddy, blackguard, knave, rascal, rogue, scoundrel.

villainous SEE **wicked**.

vindictive SEE **spiteful**.

violate *to violate a rule.* to break, to defy, to disobey, to disregard, to ignore, to infringe.

violent 1 *a violent attack.* barbaric, brutal, cruel, destructive, ferocious, fierce, murderous, savage, vicious. 2 *a violent wind.* hard, powerful, severe, strong, tempestuous. 3 *violent behaviour.* berserk, desperate, rowdy, turbulent, unruly, vehement, wild. 4 *violent emotions.* burning, intense, passionate, uncontrollable.

violin fiddle.

virile manly, masculine.

virtue 1 *We should respect virtue and hate vice.* decency, goodness, honesty, honour, integrity, morality, nobility, principle, righteousness, sincerity. 2 *The main virtue of our car is that it doesn't use much petrol.* advantage, good point, strength.

virtuous *virtuous behaviour.* chaste, good, honest, honourable, just, law-abiding, moral, pure, right, trustworthy, upright.

virus (informal) bug, germ, microbe.

visible *The dog showed visible signs of being cruelly treated.* apparent, clear, conspicuous, evident, noticeable, obvious, perceptible, plain.

vision 1 *The optician said I had good vision.* eyesight, sight. 2 *He claims that he saw a vision.* apparition, ghost, hallucination, illusion, phantom, spirit.

visit *They visited us on Sunday.* to call, to come to see, to drop in, to go to see, to stay.

visitor 1 *We had visitors on Sunday.* callers, company, guests. 2 *The town is full of visitors.* sightseer, tourist, traveller.

vista landscape, outlook, panorama, prospect, scene, scenery, view.

visualize *Can you visualize what it was like here 100 years ago?* to conceive, to dream up, to imagine, to picture, to see.

vital *It is vital to have food.* essential, fundamental, imperative, important, indispensable, necessary.

vitality *Our dog is full of vitality.* energy, life, liveliness, sprightliness, vigour, zest.

vivacious SEE **lively.**

vivid 1 *vivid colours.* bright, brilliant, colourful, gay, gleaming, intense, shining, showy. 2 *a vivid description.* clear, lifelike, lively.

vocalist singer.

vogue 1 craze, fashion, style, taste, trend. 2 *in vogue*: fashionable, popular, (informal) trendy.

voice 1 *I recognized her voice.* speech. 2 FOR WORDS TO DO WITH USING YOUR VOICE SEE **sing, talk.**

void SEE **empty.**

volume 1 *That tank can store a large volume of oil.* amount, bulk, mass, quantity. 2 *What is the volume of that tank?* capacity, dimensions, size. SEE ALSO **measure.** 3 *How many volumes are in the library?* book.

voluntary optional.

volunteer 1 *We volunteered to clear up.* to offer. 2 *to volunteer for the army.* SEE **enlist.**

vomit to be sick, (informal) to throw up.

vote 1 *Who did you vote for?* to choose, to elect, to nominate, to opt for, to pick, to select, to settle on. 2 *We had a vote to choose a captain.* ballot, election, poll.

voucher *This voucher gives you £1 off the usual price.* coupon, ticket, token.

vow *She vowed that she was telling the truth.* to give an assurance, to give your word, to guarantee, to pledge, to promise, to swear, to take an oath.

voyage SEE **travel.**

vulgar *vulgar language.* coarse, common, crude, foul, impolite, improper, indecent, offensive, rough, rude, uncouth.

vulnerable defenceless, exposed, unguarded, unprotected, weak.

W

wad *a wad of £5 notes.* bundle, pad.

wade to paddle.

wag *A dog wags its tail.* to shake, to waggle, to wave, to wiggle.

wage 1 *wages*: earnings, income, pay, salary. 2 *to wage war.* to carry on, to fight.

wager bet, stake. SEE ALSO **gamble.**

wail to cry, to howl, to moan, to shriek.

waist *She wore a belt round her waist.* middle.

wait 1 *Wait here!* to halt, to keep still, to remain, to rest, to stay, to stop. 2 *We waited for the signal.* to delay, to hesitate, to hold back, to pause. 3 *to wait around*: to dally, to linger, to loiter, to lurk. 4 *to wait at table.* to serve.

wake *Wake me at 7.30.* to arouse, to awaken, to call, to rouse.

walk VARIOUS WAYS OF WALKING: to amble, to crawl, to creep, to dodder, to hike, to hobble, to limp, to lurch, to march, to pace, to pad, to paddle, to plod, to prowl, to ramble, to saunter, to scuttle, to shamble, to shuffle, to slink, to stagger, to stalk, to steal, to step, to stride, to stroll, to strut, to stumble, to swagger, to totter, to tramp, to trample, to trek, to troop, to trot, to trudge, to waddle, to wade.

walker hiker, pedestrian, rambler.

wall KINDS OF WALL: barrier, dam, dike, embankment, fence, paling, palisade, parapet, partition, rampart, stockade.

wallet purse.

wallop SEE **hit.**

wallow *The animals wallowed in the mud.* to flounder, to roll about.

wan *She looked wan after her illness.* pale, pasty, (informal) poorly, sickly.

wand *a magician's wand.* cane, rod, stick.

wander 1 *The sheep wander about the hills.* to drift, to ramble, to range, to roam, to rove, to stray, to travel. 2 *We wandered off course.* to curve, to swerve, to turn, to twist, to veer, to zigzag.

wane *The light waned as the sun went down.* to decline, to decrease, to diminish, to dwindle, to fade, to fail, to lessen, to weaken.

want 1 *We can't always have what we want.* to desire, to fancy, to hanker after, to long for, to wish for, to yearn for. 2 *The farmers wanted rain after the long drought.* to be short of, to lack, to need, to require.

war KINDS OF ACTION IN WAR: ambush, assault, attack, battle, blitz, blockade, bombardment, campaign, counter-attack, hostilities, invasion, manoeuvre, negotiation, operation, retreat, siege, surrender, warfare, withdrawal. SEE ALSO **armed services, fight, peace, weapon.**

ward *to ward off an attack.* to fend off, to parry, to push away, to repel, to repulse.

warden *a traffic warden.* SEE **job.**

warder *a prison warder.* guard, keeper.

warehouse depot, store.

wares *The saleswoman displayed her wares.* goods, merchandise.

warlike *warlike tribes.* aggressive, belligerent, hostile, militant, pugnacious.

warm 1 *warm weather.* close, sultry. SEE ALSO **hot.** 2 *warm water.* lukewarm, tepid. 3 *a warm welcome.* affectionate, cordial, friendly, genial, kind, loving, warm-hearted.

warn 1 *Our teacher warned us not to cheat.* to caution, to remind. 2 *The guard warned us that the train would be late.* to alert, to notify.

warning 1 *Was there any warning of trouble?* hint, indication, omen, sign, signal, threat. 2 WARNING SIGNALS: alarm, beacon, bell, fire-alarm, fog-horn, gong, red light, siren, whistle.

warp *The floor is uneven because the planks have warped.* to become deformed, to bend, to buckle, to curl, to curve, to distort, to twist.

warren *a rabbits' warren.* burrow.

warrior SEE **fighter.**

wary *Many animals are wary of strangers.* careful, cautious, distrustful, suspicious, watchful.

wash 1 to bath, to bathe, to clean, to mop, to rinse, to shampoo, to sponge down, to swill, to wipe. 2 THINGS USED IN WASHING YOURSELF: bath, flannel, nail-brush, pumice-stone, shampoo, shower, soap, sponge, toothbrush, towel, washbasin. 3 THINGS USED IN WASHING CLOTHES: clothes-horse, clothes-line, clothes-peg, detergent, iron, ironing-board, mangle, spin-drier, tumble-drier, washer, washing-machine, wringer.

washing *Hang out the washing.* laundry.

waste 1 *Don't waste time.* to fritter, to misuse, to squander. 2 *He wasted away when his dog died.* to become emaciated, to become thin, to mope, to pine, to weaken. 3 *Nowadays we try to recycle waste.* garbage, junk, litter, refuse, remnants, rubbish, scraps, trash.

wasteful *It's wasteful to throw away good food.* extravagant, prodigal, uneconomical.

watch 1 *Watch what I do.* to attend to, to concentrate on, to heed, to mark, to note, to observe, to take notice of. 2 *We watched the sunset.* to contemplate, to gaze at, to look at, to regard, to stare at. 3 *Will you watch the twins while I pop out for a minute?* to care for, to guard, to keep an eye on, to look after, to mind, to protect, to supervise, to tend. 4 *Who's got a watch?* digital watch, stop-watch. SEE ALSO **clock.**

watchman guard, look-out, night-watchman, sentinel, sentry.

water 1 VARIOUS STRETCHES OF WATER: lake, ocean, pond, river, sea, SEE ALSO **stream.** 2 *The farmer waters his strawberry fields.* to irrigate, to soak, to sprinkle, to wet. 3 *It's illegal for a farmer to water down his milk.* to dilute, to thin, to weaken.

water-closet lavatory, (informal) loo, toilet, WC.

web

waterfall cataract, rapids.

waterlogged *a waterlogged pitch.* full of water, saturated, soaked.

water plant VARIOUS WATER PLANTS: reeds, rushes, seaweed, watercress, water-lily.

waterproof watertight.

waterway canal, channel, river, stream.

watery 1 *watery eyes.* damp, moist, wet. 2 *watery gravy.* thin, weak.

wave 1 *She waved to me.* SEE **gesture.** 2 *He waved his stick.* to brandish, to flourish, to swing, to twirl. 3 *The trees waved in the wind.* to flap, to move to and fro, to shake, to wag, to waggle, to wiggle. 4 *the waves on the sea.* breaker, ripple, surf, swell. 5 *radio waves.* pulse, vibration.

wavelength *You have to tune your TV to the right wavelength.* channel, station, waveband.

waver 1 *The light from the candle wavered.* to flicker, to quake, to quaver, to quiver, to shake, to shiver, to shudder, to tremble. 2 *I wavered when I saw the fierce dog.* to falter, to hesitate, to pause, to think twice. 3 *His determination never wavered.* to change, to vary.

way 1 SEE **road.** 2 *Which way will you go?* course, direction, route. 3 *She showed me the way to mend a fuse.* knack, means, method, procedure, process, system, technique. 4 *Why does he dress in that odd way?* fashion, manner, mode, style. 5 *It's our way to have mint sauce with lamb.* custom, habit, practice, routine, tradition.

wayfarer SEE **travel.**

weak 1 *a weak person.* delicate, feeble, flabby, frail, helpless, ill, listless, poorly, sickly, weedy. 2 *a weak branch.* brittle, flimsy, fragile, rickety, shaky, slight, thin, watery.

weaken 1 *The flood weakened the foundations.* to destroy, to erode, to ruin, to undermine. 2 *Our enthusiasm weakened as the day went on.* to decline, to decrease, to diminish, to dwindle, to fade, to flag, to lessen, to reduce, to wane.

weakness *The crash was due to a weakness in the design of the aircraft.* defect, failing, fault, flaw, imperfection.

wealth SEE **money.**

wealthy affluent, prosperous, rich, well off, well-to-do.

weapon 1 *weapons:* armaments. 2 VARIOUS WEAPONS: airgun, arrow, artillery, atom bomb, automatic weapon, battering-ram, battle-axe, bayonet, blunderbuss, bomb, boomerang, bow and arrow, cannon, cannonball, catapult, crossbow, cutlass, dagger, foil, grenade, harpoon, H-bomb, incendiary bomb, javelin, lance, land-mine, laser beam, long-bow, machine-gun, mine, missile, mortar, musket, napalm, nuclear weapons, pike, pistol, rapier, revolver, rifle, sabre, shotgun, sling, small arms, spear, sub-machine-gun, sword, tank, tear gas, time bomb, tomahawk, torpedo, truncheon, warhead. SEE ALSO **ammunition.** 3 PLACES WHERE WEAPONS ARE STORED: armoury, arsenal, depot, magazine.

wear 1 *Which jeans shall I wear?* to be dressed in, to put on, to wrap up in. 2 *to wear away:* to eat away, to erode, to grind down, to rub away. 3 *to wear out:* to exhaust, to tire, to weary. 4 *worn: My jumper is worn at the elbows.* frayed, ragged, shabby, tattered, tatty, thin, threadbare.

weary bored, drowsy, exhausted, jaded, sleepy, tired, worn out.

weather 1 VARIOUS FEATURES OF THE WEATHER: anticyclone, blizzard, breeze, cloud, cyclone, deluge, depression, dew, downpour, drizzle, drought, fog, frost, gale, hail, haze, heat-wave, hoar-frost, hurricane, ice, lightning, mist, monsoon, rain, rainbow, shower, sleet, slush, snow, squall, storm, sunshine, temperature, tempest, thaw, thunder, tornado, typhoon, whirlwind, wind. 2 USEFUL WORDS TO DESCRIBE WEATHER: blustery, bright, brilliant, clear, close, cloudless, cloudy, drizzly, dull, fair, fine, foggy, foul, freezing, frosty, grey, hazy, icy, misty, oppressive, overcast, rainy, rough, showery, slushy, snowy, squally, stormy, sultry, sunless, sunny, sweltering, teeming, thundery, torrential, turbulent, wet, windy, wintry. SEE ALSO **cold, hot.** 3 OTHER WORDS TO DO WITH WEATHER: barometer, climate, forecast, meteorology, outlook, thermometer.

weather-beaten tanned.

web mesh, net, network.

wedding 1 marriage. 2 PEOPLE AT A WEDDING: best man, bride, bridegroom, bridesmaid, family, groom, guests, page. 3 OTHER WORDS TO DO WITH WEDDINGS: confetti, honeymoon, reception, registry office, service, trousseau, wedding-ring.

wedge *Wedge the door open.* to jam, to stick.

wee SEE **small.**

weed SOME GARDEN WEEDS: clover, dock, nettle, thistle.

weedy (informal) *You wouldn't expect that weedy boy to be a boxer!* delicate, feeble, frail, helpless, ill, (informal) poorly, sickly, weak.

weep to blubber, to cry, to grizzle, to shed tears, to snivel, to sob, to wail.

weight 1 *What is your weight?* heaviness. 2 *This suitcase is a terrible weight.* burden, load.

weighty 1 *a weighty load.* burdensome, heavy, massive, ponderous. 2 *a weighty problem.* grave, important, momentous, serious.

weir dam.

weird 1 *What a weird thing to do!* (informal) cranky, curious, eccentric, funny, odd, peculiar, queer, strange, unconventional, zany. 2 *a weird atmosphere in the dungeon.* creepy, eerie, ghostly, (informal) scary, (informal) spooky, uncanny.

welcome 1 *a friendly welcome.* greeting, reception. 2 *She welcomed us at the door.* to greet, to receive. 3 *We had a welcome rest.* SEE **pleasant.** 4 *welcoming:* SEE **friendly.**

weld SEE **fasten.**

welfare *A nurse looks after the welfare of the patients.* happiness, health.

well 1 *You look well.* healthy, hearty, lively, robust, sound, vigorous. 2 *well off:* SEE **wealthy.**

well-to-do SEE **wealthy.**

wet 1 *The soil is too wet for gardening.* saturated, soaked, sodden, soggy, waterlogged. 2 *I got wet in the storm.* bedraggled, drenched, dripping, sopping. 3 *The cellar walls were wet.* clammy, damp, dank, moist. 4 *The weather was wet.* drizzly, rainy, showery.

whack SEE **hit.**

wharf *The ship's cargo was unloaded onto the wharf.* dock, landing-stage, jetty, pier, quay.

wheel 1 KINDS OF WHEEL: castor, cog-wheel, spinning-wheel, steering-wheel. 2 PARTS OF A WHEEL: axle, hub, rim, spoke, tyre. 3 *The birds wheeled overhead.* to circle, to move in circles. 4 *He wheeled round when I called.* to change direction, to swerve, to turn, to veer.

wheeze to gasp, to pant, to puff.

whiff aroma, fragrance, odour, perfume, scent, smell, stench, stink.

while *I haven't seen my friends for a long while.* period, time.

whim impulse.

whimper to cry, to grizzle, to groan, to moan, to wail, to whine.

whine to complain, to cry, to moan, to whimper.

whinny to neigh.

whip 1 *I'd never use a whip on a horse.* crop, lash, scourge. 2 SEE **hit.**

whirl *The roundabout whirled round.* to revolve, to rotate, to spin, to turn, to twirl.

whirlpool eddy.

whisk *I whisked some eggs to make an omelette.* to beat, to mix, to stir.

whiskers bristles, hairs, moustache.

whisper SEE **talk.**

whistle to blow. SEE ALSO **sound.**

whiten to bleach, to lighten.

whole 1 *She told us the whole story.* complete, entire, full, total, unabridged. 2 *The wolf swallowed the duck whole!* intact, unbroken, undamaged, undivided.

wholesale *The bomb causes wholesale destruction.* extensive, general, global, universal, widespread.

wholesome *wholesome food.* healthy, good, nutritious.

wicked *a wicked deed, a wicked person.* base, blasphemous, evil, foul, immoral, infamous, sinful, sinister, spiteful, vicious, villainous, wrong. SEE ALSO **bad, naughty.**

wide 1 *a wide river.* broad, expansive. 2 *a wide gap.* extensive, large, open, spacious, yawning.

widen to enlarge.

widespread *widespread rain.* extensive, general, universal, wholesale.

width breadth.

wield *to wield a cricket bat.* to employ, to exercise, to handle, to manage, to use.

wiggle to fidget, to move restlessly, to sway, to wag, to waggle.

wigwam tent, tepee.

wild 1 *wild animals.* ferocious, free, natural, undomesticated, untamed. 2 *wild country.* overgrown, rough, rugged, uncultivated, uninhabited, waste. 3 *wild behaviour.* boisterous, disorderly, excited, lawless, noisy, obstreperous, reckless, rowdy, savage, uncivilized, uncontrolled, undisciplined, unruly. 4 *wild weather.* stormy, turbulent, violent, windy.

wilderness desert, wasteland.

wilful 1 *a wilful character.* determined, dogged, obstinate, stubborn. 2 *wilful disobedience.* deliberate, intentional, premeditated.

will *the will to succeed.* desire, determination, resolution, wish.

willing 1 *I'm willing to play.* disposed, eager, inclined, prepared, ready. 2 *a willing worker.* cooperative, helpful, obliging.

wilt *The plants wilted in the drought.* to become limp, to droop, to flag, to flop, to shrivel, to weaken, to wither.

wily *Foxes are supposed to be wily creatures.* artful, astute, clever, crafty, cunning, furtive, ingenious, knowing, skilful, sly, tricky.

win 1 *The stronger team won.* to be victorious, to come first, to succeed, to triumph. 2 *His performance won a round of applause.* to deserve, to earn, to gain, to get, to receive.

wind 1 *The wind blew the papers about.* blast, breeze, draught, gale, gust, puff, whirlwind. 2 *The road winds up the hill.* to bend, to curve, to twist, to zigzag. 3 *I wound the thread on to a reel.* to coil, to curl, to loop, to roll, to turn.

window French window, pane, sash window, skylight.

windswept *a windswept moor.* bare, bleak, desolate, exposed, windy.

wing *They built a new wing on to the hospital.* annexe, extension.

wink *The Christmas tree lights winked on and off.* to blink, to flash, to flicker, to twinkle.

winner champion, conqueror, medallist, victor.

winter sports VARIOUS WINTER SPORTS: bobsleigh, ice-hockey, skating, skiing, sledging, tobogganing.

wipe 1 *Wipe the dishes.* to clean, to dry, to dust, to mop, to polish, to rub, to scour, to sponge, to wash. 2 *to wipe out:* SEE **destroy.**

wire 1 *telephone wires.* cable, flex, lead. 2 *Granny sent a wire to say that she was ill.* telegram.

wireless radio, transistor.

wiry *a wiry figure.* lean, strong, thin, tough.

wise 1 *If you are wise you won't start smoking.* intelligent, knowledgeable, perceptive, prudent, reasonable, sensible, thoughtful. 2 *She made a wise decision.* advisable, appropriate, fair, just, proper, right, sound.

wish 1 *We couldn't have wished for nicer weather.* to desire, to fancy, to hanker after, to long for, to want, to yearn for. 2 *My secret wish is to be an Olympic gymnast.* ambition, craving, desire, goal, hope, longing, objective.

wistful *a wistful expression.* forlorn, pathetic, sad.

wit 1 *We laughed at the comedian's wit.* cleverness, humour, jokes, quickness. 2 *He didn't have the wit to see that we were only teasing.* brains, intellect, intelligence, reason, sense. 3 *Dad is quite a wit sometimes.* comedian, comic, jester, joker.

witch, witchcraft SEE **magic.**

withdraw

212

withdraw 1 *The general withdrew his troops.* to call back, to recall, to remove, to take away. 2 *The troops withdrew.* to back away, to fall back, to leave, to move back, to retire, to retreat, to run away.

wither *The plants withered in the drought.* to dry, to shrink, to shrivel, to wilt.

withhold *to withhold information from the police.* to conceal, to hold back, to keep back, to keep secret.

withstand *The town withstood a long siege.* to cope with, to endure, to oppose, to resist, to stand up to, to tolerate.

witness 1 *a witness of an accident.* bystander, eyewitness, observer, onlooker, spectator. 2 *I witnessed the accident.* to attend, to behold, to be present at, to observe, to see, to view.

witty *a witty story-teller.* amusing, clever, comic funny, humorous, quick-witted, sharp-witted.

wobble *The jelly wobbles when you touch the plate.* to be unsteady, to quake, to shake, to sway, to totter, to tremble, to waver.

wobbly SEE **shaky.**

woe distress, grief, misery, sorrow, unhappiness.

woeful SEE **sad.**

woman (old-fashioned) dame, lady.

wonder 1 *We gazed with wonder at the huge spacecraft.* admiration, amazement, awe, respect, reverence. 2 *We wondered at the size of the spacecraft.* to be amazed by, to gape at, to marvel at. 3 *I wondered whether it was time for dinner.* to ask yourself, to be curious about, to question yourself.

woo to court, to make love to.

wood 1 *A carpenter makes things out of wood.* KINDS OF WOOD: balsa, beech, cedar, chestnut, ebony, elm, mahogony, oak, pine, rosewood, teak, walnut. SEE ALSO **timber.** 2 *We got lost in the wood.* coppice, copse, forest, grove, jungle, orchard, thicket, trees, woodland.

woodwind WOODWIND INSTRUMENTS: bassoon, clarinet, flute, oboe, piccolo, recorder.

woolly 1 *a woolly teddy-bear.* downy, fleecy, furry, fuzzy. 2 *woolly ideas.* ambiguous, confused, indefinite, uncertain, unclear, vague.

word *A thesaurus is a book of words.* expression, term.

work 1 *Gardening can be hard work.* chore, drudgery, effort, exertion, labour, slavery, toil. 2 *Mum leaves for work at 8.30.* business, employment, job, occupation, profession, trade. FOR VARIOUS KINDS OF WORK SEE **job.** 3 *Our teacher set us some work.* assignment, homework, project, task. 4 *We worked at our maths until dinner.* to be busy, to exert yourself, to labour, to slave, to toil. 5 *How does this machine work?* to act, to function, to go, to operate, to perform, to run. 6 *Did your plan work?* to be effective, to succeed, to thrive. 7 *to work out:* SEE **calculate.**

workmanship *We admired the blacksmith's workmanship.* art, craft, handicraft, skill, technique.

world earth, globe, planet.

worm *I wormed my way through the undergrowth.* to crawl, to creep, to slither, to squirm, to wriggle, to writhe.

worn *My shirt was worn at the cuffs.* frayed, ragged, scruffy, shabby, tattered, tatty, threadbare.

worry 1 *Don't worry granny while she's reading.* to annoy, to bother, to disturb, to molest, to pester, to trouble, to upset, to vex. 2 *Don't worry about us: we'll be all right.* to be anxious, to feel uneasy, to fret. 3 *The bad weather is a worry to the farmers.* anxiety, burden, care, concern, problem, trouble.

worsen 1 *They worsened the situation by being rude to the referee.* to aggravate, to make worse. 2 *The referee's temper worsened as the game went on.* to decline, to degenerate, to deteriorate, to get worse.

worship 1 *She worships her grandad.* to adore, to dote on, to idolize, to love, to revere. 2 *to worship God.* to praise. 3 BUILDINGS WHERE PEOPLE WORSHIP: abbey, cathedral, chapel, church, mosque, pagoda, synagogue, temple.

worth 1 *Is this stamp of any worth?* importance, merit, usefulness, value. 2 *to be worth:* to be priced at, to cost, to have a value of.

worthless *Don't waste money on worthless junk.* frivolous, futile, pointless, trivial, unimportant, useless, valueless.

worthwhile 1 *Our collection for OXFAM raised a worthwhile amount.* biggish, considerable, noticeable, significant, sizeable, substantial, useful, valuable. 2 *Is it worthwhile doing a paper round?* advantageous, beneficial, profitable, rewarding.

worthy *a worthy cause, a worthy winner.* admirable, commendable, creditable, decent, deserving, honest, honourable, praiseworthy, respectable.

wound 1 *The explosion wounded several people.* to cause pain to, to damage, to harm, to hurt, to injure. 2 VARIOUS KINDS OF WOUNDING: to bite, to bruise, to burn, to crush, to cut, to fracture, to gore, to graze, to impale, to knife, to make sore, to mangle, to maul, to mutilate, to scratch, to sprain, to strain, to stab, to sting, to torture.

wrap *We wrapped it in a bandage. The mountains were wrapped in mist.* to bind, to cloak, to conceal, to cover, to enclose, to envelop, to hide, to insulate, to lag, to muffle, to shroud, to wind.

wrath anger, exasperation, fury, rage, temper.

wrathful SEE **angry**.

wreck 1 *The ship was wrecked on the rocks.* to break up, to crumple, to crush, to demolish, to destroy, to shatter, to smash. 2 *The storm wrecked our picnic.* to ruin, to spoil.

wreckage bits, debris, pieces, remains, rubble, ruins.

wrench *I wrenched the lid off.* to force, to jerk, to lever, to prize, to pull, to twist.

wrestle to fight, to grapple, to struggle.

wretched 1 *a wretched expression.* SEE **miserable**. 2 *a wretched cold.* SEE **unpleasant**.

wriggle *The snake wriggled away.* to squirm, to twist, to writhe.

wring 1 *He wrung my hand.* to clasp, to grip, to shake. 2 *I wrung the water out of my wet swimming things.* to compress, to crush, to press, to squeeze, to twist.

wrinkle 1 *wrinkles in a piece of cloth.* crease, fold, furrow, line, pleat. 2 *Try not to wrinkle the new curtains.* to crease, to crinkle, to crumple.

write 1 WAYS OF WRITING: to compose, to doodle, to engrave, to inscribe, to jot, to note, to print, to record, to scrawl, to scribble, to type. 2 THINGS YOU WRITE WITH: ball-point, chalk, crayon, felt-tip, fountain pen, ink, pen, pencil, typewriter, word-processor. 3 THINGS YOU WRITE ON: blackboard, card, exercise book, form, jotter, notepaper, pad, paper, papyrus, parchment, postcard, stationery.

writer VARIOUS WRITERS: author, bard, composer, correspondent, dramatist, editor, journalist, novelist, playwright, poet, reporter, scriptwriter.

writhe to squirm, to twist, to wriggle.

writing 1 *Can you read this writing?* alphabet, handwriting, hieroglyphics, italics, letters, printing, shorthand. 2 *An author sells his writings to make a living.* literature. 3 VARIOUS WRITINGS: article, autobiography, biography, comedy, diary, editorial, epic, essay, fable, fairy tale, folk-tale, journalism, legend, letter, lyric, myth, novel, parable, play, prose, romance, saga, satire, science fiction, script, SF, sketch, story, tale, thriller, tragedy, verse, yarn. SEE ALSO **book, poem**.

wrong 1 *the wrong answer.* false, inaccurate, incorrect, mistaken, untrue. 2 *the wrong decision.* improper, inappropriate, incongruous, unfair, unjust, wrongful. 3 *It is wrong to steal.* corrupt, criminal, crooked, deceitful, dishonest, illegal, naughty, reprehensible, unscrupulous. 4 *Cruelty to animals is wrong.* base, evil, immoral, sinful, vicious, villainous, wicked. SEE ALSO **bad**. 5 *The car has gone wrong.* broken down, faulty, out of order, unusable. 6 *We wronged him by accusing him unjustly.* to abuse, to be unfair to, to treat unfairly.

wry *a wry smile.* crooked, twisted.

X

xylophone glockenspiel.

Y

yard courtyard, enclosure, garden, quadrangle.

yarn *She told us an old yarn.* narrative, story, tale.

yawn 1 SEE **expression.** 2 *yawning: a yawning hole.* open, wide.

yearn 1 *We yearned for some warmer weather.* to desire, to fancy, to hanker after, to long for, to want, to wish for. 2 *a yearning:* craving, desire, itch, longing, urge, wish.

yell to bawl, to bellow, to call, to shout.

yield 1 *After a long siege they yielded to the enemy.* to capitulate, to give in, to submit, to surrender. 2 *Our pear tree yielded a huge crop.* to bear, to give, to grow, to produce.

young 1 *young people, young trees, etc.* growing, undeveloped, youthful. 2 *He seems young for his age.* babyish, childish, immature, infantile. 3 YOUNG PEOPLE: adolescent, baby, boy, (insulting) brat, child, girl, infant, juvenile, (informal) kid, lad, lass, (informal) nipper, teenager, toddler, (insulting) urchin, youngster, youth. 4 YOUNG ANIMALS: calf, colt, cub, fawn, foal, heifer, kid, kitten, lamb, puppy. 5 YOUNG BIRDS: chick, cygnet, duckling, fledgling, gosling, nestling, pullet. 6 YOUNG PLANTS: cutting, sapling, seedling.

youth, youthful SEE **young.**

yule, yuletide Christmas.

Z

zany *We enjoyed the clowns' zany humour.* absurd, (informal) cranky, crazy, eccentric, ludicrous, mad, odd, preposterous, ridiculous, unconventional, weird.

zeal SEE **zest.**

zealous *There's no need for that traffic warden to be so zealous!* conscientious, diligent, eager, earnest, enthusiastic, keen.

zero SEE **nothing.**

zest *We finished off the ice-cream with great zest.* eagerness, energy, enjoyment, enthusiasm, liveliness, zeal.

zigzag 1 *a zigzag line.* bendy, crooked, twisting. 2 *The road zigzags up the hill.* to bend, to curve, to twist, to wind.

zone area, district, locality, neighbourhood, region, sector, territory, vicinity.

zoo 1 menagerie, safari park, wildlife park. 2 PARTS OF A ZOO WHERE ANIMALS LIVE: animal house (*monkey house, reptile house, etc.*), aquarium, aviary, bear pit, cage, dolphinarium, enclosure, lake, pen, pool. 3 FOR NAMES OF VARIOUS CREATURES SEE **animal, bird, fish, reptile.**

zoom (informal) *She zoomed home with her good news.* to dash, to hurry, to hurtle, to rush, to speed.

Notes

Notes

Notes

Notes